Gender Across Languages

Impact: Studies in language and society

IMPACT publishes monographs, collective volumes, and text books on topics in sociolinguistics and language pedagogy. The scope of the series is broad, with special emphasis on areas such as language planning and language policies; language conflict and language death; language standards and language change; dialectology; diglossia; discourse studies; language and social identity (gender, ethnicity, class, ideology); and history and methods of sociolinguistics

General editor

Annick De Houwer
University of Antwerp

Advisory board

Volume 9

Gender Across Languages: The linguistic representation of women and men
Volume I
Edited by Marlis Hellinger and Hadumod Bußmann

Gender Across Languages

The linguistic representation of women and men

VOLUME I

Edited by

Marlis Hellinger

University of Frankfurt am Main

Hadumod Bußmann

University of Munich

John Benjamins Publishing Company
Amsterdam/Philadelphia

TM The paper used in this publication meets the minimum requirements of American National Standard for Information Sciences – Permanence of Paper for Printed Library Materials, ANSI z39.48-1984.

Library of Congress Cataloging-in-Publication Data

Gender Across Languages : The linguistic representation of women and men Volume I / edited by Marlis Hellinger, Hadumod Bußmann.
    p. cm. (Impact, Studies in language and society, ISSN 1385–7908 ; v. 9)
    Includes bibliographical references and indexes.
    1. Grammar, Comparative and general--Gender. I. Hellinger, Marlis. II. Bußmann, Hadumod. III. Impact, studies in language and society ; 9.

P240.7 .G45 2001
415--dc21   2001037888
ISBN 90 272 1840 4 (Eur.) / 1 58811 082 6 (US) (Hb; alk. paper)
ISBN 90 272 1841 2 (Eur.) / 1 58811 083 4 (US) (Pb; alk. paper)

John Benjamins Publishing Co. · P.O. Box 36224 · 1020 ME Amsterdam · The Netherlands
John Benjamins North America · P.O. Box 27519 · Philadelphia PA 19118-0519 · USA

Contents

Languages of Volume II

Chinese
Marjorie K. M. Chan
Charles Ettner
Hong Zhang

Dutch
Marinel Gerritsen

Finnish
Mila Engelberg

Hindi
Kira Hall

Icelandic
Anna Gunnarsdotter Grönberg

Italian
Gianna Marcato & Eva-Maria Thüne

Norwegian
Tove Bull & Toril Swan

Spanish
Uwe Kjær Nissen

Vietnamese
Hoa Pham

Welsh
Gwenllian Awbery & Kathryn Jones & Delyth Morris

Languages of Volume III

Czech
Jana Valdrová

Danish
Kirsten Gomard & Mette Kunøe

French
Elisabeth Burr
Elmar Schafroth

German
Marlis Hellinger & Hadumod Bußmann

Greek
Theodossia-Soula Pavlidou

Japanese
Sachiko Ide
Janet S. (Shibamoto) Smith

Oriya
Kalyanamalini Sahoo

Polish
Gabriela Koniuszaniec & Hanka Błaszkowska

Serbian/Croatian/Bosnian
Elke Hentschel

Swahili
Rose Marie Beck

Swedish
Antje Hornscheidt

Preface

The series *Gender across languages* is an ongoing project with potential follow-up publications. Our main goal has been to provide a comprehensive collection of in-depth descriptions of gender-related issues in languages with very diverse structural foundations and socio-cultural backgrounds. The project is designed to have an explicit contrastive orientation in that basically the same issues are discussed for each language within the same terminological and methodological framework. This framework, whose central notion is, of course, the multidimensional concept of "gender", is discussed in the introductory chapter of "Gender across languages – The linguistic representation of women and men". Care has been taken not to impose a narrow western perspective on other languages.

This is the first of three volumes which comprise a total of thirty languages: Arabic, Belizean Creole, Chinese, Czech, Danish, Dutch, Eastern Maroon Creole, English, Finnish, French, German, Greek, Hebrew, Hindi, Icelandic, Indonesian, Italian, Japanese, Norwegian, Oriya, Polish, Romanian, Russian, Serbian/Croatian/Bosnian, Spanish, Swahili, Swedish, Turkish, Vietnamese, Welsh.

All contributions were specifically written for this project, in close collaboration with the editors over a period of three years. Unfortunately, a few languages (Bulgarian, Hungarian, Korean, Portuguese, and one Native American language) dropped out of the project for various reasons. These languages should be included in a potential future volume.

The basis on which particular languages should be brought together in one volume has been a problematic one to define. Rather than categorizing languages according to language family (areal, typological or historical), or according to whether the language has or does not have grammatical gender, or using an overall alphabetical ordering, we decided – in agreement with the publisher – that each volume should contain a balanced selection of languages, so that each volume will provide readers with sufficient material to illustrate the diversity and complexity of linguistic representations of gender across languages. Thus, each volume will contain both languages with grammatical gender as well as "genderless" languages, and languages with different areal, typological and historical affiliations.

"Gender across languages" is, of course, a selection, and no claims can be made that the three volumes will cover all language groups adequately. Critics will find it easy to identify those language areas or families that are under-represented in the project. In particular, future work should consider the immense number of African, Asian and Austronesian languages which have so far received little or no attention from a gender perspective.

Though we are aware of the fact that most languages of the project have developed a number of regional and social varieties, with different implications for the representation and communication of "gender", we supported authors in their unanimous decision to concentrate on standard varieties (where these exist). This decision is particularly well-founded for those languages for which gender-related issues are being described here for the very first time. Only in the case of English, which has developed major regional standards with consider-able differences in usage, did we decide to make explicit reference to four different varieties (British English, American English, New Zealand English and Australian English).

We took care that each chapter did address most of the questions we had formulated as original guidelines which, however, were not intended (nor inter-preted by authors) to impose our own expectations of how "gender" is repre-sented in a particular culture. Thus, chapters basically have the same overall structure, with variation due to language-specific properties as well as to the state of research on language and gender in the respective country. In some cases, we encouraged authors to include some of their own empirical research where this has implications for the analysis of "gender" in the respective language.

Marlis Hellinger
Hadumod Bußmann

Acknowledgments

Assembling a work of this scope requires the collaboration of many. The editors were the fortunate recipients of a large amount of support: financial, scholarly, technical, and moral. Therefore, it is a pleasure to record our gratitude to all those who have been generous with their time, attentention and expertise in providing advice, references and data, or have supplied helpful comments on particular languages. We wish to thank specifically

- all contributors for their active cooperation and patience with our ongoing demands during the preparation period over three years. Particularly those colleagues who sent in their papers early had to endure a long wait for the publication;
- all anonymous native-speaker reviewers, mainly members of the Board, for their thorough data check und thoughtful council;
- our colleague Dr. Friederike Braun of the University of Kiel, Germany, a professional general linguist and, in addition, a specialist on linguistic gender studies, for her meticulous reading, expert editorial assistance and insightful comments;
- our colleague Dr. Kerstin Kazzazi of the University of Eichstätt, Germany, a professional general linguist and native speaker of English, for thoroughly checking on the use of English;
- the staff of the Linguistics Department of the Institute of English and American Studies at the University of Frankfurt: Helena McKenzie, Dr. Bettina Migge, Dr. Susanne Mühleisen, Stephanie Schnurr, and Eva Tripp MA, for their assistance with the final preparation of the manuscript;
- the Deutsche Forschungsgemeinschaft (DFG) for financial support over the period of two years.

Finally we would like to thank the team of John Benjamins Publishing Company, especially Cornelis H. J. Vaes (Acquisition Editor), and the General Editor of IMPACT, Annick De Houwer, PhD (University of Antwerp), who were both demanding and encouraging editors, and from whose sympathetic enthusiasm and efficient expertise the final processing of the text has profited tremendously.

Marlis Hellinger, Frankfurt am Main   Summer 2001
Hadumod Bußmann, München

List of abbreviations

ABL	ablative		INESS	inessive
ACC	accusative		INF	infinitive
ADJ	adjective		INSTR	instrumental
ADV	adverb		IPF	imperfective
AGR	agreement		LOC	locative
ALLAT	allative		MASC/m	masculine
ANIM	animate		N	noun
ANT	anterior		NEG	negation
AOR	aorist		NEUT/n	neuter
ASP	aspect		NOM	nominative
ATT	attributive		NP	noun phrase
AUX	auxiliary		OBJ	object
CAUS	causative		OBL	oblique
CL	classifier		PART	participle
COM	comitative		PARTT	partitive
COMP	comparative		PASS	passive
COND	conditional		PAST	past
CONJ	conjunction		PERS	personal pronoun
COP	copula		PF	perfective
DAT	dative		PL/pl	plural
DEF	definite		POL	polite
DEM	demonstrative		POSS	possessive
DER	derivational affix		PREP	preposition
DET	determiner		PRES	present
DUR	durative		PROG	progressive
ELAT	elative		PRON	pronoun
ERG	ergative		PRT	particle
ESS	essive		REFL	reflexive
EVID	evidential		REL	relative pronoun/affix
EXPL	expletive		SG/sg	singular
FEM/f	feminine		SUBJ	subject
FUT	future		TOP	topic
GEN	genitive		TRANS	transitive
GER	gerund		TRNS	translative
HAB	habitual		VERB	verb
ILLAT	illative		VOC	vocative
IMP	imperative		1	first person
INAN	inanimate		2	second person
INDEF	indefinite		3	third person

Gender across languages

The linguistic representation of women and men[*]

Marlis Hellinger
University of Frankfurt am Main, Germany

Hadumod Bußmann
University of Munich, Germany

1.   Aims and scope of "Gender across languages"

"Gender across languages" systematically investigates the linguistic representation of women and men in 30 languages of very different structural and socio-cultural backgrounds. Fundamental to the project is the hypothesis that the formal and functional manifestations of gender in the area of human reference follow general, and perhaps universal principles in the world's languages. We will outline these principles and specify the theoretical and empirical foundations on which statements about gendered structures in languages can be made.

A major concern of "Gender across languages" is with the structural properties of the individual language:

–   Does the language have grammatical gender, and – if so – what are the consequences for agreement, coordination, pronominalization and word-formation, and more specifically, for the linguistic representation of women and men?
–   In the absence of grammatical gender, what are possible ways of expressing female-specific, male-specific or gender-indefinite personal reference?
–   Can asymmetries be identified in the area of human reference which may be interpreted as the result of the choice of the masculine/male as the default gender?
–   What is the empirical evidence for the claim that in neutral contexts masculine/male expressions are perceived as generic and bias-free?
–   Does the language contain idiomatic expressions, metaphors, proverbs and the like which are indicative of gender-related socio-cultural hierarchies or stereotypes?

In addition, the project will outline gender-related tendencies of variation and change, and – where applicable – language reform, seeking to identify the ways in which the structural/linguistic prerequisites interact with the respective social, cultural and political conditions that determine the relationships between women and men in a community.

"Gender across languages" will focus on personal nouns and pronouns, which have emerged as a central issue in debates about language and gender. In any language, personal nouns constitute a basic and culturally significant lexical field. They are needed to communicate about the self and others, they are used to identify people as individuals or members of various groups, and they may transmit positive or negative attitudes. In addition, they contain schemata of, e.g., occupational activities and (proto- or stereotypical) performers of such activities. On a psychological level, an appropriate use of personal nouns may contribute towards the maintenance of an individual's identity, while inappropriate use, for example identifying someone repeatedly (either by mistake or by intention) by a false name, by using derogatory or discriminatory language, or by not addressing someone at all, may cause irritation, anger or feelings of inferiority. And since an individual's sense of self includes an awareness of being female or male, it is important to develop an understanding of the ways in which gender is negotiated in a language. This understanding must, of course, be based on adequate descriptions of the relevant structural and functional properties of the respective language.

In communication, parameters like ethnicity, culture, social status, setting, and discourse functions may in fact be as important as extra-linguistic gender, and none of these parameters is represented in a language in any direct or unambiguous way (cf. Bing & Bergvall 1996:5). Only a multidimensional theory of communication will be able to spell out the ways in which these parameters interact with linguistic expressions. By interpreting linguistic manifestations of gender as the discursive result of "doing gender" in specific socio-cultural contexts, the analysis of gender across languages can contribute to such a theory.

Structure-oriented gender research has focused primarily on formal, semantic and historical issues. On a formal level, systems of gender and nominal classification were analyzed, with an emphasis on the phonological and morphological conditions of gender assignment and agreement (cf. Section 4.2).[1]

From a semantic perspective, a major issue was the question as to whether the classification of nouns in a language follows semantic principles rather than being arbitrary.[2] While gender assignment in the field of personal nouns is at least partially non-arbitrary, the classification of inanimate nouns, e.g. words denoting celestial bodies, varies across languages. Thus, the word for 'sun' is grammatically feminine in German and Lithuanian, but masculine in Greek, Latin and the Romance languages, and neuter gender in Old Indic, Old Iranic and Russian. Correspondingly, metaphorical conceptualizations of the sun and the moon as female or male deities, or as the stereotypical human couple, will also show variation.

Nominal class membership may be determined by conceptual principles according to which speakers categorize the objects of their universe. The underlying principles may not be immediately comprehensible to outsiders to a particular culture. For example, the words for female humans, water, fire and fighting are all in one nominal category in Dyirbal, an Australian language (cf.

Dixon 1972). The assignment of, say, some birds' names to the same category can only be explained by recourse to mythological association.[3] – Finally, historical issues in the study of linguistic gender concerned the origin, change and loss of gender categories.[4]

Corbett's account of over 200 languages is a major source for any discussion of gender as a formal category. However, since Corbett analyzes entire noun class systems, while we concentrate on personal nouns and pronouns, "sexism in language" (Corbett 1991:3) is not one of his concerns. But Corbett does in fact contribute to that debate in various ways, in particular, by introducing richness and diversity to a field which has been dominated by the study of a few Western languages.

2.   Gender classes as a special case of noun classes

Considering the lack of terminological precision and consistency in the debate about language and gender, the terms "gender class" and "gender language" need to be defined more precisely and with a more explicit reference to the wider framework of nominal classification. Of course, it must be noted that not all languages possess a system of nominal classification. In the project, Belizean Creole, Eastern Maroon Creole, English, Finnish and Turkish[5] represent this group of languages. Other languages may divide their nominal lexicon into groups or classes according to various criteria. Among the languages which exhibit such nominal classification, classifier languages and noun class languages (including languages with grammatical gender) constitute the two major types.[6]

2.1 Classifier languages

A prototypical case of classifier systems are numeral classifiers. In languages with such a system, a numeral (e.g. 'three') cannot be combined with a noun (e.g. 'book') directly, but requires the additional use of a classifier. Classifiers are separate words which often indicate the shape of the quantified object(s). The resulting phrase of numeral, classifier, and noun could, for example, be translated as 'three flat-object book' (cf. Greenberg 1972:5). Numeral classifiers are thus independent functional elements which specify the noun's class membership in certain contexts. In addition, the use of classifiers may be indicative of stylistic variation.

In languages with (numeral) classifiers, nouns do not show agreement with other word classes, although classifiers may perform discourse functions such as reference-tracking, which in gender languages are achieved by agreement. On average, classifier languages have from 50 to 100 classifiers (cf. Dixon 1982: 215).[7] Classifier systems are rather frequent in East Asian languages, and in "Gender across languages" are represented by Chinese, Indonesian, Japanese, Oriya and Vietnamese.

2.2 Noun class languages

While in numeral classifier systems the class membership of nouns is marked only in restricted syntactic contexts (mainly in the area of quantification), class membership in noun class languages triggers agreement on a range of elements inside and outside the noun phrase. Noun class languages have a comparatively small number of classes (hardly more than 20). These classes consistently structure the entire nominal lexicon, i.e. each noun belongs to one of these classes (there are exceptional cases of double or multiple class membership). French, German, Swahili and many others are noun class languages, but we find these languages also referred to as "gender languages".[8] In accordance with Craig (1994), we will not use the terms "gender language" and "noun class language" synonymously, but will define them as two different types of noun class languages based on grammatical and semantic considerations. This distinction is also motivated by our interest in the linguistic representation of the categories "female" and "male".

"Gender languages"

This type is illustrated by many Indo-European languages, but also Semitic languages. These languages have only a very small number of "gender classes", typically two or three. Nouns do not necessarily carry markers of class member-ship, but, of course, there is (obligatory) agreement with other word classes, both inside and outside the noun phrase. Most importantly – for our distinc-tion – class membership is anything but arbitrary in the field of ani-mate/personal reference.

For a large number of personal nouns there is a correspondence between the "feminine" and the "masculine" gender class and the lexical specification of a noun as female-specific or male-specific. Languages of this type will be called "gender languages" or "languages with grammatical gender".[9] The majority of languages included in the project belong to this group: Arabic, Czech, Danish,

Dutch, French, German, Greek, Hebrew, Hindi, Icelandic, Italian, Norwegian, Polish, Romanian, Russian, Serbian/Croatian/Bosnian, Spanish, Swedish, and Welsh. As the examples of Oriya and English show, a gender system of this type can erode (Oriya) and eventually be lost (English); cf. also Section 3.1.

"Noun class languages"

This type displays no obvious correspondence between class membership and a noun's specification as female-specific or male-specific in the field of personal nouns. These languages, represented in the project by Swahili,[10] have a larger number of classes than gender languages. Often class membership is explicitly marked on the noun itself (cf. the class prefixes in Bantu languages), and there is extensive agreement on other word classes.

To summarize, we will speak of a "gender language" when there are just two or three gender classes, with considerable correspondence between the class membership and lexical/referential gender in the field of animate/ personal nouns. Languages with grammatical gender represent only one type of nominal classification requiring the interaction of at least two elements, i.e. of the noun itself and some satellite element that expresses the class to which the noun belongs.

The lack of grammatical gender in a language does not mean that "gender" in the broader sense cannot be communicated. There are various other categories of gender, e.g. "lexical" and "social" gender, which may be employed to transmit gendered messages. Thus, "gender languages", languages with classifiers or noun classes, as well as those languages that lack noun classification completely (English, Finnish, Turkish), can resort to a variety of linguistic means to construct gender-related messages.

3. Categories of gender

Having established the difference between the more comprehensive concept of "noun class language" and the concept of "gender language", it is necessary to introduce a number of terminological distinctions beyond the typological level which will focus more directly on the representation of women and men in a language: *grammatical gender, lexical gender, referential gender* and *social gender.*

3.1 Grammatical gender

A central issue in any cross-linguistic analysis of gender is, of course, the category of grammatical gender. Typically, gender languages as defined in Section 2.2 have two or three gender classes – among them frequently "feminine" and "masculine". Sometimes the emergence of new subclasses presents problems of analysis, examples being Serbian/Croatian/Bosnian and Russian (cf. Corbett 1991: 161–168). By contrast, a language may reduce the number of its grammatical gender classes, as in the case of some Germanic, Romance, and most Iranian languages, or lose its original gender system completely, as happened in English and Persian.[11]

Unlike case or number, grammatical gender is an inherent property of the noun which controls agreement between the noun (the controller) and some (gender-variable) satellite element (the target) which may be an article, adjective, pronoun, verb, numeral or preposition. Nominal gender typically has only one value, which is determined by an interaction of formal and semantic assignment rules.

3.2 Lexical gender

In debates on language and gender, the term "gender" usually relates to the property of extra-linguistic (i.e. "natural" or "biological") femaleness or maleness. Thus, in English, personal nouns such as *mother, sister, son* and *boy* are lexically specified as carrying the semantic property [female] or [male] respectively, which may in turn relate to the extra-linguistic category of referential gender (or "sex of referent"). Such nouns may be described as "gender-specific" (female-specific or male-specific), in contrast to nouns such as *citizen, patient* or *individual,* which are considered to be "gender-indefinite" or "gender-neutral". Typically, gender-specific terms require the choice of semantically corresponding satellite forms, e.g., the English anaphoric pronouns *she* or *he,* while in the case of gender-indefinite nouns, pronominal choice may be determined by reference (e.g., to a known individual), tradition (choice of "false generics"; cf. Section 3.4) or speaker attitude (as evident, e.g., from a positive evaluation of "gender-fair" language). In languages with grammatical gender, a considerable correspondence can be observed between a noun's grammatical gender class and its lexical specification, most consistently in the field of kinship terms: Germ. *Tante* (f) 'aunt' and *Onkel* (m) 'uncle' have a lexical specification as [female] and [male], respectively. Such nouns require the use of the corresponding pronouns *sie* (f) and *er* (m). For terms without lexical gender, i.e. gender-indefinite nouns such as *Individuum* (n) 'indivdual' or *Person* (f) 'person', pronominal choice is usually, but not always, determined by the grammatical gender of the antecedent (see Bußmann & Hellinger, vol. III).

We do not wish to imply that the terms "female-specific" and "male-specific" correspond to a binary objectivist view that categorizes people neatly into females and males. For example, anthropologists have discussed the Hindi-speaking *hijras* as a "third gender": "[…] most *hijras* were raised as boys before taking up residence in one of India's many hijra communities and adopting the feminine dress, speech, and mannerisms associated with membership" (Hall, vol. II).[12] Although the terms "female" and "male" contribute to the construction of people's everyday experience, they might perhaps be more adequately placed on a continuum, which allows for variation, fuzzy category boundaries, and prototype effects (cf. Lakoff 1987). In spite of this insight, we will continue to use the terms "female" and "male" as valuable descriptive tools.

In any language, lexical gender is an important parameter in the structure of kinship terminologies, address terms, and a number of basic, i.e. frequently used personal nouns. Lexical gender may or may not be marked morphologically. In English, most human nouns are not formally marked for lexical gender, with exceptions such as *widow* – *widower* or *steward* – *stewardess*, which show overt gender marking by suffixation. Only in principle is such markedness independent of grammatical gender. Languages with grammatical gender generally possess a much larger number of devices of overt gender marking. Thus, in the highly inflected Slavic languages, overt lexical gender marking (as a result of the correspondence with grammatical gender) is much more visible than in most Germanic languages, simply because satellite elements have more gender-variable forms.

3.3 Referential gender

"Referential gender" relates linguistic expressions to the non-linguistic reality; more specifically, referential gender identifies a referent as "female", "male" or "gender-indefinite". For example, a personal noun like Germ. *Mädchen* 'girl' is grammatically neuter, has a lexical-semantic specification as [female], and is generally used to refer to females. However, an idiomatic expression like *Mädchen für alles* lit. 'girl for everything'; 'maid of all work', may be used to refer to males also. In this example, while the metaphor seems to neutralize the lexical specificity of *Mädchen*, a gendered message is nevertheless transmitted:

the expression has explicitly derogatory connotations.

In gender languages, a complex relationship between grammatical gender and referential gender obtains for the majority of personal nouns, with typical gender-related asymmetries in pronominalization and coordination (cf. Sections 4.3 and 4.4 below). For example, when reference is made to a particular known individual, the choice of anaphoric pronouns may be referentially motivated and may thus override the noun's grammatical gender, as in Germ. *Tennisstar* (m) ... *sie* (f) (cf. Oelkers 1996).

3.4 "False generics": Generic masculines and male generics

All the gender languages of the project illustrate the traditional (and often prescriptive) practice which requires the use of so-called "generic masculines" to refer to males as well as females.[13] With reference to languages with grammatical gender we will talk about "generic masculines" (where "masculine" denotes grammatical gender), while for languages without grammatical gender, such as English or Japanese, the term "male generics" (with "male" denoting a lexical-semantic property) is more appropriate. This terminological distinction reflects on the different typological affiliations of the respective languages as explained in Section 2.

Grammatically feminine personal nouns tend to be female-specific (with only few exceptions), while grammatically masculine nouns have a wider lexical and referential potential. For example, masculine nouns such as Russ. *vrač* (m) 'physician', Fr. *ministre* (m) 'minister', or Arab. *muḥami* (m) 'lawyer' may be used to refer to males, groups of people whose gender is unknown or unimportant in the context, or even female referents, illustrating the function of the so-called "generic masculine" usage. The reverse, i.e. the use of feminine nouns with gender-indefinite reference, is the rare exception. For example, in Seneca, an Iroquoian language, the feminine has been attested for indefinite reference to people in general (cf. Chafe 1967). In Oneida, also an Iroquoian language, gender-indefinite reference may be achieved by feminine pronouns. But then, speakers may make other choices (including the masculine gender) which are determined by highly complex semantic and pragmatic constraints (cf. Abbott 1984: 126). In a number of Australian Aboriginal languages, the feminine is used as the unmarked gender – in restricted contexts –, while other languages from the same family exhibit the opposite configuration (Alpher 1987: 175). Clearly, further research is necessary which must bring together the anthropological and linguistic evidence. Of primary importance will be the question in which way a relationship can be identified between the existence of feminine/female generics and underlying matriarchal structures.

In languages without grammatical gender, but with some gender-variable pronouns, male generic usage is the traditional androcentric practice in cases of gender-indefinite reference. E.g., in English, where gendered third person singular pronominal distinctions remain of an original grammatical gender system, "generic *he*" – including *him(self)* – is the prescriptive choice in such cases as *an American drinks his coffee black*. Since the use of male-biased pronouns may create referential ambiguities and misunderstandings, alternative formulations have been suggested to replace male generic expressions, e.g. *Americans drink their coffee black* (cf. Section 6). In languages without pronominal gender distinctions, male generic usage is found with the nouns themselves. In Finnish, for example, occupational terms ending in *-mies* 'man' are used for men as well as women (e.g. *lakimies* lit. 'law-man'; 'lawyer') and are officially claimed to be gender-neutral. Empirical findings reported by Engelberg (cf. vol. II), however, show that this claim is more than doubtful.

The prescription of "generic masculines" or "male generics" has long been the center of debates about linguistic sexism in English and other languages. The asymmetries involved here, i.e. the choice of masculine/male expressions as the normal or "unmarked" case with the resulting invisibility of feminine/female expressions are reflections of an underlying gender belief system, which in turn creates expectations about appropriate female and male behavior. Such expectations will prevent a genuinely generic interpretation of gender-indefinite personal nouns, and can also be related to the fact that masculine/male pronouns occur three times as frequently as the corresponding feminine/female pronouns in some languages, e.g. in English and Russian.[14] There is empirical evidence for English, but also for Turkish, Finnish, and German, that most human nouns are in fact not neutral, which supports the assumption that gender-related socio-cultural parameters are a powerful force in shaping the semantics of personal reference.[15]

3.5 Social gender

"Social gender" is a category that refers "to the socially imposed dichotomy of masculine and feminine roles and character traits" (Kramarae & Treichler 1985:173). Personal nouns are specified for social gender if the behavior of associated words can neither be explained by grammatical nor by lexical gender. An illustration of social gender in English is the fact that many higher-status occupational terms such as *lawyer, surgeon,* or *scientist* will frequently be pronominalized by the male-specific pronoun *he* in contexts where referential gender is either not known or irrelevant. On the other hand, low-status occupational titles such as *secretary, nurse,* or *schoolteacher* will often be followed by anaphoric *she.* But even for general human nouns such as *pedestrian, consumer* or *patient,* traditional practice prescribes the choice of *he* in neutral contexts.

Social gender has to do with stereotypical assumptions about what are appropriate social roles for women and men, including expectations about who will be a typical member of the class of, say, *surgeon* or *nurse.* Deviations from such assumptions will often require overt formal markings, as in Engl. *female surgeon* or *male nurse.* However, since the majority of general personal nouns can be assumed to have a male bias, it seems plausible to suggest that – irrespective of whether the language does or does not have grammatical gender – underlying is the principle "male as norm".

Social gender is a particularly salient category in a language like Turkish which lacks even gender-variable pronouns. Frequently, gender-related associations remain hidden on a deeper semantic level. E.g., the Turkish occupational term *kuyumcu* 'goldseller' is lexically gender-indefinite, but is invariably associated with male referents, although theoretically, a female goldseller could also be referred to as *kuyumcu.* The word can be said to have a covert male bias which derives from sociocultural assumptions and expectations about the relationships between women and men (cf. Braun, this vol., Section 3.1).

4. Gender-related structures

4.1 Word-formation

Word-formation is a particularly sensitive area in which gender may be communicated. In languages with or without grammatical gender, processes of derivation and compounding have an important function in the formation of gendered personal nouns, particularly in the use of existing and the creation of new feminine/female terms, e.g. in the area of occupational terms, cf. (1) and (2):

(1) **Derivation**

	Masculine/male	Feminine/female	
Norw.	*forfatter*	*forfatter-inne*	'author'
Arab.	*katib*	*katib-a*	'secretary'
Rom.	*pictor*	*pictor-iţă*	'painter'
Engl.	*steward*	*steward-ess*	

(2) **Compounding**

	Masculine/male	Feminine/female	
Germ.	*Geschäfts-mann*	*Geschäfts-frau*	'business man/woman'
Norw.	*politi-mann*	*politi-kvinne*	'police officer'
	lit. 'police man'	lit. 'police woman'	
EMC	*seli-man*	*seli-uman*	'trader'
	lit. 'sell-man'	lit. 'sell-woman'	
Indon.	*dokter*	*dokter perempuan*	'doctor'
	lit. 'doctor'	lit. 'doctor woman'	

Typically, female gender-specification occurs with reference to a particular individual (*Congesswoman Maxine Waters*) or in contexts of contrastive emphasis (*male and female delegates*). Female linguistic visibility is often a marked and loaded concept, and we find considerable variation concerning the status and productivity of feminine/female word-formation processes across languages. Thus, German has a well-established and extremely productive process for the formation of personal feminines ending in -*in*: *Punkerin* 'female punk', *Bundeskanzlerin* 'female chancellor', *Bischöfin* 'female bishop', etc. By contrast, Welsh, also a gender language, has no such instrument for morphological gender-specification. Very few derived feminines exist, i.e. most occupational and other personal nouns in Welsh are grammatically masculine and have no feminine counterparts.

In English, the few derivational patterns that exist for the formation of female-specific terms have low productivity, and more often than not produce semantically asymmetric pairs in which the female represents the lesser category, illustrating what Schulz (1975) has called "semantic derogation". Notorious examples are Engl. *governor/governess*, *major/majorette*. Of course, such asymmetric pairs also occur in languages with grammatical gender, cf. (3):

(3) Fr.   *couturier* (m)   'fashion designer'
            couturière (f)   'seamstress, female tailor'

Germ.   *Sekretär* (m)   'secretary of an administration, trade union or
                           the like'
        Sekretärin (f)   'secretary in an office'

Feminine/female terms are not consistently derived nor used in case of female reference; their use may be stylistically marked and in many languages carries negative connotations, which makes them unacceptable in neutral contexts. Thus, in Russian or Polish, where masculinity is highly valued, feminine/female counterparts of terms denoting prestigious occupations are avoided. By contrast, masculine/male terms are either neutral or carry positive connotations.

4.2 Agreement

In agreement, concern is with overt representations of gender. On a formal level, agreement establishes a syntactic relationship between a noun's satellite element, e.g. an article, adjective, pronominal or verbal form, and the noun's gender class. Satellite elements must be gender-variable, i.e. they must allow for a choice between at least two values (e.g., feminine and masculine, as in French and Italian, or feminine, masculine and neuter, as in Russian and German). In some languages, e.g. in Russian, discourse categories such as the gender of speaker, addressee or person talked about may all be marked morphologically on some verbal forms, cf. Doleschal & Schmid (this vol., Section 2.2):

(4) *Prišl-a   moj-a   byvš-aja   studentka,*
     came-FEM my-FEM former-FEM student.FEM
     kotor-aja očen' umn-aja.   On-a   mogl-a   by   pomoč'.
     who-FEM very intelligent-FEM she-FEM might-FEM COND help
     'A former student of mine, who is very intelligent, has come. She might help.'

In traditional grammars, agreement is described as a primarily formal and predictable phenomenon, one of whose major functions is reference-tracking. Contrary to this view, we believe that agreement may add semantic and social information to the discourse, thus taking on symbolic functions. This claim is based on the observation that agreement tends to affect masculine and feminine nouns in different ways, mainly due to the principle "male as norm": Agreement will favor the masculine in coordination (cf. Section 4.4), and, generally, masculine agreement predominates; feminine agreement is female-specific and, in many contexts, non-obligatory and irregular, depending on extralinguistic factors such as tradition, prescription or speaker attitude.

4.3 Pronominalization

Gendered pronouns are overt representations of gender both in languages with and without grammatical gender. Anaphoric gendered pronouns reveal the semantic specification of nouns with lexical gender, they may express referential gender in contradiction to grammatical gender, they may function as a means to either specify or abstract from (intended) referential gender, and they may emphasize traditional or reformed practices, as when a speaker chooses between a "false generic" (e.g., Engl. *he*) or a more gender-neutral alternative (such as Engl. "singular *they*"). Generally, pronominalization is a powerful strategy of communicating gender.

The interpretation of pronominalization as one type of agreement remains controversial. English exemplifies a type of relation between noun and pronoun which is not syntactically motivated. Only reflexes of the original grammatical gender system remain in third person singular pronouns (*he – she – it*), and the choice of anaphoric pronouns is controlled by lexical-semantic properties of the antecedent, by referential gender (including intended reference), or social gender. Corbett (1991:169) concludes that pronouns "may be the means by which particular languages divide nouns into different agreement classes". However, this classification is semantically based, and English is, of course, not a "gender language" as defined in Section 2.2.

4.4 Coordination

When a noun phrase conjoins a masculine and a feminine noun, the choice of a related target form may create a conflict between two competing genders. An example from Romanian (cf. Maurice, this vol., Section 2.3) illustrates the strategy of what Corbett (1991:279) calls "syntactic gender resolution", where agreement occurs with one conjunct only, namely the masculine, albeit in the plural:[15]

> (5) *un vizitator   și   o turistă   mult interesați*
>   a   visitor.MASC and a tourist.FEM very interested.MASC.PL
>   'a very interested (male) visitor and a very interested (female) tourist'

Corbett claims that the choice of masculine agreement forms in such cases is "evidently of the syntactic type" (Corbett 1991:ibid.), since what determines agreement is independent of the meaning of the nouns involved. In our view, however, the example illustrates the prescriptive practice that if at least one conjunct is headed by a masculine noun, masculine agreement forms are used. Another illustration of this practice involving inanimate nouns is the Hebrew example (6), cf. Tobin (this vol., Section 2.3):

(6)   *Ha-sefer*   *ve-ha-maxberet*   *nimtsaim*   *kan.*
     the-book.MASC.SG and-the-notebook.FEM.SG are.found.MASC.PL here
     'The book and the notebook are here.'

There are a number of exceptions to this regularity. For example, in some languages with three grammatical genders, the neuter gender may be employed to resolve the gender conflict in coordination, as in this example from Icelandic (cf. Grönberg, vol. II, Section 2.3):

(7)   *Óli*   *og   Elsa*   *eru ung.*
     Óli.MASC and Elsa.FEM are young.NEUT.PL
     'Óli and Elsa are young.'

In some cases the choice of the masculine target gender may be motivated by the vicinity of the nearest controller noun when this is also masculine (cf. Corbett 1991:265). However, "Gender across languages" provides numerous counter-examples. For example, in Arabic, if word order in a conjoined noun phrase is reversed to masculine first and feminine second, the choice of the feminine, as a response to the nearest controller gender, is ungrammatical; the masculine must still be chosen (cf. Hachimi, this vol., Section 4.3):

(8)   *Lab*   *u   bnat-u*   *ˁyyan-in.*
     father.MASC.SG and daughter.FEM.PL-his tired-MASC.PL
     'The father and his daughters are tired.'

Underlying such syntactic conventions may be a gender hierarchy which defines the masculine as the "most worthy gender" (Baron 1986:97).[17] As a result, masculine nouns are highly visible in gender languages and carry considerably more weight and emphasis than feminine nouns.

5.   Gender-related messages

The communication of gender-related messages may be performed by many other devices in addition to the ones discussed so far. Of primary importance in the context of "Gender across languages" are address forms, idiomatic and metaphorical expressions, proverbs, and, of course, female/male discourse.

5.1 Address terms

Languages differ considerably in the type of obligatory and optional information they encode in their address systems. English can be characterized as a language with only moderate distinctions, lacking even the *tu/vous*-distinction that is characteristic, e.g., for German, French or Russian, while languages such as Vietnamese, Japanese or Javanese have extremely complex address systems.[18]

For example, on the basis of the underlying, all-pervasive concept of *hormat* 'respect', Indonesian as spoken in Java has lexicalized numerous sociocultural and interactional dimensions such as age, gender, social status, participant relationship, and formality of the situation, which will determine a speaker's selection of an item from one of several speech styles and terms (cf. Kuntjara, this vol., Section 3). Gender will be performed in asymmetric and non-reciprocal practices. Thus, the traditional Javanese husband will address his wife by her first name or by the kinship term *dik* 'younger sister', but will receive the term *mas* 'older brother', irrespective of his age. Lexical choices generally are less constrained for males, while women are expected to use a higher, more deferential style.

Changes in address practices may be indicative of underlying changes in the social relationships between women and men. In language planning such changes will be supported as contributing to more symmetry in address systems. An example is the legislation establishing Germ. *Frau* as the only acceptable official term of address for adult women to abolish the traditional distinction between *Frau* 'Mrs' and *Fräulein* 'Miss' (cf. Bußmann & Hellinger, vol. III). Similarly, in English the address term *Ms* was introduced to abolish the distinction between *Mrs* and *Miss*. However, such a term may also be appropriated by mainstream usage to transmit (originally) unintended messages, as in the case of Australian English *Ms* 'divorced' or 'feminist' (cf. Pauwels, this vol., Section 2.1).[19]

5.2 Idiomatic expressions and proverbs

Another area of the implicit discursive negotiation of gender, irrespective of whether the language does or does not have grammatical gender, are frozen expressions such as idioms, metaphors, and proverbs.[20] Descriptions of or terms for women – when these are part of such expressions – tend to have negative, and frequently sexual and moral implications which are not found for corresponding male terms (where these exist).

For example, Moroccan Arabic provides a number of honorific terms, phrases, and proverbs which are indicative of the glorification of the mother-concept in Moroccan culture, as in 'the mother is the light of the house' or 'paradise lies under mothers' feet'. At the same time, mothers of daughters are evaluated negatively, reflecting on the unequal status of girls and boys (cf. Hachimi, this vol., Section 7). Representative of the genre of proverbs is the following Turkish example (cf. Braun, this vol., Section 6):

(9)   *Oğlan doğuran övünsün, kız doğuran dövünsün.*
      'Let the one who bears a son be proud, let the one who bears a daughter beat herself.'

This is the message of numerous idiomatic expressions and proverbs from many languages of "Gender across languages": Arabic, Chinese, Danish, Finnish, Italian, Norwegian, Russian, and Turkish.

In Russian, the woman-as-mother concept is practically the only positive female image in proverbs (cf. Doleschal & Schmid, this vol., Section 6.1). The extreme opposite is obscene language with expressions of "mother-fucking", a misogynist practice which has also been attested for many languages, with Russian, Chinese, Turkish, and Danish representing examples in "Gender across languages". Such frozen expressions embody fundamental collective beliefs and stereotypes which are available for continued practices of communicating gender.

5.3   Female and male discourse

A major concern of studies on language and gender in the 1990s has been the search for an empirical foundation on which statements could be made on discourse practices in diverse types of interaction (cf. Wodak & Benke 1997).

On a theoretical level the inadequacy of binary categories (*women* vs. *men*, *female* vs. *male*) has been criticized. These categories show internal diversification and must be described to a considerable extent as social constructs. Also statements about female and male verbal behavior have been criticized for making inappropriate generalizations. Explanatory theories (cf. the deficit, dominance, difference, and diversity models) developed with reference to English cannot be applied to other languages without taking into account dimensions of sociocultural difference (cf. also Pauwels 1998, Bergvall 1999).

Investigations of gender and discourse have primarily focussed on the identification of differences between female and male speech.[20] For a number of languages, among them English, Chinese and Japanese, some differences were indeed found, but quantitative evidence remains controversial. For example, higher frequencies of "uncertainty phenomena" were found in some types of discourse (typically in experimental or more formal situations), but not in others. More importantly, the occurrence of *tag*-questions (e.g. in English) or sentence-final particles (e.g. in Chinese) may have various communicative functions in actual discourse, so that an explanation in terms of uncertainty or tentativeness is only one among several possibilities (cf. Holmes 1995). This is also true for categories of turn-taking, where a higher frequency of interruptions and overlaps as performed by male speakers is widely interpreted as indicative of conversational dominance (cf. West & Zimmerman 1983). However, Bergvall (1999) has repeatedly warned against immediately approaching discourse in terms of gender differences, suggesting that rather than categorizing people and their verbal behavior into seemingly dichotomous and opposed groups, it would be more appropriate to interpret the data in terms of a linguistic and behavioral continuum.

In "Gender across languages", discourse analysis features more prominently for those languages where – in the absence of substantial structural representations of gender – discourse emerges as a central field in which gender is negotiated, e.g., in Chinese, Japanese, English, and Belizean Creole.

6.   Language change and language reform

In all the languages represented in "Gender across languages", tendencies of variation and change in the area of personal reference can be observed. In some languages (e.g., English, German, French, Dutch and Spanish) such tendencies have been supported by language planning measures, including the publication of recommendations and guidelines, while for other languages an awareness of gendered asymmetries is only beginning to develop in both academia and the media (e.g., in Czech or Polish). To a large extent, the emergence of public discourse on language and gender depends on the socio-political background, in particular the state of the women's movement in the respective country.

Language as a tool of social practice may serve referential functions (e.g. the exchange of information); it has social-psychological functions in that it reflects social hierarchies and mechanisms of identification, and it contributes to the construction and communication of gender. More specifically, language is assumed to codify an androcentric worldview. Recommendations and guidelines for non-discriminatory language identify areas of conventional language use as sexist and offer alternatives aiming at a gender-fair (and symmetric) representation of women and men. As an instrument of language planning they reinforce tendencies of linguistic change by means of explicit directions (cf. Frank 1989: 197; Pauwels 1998, 1999; Hellinger 1995).

Gender-related language reform is a reaction to changes in the relationships between women and men, which have caused overt conflicts on the level of language comprehension and production. Reformed usage symbolizes the dissonance between traditional prescriptions such as the use of masculine/male generics and innovative alternatives. In most cases it explicitly articulates its political foundation by emphasizing that equal treatment of women and men must also be realized on the level of communication.

Guidelines are based on the assumption that a change in behavior, i.e., using more instances of non-sexist language, will be attended by a change in attitude so that positive attitudes towards non-sexist alternatives will develop (cf. Smith 1973: 97). Conversely, positive attitudes will motivate speakers to use more non-sexist language. This is not necessarily what happens in actual cases of language reform. Reformed usage has sometimes been appropriated by speakers who will use alternatives in ways that were not intended, thereby redefining and depoliticizing feminist meanings (cf. Ehrlich & King 1994).

7. Conclusion

The central function of linguistic gender in the domain of human reference is the communication of gendered messages of various types. The linguistic representation of gender is one of the dimensions on which languages can be compared, irrespective of individual structural properties and sociolinguistic diversities. However, even apparently straightforward categories such as grammatical or referential gender cannot be fully described in terms that abstract from the cultural and sociopolitical specifics of individual languages. And once the study of gender is taken beyond the level of formal manifestation to include discourse practices, the concept of gender becomes increasingly complex and multi-dimensional.

The general tendencies we have identified all center around one fundamental principle: masculine/male expressions (and practices) are the default choice for human reference in almost any context. The assumption may be plausible that gender languages offer the larger potential for the avoidance of male-biased language – simply because female visibility is more easily achieved on the level of expression. At the same time, advocating an increase in female visibility may create problematic and potentially adverse effects in languages like Russian or Hebrew, where masculine/male terms for female reference are evaluated positively even by women. In addition, consistent splitting, i.e. the explicit use of both feminine and masculine expressions when reference is made to both women and men, is considered to be stylistically cumbersome by many speakers, esp. in languages with case. Thus, a comparative view would have to investigate the ways in which structural prerequisites interact with sociolinguistic tendencies of change.

By contrast, "genderless" languages seem to provide more possibilities for egalitarian and gender-neutral expressions, by avoiding the dominant visibility of masculine terms, and stereotypical associations of feminine terms with secondary or exceptional status. However, in genderless languages it may be even more difficult to challenge the covert male bias and the exclusion of female imagery in many personal nouns.

In the study of language and gender, there is an urgent need for comparative analyses based on adequate descriptions of a large number of languages of diverse structural and sociocultural backgrounds. This includes an awareness of the fact that *white middle class North American English* cannot be regarded as representative for other languages also. "Gender across languages" contributes towards the goal of a more global view of gender by presenting a wealth of data and language-specific analyses that will allow for cross-linguistic statements on manifestations of gender. In addition, the material presented in "Gender across languages" can be expected to enrich the debate of a number of interdisciplinary issues:

From a sociolinguistic perspective, the tremendous variation found in the exchange of gendered messages must be placed more explicitly in a wider framework of communities of practice (CofP), considering the interaction between "gender" and age, ethnic membership, social status and religion.[21]

From a text-linguistic perspective, comparative investigations of gender-related structures will identify the stylistic and rhetorical potentials of grammatical gender in a given language, in particular for the construction of cohesion and textuality by a less constrained word order and for disambiguation (reference tracking).

From a historical perspective, the analysis of ongoing structural changes may shed light on the question of why manifestations of gender in historically or typologically related languages have developed in very different directions, as in the case of Germanic languages which may have two or three categories of grammatical gender – or none at all.

From a psycholinguistic perspective, further empirical evidence is needed from more languages that might contribute towards an understanding of how gendered messages are interpreted, and more generally, in which ways the perception and construction of the universe is influenced by linguistic, social and cultural parameters.

Notes

* This chapter has considerably profited from discussions with Friederike Braun.

1. Cf. Corbett (1991). Lehmann (1993) provides an informative overview of types of congruence/agreement. Rich data from various languages can be found in Barlow & Ferguson (1988).

2. Cf. Zubin & Köpcke (1984, 1986).

3. Cf. also Lakoff (1987: ch. 6), Corbett (1991: 15–18). For further examples see Grimm (1831: 349f), Royen (1929: 341–347), Strunk (1994: 151f).

4. On the origin of gender cf. Claudi (1985), Fodor (1959), Ibrahim (1973), Royen (1929), Leiss (1994); on the decay and loss of gender (systems) cf. Corbett (1995), Claudi (1985).

5. This ignores the very rudimentary numeral classification found in Turkish.

6. Cf. Unterbeck (2000) for an overview of different types of noun classification. Material from a larger number of languages can be found in Craig (1986, 1994). Royen (1929) is still an impressive study of gender and nominal classification.

7. Thus, for Vietnamese over 200 such classifiers have been identified, cf. Pham (vol. II, Section 2); on classifier languages cf. also Craig (1994).

8. For example, Corbett (1991: ch. 3.1) discusses morphological *gender assignment* jointly for Russian, Swahili and other Bantu languages; cf. also Hurskainen (2000).

9. This is the approach taken by Dixon (1982: 160); cf. also Braun (2000: 32).

10. Swahili (cf. Beck, vol. III) is one of perhaps 600 African languages with noun classes (cf. Heine 1982: 190); on noun classes in African languages cf. Hurskainen (2000). Large numbers of noun class languages are also found among Dravidian and New Guinean languages.

11. In contrast to English, Persian even lost pronominal gender distinctions. The loss of grammatical gender in English is described in Jones (1988), and more recently, Kastovsky (2000); for a diachronic perspective on gender in the Scandinavian languages cf. Braunmüller (2000), in French cf. Härmä (2000), and in the Iranian languages Corbett (1991: 315–318).

12. Practices of gender-crossing in Native American communities, e.g., the Navajo, are described in Whitehead (1991). So-called "abnormal" developments are discussed in Wodak & Benke (1997: ch. 1.2).

13. The term "false generics" was used by Kramarae & Treichler (1985: 150, 175) to refer to "generic masculines". Romaine (vol. I Section 3.2) uses the term "androcentric generics".

14. There are statistical data for English (Graham 1975) and Russian (Francis & Kučera 1967).

15. Empirical evidence for English can be found in MacKay & Fulkerson (1979), for Turkish in Braun (2000), for Finnish in Engelberg (vol. II section 5), for German in Scheele & Gauler (1993) and Irmen & Köhncke (1996). For cross-linguistic evidence cf. Batliner (1984).

16. Coordination is no problem in German which has no corresponding gender-variable satellite forms in the plural (cf. Bußmann & Hellinger, vol. III).

17. Cf. also Curzan (2000); for German, cf. Bußmann (1995).

18. On address systems, cf. Braun (1988); on the T/V distinction Brown & Gilman (1960). For Vietnamese, cf. Pham (vol. II).

19. On French legislation, cf. Burr (vol. III).

20. For German, cf. Daniels (1985), for Moroccan, cf. Webster (1982), for Chinese, cf. Zhang (vol. II). For a comparison of Finnish and German proverbs cf. Majapuro (1997).

21. For recent overviews of gendered discourse, cf. Talbot (1998), Hall & Bucholtz (1995), and Romaine (1999: chs. 6,7).

22. On the concept of CofP, cf. the special issue of *Language in Society* 28/2 (1999).

References

Abbott, Clifford. 1984. "Two feminine genders in Oneida." *Anthropological Linguistics* 26: 125–137.

Alpher, Barry. 1987. "Feminine as the unmarked grammatical gender: Buffalo girls are no fools." *Australian Journal of Linguistics* 7: 169–187.

Barlow, Michael & Charles A. Ferguson, eds. 1988. *Agreement in natural language. Approaches, theories, descriptions.* Stanford, CA: Stanford University Press.

Baron, Dennis. 1986. *Grammar and gender.* New Haven, CT: Yale University Press.

Batliner, Anton. 1984. "The comprehension of grammatical and natural gender: A cross-linguistic experiment." *Linguistics* 22: 831–856.

Bergvall, Victoria L. 1999. "An agenda for language and gender research for the start of the new millennium." *Linguistik Online.* http://viadrina.euv-frankfurt-o.de/~wjournal/1_99/bergvall.htm

Bergvall, Victoria L. & Janet M. Bing & Alice F. Freed, eds. 1996. *Rethinking language and gender research: Theory and practice.* London: Longman.

Bing, Janet M. & Victoria L. Bergvall. 1996. "The question of questions: Beyond binary thinking." In *Rethinking language and gender research: Theory and practice*, eds. Victoria L. Bergvall & Janet M. Bing & Alice F. Freed. London: Longman, 1–30.

Bittner, Dagmar. 2000. "Gender classification and the inflectional system of German." In *Gender in grammar and cognition*, eds. Barbara Unterbeck et al. Berlin: de Gruyter, 1–23.

Braun, Friederike 1988. *Terms of address. Problems of patterns and usage in various languages and cultures*. Berlin: Mouton de Gruyter.

Braun, Friederike. 2000. *Geschlecht im Türkischen. Untersuchungen zum sprachlichen Umgang mit einer sozialen Kategorie*. Wiesbaden: Harrassowitz.

Braunmüller, Kurt. 2000. "Gender in North Germanic: A diasystematic and functional approach." In *Gender in grammar and cognition*, eds. Barbara Unterbeck et al. Berlin: de Gruyter, 25–54.

Brown, Roger & Albert Gilman. 1960. "The pronouns of power and solidarity." In *Style in language*, ed. Thomas A. Sebeok. Cambridge, MA: MIT Press, 253–276.

Bußmann, Hadumod. 1995. "Das Genus, die Grammatik und – der Mensch: Geschlechterdifferenz in der Sprachwissenschaft." In *Genus: Zur Geschlechterdifferenz in den Kulturwissenschaften*, eds. Hadumod Bußmann & Renate Hof. Stuttgart: Kröner, 114–160.

Chafe, Wallace L. 1967. *Seneca morphology and dictionary*. Washington: Smithsonian Press.

Claudi, Ulrike. 1985. *Zur Entstehung von Genussystemen: Überlegungen zu einigen theoretischen Aspekten, verbunden mit einer Fallstudie des Zande*. Hamburg: Buske.

Corbett, Greville G. 1991. *Gender*. Cambridge: Cambridge University Press.

Corbett, Greville G. 1995. "Agreement." In *Syntax. Ein internationales Handbuch zeitgenössischer Forschung*, Vol. 2, eds. Joachim Jacobs & Arnim von Stechow & Wolfgang Sternefeld & Theo Vennemann. Berlin: de Gruyter, 1235–1244.

Corbett, Greville G. & Norman M. Fraser. 2000. "Default genders." In *Gender in grammar and cognition*, eds. Barbara Unterbeck et al. Berlin: de Gruyter, 55–97.

Craig, Colette G. 1986. *Noun classes and categorization*. Amsterdam: Benjamins.

Craig, Colette G. 1994. "Classifier languages." In *The encyclopedia of language and linguistics*, Vol. 2, ed. Ronald E. Asher. Oxford: Pergamon, 565–569.

Curzan, Anne. 2000. "Gender categories in early English grammars: Their message to the modern grammarian." In *Gender in grammar and cognition*, eds. Barbara Unterbeck et al. Berlin: de Gruyter, 561–576.

Daniels, Karlheinz. 1985. "Geschlechtsspezifische Stereotypen im Sprichwort." *Sprache und Literatur* 56: 18–35.

Dixon, Robert M. W. 1972. *The Dyirbal language of North Queensland*. Cambridge: Cambridge University Press.

Dixon, Robert M. W. 1982. *Where have all the adjectives gone? And other essays in semantics and syntax*. Berlin: Mouton.

Ehrlich, Susan & Ruth King. 1994. "Feminist meanings and the (de)politicization of the lexicon". *Language in Society* 23: 59–76.

Fodor, Istvan. 1959. "The origin of grammatical gender." *Lingua* 8: 1–41, 186–214.

Francis, Nelson & Henry Kučera. 1967. *Computational analysis of present-day American English*. Providence, RI: Brown University Press.

Frank, Francine W. 1989. "Language planning, language reform, and language change: A review of guidelines for nonsexist usage." In *Language, gender, and professional writing: Theoretical approaches and guidelines for nonsexist usage*, eds. Francine W. Frank & Paula A. Treichler. New York: MLA, 105–137.

Graham, Alma. 1975. "The making of a nonsexist dictionary." In *Language and sex: Difference and dominance*, eds. Barrie Thorne & Nancy Henley. Rowley, MA: Newbury House, 57–63.

Greenberg, Joseph H. 1972. "Numeral classifiers and substantival number: Problems in the genesis of a linguistic type." *Working Papers on Language Universals* 9: 1–39.

Greenberg, Joseph H. 1978. "How does a language acquire gender markers?" In *Universals of human language*, Vol. 3, ed. Joseph H. Greenberg. Stanford, CA: Stanford University Press, 47–82.

Grimm, Jacob. 1831. *Deutsche Grammatik III*. 3. Theil, 3. Buch: *Von der Wortbildung*. Göttingen: Dietrich.

Härma, Juhani. 2000. "Gender in French: A diachronic perspective." In *Gender in grammar and cognition*, eds. Barbara Unterbeck et al. Berlin: de Gruyter, 609–619.

Hall, Kira & Mary Bucholtz, eds. 1995. *Gender articulated: Language and the socially constructed self*. New York: Routledge.

Heine, Bernd. 1982. "African noun class systems." In *Apprehension: Das sprachliche Erfassen von Gegenständen*. Teil I: *Bereich und Ordnung der Phänomene*, eds. Hansjakob Seiler & Christian Lehmann. Tübingen: Narr, 189–216.

Hellinger, Marlis. 1995. "Language and gender." In *The German language in the real world*, ed. Patrick Stevenson. Oxford: Clarendon, 280–314.

Hockett, Charles F. 1958. *A course in modern linguistics*. New York: Macmillan.

Holmes, Janet. 1995. *Women, men and politeness*. London: Longman.

Hurskainen, Arvi. 2000. "Noun classification in African languages." In *Gender in grammar and cognition*, eds. Barbara Unterbeck et al. Berlin: de Gruyter, 665–688.

Ibrahim, H. Muhammad. 1973. *Grammatical gender. Its origin and development*. The Hague: Mouton.

Irmen, Lisa & Astrid Köhncke. 1996. "Zur Psychologie des "generischen" Maskulinums." *Sprache & Kognition* 15: 152–166.

Jones, Charles. 1988. *Grammatical gender in English: 950–1250*. London: Croom Helm.

Kastovsky, Dieter. 2000. "Inflectional classes, morphological restructuring, and the dissolution of Old English grammatical gender." In *Gender in grammar and cognition*, eds. Barbara Unterbeck et al. Berlin: de Gruyter, 709–727.

Kramarae, Cheris & Paula A. Treichler. 1985. *A feminist dictionary*. Boston: Pandora.

Lakoff, George. 1987. *Women, fire, and dangerous things: What categories reveal about the mind*. Chicago: University of Chicago Press.

Lehmann, Christian. 1993. "Kongruenz." In *Syntax. Ein internationales Handbuch zeitgenössischer Forschung*, Vol.1, eds. Joachim Jacobs & Arnim von Stechow & Wolfgang Sternefeld & Theo Vennemann. Berlin: de Gruyter: 722–729.

Leiss, Elisabeth. 1994. "Genus und Sexus. Kritische Anmerkungen zur Sexualisierung von Grammatik." *Linguistische Berichte* 152: 281–300.

MacKay, Donald & David Fulkerson. 1979. "On the comprehension and production of pronouns." *Journal of Verbal Learning and Verbal Behavior* 18: 661–673.

Majapuro, Anne. 1997. "Weinende Braut, lachende Frau. Geschlechtsspezifische Merkmale des Lachens und Weinens in deutschen und finnischen Sprichwörtern." In *Laughter down the centuries*, eds. Siegfried Jäckel & Asko Timonen. Turku: University of Turku, 233–248.

Oelkers, Susanne. 1996. " 'Der Sprintstar und ihre Freundinnen'. Ein empirischer Beitrag zur Diskussion um das generische Maskulinum." *Muttersprache* 106: 1–15.

Pauwels, Anne. 1998. *Women changing language*. London: Longman.

Pauwels, Anne. 1999. "Feminist language planning: Has it been worthwhile?" *Linguistik Online*. http://www.viadrina.euv-frankfurt-o.de/~wjournal/1_99/pauwels.htm

Romaine, Suzanne. 1999. *Communicating gender*. Mahwah, NJ: Lawrence Erlbaum.

Royen, Gerlach. 1929. *Die nominalen Klassifikations-Systeme in den Sprachen der Erde. Historisch-kritische Studie, mit besonderer Berücksichtigung des Indo-Germanischen*. Mödling: Anthropos.

Scheele, Brigitte & Eva Gauler. 1993. "Wählen Wissenschaftler ihre Probleme anders aus als Wissenschaftler*I*nnen? Das Genus-Sexus-Problem als paradigmatischer Fall der linguistischen Relativitätsthese." *Sprache & Kognition* 12: 59–72.

Schulz, Muriel R. 1975. "The semantic derogation of woman." In *Language and sex: Difference and dominance*, eds. Barrie Thorne & Nancy Henley. Rowley, MA: Newbury House, 64–75.

Smith, David M. 1973. "Language, speech and ideology: A conceptual framework." In *Language attitudes: Current trends and prospects*, eds. Roger W. Shuy & Ralph W. Fasold. Washington, DC: Georgetown University Press, 97–112.

Strunk, Klaus. 1994. "Grammatisches und natürliches Geschlecht in sprachwissenschaftlicher Sicht." In *Frau und Mann. Geschlechterdifferenzierung in Natur und Menschenwelt*, ed. Venanz Schubert. St. Ottilien: EOS Verlag, 141–164.

Talbot, Mary M. 1998. *Language and gender: An introduction*. Oxford: Blackwell.

Unterbeck, Barbara. 2000. "Gender: New light on an old category. An introduction." In *Gender in grammar and cognition*, eds. Barbara Unterbeck et al. Berlin: de Gruyter, xv-xlvi.

Webster, Sheila K. 1982. "Women, sex, and marriage in Moroccan proverbs." *International Journal of Middle East Studies* 14: 173–184.

West, Candace & Don H. Zimmerman. 1983. "Small insults: A study of interruptions in cross-sex conversations between unacquainted persons." In *Language, gender and society*, eds. Barrie Thorne & Cheris Kramarae & Nancy Henley. Rowley, MA: Newbury House, 113–118.

Whitehead, Harriet. 1991 [[1]1981]. "The bow and the burden strap: A new look at institutionalized homosexuality in Native North America." In *Sexual meanings. The cultural construction of gender and sexuality*, eds. Sherry B. Ortner & Harriet Whitehead. Cambridge: Cambridge University Press, 80–115.

Wodak, Ruth & Gertraud Benke. 1997. "Gender as a sociolinguistic variable: New perspectives on variation studies." In *The handbook of sociolinguistics*, ed. Florian Coulmas. Oxford: Blackwell, 127–150.

Zubin, David & Klaus-Michael Köpcke. 1984. "Affect classification in the German gender system." *Lingua* 63: 41–96.

Zubin, David & Klaus-Michael Köpcke. 1986. "Gender and folk taxonomy: The indexical relation between grammatical and lexical classification." In *Noun classes and categorization*, ed. Colette G. Craig. Amsterdam: Benjamins, 139–181.

Shifting sands

Language and gender in Moroccan Arabic[*]

Atiqa Hachimi
University of Hawaii, Honolulu, USA

1. Introduction

Moroccan Arabic (*ddariža*) is the local Arabic dialect spoken in Morocco, the westernmost country of North Africa. Like other Arabic vernaculars, Moroccan Arabic is not used for written purposes but only for informal and mundane communication. It is spoken by more than 20 million people (including second language users), i.e. about 90% of the Moroccan population.

Genetically, Moroccan Arabic belongs to the West Semitic branch of the Afroasiatic family of languages. Like other Semitic languages, it has a fairly rich inflectional and derivational morphology. One of the special properties of the morphology of Moroccan Arabic, and Semitic languages in general, is that it forms its words by slotting vowel patterns and affixes into a skeleton of consonants known as "the root". Each pattern has a distinctive meaning of its own, thus changing the meaning of the root once attached to it. No matter what changes a root undergoes, the newly derived word will bear some meaning of that root. Consider the root *k-t-b*, which is always related to writing: *ktb-at* 'she wrote', *ktəb* 'he wrote', *ktab* (m) 'book', *mktab-a* (f) 'library', *mktəb* (m) 'desk', *l-mktab* (m) 'the inscribed (by God)', i.e. 'fate'. Moroccan Arabic has two grammatical genders (feminine and masculine); adjectives, verbs, pronouns, and prepositions are in agreement with the gender of the noun. Adjectives always follow the nouns they modify and they correspond in number and gender. The Moroccan Arabic verb is very complex, it carries a substantial amount of semantic information which allows it to be an independent sentence in its own right, e.g. *ka-y-t-katb-u* (DUR-3IPF-REFL-write-they) 'they are corresponding with each other'. Prepositions govern nouns or pronouns. The unmarked word order in Moroccan Arabic is Verb-Subject-Object, although other word orders are also possible.[1]

2.   Sociolinguistic perspectives: Multiglossia and multilingualism

The importance of locating language and gender in Morocco lies in the particular sociolinguistic situation that characterizes this area: multiglossia and multi-lingualism (Youssi 1995). Multiglossia refers to the use of different varieties of a language for distinctively separate purposes. Moroccan Arabic is in a multiglossic relationship with other varieties of Arabic: (1) Classical Arabic is used for liturgical purposes, mainly, in reading or reciting the Holy Qurʔan 'Koran'; (2) Standard Arabic is used in the press, on the radio and television; it is also one of the languages of instruction in Morocco, alongside French. Only 20% of Moroccans can read and write Standard Arabic proficiently (cf. Ennaji 1991), but very few can speak it with relative ease and fluency; and (3) Educated Moroccan Arabic, which is the result of mixing different grammatical aspects of Moroccan Arabic and Standard Arabic, is used in formal spoken situations by educated Moroccans; about 40% can speak it. (For a socio-functional description of different language varieties of

Arabic see Glaß & Reuschel 1992.)

Multilingualism in Morocco, on the other hand, is reflected in the existence of other languages – Berber, French and Spanish – alongside different varieties of Arabic. Berber is the mother tongue of Berbers, the indigenous ethnic group of Morocco; it is spoken by 40% of the population (cf. Ennaji 1991). French, the former colonial language, is estimated to be spoken, read and written proficiently by only 10% of the total population. However, Youssi (1995: 30) argues that more than 50% of the population use "a more or less pidginized form" of French to communicate with Europeans visiting or living in Morocco. Spanish is used especially in the former Spanish colonies in the north and south of Morocco. According to Abbassi (1977, cited in Ennaji 1991) more than a million people speak Spanish as their second or third language in those areas. This complex socio-linguistic situation raises interesting problems in evaluating the linguistic standards, or prestige and target forms in a speech community.

A valuable contribution by Arabic sociolinguistics to the study of gender differences in language lies in advancing the idea of competing prestige forms in a speech community, thus calling for a careful examination of what constitutes the "standard" variety. Ibrahim (1986) was the first to challenge the equation of the notions "prestigious" and "standard" language, since they have proved to be problematic in interpreting results in diglossic settings. Studies on gender-based language variation in Arabic-speaking societies (Kojak 1983, Abdel Jawad 1981, Bakir 1986) came to the same conclusion, namely, that Arab women use fewer standard prestigious forms than men. This was seen as contradicting the widely reported results from studies of Western languages, where women tend to approximate standard language more than men. In a re-analysis of these findings and conclusions, Ibrahim argued that these investigators wrongly concluded that women in Arabic-speaking communities did not conform to the Western socio-linguistic model (for a critical review of which see James 1996) because in their interpretation of the data, they were using the terms "standard" and "prestigious" Arabic interchangeably. In doing that, they overlooked the fact that "Standard Arabic has a certain degree of prestige and its religious, ideological, and education-al values are undeniable, but its social evaluative connotations are much weaker than those of locally prestigious varieties" (Ibrahim 1986: 125). Further findings by Arab linguists (Abdel Jawad 1987, Haeri 1991, Jabeur 1987) confirmed this observation and indicated that women in Arabic-speaking countries employ the locally prestigious varieties more than men. This distinction between the notions of "standard" and "prestige", which was made in the study of Arabic socio-linguistics and language and gender studies, has proved useful in interpreting findings in Western societies as well (cf. Milroy & Milroy & Hartley 1995). However, Sadiqi's (1995) attitude survey also reminds us that Moroccan women will not behave as a monolithic group linguistically. Her findings indicate that Berber women, especially housewives, consider Moroccan Arabic to be prestigious, whereas working women, Berber or not, regard French as the most prestigious language. In other words, prestige is a relative concept, which is sensitive to the different classes speakers belong to. And there may be competing prestige varieties.

3. A brief comparison of Moroccan Arabic with other varieties of Arabic

Moroccan Arabic differs on many structural levels from "Literary" Arabic, i.e. Classical and Standard Arabic, (cf. Ennaji 1991). Phonologically, Moroccan Arabic has deleted or reduced many vowels that are present in these two varieties. Compare, for instance, Moroccan Arabic *drəb* 'he hit' to Literary Arabic *daraba* 'he hit'. On the morphological level, Moroccan Arabic has dispensed with the dual number (although not entirely) and case marking inflections that are present in Literary Arabic. It has also neutralized the gender distinction in the third person plural and the second person singular in the perfective tense. Table 1 below shows how in the plural it is the masculine inflection that has been retained in Moroccan Arabic, but in the singular it is the feminine ending that has been preserved.

Table 1. Gender agreement in the perfective tense in Literary and Moroccan Arabic

Root /d-x-l/	Perfective Tense/Aspect			
	3PL		2SG	
	Feminine	Masculine	Feminine	Masculine
Literary Arabic	*daxal-na*	*daxal-u*	*daxal-ti*	*daxal-ta*
	enter- they	enter-they	enter- you	enter- you
Moroccan Arabic	*dxʷl-u*	*dxʷl-u*	*dxʷl-ti*	*dxʷl-ti*
	enter- they	enter- they	enter- you	enter- you
	'they entered'	'they entered'	'you entered'	'you entered'

On the lexical level, Moroccan Arabic, like the other North African dialects (known also as Maghrebin), namely, Tunisian and Algerian Arabic, contains a substantial number of French words and phrases as a result of their contact with French, the former colonial language. This not only distinguishes them from Literary Arabic but hinders their comprehension by Arabic speakers whose dialects were not essentially influenced by French, such as Jordanian Arabic, Iraqi Arabic and Saudi Arabic, among others. Hence, mutual intelligibility between Moroccan Arabic and other Arabic dialects decreases the further east one travels. However, all of these dialects are similar and therefore intelligible on the more formal, "high" level of the Arabic dialects continuum, i.e., Literary Arabic.

4. Grammatical gender in Moroccan Arabic

4.1 Feminine and masculine gender

The gender system of modern Moroccan Arabic, which will be described in this section, differs in certain respects from Classical Arabic. For a description of grammatical gender in Classical Arabic, cf., for example, Hämeen-Anttila (2000). Moroccan Arabic has two grammatical genders, feminine and masculine. Only feminine words are morphologically marked for gender, as most, but not all of these, carry the feminine suffix -a. Masculine words, on the other hand, carry a zero suffix, they are thus unmarked for gender. Nouns in Moroccan Arabic are either feminine (e.g., *šəʒr-a* 'tree', *wsad-a* 'pillow', *kəbd-a* 'liver') or masculine (e.g., *kʋrsi* 'chair', *miləf* 'folder', *qəlb* 'heart'). Adjectives can be marked as feminine or masculine, e.g., *frħan-a* (f), *frħan* (m) 'happy'; *bʕid-a* (f), *bʕid* (m) 'far', and they must agree in gender with the noun they modify.

(1) a.   *zlaf-a   kbir-a*
          bowl-FEM big-FEM
          'a big bowl'
     b.   *ṭəbsil   kbir*
          plate.MASC big.MASC
          'a big plate'

Note that in some cases, nouns in Moroccan Arabic do not end in -a, but are nevertheless grammatically feminine, e.g., *dar* 'house', *bnt* 'girl', as are most body parts that come in pairs, such as *yəd* 'hand', *ʕin* 'eye', *wdən* 'ear'. In this case, adjectives provide information about the noun's gender class, as in (2):

(2) *l-yəd   l-iṣr-a*
     DET-hand.FEM DET-left-FEM
     'the left hand'

Adjectives are not the only part of speech that must agree with nouns in gender and number; pronouns, verbs, and prepositions must also meet this requirement. However, this is not true for the definite article *l-*, the only article in Moroccan Arabic, which is indifferent to both gender and number. Let's consider the following example:

(3) a. *wssx-at*   *dik*   *l-basl-a*   *ḥwayž-ha.*
         dirty-3PF.FEM.SG that.FEM DET-turbulent-FEM clothes-her
         'That turbulent girl dirtied her clothes.'

     b. *wssəx*   *dak*   *l-basl.*
         dirty.3PF.MASC.SG that.MASC DET-turbulent.MASC
         ḥwayž-u
         clothes-his
         'That turbulent boy dirtied his clothes.'

So far, we have looked at gender markings in the singular; let's see how the gender distinction is reflected in the plural. There are several ways of converting a singular form into the plural in Moroccan Arabic; however, patterns of pluralization are complex (for a comprehensive assessment of plural patterns in Moroccan Arabic see Heath 1987). In general, Moroccan Arabic distinguishes between two main plural forms for nouns and adjectives; the "sound" and the "broken" plural. The pair "sound" versus "broken" plural is commonly used in the literature to differentiate plurals formed by suffixation (i.e., sound plural) from those formed by internal stem changes (i.e., broken plural). Thus, in the sound plural, feminine and masculine nouns are each assigned different suffixes. The masculine plural form is achieved by adding *-in* or *-a* to the masculine singular, e.g., *muˁllim* (m.sg) '(male) teacher', *muˁllim-in* (m.pl) '(male) teachers', *bnnay* (m.sg) '(male) construction worker', *bnnay-a* (m.pl) '(male) construction workers', whereas the sound plural for feminine forms is achieved by adding *-t* to the feminine singular noun or adjective, e.g., *muˁllim-a* (f.sg) '(female) teacher', *muˁllim-a-t* (f.pl) '(female) teachers'.

The broken plural, on the other hand, is formed by applying internal modifications to the stem: *ṭbsil* (m.sg) 'plate', *ṭbasəl* (m.pl) 'plates', *wsad-a* (f.sg) 'pillow', *wsayd* (m.pl) 'pillows'. The case of the broken plural is interesting because it may change the gender of a noun from feminine to masculine as it changes its number. Again it is the masculine inflection on the adjective that provides such information.

(4) a. *xnš-a   mzwwq-a*
         sack-FEM.SG colored-FEM.SG
         'a colored sack'
     b. *xnaši mzwwq-in*
         sack.PL colored-MASC.PL
         'colored sacks'

Most adjectives modifying a plural feminine noun can carry both feminine and masculine inflections. For instance, the examples in (5) are both possible in Moroccan Arabic:

(5) a. *muˁllim-a-t   mzyan-a-t*
         teacher-FEM-PL good-FEM-PL
         'good teachers'
     b. *muˁllim-a-t   mzyan-in*
         teacher-FEM-PL good-MASC.PL
         'good teachers'

However, the adjective modifying a masculine plural noun never carries the feminine endings. Consider example (6):

(6) a. *muˁllim-in   mzyan-in*
         teacher-MASC.PL good-MASC.PL
         'good teachers'
     b. **muˁllim-in   mzyan-at*
         teacher-MASC.PL good-FEM.PL
         'good teachers'

4.2 Grammatical gender in human nouns

In principle, grammatical and lexical-referential gender may correspond in human nouns. Thus, human nouns referring to females usually end in *-a* and are feminine, e.g., *mra* 'woman', *bniya* 'little girl', while those referring to males have no special ending and are masculine, e.g., *ražəl* 'man', *wliyəd* 'little boy'. This is clearly illustrated in kinship terms such as *walid* (m) 'father', *walid-a* (f) 'mother'; *xal* (m) 'maternal uncle', *xal-a* (f) 'maternal aunt'; *ˁəm* (m) 'paternal uncle', *ˁmm-a* (f) 'paternal aunt'.

The same holds for general human nouns, i.e., non-kinship terms, and those which do not have lexical gender, such as *ṭbbax* 'cook', *ṭbbax-a* '(female) cook', *l-mriḍ* 'the-patient', *l-mriḍ-a* 'the-patient (female)'; *baṭal* 'champion', *baṭal-a* 'female champion'. Similarly, occupational titles express gender distinctions via grammatical gender, for instance, 'a male lawyer' is *muḥami* whereas 'a female lawyer' is *muḥamiy-a;* similarly, *katib* '(male) secretary', *katib-a* '(female) secretary'. Loan words are no exception, they too follow the same pattern, e.g., *kwafur* '(male) hairdresser', *kwafur-a* '(female) hairdresser', cf. French *coiffeur* (m)/*coiffeuse* (f), respectively; *frəmli* '(male) nurse', *frəmli-a* '(female) nurse', cf. French *infirmier* (m)/*infirmière* (f), respectively.

4.3 Generic reference

In Moroccan Arabic, if the referents are a group of males, the masculine term is used, e.g., *muḥamiy-in* (m) 'lawyers'. Similarly, if the referents are a group of females, the feminine term is used, e.g., *muḥamiy-at* (f) '(female) lawyers'. However, the term chosen to refer to, say, a group of female and male lawyers is the generic masculine *muḥamiy-in,* but never the feminine plural *muḥamiy-at.* In addition, when the subject includes both a grammatically masculine and a grammatically feminine word in a sentence, it is the inflectional specifications of the masculine that always win out. Thus, generic reference is achieved by opting for masculine as the norm. For instance, sentence (7a) is acceptable, but (7b) is not:

(7) a. *l-mr-a*　　　*w*　*r-ražəl*　　　*ʕyyan-in.*
         DET-woman-FEM and DET-man.MASC tired-MASC.PL
         'The woman and the man are tired.'
     b. **l-mr-a*　　　*w*　*r-ražəl*　　　*ʕyyan-a-t.*
         DET-woman-FEM and DET-man.MASC tired-FEM-PL

We should remember also that the inflectional marking on the adjective is indifferent to the number and to the position of the feminine plural noun in the sentence. In other words, the adjective will carry the masculine inflection regardless of whether the feminine plural noun is higher in number than the masculine noun. In fact, it takes the presence of only one masculine noun among a larger number of feminine nouns to convert the inflection of the adjective to the masculine gender. In addition, the order of the noun phrases – that is, which one is closer to the adjective – does not determine the pattern of the agreement marker on the adjective. It would be wrong to argue that the adjective 'tired' in example (7a) is masculine because the masculine noun *r-ražəl* 'the man' is the second noun phrase and that its gender is the one closest to the adjective. Example (8) illustrates that the choice of the masculine gender is not determined by the "nearest" gender. As we can see, the inflectional ending of the adjective in (8) is masculine despite the presence of two "closer" plural feminine nouns.

(8) *r-ražəl*   *u   bna-t-u*   *u   xwatat-u*
     DET-man.MASC.SG and daughter.FEM-PL-his and sister.FEM.PL-his
     frħan-in.
     happy-MASC.PL
     'The man and his daughters, and his sisters are happy.'

Furthermore, generic masculine words like *šiwaħəd* 'someone (male)' are chosen when the referent is an unknown person, be it a male or a female (9a). However, its feminine counterpart *šiwəhd-a* 'someone (female)' can be used only when the referent is certainly known to be a female (9b):

(9) a. *šiwaħəd*   *nsa*   *swart-u.*
         someone.MASC forget.3PF.MASC.SG keys-his
         'Someone forgot his keys.'
     b. *šiwħəd-a*   *nsa-t*   *swart-ha.*
         someone-FEM forget.3PF-FEM.SG keys-her
         'Someone forgot her keys.'

4.4 Rules of pronominalization

Personal pronouns in Moroccan Arabic belong to two types, independent and dependent pronouns. Both types of pronouns are differentiated for gender of referent. Independent subject pronouns such as *huwa* 'he' and *hiya* 'she' are reserved primarily for emphasis or clarity since the verb form itself usually indicates its subject. Dependent pronouns are clitics that attach to verbs, e.g, *-t-* (3sg imperfective feminine, *ka-t-ktəb* 'she is writing'), *-at* (3sg perfective feminine, *ktb-at* 'she wrote'), *-y-* (3sg imperfective masculine, *ka-y-ktəb* 'he is writing', the perfective masculine is not morphologically marked, *ktəb*). The masculine clitic that attaches to nouns and prepositions is *-u* (*dar-u* lit. 'house-his' 'his house'), the feminine clitic is *-ha* (*dar-ha* lit. 'house-her', 'her house'). Generic *he* in Moroccan Arabic is thus conveyed through the use of masculine clitics.

   Let's look at example (10a) where *waħəd* 'one (m)', *y-* '3sg masculine' and *-u* 'his' are supposed to include *wəhd-a* 'one (f)', *t-* '3sg feminine' and *-ha* 'her', respectively. On the other hand, (10b) has a restricted reference only to the females.

(10) a. *kul waħəd   lazəm y-šri   ktab-u.*
         every one.MASC must 3IPF.MASC.SG-buy book-his
         'Each one must buy his book.'

  b. *kul   wəħd-a lazəm t-šri   ktab-ha.*
      every one-FEM must 3IPF.FEM.SG-buy book-her
      'Each one must buy her book.'

Moroccan Arabic has an epicene term *bnadm* (m) 'person', which refers to both men and women; however, the inflectional affixes on the verbs, adjectives and prepositions are of course masculine. In fact, all epicenes in Moroccan Arabic are grammatically masculine. Interestingly, many Moroccans today use the feminine counterpart *bnadm-a* instead of *bnadm*. However, this should not be taken as a conscious critique of the language but rather as a response to structural symmetry (see Section 8 for a discussion on a critique of the Arabic language).

4.5 The morphological structure of Moroccan Arabic human nouns

In general, feminine nouns are derived from masculine nouns. Attaching -*a* to masculine nouns almost invariably turns them feminine. This process of word formation is quite heavily exploited in professional nouns, e.g., *ţbib* (m), *ţbib-a* (f) 'physician', *xyyaţ* (m), *xyyaţ-a* (f) 'tailor', and in kinship terms as we have seen in Section 4.2 above.

As far as compounding in Moroccan Arabic is concerned, combining the word *mul* (m) or *mulat* (f) lit. 'master' with a noun, is a common and very productive pattern, e.g., *mul-l-kra, mulat-l-kra* (lit. master-the-rent) 'landlord/-lady'; *mul-ttarix, mulat-ttarix* (lit. master-history) 'history teacher'; *mul-ssnan, mulat-ssnan* (lit. master-teeth) 'dentist'.

Some female names are derived from male names. These names conform to the productive rule that derives feminine words by attaching the feminine suffix -*a* to the masculine form. Consider the following pairs of given names, where the first name in the pair is masculine and the second is feminine: *ʔamin/ʔamina, Samir/Samira, Saʕid/Saʕida*. However, in cases where the masculine name has a syllable structure different from CaCiC, such as CaCCi (e.g., *faţmi*), CaCa:C (e.g., *žama:l*) or CCCa:C (e.g., *ftta:ħ*), the process of derivation involves some internal changes in the stem to fit the CaCiCa pattern of female names. Thus, *Faţmi* becomes *Faţima*, *žamal* becomes *žamila*, and *Ftta:ħ* becomes *Fatiħa*. One might argue, however, that in this case feminine names are not necessarily derived from masculine names, rather the roots *f-t-m*, *ž-m-l* and *f-t-ħ* are simply slotted on the feminine vowel pattern *a-i-a* to produce feminine names.

In addition, there are some masculine names that end in -*a*; interestingly, none of them conform to the feminine C*a*C*i*C*a* pattern, e.g., *ħmza*, *Zakaria* and *Rida*.

Many Moroccan male names, and Arabo-Muslim male names in general, are in the form of a compound. They are composed of the word *ˤəbd* 'slave (m)' plus one of the names or attributes of Allah (God) such as *L-ləṭif* 'The-Gentle (m)', *L-munˤim* 'The-Benefactor (m)'. Nonetheless, there are no exact feminine counterparts for these compound names. For example, *ˤəbd-a(t) L-ləṭif* 'slave-female The-Gentle' is not possible in Moroccan Arabic. Deriving the female name in this case requires deletion of the first word in the compound, deletion of the definite article of the second word in the compound and slotting the remaining consonants in the *a-i-a* vowel pattern. Thus, the feminine counterpart of *ˤəbd L-ləṭif* is *Laṭifa* and that of *ˤəbd L-munˤim* is *Naˤima*. However, this cannot apply if the second word of the compound is God's name (e.g., *Llah*, *Lʔilah* 'God'), rather than one of his attributes (e.g., *L-ħakim* 'The Wise'). Thus, male names such as *ˤəbd Llah* or *ˤəbd L-ʔilah* 'slave of Allah' never produce a female name because the derivation process, in this case, would make the word *Allah* feminine.

In recent years, it has become fashionable to break with the traditional naming system. Male names are moving away from the compound, e.g., *ˤaziz* instead of *ˤəbd L-ˤəziz*, *žalil* instead of *ˤəbd ž-žəlil*, while female names are moving away from the CaCiCa, pattern, e.g., *ʔiman* 'faith', *Sabaħ* 'morning', *Btissam* 'smiling', *ˤawaṭif* 'feelings', to name just a few. In fact, nowadays there are even names that can refer to both men and women, such as *ʔamal*.

5.   The socio-religious basis of gender issues in Morocco

Social gender is defined as the social construction of the biological category of "sex" (Eckert 1989, Crawford 1995). However, Butler (1990, 1993) or Bing & Bergvall (1996), among others, argue that "sex" itself is socially constructed in that it is also the outcome of social practices. Thus, gender (or sex) construction has to do with how social practices shape women's and men's identities in terms of social roles, expectations, language, dress and so on. Different cultures construct gender differently. Thus, examining the interaction between language and gender in a society is intimately bound up with the socio-cultural context that helps construct gendered identities. Eckert & McConnell-Ginet (1992:464) argue that an understanding of the interaction between language and gender "requires that we look locally, closely observing linguistic and gender practices in the context of a particular community's social practices." In light of this, it is imperative to consider the socio-religious setting that contributes to the construction of the identities of men and women in Moroccan society in order to understand the fundamental asymmetries between the way they are addressed and talked about. I will examine the implications of the sacred tradition, Qurʔan 'Koran' and Hadith, along with other politically and socially accepted practices in the lives of Moroccan women.

Qurʔan is the sacred book of Islam that contains oral revelations by God, or Allah, to his prophet Moḥammad. Hadith, which is a complement to the teachings of the Qurʔan, records in detail the sayings and deeds of the prophet. Together they constitute the standard by which believers in the modern Islamic world profess their faith and distinguish right from wrong, truth from falsehood and the accepted from the illicit. They have shaped Muslim ethics and values and still exert an extraordinary power over ordinary Muslim citizens today.

More importantly, Qurʔan and Hadith constitute the source of law in Arab Muslim societies. Being a Muslim in Morocco means far more than abiding by the five pillars of Islam; rather it is "a civil matter, a national identity, a passport, a family code of law, a code of public rights" (Mernissi 1991:21). Since religion has the power of legitimation, it has been exploited for social, political and economic ends. Consequently, the sayings and authority of the Qurʔan and Hadith can be shown to have direct effects on women's lives. Qurʔan and Hadith shape legislation which constructs further discrimination between women and men in Moroccan society. It is in light of this that we must account for the nature and influence of legislation that bears on issues concerning the gender arrangement, such as marriage, divorce, child custody, and unequal rights of inheritance as they are practiced in Moroccan society. Let's consider the following examples:

– Marriage: a woman cannot conclude an act of marriage. A *wali* 'male guardian' is the one who contracts marriage for her (Mernissi 1987). Furthermore, a Muslim woman does not have the right to marry outside her religion whereas a man can marry a non-Muslim woman without her conversion to Islam.
– Repudiation allows a man to divorce his wife without her consent. In case of divorce, a woman gets custody of the children unless she remarries, in which case she loses all claims to the children; this is in sharp contrast with a man's right to remarry and keep the children should his ex-wife remarry.
– Women are not responsible in a court of law; they cannot act as witnesses.
– A woman inherits only half of what her brothers inherit.

- Financial dependence on men: traditionally, a woman depends on her husband for financial support; unmarried women and widows depend on their fathers or sons.
- Women need permission from their *wali* or twelve male witnesses to have a passport.

Furthermore, socially accepted practices can obviously have a power which is independent of the legitimating force of the sacred texts. This is clearly reflected in the divergence between Islamic law and social practice in Moroccan society concerning women's and men's status. A case in point is the sexual double standard prevalent in Moroccan society despite Qurʔanic prohibition of fornication and adultery for all. Men have conveniently disregarded this Islamic principle, as they have many others, and permit themselves what they forbid to women. While righteousness is considered essential for women, licentiousness is considered natural for men.

6.   Women and men in religious texts

This section examines religious sayings as a very powerful linguistic strategy used to maintain the *status quo* of gender relations in Moroccan society. Invoking sayings from Qurʔan and Hadith is a sufficient argument to legitimize female subjugation and perpetuate the ethic of male superiority and female inferiority. In other words, by passing off the inequality between women and men as an Islamic ideal, it becomes a God-given state of affairs that must not be disputed or challenged. The following quotes are commonly used by men and women alike to justify men's supremacy and authority over women.

(11)   *wa li-r-riža:l-i   ʕalay-hinn-a   daraž-a.*
       and for-DET-men-GEN over-them-FEM degree-FEM.SG
       'The men are superior to them (women) by a degree.' (Sura 2: 228)

(12)   *ʔar-riža:l-u   qawwa:m-u:na   ʕala n-nisa:ʔ-i   [bi-ma:*
       DET-men-NOM powerful-PL.ACC over DET-women-GEN for-what
       faḍḍal-a   l-La:h-u   baʕḍ-a-hum   ʕala: baʕḍ-i-n
       prefer-ACC DET-God-NOM some-ACC-PL.MASC over some-GEN-INDEF
       wa bi-ma: ʔanfaq-u: min ʔamwa:l-i-h-im].
       and for-what spent-they.MASC from money-PL-GEN-3PL.MASC
       'Men have more power than women [because Allah has made the one of them to excel over the other and because they (the men) spend of their money].' (Sura 4: 34)

(13) *ʕan-nisa:ʔ-u*   *na:qis-a:t-u*   *ʕaql-i-n*   *wa di:n.*
      DET-women-NOM defective-FEM.PL-NOM brain-GEN-INDEF and religion
      'Women are defective in understanding and religion.' (Hadith)

These verses and sayings not only relegate women to a secondary position vis-à-vis men, but they issue a decree of female inferiority which, because of its divine origin, is impossible to resist. We should bear in mind, however, that the interpretation of these sayings is far from being free from the ideologies of the dominant group, which, in this case, is obviously men. Consider the Qurʔanic verse in (12), for instance. Decontextualization of this verse has resulted in a sweeping interpretation of men's unlimited authority over women instead of the limited power they have in case they are financially supporting the woman (for a review of different readings of this verse see Stowasser 1998).

Furthermore, interpretation of (13) is controversial among Muslim scholars due to the polysemous nature of the word *ʕaql* (m) in Classical Arabic; it can mean 'brain' or 'steadfastness'. However, in Moroccan Arabic only the first meaning for the word *ʕaql* ('brain') has been retained and the saying can only be understood by the average Moroccan as meaning that women naturally have less brains than men. In fact, this saying is one of the most frequently used in order to defend the social, political and economic segregation of women and men in Morocco.

The practices codified in legislation or legitimated by common consent perpetuate negative stereotypes associated with Moroccan women. These stereotypes are the basis for many of the aphorisms about women in Moroccan Arabic as well as the fundamental asymmetries in how women and men are talked about. For instance, *hadik Rir mra* 'that's *only* a woman' is a common expression that is used to convey the inferiority of women. Its equivalent *hadak Rir ražəl* 'that's *only* a man' is never used in this respect; on the contrary, it is used to emphasize the superiority of men and to excuse them from women's supposed "duties and responsibilities": household chores and child care. Similarly, *klma dlʕyalat* 'women's word' has the connotation of a promise never kept or a deed never accomplished, whereas *klma drržal* 'men's word' implies the opposite. Also, while *bnt zznqa* 'a girl of the street' means a loose girl or a prostitute, *wld zznqa* 'a boy of the street' has the positive meaning of 'street smart' (for more on asymmetrical pairs see Sadiqi 1995).

7.   How are women addressed and talked about in Moroccan society?[2]

In Moroccan society, it is women's socio-political and sexual status that are at the heart of many of the asymmetries of addressing and talking about women and men. A close investigation of the dynamics of forms of address and reference reveals that a Moroccan woman's social status takes different dimensions with age. Webster (1982) was right in noting that the life of a Moroccan woman can be divided into three phases: pre-child bearing phase, child-bearing phase and post-child-bearing phase. What is of great importance here is that each phase in the life of the woman is carefully observed and reflected in cultural idioms and Moroccan folk wisdom. This section looks into the different social identities that a woman acquires throughout her life span and examines how these identities are reflected in language use via terms of address and reference.

7.1   Pre-child-bearing phase: The virgin female

In English-speaking societies, to use the term *girl* to refer to females over 21 years of age is inappropriate and may be considered sexist because it stresses a woman's immaturity. However, in Morocco and other Arabic-speaking societies the term *bnt* (f) '(presumably virgin) girl' is not only appropriate but is compulsory when referring to an unmarried female regardless of how old she is. *Bnt* is heavily loaded with information about a woman's social and moral status (cf. Dwyer 1978). In Moroccan society, maintaining one's virginity until marriage is a strict moral code that applies to girls only, and a girl who does not preserve her virginity is liable to severe punishments, since she is considered to have sullied the honor of her family. Ironically, a man's honor in Morocco depends primarily on whether the female members of his family can keep their sexual integrity; his own behavior is only remotely related to his honor (for similar views in Turkish society, cf. Braun, this vol.).

The terms *bnt* 'girl' and *mra* (f) 'woman' have more than purely referential meaning. By calling a woman *mra*, a speaker asserts information about her personal behavior. In a sense, use of the terms *bnt* and *mra* might be seen as performative speech acts, akin to dubbing: *mra* dubs a woman as being sexually active. Therefore, knowingly addressing an unmarried female as *mra* is a direct blow to her family's honor. By comparison, using the term *ražəl* (m) 'man' to refer to a 12 or 13 year old young unmarried male instead of using *drri* (m) 'boy' is required in order to bolster his masculine pride and to prove his virility.

Even a male child is sometimes addressed and referred to as *ražəl* (m) whereas *mra* is obviously never used to refer to a female child. Instead, she might be addressed and referred to as *bniyya* (f, diminutive of *bnt*) 'little girl' or *ˤziba* (f, diminutive of *ˤzba* 'single') 'single little girl'.

Since by Qurʔanic decree and common consent, it is men who have power over women, they may allow themselves certain privileges that are denied to women and sanction women if they claim access to them. While sexual promiscuity is admired in men, chastity and virginity are strongly required of women. This sexual double standard in Moroccan society is reflected in a variety of cultural idioms. *Bnt dar-hum* (lit. girl house-their) 'a good girl' and *bnt l-ˤarad* (lit. girl the-honor) 'a girl of honor' both have very positive sexual implications for the female. However, *wld dar-hum* (lit. boy house-their) 'a good boy' has negative connotations, suggesting that a man is inexperienced, unwieldy and lacking virility. *Wld l-ˤarad* (lit. boy the-honor) 'a boy of honor', on the other hand, is nonexistent and would sound ridiculous if used to refer to an honorable and chaste man.

Furthermore, young unmarried women are viewed and talked about negatively because society endows them with a destructive potential. It is believed that their sexual appeal is threatening to the social and moral order because they can create *fitna* (f) 'chaos' among men (Mernissi 1989). Fear of young unmarried women's sexual potential finds expression in popular sayings; consider examples (14) and (15):

(14) *l-bnat   xatar.*
      DET-girls danger.MASC
      'Girls are dangerous.'

(15) *l-bnat   ma-ka-y-str-hum   Rir   trab.*
      DET-girls not-DUR-3IMP-cover-IPF-3PL only soil
      'Only death is able to control girls.'

As might be expected, there are no equivalent expressions for young unmarried men.

7.2 The child-bearing phase: The woman as wife and mother

Marriage is valued in Islamic tradition, as it is the only legitimate way for both men and women to engage in sexual activity. In Moroccan tradition, however, marriage is considered essential for women but less so for men. As we have seen, there are a variety of terms that distinguish unmarried from married women, while there is an absence of terms serving the same function for men. It is undeniable that a Moroccan woman gains social status and prestige when she gets married. However, her social standing is at stake if she fails to become a mother, primarily a producer of sons. In Muslim societies women are favored as mothers; mothers are talked about in a very positive way in Qurʔan and Hadith. The following epithets reflect the incomparable position and social prestige allocated to mothers.

(16) *ʔumm-uk*   *θumma ʔumm-uk*   *θumma*
       mother-your.MASC then   mother-your.MASC. then
       ʔumm-uk   *θumma ʔab-uːk.*
       mother-your.MASC then   father-your.MASC
       'Your mother, then your mother, then your mother and then your father.' (Hadith)

(17) *ʔal-žannat-u*   *taħta ʔaqdaːm-i l-ʔumm-ah-aːt.*
       DET-paradise-NOM under feet-GEN DET-mother-ACC-FEM.PL
       'Paradise lies under mothers' feet.' (Hadith)

Glorification of mothers is not limited to sacred written texts but is also reflected in Moroccan oral tradition. Many cultural idioms attest to the unique role of mothers: *ləm hia kulši* 'the mother is everything', *ləm hia rras dlgsda* 'the mother is the head of the body', *ləm hia nwwart ddar* 'the mother is the light of the house'. This sudden and marked change in how women are perceived only accentuates how feminine ideals are limited and externally imposed. Women of the child-bearing phase "… presumably are sexually active, as most are married; ideally they are pregnant or nursing most of the time." (Webster 1982: 182). In other words, a woman's worth depends primarily on her legitimate sexual agentivity and her reproductive capacity.

Mothers are addressed and referred to with terms of respect such as *lħažža* (f) as honorific for 'one who has visited Mecca'; *lalla* (f) 'my mistress' and *šrifa* (f) 'lady with noble blood' are more general honorifics for mothers. In some Arabic-speaking communities mothers are addressed as 'mother' + name of her (eldest) son; for example, *umm Ahmed* 'mother of Ahmed' (Minai 1981). A Moroccan mother is never addressed in this way. In traditional Moroccan families, especially ultra-religious ones, proper names are not allowed when addressing or referring to somebody else's wife or mother because of their perceived intimacy. The wife or mother is therefore referred to as *mallin ddar* 'owners [sic] of the house' or *drari* which literally means 'children'. Used in this context, *drari* is inclusive of both the wife and the children (if there are any).

Nontraditional married women, on the other hand, are addressed and referred to by their proper names. Traditionally, married women in Morocco, unlike Western women, do not take their husband's family name, they keep their father's name all their lives. However, it has become common practice among young Moroccan wives to adopt the family name of their husbands and to be addressed as *ssəyda* or *madame*, the loan words for 'Mrs.' from Standard Arabic and French, respectively.

7.3 Post child-bearing phase: Elderly women

Although women are highly esteemed in their role as mothers in Moroccan society, motherhood cannot forever fend off negative associations, ultimately associations with the devil, the destructive force in the religio-social belief system (Mernissi 1989). Elderly women are viewed and talked about in a negative way. Their association with the devil is bluntly expressed in Moroccan folklore:

(18)   *l-ʕguz-a   ktər mən š-šitan.*
       DET-old-FEM more than DET-Satan
       'The old woman is worse than the devil.'

(19)   *lli   ka-y-dir-u   iblis   f-ʕam*
       what DUR-MASC-do-IPF.3SG devil.MASC in-year.MASC
       ka-d-dir-u   l-ʕguz-a   f-saʕ-a.
       DUR-FEM-do-IPF.3SG DET-old-FEM in-hour-FEM
       'What Satan does in a year, the old hag does in an hour.'

The word *ʕguza* (f) translates into 'old woman' as well as 'mother-in-law'. Much of the bad press about old women is related to their acquired status as mothers-in-law. It is believed that menopausal women, having lost all their assets, i.e., their reproductive capacity, their physical attractiveness and with it their sexuality, exploit the young daughter-in-law out of jealousy and envy. Thus, the word *ʕguza* has become a synonym for wicked behavior and insatiability.

Moroccan folk tradition views advanced age as having totally opposite effects on men and women:

(20)   *r-ražəl   ila wsəl   l-tman-in   ʕla bal-u*
       DET-man if reaches to-eighties-MASC on mind-his
       waliy l-lah,   u   l-mra   ila wṣl-at
       saint DET-God and DET-woman if reach-PERF

l-stt-in   *ržli-ha f-nnar.*
to-sixty-MASC leg-her in-fire
'A man who reaches eighty becomes a saint and a woman who reaches
sixty has her legs in hell.'

The divergence between how old women and old men are talked about is also
reflected in the abundance of abusive terms that describe old women, e.g.,
ħənnqriša (f) 'scorpion', *ʕqruša* (f) 'ugly old witch', *naqma* (f) 'plague' etc., and
the lack of equivalent terms for elder men.

8.   Interactional practices

The fundamental differences in the way women and men are represented in
religious, legislative and social domains attest to the unequal power relationship
between them. As we have seen, Moroccan folk tradition reflects this inequality
and at the same time helps sustain it. However, the extent to which this inequality is reflected in interaction between women and men requires close scrutiny.
There is a general paucity of empirical studies on differences in women's and
men's discourse and conversational norms in Arabic-speaking communities,
including Morocco. Therefore, no general statements can be made about
certain issues, e.g., who holds the floor, who controls the topic, who interrupts,
who challenges other speakers' statements, who remains silent and so on.

However, there are certain linguistic practices which clearly reflect a
gendered power dynamic. A case in point is women's tendency to use more
oaths than men. Because of women's secondary position in society and their
association with the futile, they frequently resort to the powerful and efficient
oaths to validate their statements. In other words, women invoke the power of
Allah 'God' to support and give credibility to what they say, something men do
not need to do in view of their institutionalized power. In a scenario where,
other things being equal, a woman and a man are asked about the validity of
their statement, a woman's more likely response would be *wllah ila bṣṣəħ* 'By
God it is true' or a longer phrase such as *wa həq llah lʕaliy lʕaḍim ila bṣṣəħ* 'By
the truth of God the glorious and the great, it is true'. A man's more likely
response, on the other hand, would be *wa rah hdərt mʕak* 'I am telling you!'
Moreover, this is not unique to Moroccan women: Trabelsi (1991) has made a
similar observation regarding women in Tunisia. If the type of oath chosen is in

fact dependent on the speaker's social status, empirical studies will be useful in uncovering the extent to which women and men use oaths (a) in all-female or all-male interactions, (b) in mixed interactions and (c) in the workplace, especially in cases where women are superiors.

9.   Concluding remarks

Despite the pre-eminent traditional values and norms in Moroccan society which view change as an external threat, change is taking place nevertheless. Change can be seen especially in the lives and experiences of women, and this is most obvious in the new roles they have come to play in society. In recent decades, Moroccan women have invaded what used to be exclusively male domains such as the street, education, employment, and even the world of oral performance in the marketplace (see Kapchan 1996). Nowadays, some women are in positions of power (thus, 20% of Moroccan judges are women). Furthermore, women's status and roles in society reached new dimensions when the first two women were elected to parliament in 1993. Although insignificant in number, their election marks a milestone in women's rights in Morocco. In 1997, four women held the position of secretary of state, some became ministers, and in 1999 one woman (Zoulikha Nassiri) was appointed advisor to the king. However, despite the eminent positions these women hold, they cannot testify in a court room, but would need another woman to confirm their testimony (because the testimony of two women equals the testimony of one man). Furthermore, these highly positioned women would lose custody of their children if they remarried, they would need a *wali* to contract marriage for them and they would also need authorization from their husbands to leave the country. Despite the many changes that have taken place in Moroccan society since the seventies women are still seen as eternal minors in the eyes of the law.

The feminist movement is still in its infancy in Morocco. It is important to point out, however, that Moroccan women, and Arabo-Muslim women in general, distance themselves from any association with feminism, because the word "feminist" has become a synonym for loose morals and values for women (cf. Fernea 1997). There are quite a few feminist movements, most of which would be reluctant to identify themselves as such. One of the most, if not the most, powerful women's movement in Morocco is Union de l'Action Féminine. This women's action group was instrumental in demanding legal reforms in

Mudawwana 'Family law' (for a brief history of women's movements in Morocco and an outline of changes in *Mudawwana* see Brand 1998). The reforms have as objective the regulation of laws pertinent to marriage, child custody, divorce and inheritance, issues which reflect overt inequalities between women and men. However, language reform does not seem to be a pressing issue among Moroccan feminists, and even if it is, nothing is being done about it. In light of this, I want to stress the importance of ensuring women's inclusion in all facets of human experience, be it political, social, economic or linguistic. I agree with Cameron (1990:90) that

> [...] a change in linguistic practice is not just a reflection of some more fundamental social change: it is, itself, a social change ... Eliminating generic masculine pronouns precisely eliminates generic masculine pronouns. And in so doing it changes the repertoire of social meanings and choices available to social actors.

In general, very few Arab scholars have voiced their concern regarding the use of masculine words or pronouns for inclusive or gender-indefinite reference. To my knowledge Jalal Al-Azm (1974, cited in Mernissi 1987) is the only Arab male social scientist who felt apprehensive using the Arabic equivalent of generic *he* in reporting findings which included both women and men. He was apologetic for misconstruing reality by adhering to gender-biased Arabic grammar. Mernissi (1987:176), a Moroccan female scholar, recognizes the necessity of addressing this issue since it is part of "a revolutionary reorganization of the entire society." Interesting though this is, it can hardly mark the beginning of a feminist critique of language in the Arab world.

The beginning of a feminist critique of the Arabic language, and maybe language in general, goes back to the seventh century during the time of the prophet Moḥammad. Arab women, then, protested against the use of the masculine gender in verses of the Qurʔan 'Koran'. They objected to the use of the masculine plural inflection *-in* (as in *Muslim-in* 'Muslims') when the referents were men and women. A decidedly militant and feminist voice is heard through their questioning words: "We have proclaimed our belief in Islam, and done as you have done. How is it then that you men should be mentioned in the Koran while we are ignored!" (quoted in El Saadawi, 1982: 212). According to El Saadawi (1982), it seems that women's protest against their exclusion might have brought about changes that are evident in the Qurʔan. Consider for instance (Sura 33:35):

(21)   *inna l-Muslim-in   wa l-Muslim-at   wa
       Lo!   DET-Muslims-MASC and DET-Muslims-FEM and
       l-Muʿmin-in   wa l-muʿmin-at   wa
       DET-Believers-MASC and DET-Believers-FEM and
       l-qanit-in   wa l-qanit-at   wa
       DET-obedient-MASC and DET-obedient-FEM and
       ṣ-ṣadiq-in   wa ṣ-ṣadiq-at [...]
       DET-truthful-MASC and DET-truthful-FEM
       'Lo! The Muslims and the believers, and the obedient and the truthful [...]'

I want to conclude by drawing attention to some changes that are germane to language and gender in Moroccan society. For instance, some derogatory sayings, such as *lmra ḥašak*, are wearing out (*ḥašak* is an apologetic term that usually accompanies mention of things associated with dirt, excrement, a water closet or an animal like a donkey). Using *l-mra* 'the-woman' in association with *ḥašak* is no doubt disappearing from language usage in Moroccan society nowadays. Furthermore, some women are becoming aware of the sexist implications in Moroccan folk wisdom, thus they engage in reversing the meanings of old sayings. For instance, *klma dlʿyalat* 'women's word' has always been used to deprecate women's promises and intended actions. But now *klma dlʿyalat* is used by some women to emphasize that a promise will be carried out beyond doubt.

Notes

*   My deepest gratitude goes to Miriam Meyerhoff for her insightful comments, suggestions, and repeated revision of earlier versions of this paper. I must thank the editors of this volume for their invaluable help in producing the final version of this manuscript.

1.   For an overview of Moroccan Arabic grammar cf. Nortier (1990). For a detailed structural study cf. Harrell (1962), Abdel-Massih (1973). For phonology and morphology cf. Heath (1987), and Boudlal (1998), and for syntax cf. Ennaji (1982) and Youssi (1992). For dialectology and contact phenomena cf. Benhallam & Dahbi (1990), Messaoudi (1995), Benhallam (1998). For code switching between Moroccan Arabic and European languages cf. Nortier (1990) and Boumans (1996) on Moroccan Arabic/Dutch code switching, and Lahlou (1991) on Moroccan Arabic/French code switching. A Moroccan Arabic-English/English-Moroccan Arabic dictionary is Harrell & Sobelman (1986).

2.   This section was presented at The Second Annual Conference for Students in the College of Language, Linguistics and Literature: Language in the Age of Globalization, University of Hawaii, March 7, 1998.

References

Abbassi, Abdelaziz. 1977. *A sociolinguistic analysis of multilingualism in Morocco.* Ph.D. dissertation, University of Texas at Austin, Austin.

Abdel Jawad, Hassan R.E. 1981. *Lexical and phonological variation in spoken Arabic in Amman.* Ph.D. dissertation, University of Pennsylvania, Philadelphia.

Abdel Jawad, Hassan R.E. 1987. "Cross-dialectal variation in Arabic: Competing prestige forms." *Language in Society* 16: 359–368.

Abdel-Massih, Ernest T. 1973. *An introduction to Moroccan Arabic.* Ann Arbor: University of Michigan.

Al-Azm, Sadiq Jalal. 1974. *Fi'l-Hubb wa'l-Hubb al-Udri* [On love and Udrite love]. 2nd edition. Beirut.

Bakir, Murtadha. 1986. "Sex differences in the approximation to standard Arabic: A case study." *Anthropological Linguistics* 28: 3–10.

Benhallam, Abderrafi. 1998. "Contact and historical evolution of languages in Morocco." In *Langues et litteratures: Contact et évolution historique des langues au Maroc.* Publications de la Facultè des Lettres, Rabat, 25–34.

Benhallam, Abderrafi & Mohamed Dahbi. 1990. "Accents of Moroccan Arabic: A preliminary study". In *Maghreb Linguistics,* ed. Jochen Pleines. Rabat: Okad. 111–125.

Bing, Janet M. & Victoria L. Bergvall. 1996. "The question of questions: Beyond binary thinking." In *Rethinking language and gender research: Theory and practice,* eds. Victoria L. Bergvall & Janet M. Bing & Alice F. Freed. London: Longman, 1–30.

Boudlal, Abdelaziz. 1998. "A diachronic analysis of labialisation in Moroccan Arabic." In *Langues et litteratures: Contact et évolution historique des langues au Maroc.* Publications de la Faculté des Lettres, Rabat, 45–60.

Boumans, Louis. 1996. "Embedding verbs and collocations in Moroccan Arabic/Dutch codeswitching." In *current issues in linguistic theory* 141: *Perspectives on Arabic linguistics* IX, eds. Mushira Eid & Dilworth Parkinson. Amsterdam: Benjamins, 45–67.

Brand, Laurie A. 1998. *Women, the state, and political liberalization: Middle Eastern and North African experiences.* New York: Columbia University Press.

Butler, Judith. 1990. *Gender trouble: Feminism and the subversion of identity.* New York: Routledge.

Butler, Judith. 1993. *Bodies that matter: On the discursive limits of 'sex'.* New York: Routledge.

Cameron, Deborah. 1990. "Demythologising sociolinguistics: Why language does not reflect society." In *Politics of language,* eds. John E. Joseph & Talbot J. Taylor. London: Routledge, 79–96.

Cameron, Deborah. 1996. "The language-gender interface: Challenging co-optation." In *Rethinking language and gender research: Theory and practice,* eds. Victoria L. Bergvall & Janet M. Bing & Alice F. Freed. London: Longman, 31–53.

Crawford, Mary. 1995. *Talking difference: On language and gender.* London: Sage.

Dwyer, Daisy H. 1978. *Images and self-images: Male and female in Morocco.* New York: Columbia University Press.

Eckert, Penelope. 1989. "The whole woman: Sex and gender differences in variation." *Language Variation and Change* 1: 245–267.

Eckert, Penelope & Sally McConnell-Ginet. 1992. "Think practically and look locally: Language and gender as community based practice." *Annual Review of Anthropology* 21: 461–490.

El Saadawi, Nawal. 1982. *The hidden face of Eve: Women in the Arab world*. Translated by Sherif Hetata. Boston: Beacon.

Ennaji, Moha. 1982. *A comparative analysis of the complex sentence in English, Moroccan Arabic and Berber*. Ph.D. dissertation, University of Essex, England.

Ennaji, Moha. 1991. "Aspects of multilingualism in the Maghreb." *International Journal of the Sociology of Language* 87: 7–25.

Fernea, Elizabeth W. 1997. *In search of Islamic feminism: One woman's global journey*. New York: Doubleday.

Glaß, Dagmar & Wolfgang Reuschel. 1992. "Status types and status changes in the Arabic language." In *Status change of languages*, eds. Ulrich Ammon & Marlis Hellinger. Berlin: de Gruyter, 65–99.

Hämeen-Anttila, Jaakko. 2000. "Grammatical gender and its development in Classical Arabic." In *Gender in grammar and cognition*, eds. Barbara Unterbeck et al. Berlin: de Gruyter, 595–608.

Haeri, Niloofar. 1991. *Sociolinguistic variation in Cairene Arabic: Palatalization and the qaf in the speech of men and women*. Ph.D. dissertation, University of Pennsylvania, Philadelphia, PA.

Harrell, Richard S. 1962. *A short reference grammar of Moroccan Arabic*. Washington, DC: Georgetown University Press.

Harrell, Richard S. & Harvey Sobelman, eds. 1986. *A dictionary of Moroccan Arabic: Arabic-English/English-Arabic*. Georgetown: Georgetown University Press.

Heath, Jeffrey. 1987. *Ablaut and ambiguity: Phonology of a Moroccan Arabic dialect*. New York: SUNY Press.

Ibrahim, H. Muhammad. 1986. "Standard and prestige language: A problem in Arabic socio-linguistics." *Anthropological Linguistics* 28: 115–126.

Jabeur, Mohamed. 1987. *A sociolinguistic study in Tunisia, Rades*. Ph.D. dissertation, University of Reading, England.

James, Deborah. 1996. "Women, men and prestige speech forms: A critical review." In *Rethinking language and gender research: Theory and practice*, eds. Victoria L. Bergvall & Janet M. Bing & Alice F. Freed. London: Longman, 98–125.

Kapchan, Deborah A. 1996. *Gender on the market: Moroccan women and the revoicing of tradition*. Philadelphia: University of Pennsylvania Press.

Kojak, Wafa. 1983. *Language and sex: A case study of a group of educated Syrian speakers of Arabic*. M.A. thesis, University of Lancaster, England.

Lahlou, Moncef. 1991. *A morpho-syntactic study of code-switching between Moroccan Arabic and French*. Ph.D. dissertation, University of Texas at Austin.

Mernissi, Fatima. 1987. *Beyond the veil: Male-female dynamics in modern Muslim society*. Bloomington: Indiana University Press.

Mernissi, Fatima. 1989. *Doing daily battle: Interviews with Moroccan women*. New Brunswick, NJ: Rutgers University Press.

Mernissi, Fatima. 1991. *Women and Islam: An historical and theological enquiry*. Translated by Mary Jo Lakeland. Oxford: Blackwell.

Messaoudi, Leila. 1995. "Eléments pour une dialectologie arabe: Quelques aspects linguistiques de l'arabe dialectal marocain." In *Dialectologie et Sciences Humaines au Maroc.* Colloques et Séminaires 38, Publications de la Faculté des Lettres, Rabat, 185–224.

Milroy, James & Lesley Milroy & Sue Hartley. 1995. "Glottal stops and Tyneside glottalization: Competing patterns of variation and change in British English." *Language Variation and Change* 6: 327–357.

Minai, Naila. 1981. *Women in Islam: Tradition and transition in the Middle East.* New York: Seaview.

Nortier, Jacomine. 1990. *Dutch-Moroccan Arabic code-switching among Moroccans in the Netherlands.* Dordrecht: Foris.

Sadiqi, Fatima. 1995. "The language of women in the city of Fès, Morocco." *International Journal of the Sociology of Language* 112: 63–79.

Stowasser, Barbra. 1998. "Gender issues and contemporary Quran interpretation." In *Islam, gender, and social change*, eds. Yvonne Yazbeck Haddad & John L. Esposito. Oxford: Oxford University Press, 30–44.

Trabelsi, Chedia. 1991. "De quelques aspects du langage des femmes de Tunis." *International Journal of the Sociology of Language* 87: 87–98.

Webster, Sheila K. 1982. "Women, sex, and marriage in Moroccan proverbs." *International Journal of Middle East Studies* 14: 173–184.

Youssi, Abderrahim. 1992. *Grammaire et lexique de l'Arabe Marocain moderne.* [Grammar and lexicon of Modern Moroccan Arabic]. Casablanca: Wallada.

Youssi, Abderrahim. 1995. "The Moroccan triglossia: Facts and implications." *International Journal of the Sociology of Language* 112: 29–43.

Belizean Creole: Gender, creole, and the role of women in language change

Geneviève Escure
University of Minnesota, Minneapolis, USA

1. Problems of definition

1.1 Gender and sex in society

The role played by gender in language use and language change is still largely unexplored. Although a substantial amount of research has recently investigated *gender* in the area of variation studies, the scope of such studies is limited by two sets of problematic assumptions: first, the simple equation of *gender* with "sex", and secondly, an almost exclusive focus on homogeneous – Western, white, middle-class – populations. The issue of "sex" differentiation is addressed by a still nascent neurological research suggesting that men and women use different parts of the brain. Some of the scientific preliminary findings related to physiological differences are commonly summarized in the mass media as: "male brains are more asymmetrical than female brains", [...] "men use [when reading] a minute area in the left side of the brain while women use areas in both sides of the brain" (New York Times 2/16/95); or "women are better at verbal memory [...] while men consistently do better at spatial reasoning" (Minneapolis Star-Tribune 2/11/96). Such brain differentiation is sometimes interpreted as determining differential behavior, resulting in statements such as "men as a group excel at tasks that involve orienting objects in space; [...] women, on the other hand, seem to be more adept at communication, both verbal and nonverbal" (Time 7/17/95). However, these simplified research reports fail to identify clearly the role of *gender*.[1]

Social definitions of gender are probably irrelevant to questions of formal grammar, but they are clearly essential to any observations of language use in society, on a par with ethnicity or class, and obviously tightly intertwined with other social factors. Simply correlating linguistic variables with respondents' biological gender is inadequate (Wodak & Benke 1997). Gender must be defined as referring to a complex network of social, cultural, economic and psychological phenomena adding to or eliminating biological differences. Since gender is solidly anchored in behavior, it seems to be best observed from a pragmatic perspective that will take into account the discourse patterns representing how men and women use language, through the medium of potentially genderized strategies used to accomplish goals (directives, mitigators, disclaimers, interruptions, repetitions, minimal responses, apologies, insults, *inter alia*, which project paralinguistic phenomena such as solidarity, competitiveness, emotion, hesitation, subservience, insecurity, or dominance).

Furthermore, generalizations based on the simple comparison of men and women as observed in relatively homogeneous Western middle class contexts cannot adequately account for the spectrum of female and male roles. The few studies investigating more ethnically and socio-economically diverse groups in Western societies or in developing countries have found that gender-based differentiation is much more complex than initially thought (Cheshire 1982, Escure 1991, Escure & McClain 1999, Gal 1979, Nichols 1983).

The research to be reported here seeks to go beyond such limitations by discussing the use of items which are potential markers of gender in relation to the shifting roles of men and women in postcolonial contexts, that is, groups with a history of oppression. I will more particularly focus on Central American English-based creole communities, especially those of Belize, Central America, where traditional westernized notions of middle or working class are not directly relevant or applicable. I will address two specific issues: first pronominal reference (typically gender-marked in English), and secondly, the issue of linguistic innovation in the diffusion of linguistic change. It will be shown that absence of gender marking in specific grammatical components does not necessarily exclude the significant effect of gender as a social variable in language use.

1.2 Pidgins and creoles

Pidgins and creoles have always existed, and new varieties continue to develop throughout the world. Pidgins typically result from traumatic contacts between various ethnocultural groups, in which one group assumes sociopolitical dominance over the other(s). This sociolinguistic clash typically occurs in the course of events such as invasion, slavery, or other types of migration. Creoles develop over time when displaced populations are forced to remain (e.g., slavery, indenture in the Caribbean, Central America), or when an occupied territory remains under the tutelage of an invading force (e.g., Papua New Guinea, many parts of Africa). A new language variety has to be fully developed to mediate communication, or – to use a common definition of creoles – the creole emerges when the preliminary pidgin code acquires native speakers. Creoles can result from contact between members of any language family. However, creoles with English or French superstrates (lexical bases) and West African substrates are among the best documented to date, probably because studies of minority and nonstandard languages primarily developed in the West in the wake of the abolition of slavery, the decolonization process, and a more recent re-assessment of traditional Eurocentric perspectives on culture which had gone unchallenged until the second part of the 20th century.

Creole vernaculars are naturally assigned the low status of their speakers, and it usually takes a long time to validate creoles and elevate their status to that of national or official language. Generally, the broad range of linguistic choices available to the members of a Creole community aptly reflects the conflicting identities common to recently independent societies. The wide-ranging linguistic repertoire is commonly referred to as a linguistic (or lectal) continuum.[2] Extensive lectal shifts may be part of the decreolization process which is often assumed to be happening in the West Indies, as well as in other developing or postcolonial societies in which access to education with acquisition of the standard is increasingly common. If decreolization is viewed as internal change away from an earlier grammar, systematic formal differences observed between basilects and mesolects could be viewed as indicators of ongoing historical change, and it would then be particularly interesting to observe whether women or men are more actively involved in ongoing linguistic change.

Although an extensive literature on creole languages has developed over the last forty years, there have been strikingly few analyses focusing on gender in the context of the postcolonial societies in which pidgins and creoles developed. This may be because in creole contexts both men and women have held equally subjugated positions vis-à-vis the colonizing powers that enforced terrible living conditions upon them: this pattern does not fit well with standard explanations of gender-linked linguistic differences which applied primarily to Western white middle classes, and were furthermore assumed to be derived from the socioeconomic dominance exerted by men over the muted group of females. In societies where men and women are equally powerless, a different perspective may be in order because both groups learn similar survival mechanisms, which no doubt entail extensive lectal shifting for necessary social adjustments. If, therefore, men and women share powerlessness, does this entail a lesser degree of gender-based language differentiation?

One may raise questions such as the following: Is sexism absent in socially oppressed groups, or is it more virulent than in other groups? Do males in subjugated societies emulate the dominant roles of the higher status groups, relative to females of their groups? Are postcolonial societies more likely to allow women to exercise social participation, precisely because men are equally powerless? Are the languages of marginalized groups involved in greater variability because of the overt prestige of a standard that is not the vernacular of the groups in question? The socio-economic interpretation of linguistic exchanges, or linguistic market (*le marché linguistique*) outlined by Bourdieu (1982) is directly applicable to societies in which the social and gender dynamics is in rapid flux: linguistic codes are ranked in terms of their social values, and what must be examined is the relation between superficial linguistic behavior (*l'habitus linguistique*) and the markets where speakers "sell" their products.

2. Focus on Belize

2.1 Sociolinguistic background

Belize, the former British colony of British Honduras, is a complex society in spite of its small size: it has the lowest population density in Central America (240,204 according to the 2000 Population Census) for a territory covering barely 13,000 square kilometers. Because of its pivotal geographical position at the juncture of Central America and the West Indies, and its complicated history, it exhibits both multiculturalism and multilingualism. It can be assumed that there are about 68,000 L1-speakers of Belizean Creole. No reliable data are available for L1-speakers in the U. S., nor for L2-speakers overall.

The diverse Belizean population results from repeated waves of immigrants, who combined with the indigenous Amerindian population of Mayas and Kekchis: they include African slaves; Miskito Indians brought from the British Settlement of the Miskito Coast (now Nicaragua); a group of Afro-Indians, the Black Carib (or Garifuna) originally deported by the British from St. Vincent to Honduras; Mestizos (Spanish and Indian), refugees of the Indian Caste War in Mexico; Mennonites looking for fresh settlements; indentured servants from India; and more recently Salvadorans and Guatemalans fleeing civil wars. The current population includes four major groups: Mestizos, Creoles, Amerindians, and Garifuna. Other smaller groups include Chinese, Middle Eastern ("Syrian/Lebanese"), and White (English/American) populations. The last population count taking ethnicity into account was conducted in April 1999, and as of May 2001, the following figures were made available by the Belize Census Bureau (Belize Population Count 2000)

Table 1. Ethnic groups in Belize in 1999 (Belize Population Count 2000)
[Total population April 1999: 243,390]

Ethnic group	Population	(%)
Mestizo	112,935	46.3
Creole	67,480	27.7
Maya	24,400	10.0
Garifuna	15,685	6.4
Mennonite	8,125	3.3
East Indian	8,020	3.3

The most striking observation involves an increase in the Mestizo (Spanish-speaking) population which is steadily gaining over the Creole population. The 1970 Census indicated equal amounts of Creoles and Mestizos – about 30% each of the overall population – (Escure 1983:32), whereas the 1991 Census showed the surge in Mestizos, 43.6% contrasted to 29.8% of Creoles (Escure 1997:29).

The most recent Census results provide a breakdown of the population in each of the six districts of Belize but do not represent ethnicity in each district. The right column in Table 2 presents an estimate based on the 1991 Census (Escure 1997:31)

Table 2. Population in the six Belize districts (Belize Census 2000)
[northern to southern locations]
[Total population as of May 2000: 240,204—1991 Census: 189,392].

Districts	Population	Ethnicity
Corozal District	32,708	mostly Mestizo (about 80%)
Orange Walk District	38,890	mostly Mestizo (about 70%)
Belize District	68,197	mostly Creole (about 70%)
Cayo District	52,564	mostly Mestizo (about 70%)
Stann Creek District[3]	24,548	Garifuna (40%), Creole and Mestizo (about 30% each)
Toledo District	23,297	Maya (60%), Garifuna and Mestizo (about 15% each)

A large segment of the population has emigrated abroad, most to the United States, in search of better economic opportunities. The number of emigrants over the last 30 years may have reached as much as 150,000, thus closely matching the population currently residing in Belize. High emigration patterns are reflected in the relative youth of the Belizean population: 65% is under the age of 24, whereas the most productive segment of the population (age 25–54) amounts to 28%, and individuals over 54 constitute only 8% of the population. This pattern suggests that the breadwinners live abroad (sending home regular checks to the grandmothers), and have only limited influence on the linguistic and behavioral development of the younger generation, except perhaps when they make occasional visits. Although those emigrants may have acquired some version of American English, it is doubtful that their short term visits home would have a significant impact on the development of the Belizean continuum, beyond some American lexical items or phrases that are readily available on television.

2.2 English influence on Belizean Creole

Since the lexical base of Belizean Creole is English, it is unavoidable here to refer to specific issues of language and gender that have been highly debated for English, the lexifier of English creoles.

However, the special relation of Creole to English must be briefly examined before focusing on aspects of Belizean Creole per se. Belize is not unique in displaying the co-existence and extensive overlap of two varieties, one carrying overt prestige, and the other covert prestige. This is typical of any societies displaying a socio-economic differential. Differences are more marked and extensive in the case of co-existent distinct varieties in a creole context, a situation typically spanning a vast multi-dimensional space (LePage & Tabouret-Keller 1985).

In spite of the official status of English in Belize, it is not anyone's native language, as illustrated in Table 2. English may be unanimously recognized as the language that one must acquire to participate in official government activities, but it is not commonly used in its external (American or British) standard form. This fact is largely ignored or unidentified by both language users and language planners. Although there is a general, informal agreement as far as the creole end of the continuum is concerned, what constitutes the "correct" norm called *English* – the acrolect – is realized differently by various people who are not necessarily aware of such variations. The persistent legacy of colonialism is still reflected in the widespread belief that any "non-English" variety is *brokop* – broken English – which often includes the creole varieties as well as the mesolectal area of the continuum.

Official directives to instruct in the overtly prestigious model are naturally passed on to educators who themselves have learned English as a second language and present their own version to the children, and in the process frequently switch to creole in the classroom to encourage active participation. The overlap of the model and the vernacular predictably accounts for the linguistic complexity encountered by children in the classroom. Unfortunately, the overlap issue is never truly articulated, and consequently there is great confusion as to what constitutes the appropriate linguistic model for education and general communication purposes, as illustrated in the following statement made by D, a Garifuna teacher:[4]

Text one: Teaching (Acrolect)

You start speaking English to dem [the children], then you give dem de
definition in Creole which is much easier to dem because dats what dey hear
around dem. Outside you find dat de majority of people, deir parents speak
Creole, dey speak Carib and Creole. When I first started teaching, while I spoke
Creole intermittent, and finally I found out dat I spoke too much Creole, and
den I put a stop to it because I had learned English. So I practice my English
more. I practice it more even when I speak to my friends. So you would find
out when I would stand in front of a class and I speak to dem, I try to speak as
fluent as I can. When dey [my friends] speak Carib to me, I speak Carib. When
dey speak Creole, I speak English to dem, dat's de way I treat dem, right?
(Escure 1997: 38).

But, later in the conversation, he says:

Let's say I go among some friends and, like, we going to have a fine time. Okay,
de boys start talking and all everybody just discussing Creole. So instead of
trying to make myself feel, or try to show off myself dat I am a better man or I
am different dan all o' dem, I associate myself wid dem. So I speak Creole,
understan'? So nobody can just say he talk funny, he must be from a different
land. Ya understan'? I play when you are in Rome you do like de Romans do.
(Escure 1997: 38).

Teacher D's spontaneous assessment highlights the ambiguous co-existence of
English and (Belizean) Creole. It is clear that even native speakers of other
languages (D's native language is Garifuna, a language claimed to be a variety of
Arawak that he calls "Carib") have to control both. English has a strong
conscious presence in Belize, holding overt prestige and official recognition,
whereas Creole, the *lingua franca* among ethnic groups, and informal code, is
overtly claimed to be inferior, in spite of its covert identity value. The paradoxi-
cal opposition of prescriptivism and naturalness is represented in the teacher's
conflicting statements – first representing the official educator's concern for
good English – *when they speak Creole* [...] *I speak English* – then the average
Belizean perspective – *I speak Creole* [...] *so nobody can just say "he talk funny"*.
A subtle shifting across varieties can be triggered by a topic change, as clearly
illustrated in Text One: The first part of the teacher's statement (educational
topic) includes only standard instances of the copula/auxiliary (*dat's what dey
hear*) and past verbal forms, whereas the second part (social interaction with
friends) includes nonstandard instances of the zero-copula (*we going to have a
fine time*) beside the standard forms (*we are in Rome*).

Since most native speakers of the creole vernacular – even those who are not educators – get some exposure to Standard English or some variant thereof, it is likely that English influences the creole continuum now, as it has before, at least as far as the development of mesolects and acrolects is involved. This diglossic situation is characteristic of creole continua, and is typically represented through extensive stylistic shifts. Lectal shifting is an extension of individual repertoires, that is, the addition of acquired second dialects to native vernacular basilects, rather than the substitution of more standardized varieties for nonstandard lects. This interpretation is supported by the fact that most Creole speakers control a broad repertoire which keeps expanding during their lifetime. However, there is no absolute definition of lectal boundaries, and the overlapping nature of varieties inevitably leads to the confusion of English Creole and Standard English.

Creole studies, as well as gender studies present the crucial problem of methodological scope: explanations are directly dependent on the kind and range of speech data collected, and analyses based on socially restricted cross-sections of men and women can hardly provide universal explanations of gender behavior.

2.3 Previous studies of gender in Belize

Early studies of creoles rarely focused on gender issues. It is generally taken for granted that creoles (especially West Indian) have "no gender, no case", as stated for example by Alleyne (1980: 13, 151) in his overview of similarities in Afro-American speech (including varieties with English, French, Iberian and mixed lexical bases).

The goal of creolistics, which developed in the 1960s, is still primarily to describe and explain the complexity of linguistic variability in the historical context of decolonization. In the case of Belize, a particular challenge derived from the multiethnic and multilingual situation in which the creole functioned as a necessary *lingua franca*. Thus preliminary analyses of the Belizean linguistic situation provided a general analysis of the creole continuum (Escure 1978, 1979, 1981, 1982, 1983; Hellinger 1972, LePage & Tabouret-Keller 1998, LePage & Tabouret-Keller 1985, Young 1973). Young focused on the Creole spoken in Belize City, a semi-urban environment in the Belize District in which the Creole group is the overwhelming majority; LePage & Tabouret-Keller investigated specifically the Cayo District in the West of the country at the Guatemalan border, in which Spanish speakers dominate Creole speakers; Escure worked in the Stann Creek District, in which the three major groups (Creole, Mestizo and

Garifuna) co-exist in comparable proportions (see Table 2), but conducted fieldwork in two rural coastal communities, one Creole (Placencia), and the other Garifuna (Seine Bight).

Escure (1991, 1993, 1998) addresses more specifically gender issues (to be discussed below). Hellinger (1997) provides an excellent argumentation for the necessity to incorporate gender in creole studies: She emphasizes the importance of pronouns in studies of linguistic change because they carry simultaneously deictic and anaphoric functions, thus requiring reference to a discourse-specific perspective. This social dimension is crucial in defining the role of gender in a creole context. Hellinger accurately points out the relevance of the superstrate English as mesolectal systems develop beside basilectal systems, and the ambiguous nature of creole continua involving the interaction of two systems: on the one hand, developing mesolects acquire more elaborated pronominal systems, but on the other hand, they are exposed to the introduction of male bias in generic pronouns (assuming there is no such thing in gender-inclusive creole systems).

2.4 Gender in nominal reference and proverbs

As indicated above, this study of gender in Belizean varieties focuses on the specific issues of (a) putative gender marking in pronominal reference and (b) the role of women in linguistic diffusion. There are of course other areas of language in which gender may be manifested, although they are not covered in this study. The specification of referent gender may be particularly represented in nominal word-formation, address forms and traditional proverbs or idiomatic expressions.

The gender of children (and sometimes animals) is occasionally marked through compounds such as *man-pikni* 'little boy' or *gyal-pikni* 'little girl' (as indicated by Marlis Hellinger, p.c.), but those items were not as commonly used in my Belizean sample as lexical gender terms such as 'boy' or 'girl'.

In casual conversations, certain gender-marked terms of address are extremely frequent – although no quantitative analysis has been conducted to attest such impressions. Thus, the familiar – and respectful – term applied to women, especially older women, is *Miss* followed by her first name (*good manin miss Cordelia* 'Good morning Miss Cordelia'; *Miss Doris gone a Belize las week* 'Miss Doris went to Belize City last week', or *Miss Lucille im got eight pikni* 'Miss Lucille has eight children'). Even the female monster (Text Two below) is referred to as *Miss Suzi*. The term *Miss* carries no reference to marital status, and in fact the term *Mrs* appears to be rarely used. The counterpart for males is *Mister*, with similar connotations of respect, age and affection.

A more casual term of address (toward younger women, or among younger women) is *gal* (*gyal*) 'girl'. This is not considered a derogatory term in the creole community, but on the contrary carries an affective connotation of friendship and familiarity. For young men, the term *bway* 'boy' is widely used with the same level of familiarity, and not just restricted to children. The word *man* is widely used as an exclamatory term, or a term of address, and equally used among women, as in *Man, i hot today* 'Man, it's hot today' (see also Hellinger 1997:348). It is therefore a clear case of semantically bleached gender reference, thus not obviously reflecting gender bias – although one can argue that there is no female-marked generic counterpart such as *Gal, i hot today* (as uttered among men)!

Traditional proverbs provide plentiful evidence that *man* is also used as 'person'. This further supports the hypothesis that "female invisibility may also be found in creole societies" (Hellinger 1997:348). Other proverbs can be found in Young (1980) and McKesey (1974).

(1) *Evry man know we   part i   own house leak.*
     every man know which part his own house leak
     'Every man knows where his house leaks.'
     [Every man knows his weaknesses.] (McKesey 1974:100)

(2) *Man hate you, i   give you basket fu   back wata.*
     man hate you he give you basket for back water
     'If a man hates you he gives you a basket to carry water.'
     [If a man hates you he makes things difficult for you.]
     (McKesey 1974:101)

(3) *When man dead, grass grow da i   door mout.*
     when man dead grass grow at his door mouth
     'When a man is dead, grass grows in front of his door.'
     [A dead man is soon forgotten.] (McKesey 1974:102)

The traditional Anansi stories can also be interpreted as a prime example of undisguised male bias. The hero Anansi – or *Bra Anansi* (Brother Anansi) – is regularly referred to as *a sma(r)t man*, and all animal characters are similarly marked with male referents (*Bra Alligator, Bra Rat, Bra Hon* 'hound/dog', *Bra Crab, Bra Taiga* 'tiger').

3. Gender in Belizean conversation

The speech data that make up the corpus to be discussed here result from years of participant-observation in the Creole village of Placencia, located on an isolated peninsula of the Stann Creek District, on the Caribbean coast of Central America.

The Stann Creek District is unique in Belize with respect to its demographic distribution of ethnic groups. In particular, it harbors most of the Carib/ Garifuna (Afro-Indian) population, which amounts to as much as 36% of the district's population. Issues of ethnic interaction are addressed in Escure (1979, 1982, 1997), but the following discussion of creole usage is based on the Placencia corpus, which includes only Creole speakers. Spontaneous conversations were recorded either by a local fieldworker or by myself, and were conducted in natural settings, such as private homes, the beach, the school, the church, or local shops. Basilects and mesolects are most commonly used, whereas acrolects are relatively rare in a natural local context, most likely produced by teachers or officials. Local speakers in formal contexts are much more likely to produce meso-acrolects, that is, highly volatile varieties sharing various lectal features (see Escure 1979, 1981, 1997 for methodological details).

3.1 Absence of referential gender-marking (generic pronouns)

The personal pronoun, and in particular the generic pronoun *he* (and possessive *his*) has been one of the most hotly discussed linguistic items, because of its identification as a marker of sexism in English, as in: *As soon as a doctor gets his license, he can work in a hospital.* Over the last twenty years, this generic pronoun has become the focus of an extensive language planning campaign, a symbol of reaction to the social invisibility of women, and targeted for extinction. In a language such as English, which is deprived of grammatical gender, and in which the only regular marker of gender differentiation is the third person singular pronoun, language planning appears to have been successful and to have effectively removed generic *he* from common usage (Bennett-Kastor 1996: 298).[5] There is now general avoidance of *he* in the case of nonspecific reference. Alternative strategies include the use of plural forms, of generic *you*, and even of a singular *they* (or corresponding possessive adjectives), which are found to be most commonly used by children (Bennett-Kastor 1996: 298). This is briefly illustrated in the following excerpt from a popular American magazine, which displays various uses of indefinite *you/your* and *their* (with non-plural reference). But note also the use of *she* as generic pronoun, anaphor of *your kid* (there is no reference in the text to the gender of the child to be married).

> When *your* book gets sold for a movie, I suspect *you* feel the way *you* feel when *your* child gets married. Unless the intended is a real mope, *you're* joyous. [...] *Everyone* shuddered in horror at the thought of such a fate befalling *their* own works. [...] It would be like trying to live with your kid after she was married. (*Seeing your book on the big screen*: Newsweek, March 1, 1999: 16)

The question arises as to whether Belizean varieties are representing this trend, at least in their acrolects. In all the samples of Belizean varieties I have reviewed for this feature, the only clear cases of a gender-marked generic pronoun equivalent to English *he* have been restricted to religious discussions and biblical contexts, as shown in the following excerpt from a sermon in the local Anglican church which displays a combination of *it*, referring to the Church; *they/dey*, referring to preachers, then to parishioners (members), and finally generic *he*, referring to *man* in the biblical fashion, perhaps to avoid implicating local church members too directly. The inevitable conclusion is of course that missionaries may have introduced linguistic bias to the Creole community:

> But also I believe, regardless of the financial problem, that the church is losing *its* influence for basic reasons: One, the preachers now – I'm talking general – do not live to de gospel dat *dey* preach, dat's one. Two, de members do not reflect what *dey* believe, And three, because Man sees *himself* as *his* god, *he* no longer wants anyone else to come into *his* life [...]. As long as *he* has money and *his* wealth, *he* needs not God, dat's what *he* says.

However, no instances of the generic pronouns were found in non-religious contexts of the samples collected in this corpus. In contrast, *you* (and variant *ya*) occur widely as indefinite pronouns as in English: Text One representing the teacher's acrolect begins with a series of generic *you* ("*you* start speaking English [...] then *you* give dem [...]"). On the other hand, the use of *he* in Text One ("So nobody can just say *he* talk funny *he* must be from a different land") may appear to display a case of generic *he*, but it can also be interpreted as the (male) speaker referring to himself as an example.

In non-acrolectal varieties, the situation is complicated by the fact that creole basilects and mesolects, and Belizean varieties in particular, primarily use multifunctional pronouns unspecified for gender, case and number:

(4) *You come one day, you got a good time wid dem, an i done.*
   you come one day you got a good time with them and it done
   'You come one day, you have a good time with them, and it's over.'
   (Holm 1983:102f)

(5) *When a de   work lang di key ya   hear one li*
   when I HAB work along the caye you hear a   little
   "kiling kiling".
   "kiling kiling"
   'When I work along the caye, you hear a ringing noise.'
   (Escure 1983:34)

Belizean Creole has been associated with the pronominal system represented in Table 3 (Dayley 1979, Hellinger 1997) which presents the basic subjective and objective pronouns in Creole and English. The creole uses eight distinct pronouns (no case distinctions in the plural), whereas English has twelve, with case and number distinctions, except for the second person pronoun which has no number/case marking – also a feature of creoles.

   Creoles are characterized by minimal systems due to the absence of grammatical gender (cf. also Migge, this vol., Section 3), and of gender-marked pronouns, and a marked reduction in case and number distinctions. An exception is the distinctive second plural form *unu* which has no equivalent in English (except dialectal *y'all; you all; yu's*). *Unu* occurs widely in English-based creoles, and is traceable to West African substrates, such as Igbo (Alleyne 1980:111).

   The following discussion focuses on third person pronouns which are the only potentially gender-specific pronouns. There are four creole pronouns and variants representing third person anaphoric reference, each holding several functions, and primarily involving a bleaching of case and gender distinctions, although minimal number marking is present. The number of pronouns greatly

Table 3. Pronouns in Belizean Creole and English (Dayley 1979, Hellinger 1997)

| | Subjective | | | | | | Objective | | | | | |
| | Singular | | | Plural | | | Singular | | | Plural | | |
	1	2	3	1	2	3	1	2	3	1	2	3
Belizean	a	yu	i	wi	unu	den	mi	yu	an	wi	unu	den
English	I	you	he/she/it	wo	you	they	me	you	him/her/it	us	you	them

Table 4. Third person pronouns in Belizean Creole and their English counterparts

	3rd singular subj/obj	3rd singular obj	3rd plural subj/obj
Belizean	i/i/im da	a/a/an	den/dem/de
English	he/she/it that	him/her/it	they/them

varies from basilects to mesolects. Table 4 shows diversified variants not all represented in Table 3 (slashes indicate optional use in each case).

The most widespread anaphoric pronoun is *i/im*, a subject pronoun which can refer to males – see also (6), females – see Text Two, as well as inanimate objects, general statements, or abstract concepts – see (4) and (7–8), thus occasionally alternating with *it* (Text Three). It also functions as possessive adjective (*only i head come out of di mud* 'only its [bottle] top was sticking out of the wet sand'), and can be combined with the reflexive suffix (*di rope wan tie up i own self* 'the rope was folded on itself' Text Three). An alternate form *da/dat* derived from *that* functions as deictic pronoun (Hellinger 1997: 344). *Da* also occurs as a simple anaphoric pronoun, especially with abstract, inanimate or noncountable referents, thus generally as a substitute for *it* (that is, bleached from its orientation function), as shown in (7). In addition, both *i* and *da* as well as other forms such as *have* or *ga/gat* in (9) may be used as presentative items in existential structures of the type represented in (8), and Text Two: *When i mos happen dat ina Len* (literally; 'when it must happen, that (is) at Lent').

The pronoun *i* often overlaps with *im* (derived from the objective *him*), and thus the case distinction disappears, as seen in (10–12). *Im* is also unspecified for gender (*We no wait fa him* 'We don't wait for her') in Text Two. Like *i/im*, the singular objective pronoun *a* (represented in Text Two and other examples) is clearly gender-indefinite, but unlike *i*, it can also function as generic pronoun as in Texts Two (*i get a* 'he gets you'), and Three (*you see an* 'you see it'). Text Four also illustrates the juxtaposition of two instances of *i tel a*, in which both anaphoric pronouns have opposite referential gender (*i tel a* 'he told her' vs. *i tel a* 'she told him').

Text two: Monsters (Miss Suzi and Tatabuhende): Basilect[6]
(Escure 1983:41)

[Miss Suzi]
i come an i bounce up front of you an *i* say
["…"], *i* hide over *i* head like *i* crazy. […]

Wi no wait for *im* tel wi ["…"], wi run bica wi
fraid fa *a* [her]; […] wi hear di tree de crack up
[…] an when wi look up wi see *a* up da top, an
wi run lef *a* [her]. […]
Di li bway me run fa *a* [her] but Miss Suzi can
run fas. When *i* mos happen *dat* ina Len(t). Den
when Len(t) mos, beka da den bad ting happen.
You usually, somting happen to you, you get cut
an like dat, so … – *i* get *a*.
Well, like, a mean, when you get cut, like, when
you go ina bush pa Len(t), beka wi usually go an
wi carry machete go chop wood, an like dat so,
an den you get chop quick;
da *him* mek *a*, da Tatabuhende mek you get
chop, mek you get chop beka da Len(t) gi you
bad luck.

[Miss Suzi]
'She suddenly appears in front of you and she says
["…"], she hides overhead [in the trees] as if she
was crazy. […]
We didn't wait for her to tell us ["…"], we ran because we were afraid of her; we heard the tree
cracking and when we looked up we saw her on
top, and we ran away from her. […]
The little boy ran really fast from her, but Miss
Suzi can run faster It mostly happens around Lent.
They [those things] occur around Lent mostly,
because that's when bad things happen.
Usually something happens to you, you get cut or
something like that – He/she/they get you.
When you get cut, when you go in the bush at
Lent,
because we usually take a machete to chop wood,
and so, you get chopped up;

he makes it happen, it's Tatabuhende who causes
you to be chopped because Lent brings bad luck.'

Text three: The Mangrove: Basilect (Escure 1983:34–36)

Sometime you hear like somting de "krich-
krich" ina mangru, *dat* a stereofom,
you know, you hafu check *dat* out, bica *dat*
could be anytin,
you hafu go check out da sound fi go beach-
combin.[…]
Di rope wan tie up ina *i* own self. – well […] if
you see *an* high pan top a mangru, no go look.

[…] *i* gone long time. – somebody me wan pick
it in, dig?
Somebody me wan pick *it* in, dig? – ya, but once
you see an ina seaweed, da good rope.

'Sometimes you hear some screeching sound in
the mangrove, it is styrofoam,
you know, you have to check it out, because it
could be anything,
you have to go check out that sound when you go
beachcombing' […]
The rope is folded [will be tied on itself]. – Well if
you see it high on the mangrove, don't go look;
it's no good – Somebody would have picked it in,
dig?
– Yes, but if you see it in the seaweed, it is good
rope.'

(6) *I hear i   me nearly had to get a psychiatric treatment*
     I hear he ANT nearly had to get a psychiatric treatment
     a de rass.
     [EXPL]
     'I heard that he was almost forced to undergo some damned psychiatric
     treatment.'

(7) *No fret bout   dat place, **dat** gon   clean, a gon   clean i.*
     no fret about that place that going clean I going clean it
     'Don't worry about that place, it will be cleaned, I will clean it.'
     (Miskito Coast Creole; Holm 1983: 102]

(8) ***Da** me   wan propaganda ting; an i come wan time wen   dis*
     that ANT one propaganda thing and it come one time when this
     Guatemala question me kinda   hot.
     Guatemala question ANT kind.of hot
     'That was pure propaganda, and it came at the height of the problems
     with Guatemala.'

(9) *Yeah **ga** li   oysters we   grow pan   dem, but i ga one different*
     yes   got little oysters which grow upon them but it got one different
     idea bout   dat, too i de   look bout   seaweed dem.
     idea about that too it PROG look about seaweed them
     'Yes, there are small oysters growing (on the mangrove trees), but there
     is another thing [to do], that's to look around the seaweed.'

(10) *Since i   have wife an   children now, **im** look like im no*
     since he have wife and children now he look like he no
     de   hardly worry wid i, but i pick it up.
     PROG hardly worry with it but he pick it up
     'Ever since he has had a wife and children, he hardly bothered with it
     [drinking], but he started it again.'

(11) ***Im** believe say a no comin   back.*
     he believe say I no coming back
     'He thought that I would not come back.'

(12) *We   **im** work de   now? From dat night a no see **im**.*
     where he work there now from that night I no see him
     'Where does he work now? I haven't seen him since that night.'
     (Miskito Coast Creole; Holm 1983: 103)

Text four: The Healer (Escure 1983: 50)

So *i* happen dat *he* hear bout one lady we could cure any kinda sickness. So di fellow gone to di old lady and *i* tell *a*:

"Look ya, I come to – I hear you could cure anytin",

den *i* say, den *i* tell *a*:
"Well yes, da we happen to you?" […]
you see *i* put *i* hand but, as di uman start *i* pray, de man put *i* hand ya because dis was what was sick.

'So it so happened that he heard about a lady who could cure any kind of disease. So that fellow went to see the old lady and he told her:

"Look, I come to – I hear that you can cure anything",

then she said, then she told him:
"Well, yes, what happened to you?" […]
You see he put his hand but, as the woman started her prayer, the man put his hand there because this was what was sick.'

Considering the ambiguity of personal pronouns, the interpretation (male, female, neutral; subjective or objective) of multifunctional pronouns is highly dependent on the context. A similar pattern affects the plural forms *den/dem/de*, which are markers of objective case in the acrolect and in English. In basilects and mesolects, *den/dem* also function as subject anaphoric pronoun variant, sometimes with additional deictic function or as presentative – in left dislocation and other structures, as in (13). *Dem* also occurs in structures with an objective function and plural value as adjective or pronoun. Both case values are represented below as well as the pronoun *dey*, obviously a reflex of English *they*. The form *den/dem* is normally present in emphatic contexts.

(13)   *Some a **dem** bway wuda   go out, an   dey   look fu **dem** old*
        some of them boy   would go out and they look for them old
        *quart bottle right? Well, bway, **dem** dey   hard to find.*
        quart bottle right well   boy   them they hard to find
        'Some of those boys would go out […] and they look for those old bottles, right? Well, boy, them they are hard to find.'

(14)   *When a da   me   one group leader de,   a know **dem** girl*
        when I TOP ANT one group leader there I know them girl
        dey   like, well, steady go-run-go-tell, run-go-tell pan dis girl, a try
        they like well steady go-run-go-tell run-go-tell on this girl I try
        *cover up fu **dem** all de time.*
        cover up for them all the time
        'When I was group leader, I knew that those girls [officeworkers] always liked to tell on other girls. I tried to cover for them all the time.'

3.2 Comparative distribution of pronouns in Belizean and other Central American Creoles

Table 5 shows that *i/im* is the most widely distributed pronoun in this sample of Belizean basilectal and mesolectal varieties, amounting to 40% of all pronominal anaphora (3sg). A related basilect was examined for comparison – namely, Miskito Coast Creole (Holm 1983), and in this text the incidence of this pronoun was even higher (60%).

On the other hand, two Belizean acrolectal samples (a sermon mentioned above, and a young man's discussion of language bias when he was a student in England) display mostly standard pronouns contrasting in case and number – that is, *dey/they* functions as subjective, and *dem/them* as objective. As indicated above, the sermon also includes 15 generic anaphoric pronouns (referent is *man*). A related acrolect – spoken on the island of Utila in the Bay Islands of Honduras (Warantz 1983) – was also included for comparison, and shows a pronominal distribution similar to that of the Belizean acrolect.

There is, however, some minimal incidence of English gender-marked pronouns even at the basilectal level, which clearly demonstrates the influence of the co-existent superstrate: the occurrence of *he* and *she* in basilects and mesolects (5% in Belize, 11% in Nicaragua) is low compared to the 45.5% to 66% represented in the Placencia and the Utila (Honduran) acrolects. The difference between the Belizean and the Honduran acrolects is related to the incidence of *da/dat* as anaphoric pronoun in Belize (but it does not appear in the Utila English text):

Table 5. Comparative distribution of pronouns in Belizean and other Central American Creoles (Miskito Coast Creole [MCC] and Utila English [UE])

	N	i/im	da/dat	a/an	de/dem	he/she/it/him/her/his
Basilects						
Belize	[207]	40.1% (83)	16.9% (35)	13% (27)	24.6% (51)	5.3% (11)
MCC	[82]	61% (50)	1.2% (1)	11% (9)	15.9% (13)	11% (9)
Acrolects						
Belize	[165]	0	15.2% (25)	0	39.4% (65)*	45.5% (75)
UE	[201]	18.9% (38)	0	0	15.4%(31)	65.7% (132)

Note: * includes 15 generic pronouns

Table 6 illustrates the distribution of pronouns in terms of their case values (not represented in Table 5). The pronoun *i* mostly occurs in subject position, and its variant *im*[7] is rare in Belize, whereas *a/an* is always restricted to objects, at least in the Belizean corpus examined.

Table 6. Distribution of Belizean Creole 3rd person pronouns (excluding English pronouns)

N	Subjective			Objective			
	i/im	da/dat	de/dem	i/im	a/an	da/dat	de/dem
[180]	33.9%(61)	12.8%(23)	10.6%(19)	3.3%(6)	15%(27)	6.7%(12)	17.8%(32)

Table 7 shows a more detailed distribution of *i/im* in Belizean varieties, and Miskito Creole, with reference to its male, female and neutral values. It is clearly an all-purpose item which occurs more frequently with a male referent, and more so in Miskito Creole than in Belizean, although this discrepancy is obviously a function of the texts and topics discussed, not an intrinsic property of each language. What clearly surfaces from this comparison is the fact that *i/im* has no association with gender, either in its simple pronominal form, or its possessive and reflexive forms.

Table 7. Distribution of anaphoric *i/im* in basilects

	N	Pers Pron (72%)			Poss Pron (27.7%)			Refl Pron (1.2%)
		M he/him	F she/her	N it	M his	F her	N its	N itself
Belize	83	43	15	2	10	10	2	1
MCC	50	43	1	3	3	0	0	0

Belize is not unique in its multifunctional use of pronouns. This is a feature characteristic of creoles in general, and represented at various levels of the language. It entails the absence of gender marking in Belizean basilects and mesolects. But the influence of the superstrate is likely, as some gender-marked pronouns appear in those varieties, often displaying the co-existence of different lectal variants, such as *she/i* in the same sentence:

(15) *Elvita, **she** no come de? – No. We **i** de?*
      Elvita she no come there   no where she there

We   she de?
where she there
'Elvita, she is not coming? – No. Where is she? Where is she?'
(Holm 1983:104)

(16) *So i happen dat he hear bout   one lady we   could cure*
so it happen that he hear about one lady who could cure
any kinda   sickness. So di fellow gone to di   old lady
any kind.of sickness so the fellow gone to the old lady
and i   tell a   […]
and he tell her
'He happened to hear about a woman who could cure any disease. So the fellow went to see that woman and he told her […]'

(17) *If you see an high pan   top a mangru,   no go look*
if you see it   high upon top of mangrove no go look
i gone long time – Somebody me   wan pick i in, dig?
it gone long time – somebody ANT FUT pick it in dig
'If you see it [rope] on the mangrove [roots], don't bother looking […]
it's no good – Somebody would have picked it up already.'

The insertion of acrolectal pronouns in basilects and mesolects merely adds to the pronominal multifunctionality represented in the texts and tables presented above. There is no evidence that either *she* or *he* have gained any gender-specific value in vernaculars outside of formal acrolectal contexts.

4.   Gender and linguistic change

One of the most widely accepted claims regarding gender holds that women as members of the muted group favor prestige varieties as a way to compensate for their lack of power, whereas men – members of the socially dominant group – assign social prestige and solidarity values to vernacular variants (Trudgill 1998:21–28). This implies that women may initiate change in the direction of the standard, and would thus facilitate a leveling of language variation with loss of the most distinctive local or basilectal variants, which in creole situations would lead to decreolization. If this turned out to be true, women would be promoters of the standardization of the continuum, but would also be responsible for the loss of varieties which represent local identity. Such possibilities were evaluated with detailed references to two sets of linguistic features affecting crucial tense and aspect components of the verb phrase.

4.1 Linguistic change: The copula

I examined creole morphemes and their standard reflexes corresponding to the copula or auxiliary *be* variable in English, because this feature holds core functions both in Belizean Creole and in English. It thus constitutes an excellent diagnostic indicator of linguistic change. Three copular variants are identified: the preverbal morpheme *de* (exclusively basilectal); zero-morpheme (copula absence may occur at all levels depending on grammatical environments); and inflected forms of English *be* (mesolectal and acrolectal). As speakers acquire acrolects, they learn to insert inflected *be* in preverbal position (whereas zero occurs in the L1 creole). Given that all speakers are able to shift at least between native vernacular styles (basilects), and less casual varieties approaching Standard English in variable ways (mesolects or meso-acrolects), speakers' choices are determined by the context as well as by their own interpretation of stylistic appropriateness, and this may vary from one individual to another.

Relative frequencies of those variants permit an assessment of lectal level, which can independently be confirmed by other linguistic or extralinguistic features, such as phonological variation, and contextual knowledge. As stated above, there is no absolute definition of lectal boundaries. No single copular variant is exclusively confined to one lect, because the relative proportion of the three morphemes differs according to stylistic level, as represented in the following examples. The acrolect in Text One illustrates the co-occurrence of the zero-copula and inflected *be*; the basilect in Text Two uses both zero-copula and *de*; and all three variants can even co-occur in a basilectal text, as in Text Three;[8] a mesolect, on the other hand, is more likely to exclude *de* altogether, and to include a higher incidence of zero-copula than an acrolect. Generally, the definition of lects is identifiable in terms of relative variant frequencies, and of course, the stylistic context (see Table 9 and discussion).

Text One Acrolect (Teaching):
zero-copula: *All everybody* [zero] *just discussing creole*
                'Everybody argues in creole'
be: *I am a better man.*

Text Two Basilect (Monsters):
de: *We hear di tree de crack up*
                'We heard the tree cracking'

zero copula: *We* [zero] *fraid*
                 'We were afraid'

Text Three Basilect (Mangrove):
de: *You hear somting de "krich"*
                 'you hear something screeching'
zero copula: *Da* [zero] *good rope*
                 'That's good rope'
be: *Dat could be anytin*

Text Four Mesolect (Healer):
be: *Dat was what was sick*

Table 8 presents an overall distribution of the three variants as observed in Placencia. In its simple reference to a binary gender system, it displays gender-based differentiation, thus confirming the hypothesis that females are promoters of standard varieties, because they use more of the standard copula (63.5%) than men (45.7%), and less of the basilectal copula (9%) whereas men use as much as 16.5%:

Table 8. Gender and choice of copular variants

	N	Basilectal *de*	Zero	Standard *be*
Women	961	9.0%	27.3%	63.5%
Men	2034	16.5%	37.0%	45.7%

However, a simple comparison of the linguistic behavior of men and women can be misleading if there is no reference to individual and group performance and to the range of stylistic variation. This is particularly applicable to creole continua where most speakers control wide-ranging repertoires (Escure 1991, 1997). But when separating basilects from mesolects (as in Table 9), the picture that surfaces shows far less gender-linked differentiation, and more subtle patterns of variant distribution. Women and men implement similar frequencies in basilects, which means that they broadly agree on their realizations of copular variants at each lectal level.

Table 9 must be interpreted in terms of the co-existence of variants illustrated above: a high frequency of *de* (around or over 30%) characterizes the basilect, but a mesolect will display minimal instances of this variant. Inversely, the mesolect – unlike a basilect – will include high frequencies (over 50%) of *be*. The unmarked variant (zero copula) will occur in intermediate amounts. The fallacy reflected in Table 8 is a result of merging basilects with mesolects, and it

Table 9. Copular use and lectal variation

	Basilects		Mesolects	
	Women (8)	Men (6)	Women (9)	Men (14)
be	10.5%	5.5%	76.5%	80.5%
zero	54.2%	61.1%	20.7%	17.5%
de	34.7%	33.4%	2.7%	2.0%

is also due to a differential amount of speech production by men and women (men in this sample roughly produced twice as much discourse as women; see Table 8). Most importantly, it is due to the pragmatic fact that women (in this sample) were more likely than men to exercise style-shifting (they use basilects and meso-acrolects equally) than men, who primarily use the creole vernacular. Consequently, women overall use standard variants more often than men, but this does not mean that they do not use the same basilectal codes as men in certain contexts.

Methodological details show that women extensively use the vernacular (creole basilects) in community activities and thus cooperate with men to preserve local identity and the traditional values rooted in the creole vernacular (Escure 1991). Although men and women in a fishing community such as Placencia appear to function according to traditional roles (men make a living, women raise children) women often participate actively in authoritative and dominant roles in local matters as well as in matters of child-rearing. This is due to the peculiar economic situation which exists in some fishing communities which – at least until recently – resulted in extended absences at sea of the sailors and fishermen, during which their wives were in charge of the village administration. Age appears to be a relevant factor which intersects with gender, since it is a particular group of middle-aged women (the wives of village officials) that are in charge of the village administration, and exhibit especially extensive style-shifting, thereby demonstrating that they value the creole vernacular as marker of local identity, yet are able and willing to switch to the overt standard for official functions. Other age groups evidence no gender-based language differentiation. In conclusion, linguistic differences appear to be related to local social status, which defines gender roles, more than to gender per se. In the case of Placencia, officials' wives effectively exert dominant officials' roles, which results in a quasi-overt matriarchal society.

In a related study, it was noted that women and men implement change differently. De has two functions in creole, but it is clear that as a locative verb, as in *We she de?* 'Where is she?' (15), it is disappearing even in basilects, unlike aspectual *de* (progressive and habitual marker), which is widely represented in the above examples. The depletion of locative *de* (replaced by English *be*) is more actively implemented by women, which suggests that women are more sensitive to the general directionality of change in this community (Escure 1993: 126–129).

4.2 Linguistic change: Past tense

A study of another linguistic feature – the use of past tense forms – also appears at first to confirm claims that men use more vernacular forms than women, at least assuming again that the most basilectal forms represent the vernacular. The three variants include *me*, the preverbal basilectal marker of past;[9] un-marked verb forms [zero-past]; and standard preterite forms [past], all illustrated below and scattered throughout the texts shown above:

Text One Acrolect (Teaching):
past:　　　　　*I first started teaching* [...] *I spoke* [...] *I found* [...]

Text Two Basilect (Monsters):
me:　　　　　*Di li bway me run fa a*
　　　　　　　'The little boy ran from her'
zero past:　　*We run because we* [zero] *fraid*
　　　　　　　'We ran because we were afraid'

Text Four Mesolect (Healer):
me:　　　　　*di man me done gone*
zero past:　　*i hear bout one lady we could cure any type of sickness*[10]
past:　　　　　*dat was what was sick*

Table 10. Use of past tense variants

	N	Basilectal *me*	Zero	Standard Past
Women	1067	39 (3.7%)	447 (41.9%)	581 (54.5%)
Men	536	165 (30.8%)	177 (33%)	194 (36.2%)

Table 10 displays a pattern somewhat similar to that representing copular variants (Table 8), in the sense that men are greater users of the basilectal variant than women (30.8% vs. 3.7%). Men use each of the three variants about equally (about 30%), whereas women frequently mark past verbs in the standard manner (54.5%). When contrasting basilectal and mesolectal patterns, the emerging picture is entirely different, and this may be related to the fact that women produce a larger speech corpus than men – a reversal of the copular sample presented above. Men are the only ones to use high frequencies of *me* in basilects, but they don't use it at all in mesolects, whereas women use small amounts in both lects:

Table 11. Past tense marking and lectal variation

	Basilects		Mesolects	
	Women (2)	Men (2)	Women (4)	Men (3)
Past	35.0%	16.6%	65.0%	75.0%
zero	62.0%	36.9%	31.0%	25.4%
me	2.9%	46.5%	4.1%	0

The pattern of past variation is clearly different across lects, but men and women represent mesolects in similar ways as a group. However, when reviewing individual behavior, another interesting pattern emerged: the six women studied display relatively homogeneous usage of past variants, whereas men contrast much more sharply in their relative use of past, the younger men favoring the vernacular variants (Escure 1998: 36). In this case, men show more flexibility than women, in contrast to the previous copular study, suggesting again that age is an important factor in issues of language choice. Because the female group uses fewer vernacular variants in basilects than the male group, women may be interpreted as innovators in the past tense case, as in the copular case (assuming that the bleaching of the basilectal morpheme is considered a sign of innovation).

Yet, there is no clear movement toward the standard on the women's part. Although they use more unmarking than men, replacing a nonstandard basilectal feature by another one (zero marking), which suggests a move away from the creole, because it is more neutral, more mesolectal, and thus less marked, less stigmatized than the creole morpheme, it does not necessarily follow that such unmarking reveals an intent to conform to the standard. Both copular and past cases of unmarking suggest a diplomatic attempt at bridging the gap between two (or more) linguistic codes, two cultures, and two identities. The analogy can be drawn with the loss of locative *de*, more actively actuated by women, and contrasted with the relative stability of aspectual *de*.

What clearly emerges is the picture of women defining their gender roles in the community as mediators.

5. Explanations

The differential patterning of male and female linguistic usage suggests that different strategies may be at work, but that there is no simple way to relate gender to linguistic change. A deep understanding of the local social dynamics, and an in-depth empirical analysis of speakers' repertoires are both essential in the interpretation of language patterns. The reported observations of the Belizean community are mostly in support of previous claims about genderized language use, summarized in Holmes (1998):

> 1. Women are stylistically more flexible than men (Holmes 1998:475)
>
> 2. Women tend to use more standard forms than men from the same social group in the same social context (Holmes 1998:473)
>
> 3. Women tend to interact in ways which maintain and stress solidarity while men (especially in formal contexts) will tend to interact in ways which will maintain and increase their power and status (Holmes 1998:472)

It has indeed been generally suggested that women develop a greater diversity of interactional skills than men, and a greater adaptability to contextual variation, probably necessitated by their lower social status. Local social considerations in the definition of gender roles must be taken into account, and language change is likely to be linked to issues of ethnic identity and vernacular loyalty, or on the contrary, to a desire of conformity to the standard and denial of the existence and value of broken English reflecting the colonial heritage.

This interpretation fits a Creole community constantly shifting values and roles. The ambiguous pattern identified in the Placencia community suggests a conflict between the necessity to learn the standard and the allegiance to the local vernacular. This is particularly vivid in a postcolonial context with a history of oppression, in which some degree of conformity to social standard expectations would have been necessary to ensure survival, yet total assimilation would have resulted in loss of identity, and been tantamount to ethnic suicide. In this case men and women are subjected to the same sociopolitical pressures and psychological dilemmas. This implies that a wide range of social and linguistic choices is available, and that individuals make personal decisions depending on their assessments and psychological or economic aspirations.

Women may be more aware than men of the power inherent in language appropriateness, and more willing to serve as interpreters or mediators in a conflicted world. Women, especially those in the 40–50 age range, fulfill ubiquitous social functions, combining traditional child-rearing female roles and dominant governing male roles. They are thus likely to regard linguistic bipolarity as an essential aspect of dynamic social relations benefiting the village both psychologically and economically (Escure 1991, 1997).

Bourdieu's model of linguistic acts as symbolic interactions which actualize the power relations among speakers is quoted below because it characterizes precisely the dynamics of creole societies, and explains how social beings define their identities, including gender identity:

> […] les rapports de communication par excellence que sont les échanges linguistiques sont aussi des rapports de pouvoir symbolique où s'actualisent les rapports de force entre les locuteurs et leurs groupes respectifs.
> (Bourdieu 1982: 14)

> '[…] linguistic exchanges constitute not only the ultimate communicative acts, but they also represent symbolic acts of power that actualize hierarchical power relations between speakers and their social groups.'

The flexible distribution of gender roles observed in Belize may be typical of many low status or minority groups, such as communities featuring massive emigration due to economic reasons (Belize); temporary or seasonal drains of the male working force (Hispanic migrants in the U.S.; Turkish or North African "guest" workers in Europe); as well as historically and forcefully transported minority groups (African Americans in the U.S.). All constitute the modern economic equivalents of colonization, in which women find themselves forced to fend for themselves. Such demographic change entails new responsibilities and some degree of ingroup power, because men have left in the pursuit of economic benefits, either physically, or psychologically (sometimes even moving to criminal gang activities which in some cases are perceived as the only means to achieve status and power). It is clearly essential to incorporate the dynamics of low status groups in any interpretation of the function of gender in language use. Economic opportunities determine differential gender roles and trigger the use of distinct linguistic codes adapted to the options available to men and women, as illustrated in widely different groups such as the Gullah in the southern United States (Nichols 1983), Hungarian peasants in Austria (Gal 1979), or Creole fishing communities in Belize.

6. Conclusion

The present data confirm my earlier hypothesis that in a Creole (postcolonial) community with earlier social leveling due to the historical subjugation of both women and men, the definition of gender roles is a variable factor determining linguistic choices in the context of the extensive range of linguistic variability available to most creole speakers.

Although the feminist debate about women's place is not unknown in Central American and Caribbean societies, it is likely to be viewed as reductionist and inapplicable to creole communities as long as both men and women struggle equally toward economic survival. Although there is little indication that gender per se has any direct effect on linguistic choices in a postcolonial Caribbean/Central American society like Placencia, there is a strong indication that the evolution of gender roles – as they are linked to issues of power and dominance – has a significant impact on linguistic development.

Notes

1. Grammatical gender, the assignment of nouns to grammatical classes, with implications for agreement phenomena, does not exist in English-based creoles (no more than it does in English), it will therefore be excluded from the following discussion. See Hellinger (1995: 287–290) for a summary of the various meanings associated with categories of gender.

2. The varieties co-occurring (and overlapping) in the creole continuum are called *lects* and range from *basilects* (most vernacular) to *acrolects* (most standard) with intermediate *mesolects*.

3. This district is the focus of the present analysis.

4. To represent acrolects, the orthographic representation of Standard English has been maintained as much as possible, but various idiosyncrasies of Belizean English are indicated: for example, the absence of interdentals as in *dem* for *the*, the use of zero-copula (*everybody just discussing*), or the absence of certain inflections (*he talk funny*).

5. The same trend has been observed in other areas such as the use of titles, first names, or a middle initial in references to men and women (Fasold & Yamada & Robinson & Barish 1990).

6. The orthographical representations *mi* and *wi* are used to differentiate pronouns from the creole markers *me* (past tense preverbal marker ANT) as in *da me wan propaganda ting* (8); and *we* (relative pronoun or locative marker) as in *oysters we grow* (9). Generally, regular English orthography is preserved, in spite of important phonetic realizations, except in cases involving crucial grammatical distinctions.

7. However, the Miskito Creole text displays a preferential use of *im* – both as subject and object (see 10–12) – whereas *a/an* is rarely used. Different varieties use various strategies, and speakers may make different choices. In spite of the similar orthographic representation, 3rd

person singular pronoun *a* is phonetically different from the 1st person singular pronoun *a* (derived from *I* [ay]). The 3rd person pronoun is consistently nasalized, with a greater degree of nasalization in *an*.

8. The post-modal context is the only one requiring the use of non finite *be* in Belizean basilects, as in *dat could be anytin* (Text Three).

9. The negative equivalent of *me* is *neva*, a preverbal marker of past in a negative proposition. *Neva* can be used for specific as well as universal negative reference. Those items are incorporated in the table (see Escure 1998). Creole *neva* is a remnant of a Middle English item *never*, which also carried the dual specific/universal meaning. This dual function still exists in various British dialects (Cheshire 1998: 138).

10. In Creole *could* [ku] is NOT a past form, it is simply equivalent to the modal 'can', and unmarked for tense. Several creole verbs are the result of the relexification of a past as non tense marked, e.g. *lef* 'leave'.

References

Alleyne, Mervyn. 1980. *Comparative Afro-American*. Ann Arbor: Karoma.

Belize Census. 2000. Report no. 1: *National population and housing census*. Belmopan.

Belize Population Count. 2000. Belmopan.

Bennett-Kastor, Tina. 1996. "Anaphora, nonanaphora, and the generic use of pronouns by children." *American Speech* 71: 285–301.

Bourdieu, Pierre. 1982. *Ce que parler veut dire: L'économie des échanges linguistiques*. Paris: Fayard.

Cheshire, Jenny. 1982. *Variation in an English dialect: A sociolinguistic study*. Cambridge: Cambridge University Press.

Cheshire, Jenny. 1998. "English negation from an interactional perspective." In *The sociolinguistics reader: Multilingualism and variation*, eds. Peter Trudgill & Jenny Cheshire. London: Arnold, 127–144.

Dayley, Jon P. 1979. *Belizean Creole grammar handbook*. Brattleboro, VT: Peace Corps Language Handbook Series.

Escure, Geneviève. 1978. "Vocalic change in the Belizean English Creole continuum and markedness theory." *Berkeley Linguistics Society* 4: 158–167.

Escure, Geneviève. 1979. "Linguistic variation and ethnic interaction in Belize: Creole/ Carib." In *Language and ethnic relations*, eds. Howard Giles & Bernard St Jacques. Oxford: Pergamon, 101–116.

Escure, Geneviève. 1981. "Decreolization in a creole continuum: Belize." In *Historicity and variation in creole studies*, eds. Arnold Highfield & Albert Valdman. Ann Arbor: Karoma, 27–49.

Escure, Geneviève. 1982. "Contrastive patterns of intragroup and intergroup interaction in the creole continuum of Belize." *Language in Society* 11: 239–264.

Escure, Geneviève. 1983. "Belizean Creole." In *Central American English*, ed. John Holm. Amsterdam: Benjamins, 29–70.

Escure, Geneviève. 1991. "Gender roles and linguistic variation in the Belize Creole community." In *English around the world: Sociolinguistic perspectives*, ed. Jenny Cheshire. Cambridge: Cambridge University Press, 595–608.

Escure, Geneviève. 1993. "Gender and linguistic change in Belize." In *Locating power*, eds. Kira Hall & Mary Bucholtz. Berkeley: University of California Press, 118–131.

Escure, Geneviève. 1997. *Creole and dialect continua: Standard acquisition processes in Belize and China (PRC)*. Amsterdam: Benjamins.

Escure, Geneviève. 1998. "Language contact: Gender and tense/aspect in Belizean Creole." In *SICOL (Proceedings of the Second International Conference on Oceanic Linguistics)*, eds. Jan Tent & France Mugler. Canberra: Pacific Linguistics, 27–41.

Escure, Geneviève & Portia McClain. 1999. *Habitual aspect and migration in African American pre-adolescents in Minneapolis*. Unpublished manuscript.

Fasold, Ralph & Haru Yamada & David Robinson & Steven Barish. 1990. "The language planning effect of newspaper editorial policy: Gender differences in the Washington Post." *Language in Society* 19: 521–539.

Gal, Susan. 1979. "Peasant men can't get wives: Language change and sex roles in a bilingual community." *Language in Society* 7: 1–16.

Hellinger, Marlis. 1972. "Aspects of Belizean Creole." *Folia Linguistica (Acta Societatis Linguisticae Europaeae)* 6: 118–135.

Hellinger, Marlis. 1995. "Language and gender." In *The German language in the real world*, ed. Patrick Stevenson. Oxford: Clarendon, 280–314.

Hellinger, Marlis. 1997. "Variation and change in creole pronominal systems: What does *i(m)* mean?" In *Anglistentag 1996 Proceedings*, eds. Uwe Böker & Hans Sauer. Trier: Wissenschaftlicher Verlag Trier, 343–350.

Holm, John. 1983. "Nicaragua's Miskito Coast Creole English." In *Central American English*, ed. John Holm. Amsterdam: Benjamins, 101–105.

Holmes, Janet. 1998. "Women's talk: The question of sociolinguistic universals." In *Language and gender: A reader*, ed. Jennifer Coates. London: Blackwell, 461–483.

LePage, Robert B. & Andrée Tabouret-Keller. 1985. *Acts of identity: Creole-based approaches to language and ethnicity*. Cambridge: Cambridge University Press.

LePage, Robert B. & Andrée Tabouret-Keller. 1998. "'You can never tell where a word comes from': Language contact in a diffuse setting." In *The sociolinguistics reader: Multilingualism and variation*, eds. Peter Trudgill & Jenny Cheshire. London: Arnold, 67–89.

McKesey, George. 1974. *The Belizean lingo*. Belize: National Printers.

Nichols, Patricia C. 1983. "Linguistic options and choices for black women in the rural South." In *Language, gender and society*, eds. Barrie Thorne & Cheris Kramarae & Nancy Henley. Rowley, MASS: Newbury House, 54–68.

Trudgill, Peter. 1998. "Sex and covert prestige". In *Language and gender: A reader*, ed. Jennifer Coates. Oxford: Blackwell, 21–28.

Trudgill, Peter & Jenny Cheshire, eds. 1998. *The sociolinguistics reader: Multilingualism and variation*. Vol. 1. London: Arnold.

Warantz, Elissa. 1983. "The Bay Islands English of Honduras." In *Central American English*, ed. John Holm. Amsterdam: Benjamins, 71–94.

Wodak, Ruth & Gertraud Benke. 1997. "Gender as a sociolinguistic variable: New perspectives on variation studies." In *The handbook of sociolinguistics*, ed. Florian Coulmas. Oxford: Blackwell, 127–150.

Young, Colville. 1973. *Belize Creole: A study of the creolized English spoken in the city of Belize, in its cultural and social setting*, University of York, York, England.

Young, Colville. 1980. *Creole proverbs of Belize*. Belize City: Angelus Press.

Communicating gender in the Eastern Maroon Creole of Suriname

Bettina Migge
University of Frankfurt am Main, Germany

1. Introduction

The Eastern Maroon Creole (EMC) is the native language of the members of four Eastern Maroon communities, the Aluku-Boni, the Paamaka, the Okanisi, and the Kwinti.[1] The majority of the villages of these semi-autonomous matrilineal communities are located along the Marowjine river (Aluku-Boni, Okanisi, and Paamaka) and its tributaries the Lawa river (Aluku-Boni) and the Tapa(n)ahoni river (Okanisi) in the interior of the South American rain forest on the territory of the Republic of Suriname and the French overseas territory French Guiana. Some Okanisi villages are also located along the Cottika river and the Sara creek. The Kwinti villages are situated along the Coppename and the Saramacca river on the other side of Suriname. The Okanisi are the largest Eastern Maroon community, numbering about 20000 people. The Paamaka number 3000 and the Aluku-Boni about 2000 people, and the Kwinti community have at the most 500 members.[2] The different Eastern Maroon communities were founded between 1710 and 1760 by West African slaves who had fled the Surinamese sugar plantations (Hoogbergen 1990).

Traditionally, Eastern Maroons are subsistence farmers and only young men used to engage in temporary cash-labor. Since about the 1960s, young Eastern Maroons have, however, increasingly been moving permanently or semi-permanently to the regional urban centers in search of permanent cash employment and better living conditions. Until the 1980s, most Eastern Maroons migrated to the Surinamese towns of Albina and Paramaribo, the capital of Suriname. Since Suriname's drastic economic decline following its independence from the Netherlands in 1975 and the civil war during the 1980s, Eastern Maroons have in the majority been migrating to the French Guianese towns of St. Laurent du Maroni, Mana, Kourou, and Cayenne. Today, members of the Okanisi and Paamaka communities are permanently and semi-permanently settled in all the Surinamese and French Guianese urban centers, while members of the Aluku-Boni community are mainly found in the French Guianese towns and in Paramaribo. Kwintis mainly reside in Paramaribo.

Varieties of the EMC enjoy a high prestige in the villages and are employed in all interactions. Most people either do not speak any of the other main languages in the region such as Dutch, French, Creole (French Guianese Creole) or the related coastal creole Sranan Tongo, or they have only a minimal, mainly passive knowledge of one of these, most typically Sranan Tongo. Urbanized young Eastern Maroons usually also speak Sranan Tongo and some Creole if they live in French Guiana and, depending on the amount of formal education they have enjoyed, also display varying degrees of knowledge of Dutch and/or French. In-group interactions in the urban centers are, however, still primarily carried out in varieties of the EMC.

The EMC is classified as a conservative English-lexified creole, since the overwhelming majority of its lexicon is derived from English. Significantly smaller numbers of its lexical items come from Portuguese, West African languages such as Gbe, Kikongo, Akan (Arends 1994, Huttar 1985), Amerindian languages of the region (Goury 1999), and, particularly in recent years, also from Dutch and somewhat from French. Structurally, it shares a great number of similarities with its West African input languages, particularly the Gbe group of languages (Migge 1998a, 1998b, 2000, in press), and it is not mutually intelligible with varieties of English. It is partially mutually intelligible with its sister languages, the central and western maroon creoles Saamaka and Matawai, and Sranan Tongo, since they all descend from a common predecessor which developed roughly between 1680 and 1720 on the Surinamese sugar plantations in the interactions between West African slaves (Arends 1994, Migge 1998a). Huttar & Huttar (1994) is a detailed grammatical description of the EMC and a preliminary EMC-English dictionary is Shanks & Koanting & Velanti (2000). Publications in the EMC include the New Testament (Beibel 1999) and a few story books and health guides cited in Huttar & Huttar (1994).

Gender, besides age, is the most salient social category in the Eastern Maroon communities. It is a major determinant of social behavior in all areas of everyday life and on all levels of public organization. For example, from very early on boys and girls are socialized to perform different tasks – boys learn to cut fields, hunt, fish, build houses, boats etc., and girls learn to plant and harvest, prepare the main food staples, cook, wash, and tend to children. Men and women do not only have clearly different rights and obligations in marriage, but also in their participation in the political decision making processes.[3] Children growing up in the urban centers are also socialized as much as possible into these gender roles.

2. Gender in the EMC

This study investigates the representation of gender in the EMC. The discussion focuses on determining (i) how gender is signaled in the EMC, (ii) in which contexts overt gender marking typically occurs, and (iii) the interpretation of overtly gender-marked and -unmarked personal nouns.[4]

The data for this study come from three sources: (i) recordings of several hours of spontaneous conversations between speakers of the Okanisi, Kwinti, and particularly the Paamaka varieties of the EMC, (ii) extensive participant-observation of Eastern Maroon and particularly Paamaka everyday life in rural and urban settings, and (iii) formal and informal questioning of selected members of the Eastern Maroon communities.

The EMC does not have grammatical gender. A great number of terms used for person reference in the EMC do not provide any formal indication of referential gender. Examples include common terms such as *mati* 'friend', *data(a)* 'medical personnel', *basia* 'assistant to lineage or village head', and pronominal forms such as *a* 'unemphatic she, he, it' and *en* 'emphatic she, he, it and her, him, his, it, its'.[5] The lack of overt gender marking leads to binary (1a) or multiple (1b) ambiguities which can only be contextually disambiguated.

(1) a. *a   kon   luku mi.*
         3SG.SUBJ come look me
         'She/He visited me.'
     b. *en   mati   kon   luku en.*
         3SG.POSS friend come look 3SG.OBJ
         'Her/His (female/male) friend visited her/him.'

The EMC does, however, also possess lexical items marked for referential gender. A word may either have lexical gender, or referential gender is expressed by combining an unmarked noun with a lexical gender noun. Below I discuss how gender is signaled in the EMC.

2.1 Personal nouns with lexical gender: Kinship terms

In the EMC gender distinctions are obligatory when referring to members of the extended family, since most kinship terms are gender-specific. Table 1 provides an overview of gender-marked kinship terms in the EMC (cf. also Huttar & Huttar 1994: 603–606).

Kinship terms combined with the personal name of a family member, such as that of the father, the mother, the husband or wife, rather than the personal name of the person in question are frequently employed when referring to a third party not present in the context. This practice is particularly common when talking about children, women, and men and women who married into the group. In such possessive-type constructions the name of a family member functions as the possessor and the kinship term functions as the possessed element (2):

(2) a. *mi si a   uman/umanpikin fu   Ba L.*
         I   see DET.SG woman/daughter POSS name
         eside.
         yesterday
         'Yesterday, I saw Mr. L.'s wife/daughter.'
     b. *mi si a   kapiten   uman   eside.*
         I   see DET.SG lineage.head woman yesterday
         'I saw the lineage or village head's wife yesterday.'

Table 1. Lexical gender in EMC kinship terms

Female	Gloss	Male	Gloss
mma	'mother'	*ppa/dda*[a], *tata*	'father'
sisa	'female child of -one's mother or father, -one's mother's or father's brothers and sisters'	*baala*	'male child of -one's mother or father, -one's mother's or father's brothers and sisters'
gaanmma *ooma*[b]	'mother of one's mother or father'	*gaanppa/dda*[a] *oopa*[b]	'father of one's mother or father'
umanpikin	'daughter'	*manpikin*	'son'
tiya, tante[b]	'one's mother's or father's -sisters, -brother's wives'	*tii(yu)*[c], *omu*[b]	'one's mother's or father's -brothers, -sister's husbands'
nikt[b]	'daughter of one's sister or brother'	*neif*[b]	'son of one's sister or brother'
uman, folow[b], *tiya sama*[d], *boliman*	'wife'	*man, masra*[b], *tii(yu)*[c] *sama*[d], *goniman*	'husband'
main	'mother-in-law' 'son's wife'	*pai*	'father in law' 'daughter's husband'
meti	'one's co-wife' 'wife of one's sister's husband' 'ex-wife of one's spouse'		
(gaan meti)	'wife's mother's mother'		

[a] *dda* is typical of Kwinti and Okanisi, while *ppa* is more common in Paamaka.
[b] These terms are (recent) borrowings from Dutch or Sranan Tongo used particularly by younger people.
[c] *Tiyu* is used among the Okanisi while *tii* is used by Paamakans.
[d] These terms are commonly used among older (50+) people.

The few other lexical gender nouns either refer to human beings (3) or to professions (4):

(3) a. *meishe*   'girl' (from Dutch)
     b. *boi*   'boy'
     c. *kiyo*   'young man (16–40 years of age)'
     d. *baya*   'female friend, i.e. woman of the same
                     age group as the speaker or referent'[6]
     e. *biya*   'male friend, i.e. man of the same age
                     group as the speaker or referent'
     f. *misi*   'beautiful, well-dressed (town) woman'

(4) a. *yefrow*   'female teacher' (from Dutch)
     b. *sikoo misi*   'female teacher'
     c. *mesta, mes(i)ti* 'male teacher' (from Dutch)
     d. *siste*   'female nurse' (from Dutch)
     e. *opasi*   'male nurse' (from Dutch)

2.2 Address forms

When directly addressing (or referring to) adult members of the Eastern
Maroon communities by their name, it is customary to combine the name either
with a title of courtesy appropriate for age and gender or with a title denoting
their social function. Most of these titles may also be used as self-referential
terms. Table 2 gives an overview of titles and their distribution in the EMC:

Combining the Eastern Maroon name and less commonly the *bakaa* or
dopu nen 'European or Christian name' of adults with a title of courtesy
appropriate for age and gender in addressing or referring is a way of paying
respect to a person.[7] Special or excessive respect is customarily expressed by
using the title of courtesy appropriate for a higher or older age group when
addressing someone. In relaxed settings, close family members, friends, and
people from the same age (and status) group often address each other only by
their Eastern Maroon name or combine it with a title of courtesy used for
addressing members of a younger age group. In official or hostile settings, the
omission of titles or the use of a title appropriate for a younger age group
conveys condescension, particularly if employed non-reciprocally. Children are
never addressed with any titles, but they always have to employ titles when
addressing adults. Younger and urbanized Eastern Maroons typically do not use
titles of courtesy when addressing each other, but they always employ such titles
when addressing older Eastern Maroons. It remains to be seen, however,
whether the omission of titles represents a change in progress or just an age-
grading effect.

In contemporary usage, the titles used for addressing people of the middle
generation, *Tiya* and *Tii(yu)*, are becoming obsolete among the younger
generations. They are being increasingly replaced by the Dutch- or Sranan
Tongo-derived terms *Tante* and *Omu* respectively. Unlike the former, the latter
are frequently not juxtaposed to a personal name, however. Younger Eastern
Maroons are also alternating between the optional titles *Gaanmma* and
Gaanppa and the Dutch- or Sranan Tongo-derived terms *Ooma* and *Oopa*
respectively when addressing and referring to the oldest generation.[8] They are

Table 2. Gender-marked titles of address in the EMC

Female	Gloss	Male	Gloss
		Titles of courtesy	
Sa + Name	'Ms'[a] for women between 16–40	*Ba* + Name	'Mr' for men between 16–40
Tiya (+ Name) *Tante* (+Name)	'Ms' for women between 40–60	*Tii(yu)*(+ Name) *Omu* (+ Name)	'Mr' for men between 40–60
Mma (+ Name)	'Ms' for women above 60	*Dda, Ppa* (+ Name)	'Mr' for men above 60
		Function-denoting titles	
mi Mma, maama	'one's mother', 'sisters and cousins of one's mother'	*mi Ppa/Dda, paapa*	'one's father', 'brothers and cousins of one's father'
mi Main	'mother-in-law', 'mother-in-law's sisters and brothers' wives', 'sons' wife(s)'	*mi Pai*	'father-in-law', 'father-in-law's brothers and sisters' husband', 'daughter's husband'
Gaanmma, Ooma	'one's grandmothers', 'women of one's grandmothers' family/ generation'	*Gaanppa, Oopa*	'one's grandfathers', 'men of one's grandfathers' family/ generation'
		Gaaman (+ Name)	'(male) head of government'
Kapiten (+Name)	'village and lineage head'	same	
Yefrow (+Name)	'female teacher'	*Mesta* (+Name)	'male teacher/head teacher'
Siste (+ Name)	'female nurse'	*Opasi* (+ Name)	'male nurse'

[a] In this context, *Ms* refers to any adult woman regardless of her marital status.

typically not juxtaposed to a name.

In the villages, professionally trained people are often addressed and referred to by their professional or function title (cf. Table 2) instead of a title of courtesy, because such titles carry a higher social prestige, since few Eastern Maroons are professionally trained. In urban centers this practice is much less common since professionally trained people are more frequent. The head of each Eastern Maroon community is always addressed by everyone, including outsiders, with the title *Gaanman* lit. 'head of community', which is rarely combined with the person's (Eastern Maroon) name.

2.3 Formation of gender-marked personal nouns from non-personal words

In the EMC, gender-specified personal nouns may be formed by combining *man* 'male, man' or *uman* 'female, woman' with a non-personal word.[9] The non-personal words come mainly from the lexical categories of nouns and verbs. Only few come from the category of adjectives, since most property-denoting items in the EMC are verbs (Migge 2000). Table 3 provides examples of such gender-specified personal nouns:

Table 3. Gender-marked personal nouns formed from non-personal words

Content word	Man	Uman	Gloss
Noun			
paandasi 'village community'	*paandasiman*	*paandasiuman*	'member of the village community'
obia 'supernatural power'	*obiaman* *witiman*	*obiauman* *witiuman*	'person who has supernatural powers'
koloku 'luck'	*kolokuman*	*kolokuuman*	'a lucky person'
Verb			
seli 'sell'	*hosel/seliman*	*hosel/seliuman*	'trader'
gongosa 'gossip'	*gongosaman*	*gongosauman*	'person who likes to gossip'
leli 'learn'	*leliman*	*leliuman*	'person who has studied/ studies'
Adjective			
faansi 'French'	*faansiman*	*faansiuman*	'French citizen'

This strategy for deriving gender-marked personal nouns is very productive in the EMC. It seems, however, that personal nouns formed with *man* are generally much more frequent and lexicalized than their counterparts involving *uman*.[10]

A couple of personal nouns may either only be formed with *uman* or only with *man* (5). They include but are not restricted to the examples in (5).

(5) a. *pangiuman* 'woman wearing a wrap-around skirt', i.e. woman of age
         **pangiman*
     b. *goniman*   'hunter, husband'
         **goniuman*
     c. *gaanman*   'head of a government'
         **gaanuman*[11]

These personal nouns are typically derived from non-personal words referring to objects or activities which are only or primarily associated with one gender.

2.4 Formation of gender-marked nouns from personal nouns

Animate nouns in the EMC which are gender-neutral may be gender-marked by compounding them with the lexical gender nouns *uman* 'female, woman' and *man* 'male, man'. In such nominal compounds the gender-specifying noun precedes the head noun (6).

(6) a. *komisasi* 'commissioner' > *uman komisasi* 'female commissioner'
                                       man komisasi 'male commissioner'
     b. *data* 'medical staff'   > *uman data* 'female medical staff'
                                       man data 'male medical staff'
     c. *kapiten* 'village head'   > *uman kapiten* 'female village head'
                                       man kapiten 'male village head'
     d. *pingo* 'wild pig'   > *uman pingo* 'female wild pig'
                                       man pingo 'male wild pig'

This way of deriving overtly gender-marked nouns is very productive, although it involves an asymmetry: It is primarily used for deriving overtly female-marked personal nouns; nominal compounds involving *man* are relatively uncommon. This strategy for overt gender-marking is commonly employed in contexts in which the gender of the referent is under discussion or plays an important role in the context. If the referents (and their gender) are known to the interlocutors, overt gender-marking is generally omitted.

The EMC also has a construction in which *uman* and *man* follow a personal noun (7).

(7) a. *data uman*   'the wife of the (male) medical staff'
     b. *gaanman uman*   'the wife of the head of government'
     c. *yefrow man*   'the husband of the teacher'

The examples in (7) are not instances of compounding like the examples in (6). The two nouns are interpreted as being in a possessive relationship meaning 'the wife/husband of X'. Possessive constructions involving *uman* are clearly more frequent and common than those involving *man* since women rather than men are seen as "belonging" to someone.

3.   The interpretation of personal nouns in discourse

3.1   Gender-unmarked personal nouns

Gender-unmarked nouns (and indefinite pronouns) in the EMC fall into two groups with respect to their (discourse) interpretation. Some of them are equally used to refer to female and male referents, while some refer primarily to men. The first group consists of a few kinship terms summarized in Table 4 and words such as *mati* 'friend', *ibiwan* 'everyone', and *sama* 'person, someone'.[12] Some of the words from this set, such as *mati*, *sama* and *pikin* 'child' may also be compounded with *uman* and *man* for gender-specific reference (cf. Section 2.4), but they are typically used generically.

Table 4. Gender-neutral kinship terms in the EMC

Kinship term	Gloss
(avo) tototo	'(great) great grand parents'
pikin	'child'
pikin pikin	'grandchild'
sisa pikin	'children of one's sisters'
baala pikin	'children of one's brothers'
swagi[a]	'spouse's sibling, sibling's spouse'

[a] *Mi Swagi* is often also used to address in-laws (and friends).

The term *sama*, for example, is frequently employed to refer to both female and male persons who are known to the interlocutors and who may even be present in the context (8a), or to attract the attention of someone known to everybody in context (8b) in order to avoid pronouncing their name. (Frequently) pronouncing a person's name (*ka(l)i nen* 'call name') is believed to bring a curse onto that person.

(8) a. [someone is complaining about another person's demand to a third
person in the presence of the demander]
"*a   sama   ya   feni taki mi mu   ondo*
DET.SG person here find say I   must move

a   gaasi ya."
DET.SG grass here
'This person (here) thinks that I have to cut this grass.'

b. [a group of people are standing around arguing when another person looks at one of the people and asks:]
"*a   sama   de,   u   na o   koti*
DET.SG person there you (polite) NEG FUT cut

a   sani de   moo?"
DET.SG thing there more
'That person (there), won't you cut that thing any more?'

Gender-unmarked personal nouns which are, however, primarily used to refer
to men include nouns denoting occupations or social functions (9) and several
general terms (10).

(9) a. *basi*   'boss'
    b. *basia*   'assistant to lineage or village chief'
    c. *data*   'medical staff'
    d. *domini*   'Protestant minister'
    e. *kapiten*   'lineage or village head'
    f. *kelepisi*   'head of burial'
    g. *sikoutu*   'police'

(10) a. *(busi)nenge*   'black person (from the interior)'
     b. *ingi*   'Amerindian'
     c. *bakaa*   'European'
     d. *gaansama*   'elder'
     e. *fositensama*   'founders of the EM communities'.[13]

Such words may be used to refer to both female and male referents as shown in
(11), but they are often interpreted as referring to male referents only.

(11) *Sa L./Ba N., na wan Albina sikoutu.*
     Ms L./Mr N. FOC one Albina police
     'Ms L./Mr N., s/he is a police officer in Albina.'

The predominantly male interpretation of such personal nouns is confirmed by
the fact that they are often compounded with the noun *uman* (cf. *uman sikoutu*

'female police officer') when referring to a female referent. When used for a male referent, on the contrary, they are generally not compounded with *man*.

In the case of professional titles, their predominant association with male referents is most likely due to the fact that these jobs are even today primarily held by men. This reasoning cannot, however, be valid for the nouns in (10), since women have always been members of the groups they refer to. The male-biased interpretation of these nouns most likely results from the fact that in the social ideology of the Eastern Maroon communities, in which male represents the socially accepted norm, men are viewed as the (proto)typical members of such groups. This in turn is related to (and contributes to) the overall higher visibility of men as opposed to women in the social life of the Eastern Maroon communities.

3.2 Words overtly marked as 'male'

When used by itself, the word *man* may be used to refer to both male (12a) and generic referents (12b) but not to overtly female-marked referents (12c).[14] In the latter case (12c), only the gender-unmarked term *sama* 'person, people' or the female gender specifying term *uman* may be employed (12d).

(12) a. *Ba D., a   wan man di   e   lobi wooko.*
          Mr D. FOC one man REL PROG like work
          'Mr D. is a man who likes to work.'

      b. *Den   tu   man de a   osu.*
          DET.PL two man COP LOC house
          '(Talking about Ms N. and Ms K./Mr J.) The two (people) are at home.'

      c. **Mma D., na   a   man di   be   dansi awasa.*
          Ms   D. FOC DET.SG man REL PAST dance awasa
          'Ms D. is the person who danced *awasa* (traditional dance).'

      d. *Mma D., na a   sama/uman   di   be*
          Ms   D. FOC DET.SG person/woman REL PAST
          dansi awasa.
          dance awasa
          'Ms D. is the person/woman who danced *awasa*.'

Personal nouns involving *man* (cf. *biibiman* 'believer, Christian' and *singiman* 'singer') are also used to refer to generic referents (13a) and to their male subsets (13b). In addition, a great number of them may also be used to refer to overtly female-marked referents (13c). Their overtly female-marked counter-parts (cf. *biibiuman* and *singiuman*) are relatively uncommon even though, for example, most of the active Christians among the Eastern Maroons are women.

(13) a. *A   goontapu   ya,   biibiman no   de.*
DET.SG ground-top here believer NEG exist
'In this world, there aren't any believers/Christians (any more).'

b. *Ppa B., na   wan biibiman.*
Mr B. FOC one believer
'Mr B. is a believer/Christian.'

c. *Mma B. e   lobi pee gaan biibiman teee.*
Ms B. PROG love play great believer very
'Ms B. likes very much to pose as a great believer/Christian.'

It seems that only those personal nouns formed with *man* can be used generi-cally or refer to women which are derived from verbs and nouns associated with activities that may be carried out by both women and men (according to the social ideology of the Eastern Maroon communities). This set includes, but is not restricted to the examples given in (14).

(14) a. *leiman*   'liar'
b. *wisiman*   'sorcerer'
c. *donman*   'stupid person'
d. *duman*   'doer'
e. *nyanman*   'glutton'
f. *kokobeman*   'leper'

Personal nouns derived from objects or activities primarily or exclusively associated with men do not appear to be used generically. The words in (15), for example, refer only, or primarily, to a male referent.[15]

(15) a. *pikiman*   'formal interlocutor at political meetings'
b. *oloman*   'grave digger'
c. *botoman*   'boat driver'
d. *hontiman*   'hunter'

Women (and men) who regularly perform activities typically associated with men (or women) are not referred to by a personal noun involving *man* (or *uman*). In such cases, an active construction is used to describe the activity (16a) or an appropriate term is borrowed from another language (16b). The word *kok* 'cook' in (16b) is a borrowing from Dutch.

(16) a. *Sa D. e   lobi honti teee.*
          Ms D. PROG love hunt very
          'Ms D. likes to hunt very much/hunts a lot.'
      b. *Ba D., na   wan kok/*boliman.*
          Mr D. FOC one cook
          'Mr D., he's a cook.'

There are also a few personal nouns in the EMC which are only or primarily formed with *man,* but which can only have a female referent.[16] The most prominent examples are given in (17):

(17) a. *boliman*   'cook, wife'
      b. *faagiman*   'menstruating person'
      c. *beeman*   'pregnant person'
      d. *mekiman*   'a person who has given birth, midwife'

3.3 Words overtly marked as 'female'

Overtly female-marked nouns can only be used to refer to female referents. They are never used generically or to refer to men.

Female-marked nouns derived by compounding with *uman* (cf. Section 2.4) are used to refer to a more restricted or a different set of functions (which are viewed as socially appropriate for women) than their male-marked or gender-unmarked counterparts (which have a male bias) if the resulting terms refer to traditional Eastern Maroon social functions, such as *basia* 'assistant to the lineage or village head' and *kapiten* 'lineage or village head'. An *uman basia*, for example, is responsible for decorating, cleaning, and preparing food for official functions. She receives orders from the (*man*) *basia* or a *kapiten*. The (*man*) *basia*, on the contrary, only receives orders from the *kapiten* or *gaanman* and typically carries out many different tasks, such as disseminating messages, acting as formal interlocutor at meetings (*pikiman*), driving boats (*botoman*), calling people together, etc.

Similarly, an *uman(pikin) kapiten* is mainly responsible for matters concerning the women of her village or lineage. She primarily represents women, and receives orders from the (*man*) *kapiten* of her village or lineage.[17] The (*man*) *kapiten*, on the other hand, deals with all matters concerning all members of the village or lineage. He represents both the women and the men of the community.

This difference in interpretation seems to be less obvious or absent in the case of nouns referring to non-traditional Eastern Maroon social functions such as *data* and *komisasi*. An *uman data* and an *uman komisasi*, for example, perform the same tasks and have the same social standing as a *(man) data* and a *(man) komisasi*.

Personal nouns formed with *uman* (cf. Section 2.3) generally refer to female referents who are equivalent to male, female, or generic referents referred to by personal nouns involving *man* (see Table 3). The former are not highly lexicalized though. There are, however, two groups of lexicalized personal nouns formed with *uman*. These nouns have partially different social interpretations than their counterparts involving *man* resulting from different social expectations for the two gender groups. In the case of one group (18), personal nouns formed with *uman* denote the functions typically performed by women in these settings:

(18) a. *olouman/man*   'woman/man responsible for a burial'
　　 b. *gowtuuman/man* 'person working in gold mining industry'
　　 c. *wookouman/man* 'worker'

The *olouman* prepares, brings, and distributes food to the *oloman* who digs the grave and buries the corpse. The *gowtuuman* sells food or her body, cooks, or serves food to the men who mine the gold (*gowtuman*). A *wookouman* is assiduously keeping up, i.e. cleaning and decorating, her domestic area, tending to the needs of her family, and performing other (respected) "womanly" tasks such as doing embroidery, helping others etc. The *wookoman*, on the contrary, regularly carries out traditional male tasks such as hunting, cutting fields, making boats etc. In urban areas or in the cash industry both terms may also be used to refer to someone who has a (regular) cash-earning job, i.e. as an employee.

Regarding the second group (19), the personal nouns involving *uman* typically have a highly sexualized and/or a more negative connotation than their male-marked counterparts. In the case of (19c-f), the nouns involving *uman* are clearly more common than those involving *man*.

(19) a. *wakauman/man*   'traveler'
　　 b. *fufuuuman/man*   'thief'
　　 c. *lasa(a)uman/man* 'cursing, i.e. promiscuous person'
　　 d. *gandauman/man* 'homeless, i.e. promiscuous person'
　　 e. *weiuman/man*   'promiscuous person'
　　 f. *kaasiuman/man*   'lascivious person'

Wakaman (lit. 'travel man'), for example, is used to refer to a man who travels from one place – usually a work site – to another and often does not have a permanent residence and/or a (permanent) wife and children.[18] Such men are prone to having sex outside of marriage, but this aspect of their life-style is hardly (an integral) part of the definition of a *wakaman*. The definition of its female counterpart (cf. *wakauman*), however, puts a primary focus on this aspect of her life-style and thus carries negative connotations. If *wakauman (wakaman)*, however, functions as a possessed element in a possessive construction in which a term referring to a man (woman) appears as the possessor, it is used to mean girlfriend, i.e. a woman (man) who is not (yet) officially recognized as a/the wife (the husband) of her male (female) sexual partner (20). This usage does not carry negative connotations.

(20) *Na a   wakauman   fu Ba K.*
      FOC DET.SG travelwoman for Mr K.
      'It's Mr K.'s girlfriend.'

In its generic usage *wakaman* means 'traveler'.

Similarly, a *fufuuuman* (lit. 'steal woman') is viewed as less respectable and more problematic than her male counterpart because women more than men have to be proper and obey the law. If a woman fails to conform to this norm, she is viewed as a threat to the prevailing social order and makes her (and her husband's) family socially unacceptable. Although also regarded negatively, breaking the law is socially much more acceptable for men.

Finally, a *kaasiuman* (lit. 'scratch woman') poses a threat to (male) society since she might be prone to engaging in extra-marital sex when her husband is unavailable and thus stir up trouble between her husband (and family) and (the) other men. By contrast, men are expected to want to have sexual relations frequently, including outside of marriage.

The negative and/or sexualized connotation of most terms involving *uman* seems to be confirmed by the fact that social functions only associated with women which carry prestige or are viewed as natural in Eastern Maroon social ideology are generally expressed by overtly male-marked terms, i.e. personal nouns formed with *man* (cf. 17). Corresponding overtly female-marked terms are either less acceptable since *uman* carries sexual or negative connotations or they do not exist.

Among the overtly female-marked personal nouns in the EMC (cf. Table 1), the word *mama* 'mother' seems to exclusively carry positive connotations. In nominal compounds such as those given in (21) it is often used to mean 'important' and 'main'.[19]

(21)   a.   *mama osu*   'family home'
       b.   *mama sooto*   'lock'[20]
       c.   *mama konde*   'native village'
       d.   *mama wataa*   'high tide, i.e. high water level'
       e.   *mama mofu*   'important or main message'
       f.   *mama liba*   'the main river'
       g.   *a mama fu a toli* 'the gist of the story'

The positive connotations of the word *mama* are due to the fact that 'mother' is a very prestigious social function in the matrilineal Eastern Maroon communities: The mother plays a vital role in the continuation of the lineage, she and her family have the primary authority over her children, and the line of descent of every lineage is determined by its women (mothers); only the (male) children of the women of certain lineages (*lo*) and sublineages (*bee*) may carry out the communities' main socio-political functions such as *gaanman, kapiten, basia*.

4. Conclusion

The investigation of gender-marking in the EMC revealed that even though the language lacks the grammatical category of gender, its speakers are still able to communicate referential gender. In the EMC referential gender is either conveyed by personal nouns with lexical gender or by compounding personal nouns which are not gender-marked with the overtly gender-marked personal nouns *man* and *uman*.

The analysis also revealed four things about the interpretation of personal nouns: First, gender-unmarked personal nouns frequently have a predominantly male interpretation. Second, a great number of those overtly marked as 'male' are also used generically, or to refer to women. Third, nouns overtly marked as 'female' cannot refer to men and tend to have a sexualized or less general social interpretation. Fourth, personal nouns overtly marked as 'male' generally carry a positive and non-sexualized connotation, particularly when they only refer to female referents.

Notes

1. The EMC is better known by the name of *Ndyuka* in the linguistic literature (cf. Huttar & Huttar 1994, Goury 1999, Migge 1998a). In this study the term *Eastern Maroon Creole* was chosen as a neutral label, since *Ndyuka* is typically used among native speakers to refer to the Okanisi people and their varieties. Members of the Paamaka and particularly the Aluku-Boni communities do not always appreciate being referred to by this name due to sociohistorical circumstances (Bilby 1999).

2. The figures are taken from http://www.sil.org/ethnologue/countries/Suri.html.

3. Men, for example, may have more than one wife and/or several girlfriends while this is not socially acceptable for women. It is widely accepted that women are somewhat subordinate to men: *ala yuu a man de a tapu (fu a uman)* 'Men are always in charge (of women)'.

4. The study does not investigate proverbs, since the author is not aware of any systematic collections and studies of proverbs (*nongo*) in the EMC. The few common ones found in the recordings do not deal with the communities' gender arrangement.

5. Long word-final vowels are characteristic of the Okanisi variety, e.g. *ondoo* 'below, under' in Okanisi versus *ondo* in the other EMC varieties. Long vowels in word-initial syllables are characteristic of the Kwinti variety, e.g. *saani* 'thing' in Kwinti versus *sani* in the other EMC varieties. The examples in the text come from the Paamaka variety and thus do not involve long final vowels. Vowel length may, however, also be distinctive in all varieties of the EMC, e.g. *baka* 'back, behind, bake' versus *bakaa* 'non-maroon' and *baaka* 'black'.

6. The difference in age between persons referring to each other by the terms *baya* or *biya* should not be more than about five years. *Biya/baya* are also used to mean 'young man/woman'.

7. Members of the Eastern Maroon communities receive an Eastern Maroon name (*busikonde* or *osu nen*) by which they are known in their communities. Such names are not necessarily differentiated according to gender and often convey some special meaning (to the name giver). Examples are *Sa(n-i)-wani* 'what do you want', *Sama-sani* 'someone's thing', and *Mi-denki* 'I think/remember'. Eastern Maroons also have a European first name (*bakaa or dopu nen*) and a last name (*famii nen*). These latter names are typically only used with government authorities and outsiders. Younger Eastern Maroons born in urban hospitals are, however, increasingly only called by names of European origin and sometimes do not even receive an *osu nen*.

8. They are optional in that their semantic space may also be covered by *Mma* and *Ppa*.

9. The main word-formation processes in the EMC are reduplication (Huttar & Huttar 1997; Migge, in press) and compounding (Huttar & Huttar 1994). It seems, however, that some free morphemes such as *man* 'male, man' and *peesi* 'location, place, space' may also be used as derivational suffixes (Goury 1999). A number of personal nouns formed with *man* as a second member in a compound, for example, may in most cases refer to male, female, and generic referents (cf. *biibiman* 'believer') or just to female referents (cf. *faagiman* 'menstruating person'), while *man* as a free morpheme may only refer to male or generic referents (cf. Section 3.2). *Peesi* is realized as *pe* and nouns formed with *pe* may only refer to a geographical location (cf. *tanpe* 'residence', *lanpe* 'location where boats arrive and are tied',

wookope 'workplace', *belipe* 'cemetary') rather than any kind of space. The word *manpeesi* 'male sexual organs', for example, may not be shortened to **manpe*.

10. Note also that the overwhelming majority of personal nouns in the EMC-English dictionary (Shanks et al. 2000) involve *man*.

11. The expression *g(g)aan uman* 'elder (50+) or important woman' exists but it does not seem to be a personal noun like *gaanman*. The intonation suggests that it is best analyzed as a noun (*uman*) modified by an adjective (*gaan*). To denote a female head of government, as sometimes found among the Amerindians, the term *uman gaanman* is used (see Section 2.4).

12. Note that the non-emphatic third person singular subject pronoun *a*, its emphatic counterpart *en*, and the third person singular object pronoun *en* are also equally used to refer to both male and female referents. The EMC does not have any means of overtly indicating their referential gender.

13. Note that these terms may not be disambiguated by preposing *uman* (or *man*) to them. They are either referred to as *den uman (sama) fu den ingi* 'the women (people) of the Amerindians' or as *den businenge uman* 'the Maroon women', or *den fositenuman* 'women ancestors'. The former constructions are homonymous with a possessive construction (cf. Section 2.4).

14. Among young men, *man* is also used as an exclamation roughly equivalent in meaning to *man* in contemporary American English:

> *Man, mi an   yee/yere den   sani de/dati   ete.*
> man I   NEG hear   DET.PL thing there/that yet
> 'Man, I hadn't heard that yet.'

This usage is probably derived from (Dutch-influenced) Sranan Tongo which much influences their speech in general.

15. Since women increasingly engage in activities traditionally associated with men only (cf. *botoman*), the social interpretation of such strongly male-biased terms may in the future also include female referents.

16. *Beeuman* and *mekiuman* are also possible but are less common. **faagiuman* and **boliuman* do not seem to be acceptable, however.

17. The institution of a *uman(pikin) kapiten* was started in the 1990s due to pressure from the central government of Suriname to accord more political power to women. Instead of opening up existing *kapiten* positions to women, new *kapiten* positions were created which can only be held by women. It seems unlikely that this was imposed by the government. Rather, it seems that it was modeled on the prevailing gender ideology. All villages (*konde*) have not yet received such a *kapiten* due to resistance from their male counterparts who have to initiate their selection.

18. Most (young) Eastern Maroon men have to leave their native communities to find cash labor, but they are expected to maintain a house there and to return to it on a regular basis. Married men are also expected to regularly visit their wife (or wives), who often remain in their native villages after they get married.

19. The term *m(a)ma* may replace *uman* in various contexts including compounds (cf. *wakamma*). It appears to give a slightly more positive connotation to the resulting compound. As a second member in a compound the word is typically pronounced *mma*. As a first member it is pronounced *mama*. When referring to one's wife/girlfriend in an endearing manner, it is pronounced *maama*.

20. In the EMC, *sooto* means 'lock' and 'key'. To distinguish the two, the 'lock' is called *mama sooto* (lit. mother lock) and the 'key' is called *pikin sooto* (lit. child lock).

References

Arends, Jacques. 1994. "De Afrikaanse wortels van de creooltalen van Suriname." *Gamma/TTT* 3: 115–128.

Beibel, Okanisi Tongo. 1999. Wycliffe Bible Translators.

Bilby, Kenneth. 1999. *Aluku: A Surinamese creole in French territory*. Paper read at the symposium on the languages of Suriname, University of Leiden, Leiden.

Goury, Laurence. 1999. *Restructuration grammaticale dans les langues créoles: Le cas du ndjuka, langue créole de base anglaise du Surinam et de Guyane française*. Ph.D. dissertation, Université Paris 7 – Denis Diderot UFRL.

Hoogbergen, Wim. 1990. "The history of the Suriname maroons." In *Resistance and rebellion in Suriname: Old and new*, ed. Gary Barna-Shute. Williamsburg: The College of William and Mary, 65–102.

Huttar, George. 1985. "Sources of Ndjuka African vocabulary." *De Nieuwe West-Indische Gids* 59: 45–71.

Huttar, George & Mary Huttar. 1994. *Ndyuka*. London: Routledge.

Huttar, Mary & George Huttar. 1997. "Reduplication in Ndyuka." In *The structure and status of pidgins and creoles*, ed. Arthur K. Spears & Donald Winford. Amsterdam: Benjamins, 395–414.

Migge, Bettina. 1998a. *Substrate influence in the formation of the Surinamese Plantation Creole: A consideration of sociohistorical data and linguistic data from Ndyuka and Gbe*. Ph.D. dissertation, Ohio State University, Columbus, Ohio.

Migge, Bettina. 1998b. "Substrate influence in creole formation: The origin of *give*-type serial verb constructions in the Surinamese Plantation Creole." *Journal of Pidgin and Creole Languages* 13: 215–265.

Migge, Bettina. 2000. "The origin of property items in the Surinamese Plantation Creole." In *Language change and language contact in pidgins and creoles*, ed. John H. McWhorter. Amsterdam: Benjamins, 201–234.

Migge, Bettina. in press. "The origin of predicate reduplication in the Surinam Eastern Maroon Creole(s)." In *Twice as meaningful. Reduplication in pidgin and creole languages*, ed. Silvia Kouwenberg. London: Battlebridge.

Shanks, Louis & Evert D. Koanting & Carlo T. Velanti, eds. 2000. *A buku fu okansi anga ingiisi wowtu* [Aukan (EMC) – English Dictionary] 2nd ed. Paramaribo: SIL.

English – Gender in a global language

Marlis Hellinger
University of Frankfurt am Main, Germany

1. Introduction

The decision to cover more than one variety of English in "Gender across languages" was motivated by the fact that English is a global language which has developed a number of major regional standards, with appr. 508 million speakers of English worldwide.[1] Some 341 million have English as their first or native language: 210 million in the USA, 55 million in the United Kingdom, 17 million in Canada, 16 million in Australia and 3 million in New Zealand, with smaller groups of speakers in the Caribbean, South Africa and elsewhere (cf. Ethnologue 2000: 707).[2]

English today serves as the lingua franca of diplomacy, government, science, commerce, and scholarship. It is the sole official language of some two dozen countries, among them Ghana, Nigeria, South Africa, Jamaica and Barbados; and along with Arabic, Chinese, French, Russian and Spanish, English is an official language of the United Nations.

Thus it is no longer meaningful to make assumptions about "English" without specifying the respective regional variety. This does not contradict the fact that varieties of English share at least part of their histories; this includes English-based creoles, in whose formative stages English functioned as a lexifier language.[3] Varieties of English also share many structural properties; individual developments occur most obviously in pronunciation (thus one can distinguish accents of Australian or Irish, Indian or Jamaican English) and lexico-semantics, primarily as a result of language contact with indigenous and/or immigrant languages (e.g., Maori in New Zealand, Spanish in the USA); borrowings are frequent in the lexical fields of plants, animals and cultural phenomena.[4]

English is also the language with the most extensive and profound history of linguistic description, and this holds true for the area of gender as well.[5] In addition, English is one of the few languages of the world for which computerized corpora of written and spoken language are available, which tremendously facilitates the empirical/quantitative analysis of usage in various contexts and styles.

English derives from the West Germanic branch of the Indo-European family of languages, along with German, Dutch and Frisian. Old English or Anglo-Saxon, i.e. the language spoken during the period from the arrival of Germanic tribes in England in the 5th century to the Norman Conquest in the 11th century, was a highly inflected language, comparable to Latin and Russian, with strong and weak inflectional paradigms, three grammatical genders (feminine, masculine, neuter), two numbers (singular and plural, with remnants of the Indo-European dual) and four cases. Old English adjectives, verbs, determiners and other word classes showed morphological agreement with their heads; the pronominal system was highly elaborated. And since grammatical relations were primarily marked by inflection, word order was variable, with a preference for SVO (subject–verb–object) in main clauses, and SOV in subordinate clauses. As a consequence of extensive phonological reduction and merging during the Middle English period, English lost much of its synthetic character; grammatical relations were now expressed by a more rigid word order and the increased use of function words such as prepositions and auxiliaries.[6]

With the Norman invasion, French became the dominant language of the upper classes in England, and a vast number of French loanwords entered the English language. Thus, the vocabulary of Middle English is approximately half Germanic and half Romance. It was not before the 14th century that Middle English lost its status as a subordinate language and that the London Court changed to English as official language. The transition from Middle to Modern English began in the 15th century, with the shift from West Saxon as the language of the cultural center of the Old English period to London English, which was the major influence in the development of a written standard. Modern English orthography is based on 15th century spelling, while pronunciation has considerably changed since then. Of the world's languages, Modern English has the largest lexicon, due to continuous borrowing from numerous other languages, and vast expansion in the 19th and 20th centuries to accommodate innovations in the sciences and technology.

2.   Gender in English

2.1 Grammatical gender

Languages differ widely in the number and morphological representation of grammatical gender, which can be defined as an inherent and invariant nominal property (cf. Corbett 1991). Thus, within the Germanic family of languages, Danish has two genders, German has three, and English has no grammatical gender at all. While Old English had three gender classes, feminine, masculine, and neuter, the category of grammatical gender was lost by the end of the 14th century due to the decay of inflectional endings and the disintegration of declensional classes (cf. Strang 1970, Kastovsky 2000). And unlike German, which has a number of elements inside and outside the noun phrase (determiners, adjectives, pronouns) which vary according to the noun's grammatical gender, Modern English shows no such morphological agreement. English is no longer a (grammatical) gender language.

2.2 Lexical and social gender

Gender in English is primarily a semantic category, with important social implications (cf. Hellinger 1990). English has a restricted class of personal nouns with lexical gender, i.e. their semantic specification includes a property [+female] or [+male]: *aunt, queen, soul sister* vs. *uncle, king, sugar daddy*. This property determines the choice of anaphoric pronouns: *she* for members of the first nominal class, *he* for members of the second. The majority of English personal nouns, however, are unspecified for gender, and can be used to refer to both female and male referents: *person, neighbor, engineer, babysitter, movie star, drug addict*; they can be pronominalised by either *she* or *he* or – in neutral, non-specific contexts – by singular *they*. In a few cases, choice of anaphoric pronouns may be determined by "psychological gender", i.e. affective attitudes of the speaker, which accounts for variation as in *baby – she* vs. *baby – it*.

However, though lacking lexical gender, the semantics of a large number of English personal nouns shows a clear gender-bias. Many high-status occupational terms, such as *lawyer, physician* or *scientist*, will traditionally be pronominalised by *he* (the so-called "generic *he*") in contexts where gender of referent is either not known or irrelevant. On the other hand, low-status occupational titles, such as *secretary, nurse* or *schoolteacher*, will often be followed by anaphoric *she*. Even for general human nouns such as *pedestrian, patient* or *driver*, as well as for indefinite pronouns (*somebody, anyone, no one*, etc.), the choice of *he* is prescribed in neutral contexts. This illustrates the category of social gender in English. Social gender has to do with stereotypical assumptions about what are appropriate social roles for women and men, including expectations about who will be a typical member of the class of, say, *surgeon* or *nurse*. Deviations from such assumptions will often require formal markings, for example by adjectival modification: *female surgeon* or *male nurse*.

The prescription of androcentric *he* has long been a central issue in debates about linguistic sexism in English (Martyna 1978, MacKay & Fulkerson 1979, Hellinger 1991). Underlying prescriptive *he* in English is the ideology of MAN (male as norm), which considers the male/masculine as the higher, more prestigious category and the female/feminine as secondary and subordinate (cf. Baron 1986: chap. 6, Curzan 2000). All of the English contributions in this volume provide evidence for this assessment.

3.   Semantic derogation

In contrast to German, English has no productive word formation patterns for the expression of referential gender (cf. Bauer 1983). Of the few suffixes of Germanic origin, *-e* (f), *-estre* (f), *-a* (m), only the second (in the shape of *-ster*) has survived in a few examples (cf. *spinster*; also the proper names *Webster, Baxter*; of more recent origin are *gangster, youngster*). Already in late OE *-estre* (which was later replaced by the French suffix *-esse*) could be used to denote both female and male referents: a *webbestre* was a person who weaves, a *baecestre* someone who bakes (cf. Rabofski 1988).

The word *spinster* is a typical illustration of what has been described as semantic derogation (Schulz 1975). In the 17th century the word was "the proper title of one still unmarried" (Baron 1986:118), already with explicitly female reference. By the 18th century the word had acquired clearly negative connotations, denoting "a woman still unmarried; esp. one beyond the usual age for marriage, an old maid" (OED 1989, s.v. *spinster*). Kramarae & Treichler (1985: 429) summarise the development of *spinster* in these words: "Originally meaning a person who tended the spinning wheel. Like most terms connected with women, it became a euphemism for *mistress* or *prostitute*".

From the 11th century, French supplied a few feminine suffixes which led to the formation of a limited number of female-specific derivations: *heroine, chorine, aviatrix, educatrix, usherette, majorette*. These patterns were usually short-lived as well as problematic: they never only denoted the female counter-part of a male referent, but generally carried additional negative connotations derived from associations with their original sources: *booklet* is a small book, a *kitchenette* is not a real kitchen, and *leatherette* is artificial leather. Thus, personal nouns carrying these suffixes tend to be associated with connotations of smallness, triviality or imitation.

Only the suffix *-ess* gained some productivity, and a number of formations are still in current use: *actress, hostess, stewardess, waitress*. The suffix entered the English language with French words such as *countess, duchess, adulteress*. Words like *authoress, goddess* and *jewess* date from Middle English. Modern English derivations include *poetess, actress, seamstress* and *stewardess*. Traditional descriptions of English word-formation (e.g., Marchand 1969, Koziol 1937) discuss phonological variation in pairs like *author/authoress* vs. *governor/governess*, but do not even mention the gender-stereotypical semantic asymmetries involved in *governor/governess, mister/mistress*, and *major/majorette*.

4. Reforming English

Many alternatives have been suggested to replace asymmetric or sexist usage in English (cf. Miller & Swift 1981, Frank & Treichler 1989, Pauwels 1998). One form such protest has taken is the development of numerous guidelines for gender-neutral language, from the McGraw-Hill guidelines of 1972 to the UNESCO guidelines of 1999 (cf. Hellinger 1995: Section 5.3). In reformed usage, the principle of neutralization has the highest priority in English, in contrast to German, where female visibility is the basic characteristic of gender-fair usage. Neutralization means the avoidance of false generics, especially usages of "generic" *man*, as in *primitive man, to man a project*, or *chairman*. Gender-inclusive wording can also be achieved by avoiding gender-marked terms for female referents, especially derivations ending in *-ess* or *-ette*.

Second in the hierarchy of English guidelines is avoidance of stereotyping (*transport will be provided for delegates and their wives*), and third the principle of symmetry, i.e. avoidance of marked forms (*female doctors*) where no parallel male forms would be used.

As a subordinate strategy, neutralization includes visibility of (potential) female referents, when the strategy of pronominal splitting is employed, as in *patient … she or he.* At the same time, this example illustrates symmetric usage, which should be observed whenever specification of referential gender is required, as in *female and male athletes; cameramen/camerawomen.* Another gender-neutral alternative is the use of singular *they* as in *a lawyer must listen to their clients.*

5.   Varieties of English represented in "Gender across languages"

Australian English and New Zealand English are both based on British regional/social dialects (South East of England), with Australian English showing more traces of Irish English, New Zealand English more of Scottish English. Both varieties share numerous properties; thus, they are both non-rhotic (i.e. post-vocalic /r/ is not pronounced), and neither shows much regional variation. There are some differences in vocabulary: New Zealand English is more influenced by the indigenous language Maori than Australian English by Aboriginal languages. And recently, i.e. since 1970, a tendency has been observed towards more individual phonetic developments, so that speakers under the age of forty can be identified as Australians or New Zealanders (cf. Collins & Blair 1989).

In the 17th century, colonies were established by Europeans in America, India and Africa, marking the beginning of a long history of colonial imperialism, with frequently dramatic linguistic consequences (cf. Phillipson 1992). American English was the earliest colonial variety to achieve linguistic and cultural independence, and 19th century frontier democracy, urbanization and non-European immigration have all contributed to create a specifically American variety of English.

Colonial settlement in New Zealand began in the first half of the 19th century, but a distinctive variety of New Zealand English did not emerge until the turn of the twentieth century. New Zealand was settled by immigrants from all over the British Isles, most of whom came from rural and upper working class or lower middle class backgrounds. In this, as in other respects, it differed from Australia, which was initially a penal colony with immigrants from largely urban backgrounds. On the other hand, while a range of varieties of British English, including London English, provided the major original sources of input to New Zealand English, Australian English is undoubtedly the single most important contact variety, and the most widely held current theory of the origins of New Zealand English is that it stems from Australian English (Bauer 1994).

The following three chapters stand out in that all employ empirical methodologies. In her analysis of gender in New Zealand English, Holmes examines address terms, occupational titles and morphological markings, in written and spoken corpora of New Zealand English, and not only compares them with data from Australian English (the Macquarie corpus) but also from British English (the LOB corpus) and American English (the Brown corpus). By contrast, Pauwels provides an in-depth analysis of one single feature, namely the adoption and spread of the courtesy title *Ms,* which has become the focus of innumerable academic and public debates about a more gender-fair usage of English. Using questionnaire and interview techniques, she discusses variation and change in Australian English, and evaluates feminist language planning on the basis of a sociolinguistic profile of *Ms*-users in Australia. Romaine takes a comparative perspective on British, American, Australian and New Zealand English. She has searched the British National Corpus for a number of issues, comparing the results with the data provided by Holmes and Pauwels, and making assumptions about different tendencies of language change in progress in the four varieties.

Notes

1. On English as a global language cf. Crystal (1995, 1997), Bailey & Görlach (1982), Trudgill & Hannah (1982).

2. Estimates of speakers using English as a second or foreign language differ widely. Based on Ethnologue (2000), the number would be ca. 170 million.

3. On English-language pidgins and creoles cf. Hymes (1971), Valdman (1977), Romaine (1988), Sebba (1997), Alleyne (1980).

4. On varieties of English cf. Ahrens & Bald & Hüllen (1995: chap. 2), Kachru (1983, 1997), Cheshire (1991), Schmied (1991). Examples of dictionaries of varieties of English are Branford (1990), Cassidy & LePage (1980), Fyle & Jones (1980).

5. Major reference works are: (a) grammars: Collins Cobuild (1990), Huddleston (1984), Leech & Svartvik (1994), Quirk & Greenbaum & Leech & Svartvik (1985); (b) dictionaries: COD (1990), Collins Cobuild (1988), OED (1989), Random House (1971), Webster's Third (1961).

6. On the history of English cf. Baugh & Cable (1992), Cambridge History (1992–1996); on the history of African American English cf. Bailey & Maynor & Cukor-Avila (1991).

References

Ahrens, Rüdiger & Wolf-Dietrich Bald & Werner Hüllen, eds. 1995. *Handbuch Englisch als Fremdsprache* (*HEF*). Berlin: Erich Schmidt.
Alleyne, Mervyn C. 1980. *Comparative Afro-American*. Ann Arbor: Karoma.
Bailey, Guy & Nathalie Maynor & Patricia Cukor-Avila. 1991. *The emergence of Black English*. Amsterdam: Benjamins.
Bailey, Richard & Manfred Görlach. 1982. *English as a world language*. Ann Arbor: University of Michigan Press.
Baron, Dennis. 1986. *Grammar and gender*. New Haven: Yale University Press.
Bauer, Laurie. 1983. *English word-formation*. Cambridge: Cambridge University Press.
Bauer, Laurie. 1994. "English in New Zealand." In *The Cambridge History of the English language*. Vol. V. Cambridge: Cambridge University Press, 382–429.
Baugh, Albert C. & Thomas Cable. 1992. *A history of the English language*. 4th ed. London: Routledge.
Branford, William. 1990. *A dictionary of South African English on historical principles*. Oxford: Oxford University Press.
Cambridge History. 1992–1996. *The Cambridge history of the English language*. 6 vols. Cambridge: Cambridge University Press.
Cassidy, Frederic G. & Robert B. LePage. 1980. *Dictionary of Jamaican English*. 2nd ed. Cambridge: Cambridge University Press.
Cheshire, Jenny, ed. 1991. *English around the world: Sociolinguistic perspectives*. Cambridge: Cambridge University Press.
COD. 1990. *The concise Oxford dictionary of current English*. 8th ed. Oxford: Clarendon.
Collins Cobuild. 1988. *Collins Cobuild English language dictionary*. Glasgow: Collins.
Collins Cobuild. 1990. *Collins Cobuild English grammar*. London: Harper Collins.
Collins, Peter & David Blair, eds. 1989. *Australian English. The language of a new society*. Brisbane: University of Queensland Press.
Corbett, Greville G. 1991. *Gender*. Cambridge: Cambridge University Press.
Crystal, David. 1995. *The Cambridge encyclopedia of the English language*. Cambridge: Cambridge University Press.
Crystal, David. 1997. *English as a global language*. Cambridge: Cambridge University Press.
Curzan, Anne. 2000. "Gender categories in early English grammars: Their message to the modern grammarian." In *Gender in grammar and cognition*, eds. Barbara Unterbeck et al. Berlin: de Gruyter, 561–576.
Frank, Francine & Paula A. Treichler. 1989. *Language, gender, and professional writing*. New York: MLA.
Fyle, Clifford & Eldred D. Jones. 1980. *A Krio – English dictionary*. Oxford: Oxford University Press.
Hellinger, Marlis. 1990. *Kontrastive feministische Linguistik. Mechanismen sprachlicher Diskriminierung im Englischen und Deutschen*. München: Hueber.

Hellinger, Marlis. 1991. "Feminist linguistics and linguistic relativity." *Working Papers on Language, Gender, and Sexism* 1: 25–37.

Hellinger, Marlis. 1995. "Language and gender." In *The German language today*, ed. Patrick Stevenson. Oxford: Clarendon, 279–314.

Huddleston, Rodney. 1984. *Introduction to the grammar of English.* Cambridge: Cambridge University Press.

Hymes, Dell, ed. 1971. *Pidginization and creolization of languages.* Cambridge: Cambridge University Press.

Kachru, Braj B. 1983. *The other tongue. English across cultures.* Oxford: Pergamon.

Kachru, Braj B. 1997. "World Englishes and English-using communities." *Annual Review of Applied Linguistics* 17: 66–87.

Kastovsky, Dieter. 2000. "Inflectional classes, morphological restructuring, and the dissolution of Old English grammatical gender." In *Gender in grammar and cognition*, eds. Barbara Unterbeck et al. Berlin: de Gruyter, 709–727.

Koziol, Herbert. 1937. *Handbuch der englischen Wortbildungslehre.* Heidelberg: Winter.

Kramarae, Cheris & Paula Treichler. 1985. *A feminist dictionary.* Boston: Pandora.

Leech, Geoffrey & Jan Svartvik. 1994. *A communicative grammar of English.* 2nd ed. London: Longman.

MacKay, Donald & David Fulkerson. 1979. "On the comprehension and production of pronouns." *Journal of Verbal Learning and Verbal Behavior* 18: 661–673.

Marchand, Hans. 1969. *The categories and types of present-day English word-formation. A synchronic-diachronic approach.* 2nd ed. München: Beck.

Martyna, Wendy. 1978. "What does 'he' mean? Use of the generic masculine." *Journal of Communication* 28: 130–139.

Miller, Casey & Kate Swift. 1981. *Handbook of non-sexist writing for writers, editors and speakers.* 2nd ed. London: The Women's Press.

OED. 1989. *Oxford English dictionary.* 2nd ed. 20 vols. Oxford: Clarendon.

Pauwels, Anne. 1998. *Women changing language.* London: Longman.

Phillipson, Robert. 1992. *Linguistic imperialism.* Oxford: Oxford University Press.

Quirk, Randolph & Sidney Greenbaum & Geoffrey Leech & Jan Svartvik. 1985. *A comprehensive grammar of the English language.* London: Longman.

Rabofski, Birgit. 1988. *Motion und Markiertheit.* Frankfurt am Main: Peter Lang.

Random House. 1971. *The Random House dictionary of the English language.* 5th ed. New York: Random House.

Romaine, Suzanne. 1988. *Pidgin and creole languages.* London: Longman.

Schmied, Josef. 1991. *English in Africa. An introduction.* London: Longman.

Schulz, Muriel. 1975. "The semantic derogation of woman." In *Language and sex: Difference and dominance*, eds. Barrie Thorne & Nancy Henley. Rowley, MA: Newbury House, 64–75.

Sebba, Mark. 1997. *Contact languages: Pidgins and creoles.* London: Macmillan.

Strang, Barbara M. H. 1970. *A history of English.* London: Methuen.

Trudgill, Peter & Jean Hannah. 1982. *International English: A guide to varieties of Standard English.* London: Longman.

Valdman, Albert. 1977. *Pidgin and creole linguistics.* Bloomington: Indiana University Press.

Webster's Third. 1961. *Webster's third international dictionary of the English language.* Springfield, MA: Merriam.

A corpus-based view of gender in New Zealand English[*]

Janet Holmes
Victoria University of Wellington, New Zealand

1. Introduction

The relationship between women and men in a community is constructed through all aspects of their language use. Gender variation in the use of particular linguistic features is as indicative as gender-differentiated patterns of interaction, or choices among alternative ways of describing and referring to women and men. This is evident in all languages, and has been well documented for English (see Romaine and Pauwels, this vol.). Research on New Zealand English (henceforth NZE), too, provides evidence of the way gender roles are constructed in all three of these areas.[1]

Social dialect analysis of a wide range of linguistic variables has demonstrated that gender is a salient variable in NZE; choice among linguistic variants is one way of signalling gender identity. New Zealand women and men can be distinguished by their patterns of use of a wide range of particular variants of phonological variables, such as initial /h/, medial and final /t/, and the short front vowels /I/ and /e/ (Holmes & Bell & Boyce 1991, Bell 1997, Batterham 1996). These sounds have social significance as markers of gender (Holmes 1998). As women and men make sociolinguistically significant phonetic choices in their daily interactions, they are constantly constructing their gender identities: "the use of phonetic variation and the construction of identities are inseparable" (Eckert & McConnell-Ginet 1995: 503).

Moreover, young women are in the forefront of much linguistic change in NZE (Holmes 1997a): for example, the widely discussed raising of New Zealand front vowels (e.g. Woods 1997, Trudgill & Gordon & Lewis 1998), the merging of the EAR/AIR diphthongs (Holmes & Bell 1993, Maclagan & Gordon 1996, Batterham 1996), the spread of the high rising terminal intonation contour (Britain 1992), and the extension of the use of the discourse tag *eh*, associated with Maori usage, into Pakeha NZE (Meyerhoff 1994, Holmes 1997b).[2] The consistency of women's role in relation to sound change across diverse speech communities has generated a number of possible explanations for the robustness of this pattern (e.g. Trudgill 1983, Eckert 1989, Labov 1990, Chambers 1995, Gordon & Heath 1998), including reference to the crucial role of language in constructing women's social identity. The New Zealand data is consistent with such an explanation; since colonisation, Pakeha women have tended to be assigned the role of guardians of linguistic usage in New Zealand. The fact that young women's usage seems likely to determine the future shape of NZE indicates the extent to which at least some women are constructed as arbiters of linguistic usage in their daily interactions (see Holmes 1997a).

Patterns of discourse provide further evidence that New Zealand women construct a particular identity as they interact with others. In New Zealand, as elsewhere, women often adopt a facilitative rather than an aggressive role in conversation and debate, as evidenced by patterns of interruption and feedback (e.g. Holmes 1995). Women tend to use particular pragmatic particles, with particular social meanings (Holmes 1997c, 1998), to construct a supportive, conversational identity, and to enact a role as helpful and interested listener rather than contestive, challenging debater. Narratives recounted by New Zealand women and men often provide even more explicit evidence of the social roles they construct for themselves within their particular spheres of interaction (Holmes 1997c). Explanations for these patterns have also exercised many researchers, with sometimes acerbic debate between those who regard the "two cultures" approach as providing a satisfactory explanation (e.g. Tannen 1990, 1992), and those who believe that women's accommodating patterns of interaction rather reflect the distribution of power in a society (Troemel-Ploetz

1991, Henley & Kramarae 1991, Holmes 1995).

A third contribution to the construction of gender-marked identities in NZE comes from the way language is used to represent categories of gender. Usages such as pseudo-generic *man* and *he* treat men as the norm, and render women invisible. Suffixes, such as *-ess* and *-ette*, are widely perceived as trivialising women's occupations (*sculptress, poetess, usherette*) and undermining their professional status. Most obviously, perhaps, gender identities are constructed, constrained and moulded by imagery which describes women and men as objects (e.g. *old bag, prick, blouse*), animals (e.g. *bitch, shark, wolf*) or food (*peach, tart, studmuffin*). Such usages reflect societal attitudes to gender roles, and ideological influence is here very overt. When speakers are faced with a range of variants, there is no neutral or unmarked choice. Rather, "every alternative is politically loaded, because the meaning of each is now defined by contrast with all other possibilities" (Cameron 1994: 26).

From this perspective, every utterance can be examined in terms of how it contributes to the construction of gender identity in the specific context in which it occurs. Recent research in this area has focussed on the fundamental issue of the extent to which language has been co-opted by a patriarchal society and turned against women, so that women feel alienated from language, and unable to articulate their experience as women.

> Like a wolf-whistle, a sexist remark has a significance above and beyond the immediate offence it gives: it is the outward manifestation of an unacceptable misogyny. But is it also, as many feminists believe, the very mechanism by which misogyny is constructed and transmitted? Can we think outside the confines of a woman-hating language? (Cameron 1985: 7)

This contribution focuses on usages representing gender categories. I review research on sexist usages, and consider what illumination they provide about the way gender roles are constructed in New Zealand society.

2.   Sexist language research in New Zealand

(1)   Context: Male local authority councillor thanking female chair of that authority.
"You have been a capable and decorative chairman."
(Austin 1990: 285)

Many New Zealanders have become sensitive over the last 25 years to the issue of sexist language, and the ideological implications and effects on gender identity perception of the categories regularly used in NZE to categorise women (and men). However, we have little reliable linguistic research which documents this change.

The overt derogation of women through negative imagery has declined, at least in public: any politician who used demeaning metaphors to refer to New Zealand women in the 1990s would certainly attract public censure. There is anecdotal evidence that people are increasingly aware of the complexities of choosing between gender-marked terms, such as *chairwoman* and *spokeswoman*, and their supposedly gender-neutral equivalents, *chairperson* and *spokesperson*.[3] *Chairperson* and *spokesperson* sound artificial and clumsy to some, and can be regarded as making women invisible, or as effectively functioning as synonyms for *chairwoman* and *spokeswomen;* but these latter are sometimes regarded as unnecessarily marking gender in contexts where it is irrelevant. Some are sensitive to the problems of choosing between terms such as the gender-marked *hostess,* with the derogatory associations of its suffix, and the unmarked, but traditionally male, term *host.* Many New Zealanders have become aware that use of a form such as *Mrs,* or using *chairman* as a generic, reflects an ideological position just as clearly as selecting forms such as *Ms* or *chairperson.*

On the other hand, the espousal of non-sexist forms has not been un-controversial. They have been attacked in the New Zealand media, not only by those unsympathetic to the goals of feminism, but also by language purists who dismiss them as newfangled and ugly, and reject them as evidence of superficial "political correctness" (cf. example (4) below). Some feminists agree with the latter judgement, regarding the use of at least some non-sexist terms as evidence simply of linguistic eugenics. They suggest that the use of such forms pays lip-service to an ideal that belies the underlying reality of continuing sexism in the wider society.

In the following, I will focus on a few selected areas of sexist and non-sexist usage in NZE where research has been undertaken: the term *Ms*, the pseudo-generic term *-man*, forms such as *chairperson*, and sexist suffixes such as *-ess* and *-ette*.[4] Finally, metaphorical reference terms will be briefly discussed.

2.1 *Ms*-usage

(2)   *Context: Bank manager to female customer.*
   "A.   Now that will be Miss, won't it?
   B.   No, Ms.
   A.   Oh, one of *those."*
   (Austin 1990:282)

The term *Ms* was intended to eliminate linguistic discrimination by providing a term for women which, like *Mr*, did not signal marital status. It was to replace *Mrs* and *Miss*, providing a parallel system of address and reference for women and men. Instead, we now have a more complex system for women, where the choice between *Miss* and *Mrs* provides information on marital status, while the choice between these two and *Ms* provides a range of further sociolinguistic information, reflecting the beliefs of those involved. In NZE, as in Australian English, where its meanings and uses have been documented by Anne Pauwels (1987, this vol.), *Ms* is regarded by some New Zealanders as signalling "feminist", by others as indicating that a woman is separated, divorced or widowed, and by still others as an address form for women in de facto relationships.[5] The social meaning of *Ms* as a term of address or reference, or as a means of self-identification, is thus far from transparent.

Two major methods have been used to study the occurrence of *Ms* as an honorific in NZE. The first involves direct questioning of people concerning their preferences, using an interview schedule or questionnaire. The second examines actual occurrences of *Ms* in the two million word Wellington Written and Spoken Corpora of New Zealand English.[6] The first provides greater insight into the intended social meanings or interpretations of *Ms* as used by individuals, but rests on restricted quantities of data in a limited range of contexts. The second promises more natural data from a broader range of speakers, but presents interpretative problems.

Two small studies of Wellington women's reported usage indicated that *Ms* was used by a substantial proportion of educated women in the early 1990s (see Table 1).

Brian Milne (1991) investigated *Ms* usage by 43 educated Wellington women working for government organisations. Almost half of these educated professional respondents (49%) reported using *Ms*. Two thirds (66.7%) of those who reported using *Ms* in his sample were unmarried, almost a quarter (24%) were married, and the remainder (9.3%) were divorced. Though *Ms* was most

Table 1. *Ms*-usage in Wellington: self-report data

	Milne (1991)		O'Brien (1993)	
	N	%	N	%
Miss	9	20.9	23	46.9
Mrs	10	23.2	10	20.4
Ms	21	48.8	16	32.6
Other	3	7.0		
Total	43	100	49	100

popular among unmarried respondents, it is worth noting that almost a third (31%) of married respondents used *Ms*, too. Perhaps predictably, no-one over fifty reported using *Ms*, but half of those in the youngest age group (16–29 years) reported using it.

Jenny O'Brien (1993) collected data from 30 student teachers and 19 practising teachers. One third of these women reported that they used *Ms*. Her results suggest that in this group *Ms*-usage reflected education and maturity. In particular, none of the primary student teachers / practising teachers reported using *Ms*, while 43% of the secondary student teachers and 58% of the secondary teachers reported using *Ms* rather than *Miss* or *Mrs*. In O'Brien's sample, 37% of married people preferred *Ms*, while only 21% of unmarried respondents used it. In general, those under 24 were more likely not to use *Ms*: it was more popular among those over 30.

These results echo those of Pauwels (1987, this vol.) for young Australian women: Pauwels found that female students over 23 were more likely to use *Ms* when filling in a form than those aged 17–22. There are at least two alternative explanations for this pattern: (i) young women may change to *Ms* as they get older, or alternatively (ii) feminism, and associated *Ms*-usage, may be regarded as passé by young people – evidence possibly of the feminist backlash described by Faludi (1991). Moreover, the fact that O'Brien's results contrast with Milne's at a number of points suggests that usage is volatile in this area.

Both these studies used relatively highly educated respondents from the capital city, Wellington, and the results cannot be treated as representative of New Zealand women more generally.[7] They also relied on self-report data and are subject to the usual caveats that, for a variety of reasons, people do not always accurately report their usage. Nevertheless, the results do suggest that this is an area where women make a conscious choice about how they present their gender identity, though the differences in usage by women of different ages and social backgrounds exemplify the need for caution in interpreting that gender identity.

An alternative approach involves examining actual occurrences of an item in a large and more representative corpus of data. Simply comparing the frequencies of occurrence of gender-differentiated address and reference titles in the recently completed Wellington Written and Spoken Corpora of New Zealand English indicates that women are not addressed or referred to by gender-marked titles as often as men.[8] Thus, for example, there are less than 100 female titles (*Mrs, Miss, Ms*) in the Wellington Corpus of Spoken New Zealand English (WCSNZE) compared to over 400 which refer to men (*Mr*). However, most instances occurred in formal settings, such as Parliamentary debate, and thus reflect men's domination of such spheres, rather than a tendency to address men more respectfully than women. There were only two instances of *Ms* in one million words of spoken NZE. Clearly, *Ms* is not a form used widely in New Zealand speech.

Ms does occur more often, however, in written NZE. The newspaper section of the Wellington Corpus of Written New Zealand English (WCWNZE), comprising 176,000 words, provided a suitable sub-corpus for more detailed investigation of its distribution, and one which it was possible to compare with a parallel corpus from the Macquarie Corpus of Australian English.[9] Table 2 provides the relative frequencies of instances of *Ms* in the press section of the WCWNZE and the Macquarie Corpus (Peters & Purvis & Martin & Jenkins 1990). Note that the table includes instances of forms only where a genuine choice between *Ms* and *Mrs* or *Ms* and *Miss* seemed possible.[10]

Table 2. Relevant *Miss/Mrs/Ms* forms in New Zealand and Australian newspapers

	WCWNZE press section		Macquarie press section	
	N	%	N	%
Ms	14	14.7	53	42.7
Mrs	77	81.1	60	48.4
Miss	4	4.2	11	8.9
Total	95	100	124	100

Clearly, *Ms* is more frequent than *Miss* in both corpora, though *Mrs* remains the most frequently occurring form. Despite its unpopularity in the 1970s, as reflected in *Letters to the Editor* of a wide range of New Zealand newspapers and magazines (describing *Ms* as an "abomination", and *Ms*-users as "predatory", for instance), *Ms* has clearly become acceptable by 1986. The numbers are small, but *Ms* occurs more than three times as often as *Miss* in the newspaper material of the WCWNZE, and *Ms* is over four times as frequent as *Miss* in the parallel section of the Macquarie Corpus.

This data will provide a useful baseline for monitoring language change in Australasia, but it is worth noting that there was not a single instance of *Ms* in either of the comparably composed million-word British LOB (Lancaster-Oslo-Bergen) or American Brown corpora of data collected in 1961. Given the unlikelihood that NZE would have been ahead of overseas trends in this area in 1961, we can safely conclude that the appearance of *Ms* in the WCWNZE is evidence of language change in NZE. And its higher frequency in the Macquarie Corpus suggests that, in 1986, Australian editors, at least, were ahead of New Zealand editors in this area of language change.[11]

Perhaps we can also infer that *Miss* is declining in popularity and being replaced at least in newspaper contexts by *Ms*, while there is no such evidence for *Mrs*. To be confident of the accuracy of this inference, we would need evidence of the marital status of all the *Ms*-users. However, it would certainly be consistent with Milne's (1991) results, described above, as well as Pauwels' (1987) analysis of student usage, as evidenced in Melbourne university files and interviews with a wide range of Australian women. Pauwels, too, noted that *Ms* was more popular with single than with married women, and she comments that married women often indicated pride in their married status and a reluctance to conceal it, or to "embarrass" or "insult" their partners by using *Ms* (Pauwels 1987: 145; see also Pauwels, this vol.).

Such comments have far-reaching implications in interpreting how Australasian women construct their gender roles. The data collected to date suggests that New Zealand women are not embracing the term *Ms* with great enthusiasm. It is possible that New Zealand constructions of female identity tend to the conservative, with married status an important component of a woman's identity (see Holmes 1997c, 1997d). Alternatively, *Ms* may be regarded as dated or "de trop" among young people, who increasingly reject the use of any title, and prefer to use full names without any garnish. These are clearly issues for further research.

2.2 Generic *man*

(3) "Man loves to hunt. He sees it as a tradition and a right. He believes
that deer herds should be managed so he and his son after him, can
hunt them. He cannot understand his brother's claim that deer diminish
the range of plants. After all his brother couldn't name a single plant
that deer had made extinct."
From *Mountain Management* (New Zealand Department of the Environment, 1986)

The extent to which an English-speaking community in the 1980s and 1990s
continues to use androcentric or pseudo-generic forms such as *man, -man* and
he is another indication of the way conservative gender roles are constructed
and maintained in the society. An American study of "androcentric generics"
showed a dramatic decline in their use in a range of American publications
between 1971 and 1979 (Cooper 1984). Using a 500,000 word corpus, Cooper
examined the use of *he, man,* and *-man* in newspapers, magazines, periodicals,
and the *Congressional Record.* The rate of use fell from 12.3 per 5000 words in
1971 to 4.3 per 5000 words in 1979.

Studies of generic forms in NZE suggest that at least some writers and
speakers are sensitive to the potential social effects of continually categorising
women as "men".[12] There is evidence of a decline in androcentric usages in
written materials, and low levels of occurrence in spoken samples of current
usage.[13] Miriam Meyerhoff (1987) analysed changes in the use of generics such
as *man* and *he* in five newspapers between 1964 and 1984. The five papers were
selected to give some social range: *The Listener, The New Zealand Woman's
Weekly, The Evening Post, Salient,* a student newspaper, and *The New Zealand
Journalist,* a monthly union newspaper. Using a 150,000 word corpus, she noted
the incidence of such usages per 1000 words and found that all five papers
showed a reduction in the use of such generics over the twenty year period. The
largest decrease occurred in *The New Zealand Journalist,* supporting the
National Business Review's claims that journalists are the driving force in moves
to non-sexist language (Holt 1988: 16), though the Wellington student newspaper *Salient* was close behind. Both these papers, however, used far more androcentric generics in the 1964 sample than the three others, and so they had more
room for improvement.

Using a sample of 176,000 words per corpus, I analysed and compared the
use of generic *man* in the press sections of the WCWNZE, the Australian
Macquarie and the British LOB corpora. Initially, a methodological problem

had to be addressed. There are some instances of *man* where the intended referent is clearly 'humankind' rather than a specifically male human being, e.g.: *fearful of what man can do to man, the right of man to life, the primitive Neanderthal man, the dawn of modern man.* These usages were classified as generics in a "narrow" sense. However, the form *man* now signals 'male' in the minds of many New Zealanders (Wilson & Ng 1988, Ng 1990, 1991). This is particularly problematic with phrases such as *the tax man, the man in the street, as good as the next man,* which have been labelled "pseudo-generics". I classified such phrases as generics in a "broad" sense.[14]

Drawing such distinctions is obviously problematic. One person's intended generic may be another's clearly male referent. One consequence is what has been called "slippage" (when an utterance starts as a generic but slips into masculinity before it ends), not only in people's usage, but also in interpreting their meaning accurately for purposes of corpus analysis (see example (3) above and example (7) below). Slippage is obviously a crucial area in the fight against sexist constructions of female identity (Cameron 1985). Identifying instances of slippage is an important means by which linguists expose the underlying assumptions which pervade a society's constructions of gender identity.

Table 3. Generic *man* from press sections

	WCWNZE Corpus 1986	Macquarie Corpus 1986	LOB Corpus 1961
man	134 (100%)	122 (100%)	151 (100%)
generic *man* (narrow sense)	11 (8.2%)	8 (6.5%)	15 (9.9%)
pseudo-generic *man* (broad sense)	10 (7.5%)	28 (22.9%)	32 (21.2%)

Table 3 presents the results of my analysis. There were few instances of generic *man* in its narrow meaning of 'humankind' in any of the three corpora. However, it appears that New Zealand usage differs from Australian in the use of the broader category of *man* as a pseudo-generic. Here, Australian press usage appears to resemble more closely the older British LOB usage; there are far fewer instances of these pseudo-generics in the New Zealand press material. Before making too much of New Zealanders' apparent avoidance of pseudo-generics (especially in the light of the fact that it reverses the trend noted in

Ms-usage), analysis of a larger and more representative sample of usage is required. However, this is obviously another area where evidence concerning the construction of gender identities and constrained perceptions of gender roles in a community can be gathered.

2.3   *Chairpersons* and *spokespersons*

(4) "Do the feminists who want to be called 'chairperson' or, even worse, 'chair' realise that the 'man' in 'chairman' has nothing to do with the male gender? It comes from the Latin *manus*, which means 'hand' … Let's drop this dreadful 'chairperson', or this article of furniture 'chair', and let a woman be 'Madam chairman'. In any case … are you not troubled by the 'son' in chairperson?"
(Letter to the *Dominion* newspaper, September 1992)

It is also possible to use corpus analysis to examine the construction of very specific social roles. An analysis of the data for *-person* vs *-man* or *-woman* forms in the whole of the WCSNZE, the WCWNZE, the LOB, and the Brown corpora provided evidence suggesting linguistic change in the use of such forms in the last 25 years, though it was not very great (Holmes 1993a). Forms such as *frontperson, sportsperson* and even *handyperson* occurred in the 1986 New Zealand data, for instance, but not in the 1961 British or American English corpora.

While most such forms occurred only once per million words, two forms, *chairperson* and *spokesperson,* occurred more often. As example (4) illustrates, these forms also attracted public comment in newspapers, and were clearly socially very salient, presumably because of the status and influence associated with the designated roles. Table 4 provides information on their frequency of occurrence in the four corpora.

The overwhelming majority of the instances of *chairman* were identifiable as male, a sad reflection of the social reality that it was men who held this position most often, even in 1986. There were four instances in the WCWNZE where a woman was referred to as *chairman*, e.g. "the chairman of the airport committee, Cr Helene Ritchie", and one in the WCSNZE, where a woman was addressed as "madam chairman" in a formal meeting. So, despite the evidence from psychologists that most people interpret *man* as indicating 'male', some New Zealanders persist with such out-dated usages.

It is noticeable that the proportion of instances of *chairperson* compared to *chairman/men* in New Zealand speech is greater than that in writing, and

Table 4. *Chair-* and *spokes-*forms in WCSNZE, WCWNZE, LOB and Brown corpora

	WCS (NZ) 1989–94	WCW (NZ) 1986–89	LOB (UK) 1961	Brown (USA) 1961
chairperson(s)	7	6	0	0
chairman/men	20	109	119	78
chairwoman/women	0	2	0	0
spokesperson(s)	7	4	0	0
spokespeople	1	1	0	0
spokesman/men	9	36	22	24
spokeswoman/women	1	2	0	0

instances of *spokesperson* in speech almost match those of *spokesman*, suggesting that these forms are gradually gaining acceptability in New Zealand usage. Moreover, in NZE, as distinct from other varieties (Romaine 1997), they are used to refer to men as well as to women (i.e., *chairperson* has not become a substitute for *chairwoman*), and also in cases where the gender of the referent is not known (Holmes 1993a).

This suggests that such social roles are no longer perceived as appropriately filled only by men. In particular, the use of terms such as *chairperson* and *spokesperson* to refer to positions to which people have yet to be elected, can be interpreted as an indication that these roles are not being exclusively constructed as male. Such trends are consistent with a perception that a wider range of social roles are available to women than in earlier eras.

2.4 Morphological marking

(5) "Good on you Barbara Ewing, for speaking out against the use of actor for actress … The current use of the word actor does nothing but clunk up the sense, and I'm surprised that the people most affected – actresses – have not spoken out about it before. Under this sexist invisibility, if television does a repeat …".
(Letter to the New Zealand *Listener*, April 1992)

The use of suffixes to mark the female form of occupations and social roles such as *aviatrix, usherette, heroine,* and *hostess,* is another means of suggesting that the male is the norm, the female a secondary, derived and even stigmatised form. If language contributes to the construction of social reality, female gender roles are here constructed as dependent on or derived from male roles.

This is another area where New Zealand usage appears to have changed over the last generation, with such affixed forms becoming less acceptable. Many theatre companies no longer use forms such as *actress*, though, as example (5) illustrates, some commentators take the view that such marked forms should be endorsed, since they make working women more visible. *Actress* is a further example, then, of the ideologically-based "feminization" vs "neutralization" problem (Hellinger 1989), mentioned above, of choosing between terms which make women visible, but which may carry derogatory connotations (e.g. *authoress*), and terms which do not distinguish women from men, but which may thereby render women invisible (e.g. *pilot*).

A search of the Wellington Corpora supported the impression that this is an area of sociolinguistic change. I compared the frequencies of occurrence of the following suffixes in the 1986 WCWNZE with those in the 1961 British LOB corpus, and also with usage in the WCSNZE:[15] *-ette, -ine, -enne, -ix*.[16]

Comparing usages in 1961 with those in 1986 for the purpose of deducing change, it was again necessary to look carefully at context in order to identify only those suffixed forms which could reasonably have been avoided.[17] Moreover, semantic change is also apparent: a form such as *hero* might once have been considered inappropriate for a female referent, yet it is used explicitly to refer to a woman in the WCWNZE, supporting the claim that *heroine* could be avoided.

Table 5 lists all those forms from the WCSNZE, WCWNZE and LOB corpora with gender-marked suffixes which, taking account of the above considerations and of the context of their occurrence, could have been replaced by the base form.

It is immediately clear that forms with gender-marked suffixes are dramatically less frequent in the spoken corpus, which suggests that people avoid such forms in current speech. Assuming New Zealand usage in the area of gender-marked suffixes was likely to be as conservative as British usage when the British LOB Corpus was collected, the table also provides evidence to support the suggestion that the use of such forms has declined in 25 years.

It is also apparent from Table 5 that the range of types occurring in both corpora of the WCNZE is considerably more restricted than in the 1961 LOB Corpus. Moreover, my analysis showed that forms which would once have been considered to refer exclusively to males (e.g. *hero* and *waiter*), were used in the WCWNZE not only generically to include women and men, but also to refer explicitly and specifically to women. Moreover, the one occurrence of *murderess* in the WCSNZE is self-corrected to "female mass murderer", indicating sensitivity to the reduced acceptability of suffix-marking as a means of signal-

Table 5. Gender-marking suffixes where base form could have been used

	WCS (NZE) 1989–94	WCW (NZE) 1986	LOB (UK) 1961
-ess			
actress(es)	–	10	17
adulteress	1	–	–
authoress	–	–	1
editress	–	–	1
goddess(es)	–	–	2
heiress	–	–	2
hostess(es)	1	10	21
manageress	–	1	1
millionairess	–	–	1
murderess	1	–	–
negress	–	–	2
peeresses	–	–	1
prophetess	–	2	–
proprietress	–	–	1
quakeress	–	–	1
shepherdess	–	1	–
villainess	–	–	1
waitress(es)	–	7	5
-ine			
heroine	–	15	9
-ix			
executrix	–	–	1
Total	3	46	67

ling gender. Together these points support the suggestion that the use of such forms is in decline in NZE. To the extent that language contributes to the construction of social reality, this is encouraging evidence that constructions of female occupational and social roles as secondary to male roles are becoming less acceptable in New Zealand.

2.5 Metaphorical terms of reference

(6)   Context: Two young women discussing an American talk show.
      "and that lady that stood up and made a real dick of herself"
      (From WCSNZE)

A further area of sexist usage which merits discussion is the use of metaphorical reference terms for women and men. This is an area which awaits systematic research in NZE. A small pilot study focussing on animal, food and object terms used for women and men indicated that New Zealanders use a range of such terms to refer to both men and women, but the connotations of the terms used for women were rather more consistently derogatory (Roberts 1997). So, for example, focussing on terms used to refer to women and men as sex objects, the students provided three terms for women (*tart, fox, crumpet*), and four terms for men (*stallion, goat, stud, studmuffin*). Mary Roberts comments that a term such as *tart* is "entirely condemnatory and carries the added meaning of someone who exchanges sex for money", while *stallion* and *stud*, superficially equivalent terms for males in that they suggest a number of sexual partners, "are not strongly pejorative", and in fact generally indicate some degree of admiration.

Table 6. Metaphorical terms identified in Roberts' (1997) student data

	Instances in WCSNZE		Instances in WCSNZE
asshole	2	*mole*	0
beef	0	*mongrel*	0
bitch	8	*nut/nutter/nutcase*	3
brick	1	*penis*	0
cabbage	0	*pig/hog*	0
carrot top	0	*prick*	3
chicken	0	*rat*	3
cockroach	4	*shark*	0
cow	1	*sheep*	3
crumpet	0	*snake*	0
cunt	8	*spunkrat*	0
daddy long legs	0	*stallion*	0
dick	7	*stud*	0
dickhead	3	*studmuffin*	0
dog	0	*tart*	3
fish	0	*tool*	0
fox	0	*twat*	0
fruit	0	*vege/vegetable*	0
goat	0	*weasel*	2
honey	1		

The search through the WCSNZE indicated that relatively few of these terms occurred in this one million word sample of naturally occurring New

Zealand speech (see Table 6). The corpus data also suggested that men were more likely than women to use such terms, at least in the contexts in which the WCSNZE was recorded. This is one obvious area where further research using a variety of methods is needed. Overall, however, the small amount of data available to date suggests this is a domain where women's identities continue to be constructed more negatively than men's, in that terms used exclusively for women (e.g. *bitch, cow, tart*) tend to be more prolific and more derogatory than those used exclusively for men (e.g. *prick*).

3. Conclusion

(7) "People won't give up power. They'll give up anything else first –
money, home, wife, children, – but not power."
(Miller & Swift 1990: 55)

The societal construction of gender identity is a complex process. Every time they speak, New Zealand women and men conform to or challenge the established gender-marked patterns of phonological variation. As they interact, women's and men's patterns of discourse similarly contribute to the construction of gender identity in the many different contexts in which they operate. There is evidence that New Zealand women and men signal gender identity very clearly in these aspects of their speech (Holmes 1995, 1997c). In this contribution, however, I have focussed on the extent to which New Zealanders make use of sexist and non-sexist categories available in English to enact or reduce overt discrimination against women. This is clearly an important area of language variation and change, where possible new gender identities may be forged and asserted. Constructive daily choices in this area can contribute to a more positive and socially equitable gender identity for New Zealand women.

The evidence I have reviewed suggests that there has been considerable change in this area of NZE in the past twenty-five years. The term *Ms* is in regular use by New Zealand women, including a reasonable proportion of educated women under 50. It is widely available as an option on official forms, and it is well established in a number of influential New Zealand newspapers. This provides an indication that New Zealand society recognises women's right to resist public classification by marital status, an important aspect of the construction of gender identity.

The use of terms such as *man* to refer to women appears to be declining in New Zealand, if the analysis of the corpus materials can be taken as a reliable indicator in this area. There is scope for much more extensive analysis of such pseudo-generics, however, including head words such as *guy, mate,* and, especially in Australasia, *joker* (a local term meaning 'guy'). Even terms such as *people* repay study, because of the potential they offer for slippage (cf. example (7) above).

The evidence reviewed also suggests that perceptions of women's occupational and social roles are changing. Forms such as *chairperson* and *spokesperson* are evident in samples of both written and spoken current NZE. Especially when such forms refer to positions to be filled, they can be interpreted as an indication that such roles are increasingly regarded as open to women. Avoidance of gender-marked trivialising terms, such as *usherette* and *aviatrix,* can similarly be interpreted as indicating a change in the perception of such occupational roles. They are no longer overtly marked with the suggestion that when women occupy such positions they are not to be taken seriously.

While changing the language will not in itself solve the problems of women's lack of power or improve their subordinate status in the wider society, the evidence presented here has suggested that the provision of non-sexist options can contribute to the construction of a more positive female identity. Similarly, avoiding sexist language and challenging sexist assumptions contributes indirectly to the construction of more positive images of women. Drawing attention to evidence of widespread male bias in conventional uses of language is a worthwhile activity in its own right. But it is also true that such changes can ultimately affect attitudes because in and of themselves they alter the status quo:

> "[...] the change in outward practice constitutes a restructuring of at least one aspect of one social relationship [...] every act reproduces or subverts a social institution." (Pateman 1980: 77)

Speakers always have a choice. "There is always room for resistance, challenge, and alternatives" (Eckert & McConnell-Ginet 1992: 482). The deliberate choice of usages which favour women and which liberate women, challenging norms of usage which discriminate against women – these are all ways in which linguistic expertise can work towards a more positive construction of gender identity in the wider society.

Notes

* I would like to thank Robert Sigley and Bernadette Vine, who ran a number of the word-frequency searches on the Wellington Corpora, and provided valuable feedback after reading this paper. I am grateful to Mary Roberts, who also read the paper and made useful comments. Completion of the Corpora was made possible by grants from Victoria University's Internal Grants Committee and the New Zealand Foundation for Research, Science and Technology. I would like to thank the editors of this volume for their help in the final preparation of the manuscript.

1.   Though generalisations about women's and men's usage are currently controversial, they are nevertheless essential (see Holmes 1993d), if we are to undertake comparative research and perceive general trends.

2.   "Pakeha" is a term borrowed from Maori and widely used in New Zealand to refer to New Zealanders with British or European ancestry.

3.   "Supposedly" because, for a period at least, the use of such -*person* terms tended to be restricted to female referents.

4.   See Holmes (1993a, 1993b, 1993c) for further discussion of sexist usages in New Zealand English.

5.   In Canada, Ehrlich & King (1994) found that *Ms* was used mainly for divorced women.

6.   Preliminary versions of the Wellington Written and Spoken Corpora of New Zealand English were used for this analysis.

7.   Only 20% of the randomly selected sample of 250 Australian women interviewed in Pauwels' 1986 survey reported that they used *Ms* (Pauwels 1987).

8.   See Bauer (1993) for a description of the composition of the Wellington Corpus of Written New Zealand English, and Holmes (1994b) for a description of the composition of the Wellington Corpus of Spoken New Zealand English.

9.   The WCWNZE (based at Victoria University of Wellington, New Zealand) and the Macquarie Corpus (based at Macquarie University in Australia) both selected 1986 as the focus date for texts, and have been constructed on similar lines using the same basic discourse categories as the pioneering Brown and LOB corpora. All four corpora consist of one million words of written English. The Brown Corpus was constructed at Brown University in the USA, and the LOB is a parallel British Corpus constructed by the Universities of Lancaster, Oslo and Bergen. Brown and LOB use written texts from 1960. Pam Peters kindly provided me with access to the press section of the Macquarie Corpus. *Micro-OCP*, a computerised concordance programme was used for the analysis.

10.   Two methodological points should be noted. Firstly, we are not dealing with random, unmonitored usage. Most newspapers have a policy on non-sexist language, though it is not always explicitly coded: e.g., some New Zealand newspapers expressly banned the use of the term *Ms* at the time the WCWNZE was collected (Holt 1988). Secondly, it is not always clear what to count. We are interested in *Ms* when it is used as an alternative to other possible terms of address or third person reference, including *Mrs* or *Miss*. This clearly excludes instances such as the names of fictional characters, or references to the *Miss Universe* contest.

But the choices are not always so clear-cut; the precise options at any point may be complicated and their social significance may require some unpacking. It is crucial to consider the significance of forms in context in order to identify genuine alternatives within the relevant universe of discourse, and in order to make valid comparisons between corpora (Holmes 1993a, 1994a).

11. There were only 4 instances of *Ms* (three of which referred to the same person) in the press section of the 1991 Freiburg Corpus, which has been designed to match the 1961 British LOB Corpus as closely as possible. This suggests that Australasian usage is also ahead of British in this area.

12. There is evidence, for instance, that such usages influence occupational choices among young people (Eakins & Eakins 1978).

13. A preliminary analysis of the WCSNZE suggests that *they* is the default pronominalisation, used in speech for 80% of heads such as *anyone, anybody, nobody, no one, person, somebody, someone, whoever* etc. Forms of *he* occur less than 10% of the time in such contexts. See Holmes & Sigley (in press).

14. I used the following criteria for the "broad" category of generics: (i) substituting *person* would not lose relevant information about the referent; (ii) substituting *person* would make it clear that this referent could be female, and that there was nothing inherently masculine about the reference to justify the use of *man*.

15. See Holmes (1993b) for a more detailed analysis of the meanings and uses of these forms in different corpora.

16. All those English words in which the suffix -*ix* occurs have roots ending in *t* and a reduced agentive suffix *r*. They all end, therefore, with the sequence -*trix*. However, -*ix* specifically marks femaleness and therefore seems the appropriate parallel to the other suffixes listed here.

17. A reference to a *suffragette* in a historical document, or to a *governess* in a biography, for instance, gives no indication that such forms are in current usage. Items referring to individuals, such as the *Duchess of York,* obviously do not provide information on changing usage in the area of sexist suffixes. Nor is there much point in comparing the frequencies of items such as *princess* at two different points in time, when there is no obvious alternative form available. Finally, it is also worth noting the witty and unique nonce form (nicely illustrating the trivialising effect of -*ette*) referring to "Barbie – the consumerette"!

18. The WCSNZE has examples of *cunt* referring to men and one example of *dick* referring to a woman. The term *bastard* occurs 19 times, referring predominantly to men.

References

Austin, Paddy. 1990. "Politeness revisited: the dark side." In *New Zealand ways of speaking English*, eds. Allan Bell & Janet Holmes. Bristol: Multilingual Matters, 276–295.

Batterham, Margaret. 1996. *"There is another type here?" Some front vowel variables in New Zealand English*. Ph.D. dissertation, La Trobe University, Bundoora, Victoria.

Bauer, Laurie. 1993. *Manual of Information to accompany the Wellington Corpus of Written New Zealand English.* Wellington: Dept of Linguistics, Victoria University of Wellington.

Bell, Allan. 1997. "The phonetics of fish, chips and ethnic identity in New Zealand." *English World-Wide* 18: 243–270.

Britain, David. 1992. "Linguistic change in intonation: the use of High Rising Terminals in New Zealand English." *Language Variation and Change* 4 (1): 77–104.

Cameron, Deborah. 1985. "What has gender got to do with sex?" *Language and Communication* 5 (1): 19–27.

Cameron, Deborah. 1994. "Problems of sexist and non-sexist language." In *Exploring Gender: Questions for English Language Education,* ed. Jane Sunderland. London: Prentice Hall, 26–33.

Chambers, Jack C. 1995. *Sociolinguistic Theory.* Oxford: Blackwell.

Cooper, Robert L. 1984. "The avoidance of androcentric generics." *International Journal of the Sociology of Language* 50: 5–20.

Eakins, Barbara W. and R. Gene Eakins. 1978. *Sex differences in human communication.* Boston: Houghton Mifflin.

Eckert, Penelope. 1989. "The whole woman: Sex and gender differences in variation." *Language Variation and Change* 1: 245–267.

Eckert, Penelope & Sally McConnell-Ginet. 1992. "Think practically and look locally: language and gender as community-based practice." *Annual Review of Anthropology* 21: 461–490.

Eckert, Penelope & Sally McConnell-Ginet. 1995. "Constructing meaning, constructing selves: snapshots of language, gender, and class from Belten High." In *Gender articulated: Language and the socially constructed self,* eds. Kira Hall & Mary Bucholtz. New York: Routledge, 469–507.

Ehrlich, Susan & Ruth King. 1994. "Feminist meanings and the (de)politicization of the lexicon." *Language in Society* 23: 59–76.

Faludi, Susan. 1991. *Backlash. The undeclared war against American women.* New York: Crown.

Gordon, Matthew & Jeffrey Heath. 1998. "Sex, sound symbolism and sociolinguistics." *Current Anthropology* 39: 1–61.

Hellinger, Marlis. 1989. "Revisiting the patriarchal paradigm. Language change and feminist politics." In *Language, power and ideology,* ed. Ruth Wodak. Amsterdam: Benjamins, 273–288.

Henley, Nancy M. & Cheris Kramarae. 1991. "Gender, power and miscommunication." In *'Miscommunication' and problematic talk,* ed. Howard Giles & John W. Wiemann & Nikolas Coupland. London: Sage, 18–43.

Holmes, Janet. 1993a. "Charpersons, chairpersons and goddesses: Sexist usages in New Zealand English." *Te Reo* 36: 99–113.

Holmes, Janet. 1993b. "Sex-marking suffixes in written New Zealand English." *American Speech* 68: 357–370.

Holmes, Janet. 1993c. "He-man beings, poetesses, and tramps: Sexist language in New Zealand." In *Of Pavlova, poetry and paradigms: Essays in honour of Harry Orsman,* eds. Laurie Bauer & Christine Franzen. Wellington: Victoria University Press, 34–49.

Holmes, Janet. 1993d. "Women's talk: The question of sociolinguistic universals." *Australian Journal of Communication* 20 (3): 125–149.

Holmes, Janet. 1994a. "Inferring language change from computer corpora: Some methodological problems." *ICAME Journal* 18: 27–40.

Holmes, Janet. 1994b. "The Wellington corpus of New Zealand English." *TESOLANZ Newsletter* 3 (3): 7.

Holmes, Janet. 1995. *Women, men and politeness.* London: Longman.

Holmes, Janet. 1997a. "Setting new standards: Sound changes and gender in New Zealand English." *English World Wide* 18: 107–142.

Holmes, Janet. 1997b. "Maori and Pakeha English: some New Zealand social dialect data." *Language in Society* 26: 65–101.

Holmes, Janet. 1997c. "Women, language and identity." *Journal of Sociolinguistics* 2: 195–223.

Holmes, Janet. 1997d. "Story-telling in New Zealand women's and men's talk." In *Gender, discourse and ideology*, ed. Ruth Wodak. London: Sage, 263–293.

Holmes, Janet. 1998. "Women's role in language change: A place for quantification." In *Gender and belief systems: Proceedings of the Fourth Berkeley Women and Language Conference, April 19–21, 1996.* eds. Natasha Warner & Jocelyn Ahlers & Leela Bilmes & Monica Oliver & Suzanne Wertheim & Melinda Chen. Berkeley, CA: Berkeley Women and Language Group, 313–330.

Holmes, Janet & Allan Bell. 1993. "On shear markets and sharing sheep: the merger of EAR and AIR in New Zealand English." *Language Variation and Change* 4: 251–273.

Holmes, Janet & Allan Bell & Mary Boyce. 1991. *Variation and change in New Zealand English: A social dialect investigation. (Project Report to the Social Sciences Committee of the Foundation for Research, Science and Technology).* Wellington: Victoria University.

Holmes, Janet & Robert Sigley. in press. "What's a word like *girl* doing in a place like this? Occupational labels, sexist usages and corpus research." In *New frontiers of corpus linguistics*, ed. Adam Smith. Sydney: Macquarie.

Holt, Vivienne. 1988. "How New Zealand newspapers name people." *Occasional Papers in Language and Linguistics* 1: 9–18.

Labov, William. 1990. "The intersection of sex and social class in the course of linguistic change." *Language Variation and Change* 2: 205–254.

Maclagan, Margaret & Elizabeth Gordon. 1996. "Out of the air and into the ear: Another view of the New Zealand diphthong merger." *Language Variation and Change* 8: 125–147.

Meyerhoff, Miriam. 1987. "Language and sex: Research in New Zealand." In *Women and language in Australian and New Zealand society*, ed. Anne Pauwels. Sydney: Australian Professional Publications, 32–44.

Meyerhoff, Miriam. 1994. "Sounds pretty ethnic, eh? – a pragmatic particle in New Zealand English." *Language in Society* 23: 367–388.

Miller, Casey & Kate Swift. 1990. *Words and women.* 2nd ed. Harmondsworth: Penguin.

Milne, Brian. 1991. *Ms-usage in the public service.* Term paper. Linguistics Department, Victoria University, Wellington.

Ng, Sik Hung. 1990. "Androcentric coding of man and his in memory by language users." *Journal of Experimental Social Psychology* 26: 455–464.

Ng, Sik Hung. 1991. "Evaluation by females and males of speeches worded in the masculine, feminine or gender-inclusive reference form." *International Journal of Applied Linguistics* 1: 186–197.

O'Brien, Jenny. 1993. *Ms, Miss or Mrs? A study of the use of titles and of interpretations of the title Ms.* Term paper. Linguistics Department, Victoria University, Wellington.

Pateman, Trevor. 1980. *Language, truth and politics.* London: Jean Stroud.

Pauwels, Anne. 1987. "Language in transition: A study of the title 'Ms' in contemporary Australian society." In *Women and language in Australian and New Zealand society*, ed. Anne Pauwels. Sydney: Australian Professional Publications, 129–154.

Peters, Pam & Harry Purvis & Cathy Martin & Robert Jenkins. 1990. *Word frequencies from the Macquarie Corpus: The newspaper files. Working Papers of the Speech Hearing and Language Research Centre.* Special joint edition with Dictionary Research Centre. North Ryde, New South Wales: School of English and Linguistics. Macquarie University.

Roberts, Mary. 1997. "Metaphor: or brick shithouses, studmuffins and horny old goats." Paper read at the Twelfth New Zealand Linguistics Society Conference, Nov 26–29, 1997. University of Otago, Dunedin.

Romaine, Suzanne. 1997. "Gender, grammar and the space in between." In *Communicating gender in context*, eds. Helga Kotthoff & Ruth Wodak. Amsterdam: Benjamins, 51–76.

Tannen, Deborah. 1990. *You just don't understand: Women and men in conversation.* New York: William Morrow.

Tannen, Deborah. 1992. "Response to Senta Troemel-Ploetz' 'Selling the apolitical.'" *Discourse and Society* 3: 249–254.

Troemel-Ploetz, Senta. 1991. "Review essay: Selling the apolitical." *Discourse and Society* 2: 489–502.

Trudgill, Peter. 1983. *On dialect.* Oxford: Blackwell.

Trudgill, Peter & Elizabeth Gordon & Gillian Lewis. 1998. "New-dialect information and Southern Hemisphere English: The New Zealand short front vowels." *Journal of Sociolinguistics* 2: 35–51.

Wilson, Edward & Ng, Sik Hung. 1988. "Sex bias in visual images evoked by generics: A New Zealand study." *Sex Roles* 18: 159–169.

Woods, Nicola. 1997. "The formation and development of New Zealand English: Interaction of gender-related variation and linguistic change." *Journal of Sociolinguistics* 1: 95–125.

Spreading the feminist word

The case of the new courtesy title *Ms* in Australian English*

Anne Pauwels
The University of Western Australia, Australia

1.   Feminism and language

There is no doubt that feminism has been and continues to be one of the main social movements of this century. Its impact is felt in many societies around the world and in many spheres of life. The feminist or women's movement strives, amongst other things, for the elimination of gender discrimination and for the greater recognition of women's contributions to society as well as aims to change many cultural and social practices which perpetuate patriarchal value systems. Language was and is seen by many feminists as a powerful instrument of patriarchy: for example, the feminist Dale Spender spoke of the English language as being "manmade" and as being an important contributor to women's oppression (Spender 1980). It is therefore not surprising that language and discourse practices were subjected to feminist scrutiny, usually leading to elaborate and detailed descriptions of how sexist practices permeate language use.

1.1   Feminism and lingustic reform

Feminists, at least in some western societies, also expressed a desire to change the patriarchal and sexist "nature" of language and therefore engaged in various types of linguistic reform or language planning. Although many feminists shared the belief that changing linguistic and discourse practices is an important element in women's liberation, this did not result in a uniform approach to linguistic reform (see Pauwels 1998a). The social, cultural, political and philosophical diversity which characterises members of the feminist movement is also reflected in the approaches to, and aims for feminist language reform. For example, not all forms of feminism interpret women's liberation as a question of achieving mere equality of women and men. Similarly, not all linguistic reform proposals have as their main aim the achievement of linguistic equality of women and men.

Some reform initiatives primarily aim at exposing the sexist nature of "patriarchal" language by causing linguistic disruptions. The strategies employed to achieve linguistic disruption frequently involve experimentation and creativity with all parts of speech. The word *herstory* is an example of linguistic disruption, i.e., a morphological boundary has been reconstituted on semantic grounds.

Creating a women-centred language capable of expressing reality from a female perspective is another prominent objective of some forms of feminist language reform. Proposed changes range from the creation of new women-centred meanings and words, graphemic innovations, to developing women-focussed discourses and even creating an entirely new language. An example of the latter is the Láadan language created by the science-fiction writer and linguist Suzette Haden Elgin "for the specific purpose of expressing the perceptions of women" (Elgin 1988: 1).

Despite this diversity in reform initiatives and objectives for feminist language planning, it is *the linguistic equality* approach which has become synonymous with feminist language planning in the eyes of the wider community, especially in English speech communities. In part, this is due to the prominence of liberal feminist approaches in the public arena which focus on achieving gender equality. Linguistic discrimination is seen as a form of gender discrimination which can be addressed in ways similar to other forms of gender discrimination (e.g. in employment). The prominence of the linguistic equality approach is also due to the media's attention to non-sexist language guidelines, the main instrument of promoting this type of feminist language reform (see e.g. Pauwels 1998a).

1.2 Evaluating feminist linguistic reform

Evaluating the outcome of linguistic reform is a crucial aspect of any form of language planning. Language planners together with the interest groups, agencies or institutions which encouraged, demanded or sanctioned the reforms are usually keen to assess the impact of planning on the linguistic behaviour of the individuals, groups or communities targeted by the reforms. Whereas advocates and/or opponents of linguistic reform are primarily interested in the extent to which the linguistic reform proposals have been adopted or rejected, for language planners the evaluation exercise also provides valuable information on the process of language planning, the factors which facilitate and/or obstruct change. A further interest for language planners who are also linguistic scholars is the possibility of comparing the process of the spread of so-called "planned" vs "unplanned" linguistic change, thus contributing to a better understanding of linguistic change.

In this contribution I discuss the evaluation stage of feminist language planning through a detailed analysis of the adoption and spread of one specific proposal – the new courtesy title for women, i.e. *Ms* – in Australian English.

1.3 Eliminating gender bias in courtesy titles: The options

Since the 1970s, the title *Ms* has been promoted as the non-sexist, feminist alternative to replace the traditional titles of *Miss* and *Mrs* in English. The latter were seen as blatant examples of gender bias in language reflecting and reinforcing patriarchal views of women as property of some man or as dependent on men for their status. The distinction between *Mrs* and *Miss* forces a categorisation on women according to their (presumed) marital status. No such categorisation occurs for men, leading some feminists to comment that "[...] men are defined in terms of what they do in the world, women in terms of the men with whom they associate" (Lakoff 1975:30), and that the practice of labelling women as married or single "[...] conveniently signals who is "fair" game from the male point of view" (Spender 1980:270).

From a language planning perspective, there are different ways in which to address the imbalance or asymmetry between female and male courtesy titles.

The imbalance can be restored, at least theoretically, by any of the following proposals:

1. developing a gender-neutral title for use by women and men;
2. making the feature of marital status relevant for men by introducing an additional courtesy title for men;
3. abandoning courtesy titles altogether;
4. abandoning the feature of marital status in women's titles.

Options (1) and (3) have been around for many years (see e.g. Bierce 1911, Hook 1977, Key 1975, Pauwels 1987): the abandoning of the common courtesy titles *Mrs*, *Miss* and *Mr* was and is seen by many as the best solution to the problem, although Key (1975) believed the option of eliminating such titles to be too radical in the 1970s. The option of a gender-neutral title has led to creations such as *M.*, or *Person*. To date, there is little evidence of the acceptance of such a gender-neutral title.

Option (2) has also led to a variety of proposals (many mainly in jest), including the introduction of titles for unmarried men such as *Mush*, abbreviated as *Mh* by Bierce (1911), *Srs* (Baker as cited in Lakoff 1975) or for married men, for example *Mrm* (Baker as cited in Lakoff 1975) or *Mrd* (Sorrels 1983). Hook (1977) proposes the re-introduction of *Master* for reference to unmarried men. To my knowledge, none of these proposals have been taken up for implementation.

Option (4) is the proposal implicitly and explicitly promoted by feminists. This proposal entails two alternative solutions: (a) abandoning one of the existing titles for women (either *Miss* or *Mrs*), leading to a semantic shift in the remaining title (no longer a marker of marital status) or (b) abandoning both titles and replacing them with a new one (i.e. *Ms*) which functions as the female equivalent to *Mr*. Whereas European speech communities other than English have generally opted for solution (a) within Option (4), English speech communities have promoted the use of the new title *Ms*. Elsewhere (Pauwels 1996, 1998a) I have explained that the latter alternative is more complex, both linguistically and socially, as it involves the elimination of two widely used and familiar titles in favour of a new and unknown title. Furthermore, the exact origin of the *Ms* title is rather vague. Kramarae and Treichler (1985:286) mention the appearance of *Ms* on the tombstone of a woman called Sarah Spooner, who was buried in Plymouth, Massachusetts in 1767. However, the authors think it unlikely that this was "an example of colonial feminism", rather an abbreviation of *mistress* in its meaning 'wife of'. Kramarae and Treichler cite

Mario Pei's (1949) book, *The Story of English,* as containing the first reference to *Ms* in its current meaning. Miller and Swift (1981) mention that the title *Ms* first appeared in secretarial handbooks in the United States in the 1940s as a title analogous to *Mr.* The introduction of computers and their application to the processing of mail orders has also been indicated as a possible source for the formation *Ms.* Stannard (1977:342) reports that *Ms* is supposed to have originated from computerised programming of mailing lists: *Ms* was the form printed out by a computer in the absence of information regarding the exact courtesy title of a female recipient. Personal communication with Australian women in the mid 1980s revealed that they were uncertain about the origin of the title *Ms* or about the timing of its introduction into Australian society.

2. Spreading the feminist word: The case of *Ms* in Australia

Here I present the findings of a small-scale study on the use of *Ms* among Australian women. The main focus is on establishing a profile of the *Ms*-users in order to gain insight into adoption patterns and ways in which the use of *Ms* spreads through a speech community. To date, research and observations on the use of *Ms* in English language communities (e.g. Atkinson 1987, Ehrlich & King 1992, Graddol & Swann 1989, Jacobson & Insko 1984, Milne 1991, O'Brien 1993, Pauwels 1987, 1996, 1998a) have provided evidence that the title *Ms* is gaining currency amongst female users, although no reliable figures are available for any of the communities. Small-scale surveys and studies have established that the use of *Ms* ranges from 20% to almost 50% amongst the female population in these communities.

In 1996, I undertook a study involving 300 women in Australian cities and regional towns which aimed to establish a profile of *Ms*-users. I decided to focus the research on women's understanding and use of the title, as women were the primary group to be affected by the proposed changes. The study involved short interviews with women in which they were questioned about their familiarity with, understanding of, as well as use of the title *Ms.* The interviews also sought some socio-demographic information including age, educational background and marital status. The interviews took place in public spaces (e.g. banks, post-offices, insurance offices) and lasted on average about 5 to 10 minutes. 387 women had been approached in 4 major cities and some regional towns, and 313 women agreed to an interview. The data of 300 interviews were usable and form the basis for the results presented below (for more details on methodology, see Pauwels 1998b).

2.1   A profile of *Ms*-users in Australia: Socio-demographic data

The interviews revealed that approximately 96% (95.7%) were familiar with the title, i.e. they knew that *Ms* was a title of address for women. Although familiarity with the actual title was very high, this was not replicated in regard to the meaning of the title *Ms*. As mentioned before, *Ms* was promoted as the female equivalent of *Mr*, i.e. a courtesy title for women which does not categorise (adult) women according to actual or presumed marital status. It is interesting to note (see Table 1) that there is still a not insignificant proportion of women who do not assign this meaning (i.e. the promoted meaning) to the title *Ms*, i.e. 25.3%.

Table 1. Meanings of *Ms*

Promoted meaning	224	(74.7%)
Separated/Divorced	26	(8.7%)
De facto relationship	11	(3.7%)
Professional women	8	(2.7%)
Feminists	14	(4.7%)
Lesbians	2	(0.7%)
Other	2	(0.7%)
NA	13	(4.3%)
Total	300	(100%)

A similar study undertaken in 1986 (Pauwels 1987) revealed that 64% of polled women were conversant with the promoted or propagated meaning of *Ms*. The findings from the 1996 study suggest an increase in women's awareness of the promoted meaning of *Ms*, i.e. from 64% to approximately 75%. Women whose understanding of *Ms* is different from the propagated meaning tend to resort to two main features for their interpretation of *Ms*:

(1)   *Marital status*: divorced, separated, living in a de facto relationship (i.e. not legally married), or possibly, living in a relationship with a woman.

(2)   *"Lifestyle"*: working women (especially professional women), feminists, and possibly lesbian.

Women who consider the title *Ms* in relation to marital status use it to label or categorise women who do not "fit" well into the existing categories of married and unmarried, i.e. separated or divorced women and women in de facto relationships. In fact, these women use *Ms* as a third title denoting some form of marital status. The feature of "lifestyle" (including ideology) is an additional feature used to explain "*Ms*-using" women. It is also interesting to note that the degree of awareness of the propagated meaning (PM) divides somewhat across urban (metropolitan) and regional (country/rural) lines: whereas the metropolitan average lies around 83%, the average of country/regional centres is approximately 63%.

In terms of usage, approximately 37% indicated that they were users of *Ms*. Given the difficulty of comparing usage results across the various English speech communities due to the different data collection procedures, I only present a comparison with Australian data on *Ms* collected in 1986 in a very similar manner (see Pauwels 1987). The 1986 study found that approximately 20% of women used *Ms*. The 1996 study records a usage pattern which is almost double. This is a remarkable increase.

The following tables provide a socio-demographic profile of *Ms*-users in terms of location, age, educational background and marital status based on the 1996 data.

Location
Women who took part in this study came from three main cities on Australia's east coast (Sydney, Melbourne and Canberra) and from the city of Adelaide on the south coast of Australia, as well as from some regional centres on the east coast.

Table 2. *Ms*-users according to location

Location	No. of informants	No. of users	%
Sydney	75	28	37.3
Melbourne	55	21	38.2
Canberra	40	23	57.5
Adelaide	30	17	56.6
Reg. Cent.	100	23	23.0
Total	300	112	37.3

Table 2 reveals a stronger use of *Ms* in metropolitan than in regional centres. In Canberra and Adelaide more than half of the women interviewed reported *Ms* use. In the two largest cities, Sydney and Melbourne, usage rates approach 40%, whereas regional towns and centres record around 23% use. Given the small number of observations across the cities and regional towns, it is difficult to interpret regional trends in the findings. Nevertheless, the high use of *Ms* in Canberra, Australia's capital city, may be partly explained by the population profile of the city. Canberra's population includes a very high proportion of government bureaucrats and public servants whose exposure to non-sexist language guidelines in the workplace may have made them more aware of *Ms*, possibly leading to a higher personal use of *Ms*. In fact, Milne (1991), who examined women working for government organisations in Wellington, the capital of New Zealand, found that 49% of women used *Ms*. The high level of use in Adelaide is more difficult to interpret. Melbourne and Sydney women seem to behave in a very similar way. In comparison with Canberra and Adelaide, these cities represent a more diverse population, both in social (e.g., occupational, socio-economic) and linguistic/cultural terms. The lower use in regional centres may reflect the more conservative attitude towards feminist issues. However, it should be noted that statistically speaking, the differences between city and country were not significant.

Age

Due to the fact that a pilot study to this project revealed many women's unwillingness to state their exact age, I decided to ask the age-related question making use of rather broad age group categories.

Table 3. *Ms*-users according to age

Age	under 25	25–40	41–65	over 65
Total no. in age group (Total = 300)	(28)	(121)	(123)	(28)
Number of *Ms*-users	9	49	49	5
% in age group	32.1	40.5	39.8	17.8

Insights into the age profile of *Ms*-users are particularly interesting from the perspective of linguistic change. Recent sociolinguistic work has shown that adolescents and young adults (often young women) are the "movers and the shakers" in phonological change (e.g. Cheshire 1998, Eckert 1988, 1989, 1998, Holmes 1997). The age profile of the *Ms*-users seems to indicate that this type of planned, lexical change does not reflect the patterns of sound change. In fact, women under 25 are not the prime users of the *Ms* title. This is reserved for women between 25 to 65. Women over 65 are least likely to use *Ms*.

The distribution of *Ms* with regard to age currently resembles a bell shaped curve. The low usage rate amongst 65+ year olds may be attributable in part to the relative recency of the title. Furthermore, it is likely that women in the 65+ age group were less affected by feminist activism during the 1970s and 1980s. Explaining the lower rate of *Ms* use among young women (under 25) is more difficult. The lower rate of use in this group could be seen as an expression of feminist backlash (Faludi 1992): in a "post-feminist" era where gender equality is considered a fact, young women no longer see the need for the linguistic expression of women's independence. An alternative explanation of the observed pattern is that *Miss* is still firmly entrenched as the courtesy title for girls (i.e. [-adult]). Although *Miss* may be losing its connotation of 'single' or 'unmarried', it seems to have maintained its connotation [-adult]. Today girls continue to be referred to and addressed by the title *Miss* rather than *Ms* in the school and the wider public environment. *Ms* like *Mrs* is considered a marker of adulthood. When reaching adulthood through rites of passage such as gaining employment or entering a relationship, girls are faced with a title choice: to remain a *Miss*, or to change to *Ms* or *Mrs*. The present sample suggests that a majority of girls and young women (53.6%) use *Miss*, possibly because they still classify themselves as [-adult]. Approximately one third of young women in this sample chose to switch to *Ms* (32.1%) and 14% (4 women) chose for *Mrs*. It was not possible to check whether those choosing to change did so because they were older than the others.

When asked how long they had been using *Ms*, most women could remember when they had started using *Ms* and what had led them to switch to *Ms*. Significant here is the observation that none of the women had always used *Ms*; rather, all women had *switched* to the title *Ms* at some stage in their lives. For women under 25 years of age the average length of use is 2.7 years. Mean length of use was 7.9 years for women in the 25–40 age group, 8.1 years for women in the 41-65 group and 10 years for the 65+ group. The maximum length of use was 15 years (recorded by 3 women in the 41-65 age group and one woman in the 65+ category). This means that for this sample of women, the earliest recorded use of *Ms* was in the 1980s. The majority of the sample started using *Ms* in the late 1980s and early 1990s. This coincides with the period in which non-sexist language guidelines were implemented and non-sexist language reform received attention in the media and the public arena (e.g. Pauwels 1998a).

Education

Another important variable in the use of *Ms* is the educational level of the informant. Table 4 provides overwhelming evidence that *Ms*-users are (highly) educated women with tertiary qualifications. In fact, the Chi square test as well as a discriminant function analysis revealed that education is the most significant factor influencing title use: women with tertiary qualifications are the most likely *Ms* users. Similar results have been noted in New Zealand, where Milne's (1991) and O'Brien's (1993) studies found that educational level had a significant impact on *Ms* use. This result is not surprising, given the nature of the change. *Ms* was in many respects the "flagship" of feminist reform initiatives. Although feminist reform is much more a question of *grassroots* language activism than *top down* language planning, the grassroots reformers were and still are mainly middle-class, well-educated women with a professional interest in language. The use of *Ms* not only originated amongst well-educated women, but is also most likely to spread first among women with similar levels of education. Furthermore, the spread of language guidelines has been first and foremost in contexts with a strong presence of professional and highly educated women (i.e. tertiary and secondary education, public service, law).

Table 4. *Ms*-users according to education

	Lower Secondary	Secondary	Tertiary
Total no. in each group	(82)	(125)	(93)
Number of users	1	30	81
% in group	1.2	24.0	87.1

Marital Status

Of specific interest in judging the successful adoption of *Ms* as well as in obtaining a profile of the prime movers of *Ms* is a breakdown of users in terms of marital status. Such a breakdown may shed light on the acceptance of *Ms* as an appropriate title for women irrespective of their marital status. Feminist researchers have commented on the "depoliticisation" and on the misuse of the term *Ms*, which mirrors the remarks about the misuse of putative gender-neutral nouns (e.g. *chairperson*). For example, Graddol & Swann (1989) and Penelope (1990) mention that in the United Kingdom and the United States respectively, the term *Ms* seems to have replaced *Miss* on official forms leading to the dichotomy *Mrs* (presumably for married women) and *Ms* (presumably for single/unmarried women). In Canada, Atkinson (1987) found that *Ms* use was associated with women who were separated and/or divorced, i.e. women who did not "fit" well into the *Mrs* or *Miss* categories.

Table 5 reveals that in Australia the *Ms*-users are found in all categories reflecting various forms of marital status. However, Australian data also show that women who do not fit well into the "married" or "unmarried" categories are the trendsetters. Women who live in heterosexual relationships, but who are not formally (legally) married (i.e., de facto) are the most likely *Ms*-users, followed by separated/divorced women and women who describe themselves as "single". Nevertheless, 31% of women who are currently married also state that they use *Ms*.

Table 5. *Ms* users and marital status

	Single	De facto	Married	Sep./Divorced	Widowed
Total no. in group	(63)	(23)	(43)	(58)	(14)
No. of users	25	14	45	58	14
% in group	39.9	60.8	31.4	44.8	14.3

The Australian data on *Ms* use do not support the observations by Graddol and Swann (1989) for the UK and Penelope (1990) for the US, that *Ms* is merely a replacement for *Miss*. The Australian findings, however, do echo the Canadian findings that *Ms* use is strongly associated with separated and divorced women.

2.2 The main triggers for change

In addition to collecting socio-demographic information, I also sought information from the *Ms*-users regarding the main trigger(s) for change. It was established that none of the women in this study had always used *Ms*. Hence, they had switched to *Ms* use at some stage in their lives. The question about who or what influenced the women to adopt the title *Ms* allowed me to explore the issue of agents of change. Replies to the question "Who or what was or is a major influence on your use of the title *Ms*?" could be categorised as follows:

– Friends, and/or close colleagues have been the main influence.
– Female family members have been the main influence (e.g. mother, daughter, sister).

- Female role models have been the main influence.
- My feminist awareness and orientation have led me to use *Ms*.
- Its use in the media has mainly triggered my own use.
- I was mainly influenced through language guidelines.
- I don't know, can't remember .

Although these categories overlap to some extent, they nevertheless represent a variety of agents or influences which have been recognised in sociolinguistic work as triggering linguistic change.

Table 6. Main triggers for *Ms* use

	Number	%
Friends/Colleagues	39	34.8
Language Guidelines	20	17.9
Feminist Orientation	13	11.6
Role Models	13	11.6
Can't remember	13	11.6
Family	9	8.0
Use in the media	5	4.46
Total	112	100.0

Changing to *Ms* under the influence of friends and colleagues is clearly the most significant trigger for change, followed by the awareness of language guidelines (non-sexist language policy). A feminist orientation as well as the impact of role models also affect the change to *Ms* use.

It is interesting to note that feminist language change, which is a form of planned language change, has in common with unplanned linguistic change the importance of peers as agents of change. I believe it is appropriate to interpret friends/colleagues as peers in the context of this research project. Comments made by the women in this research project further revealed that the change to the use of *Ms* had usually come about after some discussion with friends and colleagues who themselves were *Ms*-users. The women were also at pains to point out to me that the change had occurred of their own volition rather than under pressure from their colleagues or friends. This seems to indicate that in the context of title change the main role of peers is to "enlighten" other women (i.e. to increase awareness of linguistic discrimination) and to provide a supportive environment in which the new title can be used.

The fact that language guidelines seem to have exerted influence on the title use of a significant number of women is a promising finding from a language planning perspective: it provides some evidence that the implementation strategy of feminist language reform (i.e. language guidelines) is having some impact on usage patterns. The women who selected this option were all employed in the paid work force and had come across guidelines in the context of their work environment (mainly public sector institutions). Some commented that they had used *Ms* first in the workplace and later in other contexts.

The presence of role models who use *Ms* and the women's feminist awareness and/or orientation are further important triggers for a change in title use. The role models mentioned by the women were almost exclusively female teachers and lecturers. The women who indicated that their feminism was the main trigger for a change in title use seemed to have (had) an active involvement in women and feminist issues (they may have been activists). They could possibly be seen as the pioneers of title change. There did not seem to be a correlation between age and the importance of role models or feminist awareness in influencing title changes.

3. Conclusion

Although this is a small-scale project on title use among women in Australia which elicited limited socio-demographic information, the findings nevertheless reveal an interesting picture of the type of women likely to use *Ms*, at least in Australia. It also provides some insight into the mechanisms of the spread of this form of planned language change.

Women with tertiary education and between the ages of 25–65 (i.e. the working population) form the main group using *Ms*. Education is the most significant factor in determining title use. Age is also significant, but because of the large age groupings it is not possible to pinpoint the most significant age group for *Ms* use.

The correlation between marital status and title use shows that *Ms* is being adopted first by those who fall outside the traditional categories of "married" and "single/unmarried". However, there is some evidence that *Ms* use is also increasingly found among those who are married. Nevertheless, the findings in relation to marital status seem to imply that a (strong) motivation for *Ms* use is the inadequacy of the current title system to cope with alternative forms of marital situations rather than a desire not to reveal marital status *per se*.

Although *Ms* use is higher amongst city women, the correlation between place of living (location) and title use is not significant. This study also shows that the earliest adoption of the title *Ms* occurred in the early 1980s, although most adopted the title in the mid to late 1980s. Finally, the results of this study provide evidence that *Ms* is not yet regarded as the sole courtesy title for women, i.e. replacing both *Miss* and *Mrs.*

In terms of spread or diffusion, this form of linguistic change is most likely to spread first among women with high levels of education through contacts with friends and colleagues. The adoption of the change also seems to spread from a work-related (professional) environment to other more informal ones. Adoption and spread seem to be predicated on (a) a familiarity with the new title as well as (b) an understanding of its promoted meaning. These observations lead me to believe that the spread of planned language change significantly differs from unplanned language change, despite some common traits in terms of agents of change (e.g. peers).

Notes

* I would like to thank Ester Klimkeit for assistance with the statistical information, and Jo Winter and Janet Holmes for useful comments on earlier drafts.

References

Atkinson, Donna L. 1987. "Names and titles: Maiden name retention and the use of *Ms.*" *Women and Language* 10: 37.

Bierce, Ambrose. 1911. *The devil's dictionary.* New York: Dover.

Cameron, Deborah. 1992. *Feminism and linguistic theory.* 2nd ed. London: Macmillan.

Cheshire, Jenny. 1998. *The levellers: Adolescents and their role in language change.* Paper read at the 12th Sociolinguistics Symposium, March 1998, London.

Dubois, Betty L. & Isabel Crouch. 1987. "Linguistic disruption: *he/she, s/he, he* or *she.*" In *Women and language in transition*, ed. Joyce Penfield. Albany, NY: State University of New York, 28-35.

Eckert, Penelope. 1988. "Sound change and adolescent social structure." *Language in Society* 17: 183-207.

Eckert, Penelope. 1989. *Jocks and burnouts: Social categories and identities in high school.* New York: Teachers College Press.

Eckert, Penelope. 1998. *Variation, style and identity.* Paper read at the 12th Sociolinguistic Symposium, March 1998, London.

Ehrlich, Susan & Ruth King. 1992. "Genderbased language reform and the social construction of meaning." *Discourse and Society* 3: 151–166.

Elgin, Suzette Haden. 1988. *A first dictionary and grammar of Láadan.* Rev. ed. Madison: Society for the Furtherance and Study of Fantasy and Science Fiction.

Faludi, Susan. 1992. *Backlash. The undeclared war against women.* London: Vintage.

Graddol, David & Joan Swann. 1989. *Gender voices.* Oxford: Blackwell.

Holmes, Janet. 1997. "Setting new standards: Sound changes and gender in New Zealand English." *English World Wide* 18: 107–142.

Hook, Donald. 1977. "Sexism in English pronouns and forms of address." *General Linguistics* 14: 86–96.

Jacobson, Marsha B. & William R. Insko. 1984. "On the relationship between feminism and the use of *Ms.*" *Psychological Reports* 54: 388–390.

Key, Mary R. 1975. *Male/female language.* Metuchen, NJ: Scarecrow.

Kramarae, Cheris & Paula A. Treichler. 1985. *A feminist dictionary.* Boston: Pandora.

Lakoff, Robin. 1975. *Language and woman's place.* New York: Harper & Row.

Miller, Casey & Kate Swift. 1981. *Handbook of non-sexist writing for writers, editors and speakers.* London: The Women's Press.

Milne, Brian. 1991. *Ms-usage in the public service.* Term paper. Wellington: Linguistics Department, Victoria University.

O'Brien, Jenny. 1993. *Ms, Miss or Mrs? A study of the use of titles and of interpretations of the title Ms.* Term paper. Wellington: Linguistics Department, Victoria University.

Pauwels, Anne. 1987. "Language in transition: A study of the title 'Ms' in contemporary Australian society." In *Women and language in Australian and New Zealand society,* ed. Anne Pauwels. Sydney: Australian Professional Publications, 129–154.

Pauwels, Anne. 1996. "Feminist language planning and titles for women: Some cross-linguistic perspectives." In *Contrastive sociolinguistics,* eds. Marlis Hellinger & Ulrich Ammon. Berlin: de Gruyter, 251–269.

Pauwels, Anne. 1998a. *Women changing language.* London: Longman.

Pauwels, Anne. 1998b. *Evaluating gender-inclusive language reform in two speech communities. Female courtesy titles in English and Dutch.* Paper read at the 12th Sociolinguistics Symposium, March 1998, London.

Pei, Mario. 1949. *The story of language.* London: Allen & Unwin.

Penelope, Julia. 1990. *Speaking freely: Unlearning the lies of the fathers' tongues.* New York: Pergamon.

Schneider, Joseph W. & Sally L. Hacker. 1973. "Sex role imagery and use of the generic 'man' in introductory texts." *American Sociologist* 8: 12–18.

Sorrels, Bobbye M. 1983. *The nonsexist communicator.* Englewood Cliffs, NJ: Prentice Hall.

Spender, Dale. 1980. *Man made language.* London: Routledge.

Stannard, Una. 1977. *Mrs Man.* San Francisco: Germainbooks.

Wilson, Elizabeth & Sik Hung Ng. 1988. "Sex bias in visual images evoked by generics: A New Zealand study." *Sex Roles* 18: 159–169.

A corpus-based view of gender in British and American English

Suzanne Romaine
Merton College, University of Oxford, UK

1. Introduction

The spread of English as an international language makes it increasingly difficult to say anything which will apply to the language as a whole. The singular term *English* seems no longer adequate to describe the social, regional and other variation in a language used by millions. It is now one of a few languages whose non-native speakers outnumber its native speakers. In this chapter I concentrate mainly on British and American English, the two most important varieties, in order to complement the chapters by Holmes and Pauwels, which focus on English in New Zealand and Australia, respectively.

Section 2 provides a brief overview of English with respect to its status as an international language, and its importance as a model for international gender reform. In Section 3, I identify those sites in English grammar where gender is displayed or gender indexing occurs in order to discuss some of the reforms proposed and evaluate their comparative success or failure in a number of varieties of English. Most of the data I have collected myself comes from British and American English, particularly British English. The availability of linguistic corpora opens up linguistic phenomena to empirical investigation on a scale previously unimaginable, and I use them wherever possible, in particular, the British National Corpus (1995) consisting of 100 million words of spoken and written British English.

In Section 4 I argue that reform must be directed at discourse as a whole rather than piecemeal at gendered bits of the language such as titles, forms of address, and androcentric generics. One of the sometimes more subtle forms of discrimination against women is that they are simply not mentioned at all! Eliminating nubility titles such as *Miss* and *Mrs* in favor of *Ms* or prescribing for public use neutral forms such as *flight attendant* instead of *steward* and *steward-ess* does little to address this problem. At the moment, English usage is very much in flux, with alternatives such as *he/she, (s)he, he or she, chairman/chairwoman/chairperson*, etc. being symbolic of different values and attitudes.

2.   English as pluricentric language

In sociolinguistic terms English can be best described as a "pluricentric" language (see e.g. Clyne 1992). Such a language is one whose norms are focused in different local centers, capitals, centers of economy, publishing, education and political power. Although no variety of English has a special linguistic claim to be considered the norm against which other varieties are measured, typologi-cally as well as sociolinguistically speaking, the two most important varieties are British and American English. All other varieties, such as Australian English, Canadian English, Indian English, etc., can be clearly related to one of these two by virtue of settlement history (e.g. British colonization of Australia and New Zealand vs. American colonization of Guam, Hawai'i, etc.) and/or geographical proximity (e.g. the case of Canadian English vis-à-vis American English). American and British English were also the first two national varieties to come into existence after the unity of English was broken in the 18th century. English was not exported to South Africa, New Zealand and Australia until much later in the 18th and 19th centuries. By virtue of number of speakers, and influence as a norm for foreign learners, British and American English are also clearly the two most important varieties. Certainly, the British variety is more advanced in terms of its codification, its pedigree having been established in a long line of grammars (e.g. Quirk & Greenbaum & Leech & Svartvik 1985) and dictionaries of great influence around the English-speaking world. Although there are now many dictionaries of varieties of English other than British English, none arguably has the authoritative status of the Oxford English Dictionary (OED).

In most other respects, however, American English is the most important variety. Not long after political separation of the American colonies, Noah Webster (1758–1843) declared linguistic independence, and did much to alter spelling and propel the American variety on a different course of standardization. Webster sought no less than to validate linguistically the creation of a new nation and national identity distinct from Britain. As in Britain, dictionaries became surrogates for the language academies of other countries. Webster's lexicographical tradition was carried on after his death by a succession of direct literary heirs down to the present day. Until 1890 the title of his dictionary remained unchanged. Subsequent editions dropped the word *American* and were referred to as *International*.

By the beginning of the twentieth century, the center of gravity had already shifted to the other side of the Atlantic. As the demographic shift in the English-speaking population continued to move away from Britain, and its political influence as a world power declined, the twentieth would be declared the American century. Over time, America's linguistic independence made itself felt on the development of the English language as a whole (see Romaine 1998 for further discussion). While Webster's linguistic declaration of independence was unparalleled for more than two hundred years, it should come as no surprise that its repercussions would be felt in other corners of the empire. Australia would be the next to follow suit in time. The appearance of Baker's (1945) *The Australian Language* confidently asserted in its title the autonomy of Australian English in the same way that Mencken (1919), following in Webster's footsteps, had attempted to do for American English with his book, *The American Language*. Australia, too, now has its own dictionary, *The Australian National Dictionary* (Ramson 1988). More recently, some of the so-called New Englishes such as Singapore English followed suit.

Major telecommunicational innovations of the late 19th and 20th centuries such as the telephone, film, television and the personal computer originated largely in the English-speaking world, and not surprisingly, English has become its lingua franca. Similarly, the corporations and financial institutions of the anglophone countries have dominated world trade and made English the international language of business. Books in the English language have dominated the publishing business. There are few countries in the world where

English books cannot find a market of some kind, and anyone who uses the internet has exposure to English. Other major languages such as French and German have continued to lose ground against English over the course of this century as mediums of scholarly publication. If the medium is the message, as McLuhan (1989) tells us, then the language of his global village is indeed English. This means that the issue of gender reform in English provides a potential model for users of other languages around the world.

3.   English as a gendered language

Dale Spender (1980) made headlines with her provocatively titled book, *Man-Made Language*. Others such as Luise Pusch (1984) soon followed her lead in a discussion of the male bias in other languages, such as German. By contrast, I have called this section English as a gendered language because I want to draw attention primarily to the structural points at which gender distinctions are made in English, rather than to the male bias identified by Spender and others (see 4. for a fuller discussion of discourse).

I do this for two reasons: Firstly, it is of empirical interest to identify those sites in grammar where gender is displayed or gender indexing occurs. Secondly, the verbally represented world is gendered in different ways. Thus, languages vary in terms of the amount and type of sexism they display, which implies they will require different types of reform (see Hellinger 1990). The primary strategy adopted by English-speaking feminists has focused on gender neutralization (degendering), while German and French reformers have more often campaigned for visibility through feminization (engendering or regendering). This difference has at least partly to do with the absence of grammatical gender in the English language (see Romaine 1997 and Romaine 1999 for fuller treatment).

Differences between Anglo-Saxon and continental European feminist theories may also have some influence on the direction of reform. Although language has received much critical attention by English-speaking feminists, it has been at the very heart of the French feminist debate. If the world is constructed and given meaning through language, then our history, philosophy, government, laws and religion are the products of a male way of perceiving and organizing the world. Because the male world view has been transmitted for centuries, it appears "natural", "objective", a "master" discourse beyond question. In this way male values become "normal" as well as normative. Our ideas about what is "normal" are deeply embedded in linguistic practices.

Language thus holds the key to challenging and changing male hegemony. For French feminists women's oppression has to be understood linguistically. Any and all representations, whether of women or men, are embedded first in language, and then in politics, culture, economics, history etc. This is at least one interpretation of Donna Haraway's (1991:3) claim that "grammar is politics by other means".

3.1 Titles and forms of address

For some people, feminism has been equated with what is perceived as a pointless and at times amusing or irksome insistence on the replacement of titles, such as *Mrs* and *Miss* with *Ms* and other gender-marked terms, such as *chairman* with *chairperson* or *chair*. Yet, it is easy to see why women all over the world have been especially sensitive to gender differences in naming practices and forms of address, since these are a particularly telling indicator of women's social status. To be referred to as 'the Mrs.' or 'the little woman' indicates the inferior status to which men have allocated women. This is one reason why language reform has been critical in feminist theories. Women wish to decide how to represent themselves.

When Yvette Roudy became Minister for Women's Rights in France following a 1983 law making sexual discrimination illegal, she observed that women had not yet won the political right to be titled accurately. Men have the right to be referred to as 'writers' or 'doctors'. Women who occupy these professions are frequently marked with special titles such as 'lady/woman doctor' or 'female/woman writer'. In the British National Corpus (hereafter BNC), for instance, I found the following usages: *lady doctor* (125 times), *woman doctor* (20 times), *female doctor* (10 times) compared to *male doctor* (14 times). There were no occurrences of *gentlemen doctor* and only one case of *man doctor*.

Decades ago Fowler (1927) noted the "inconvenience" of not knowing whether one is dealing with a woman, in his argument in favor of the word *doctoress*: "Everyone knows the inconvenience of being uncertain whether a doctor is a man or a woman; hesitation in establishing the word *doctoress* is amazing in a people regarded as nothing if not practical" (cited in Baron 1986:131). Presumably, most of the seemingly gender-neutral "people" referred to here are, in fact, male. Fowler wanted to revive certain -*ess* forms which had declined in use, e.g. *editress* (3 occurrences in BNC), and *inspectress*, and to create new ones for words which had none, such as *lecturer, cyclist,* etc. Evidently, some men still feel able to revive old words ending in -*ess* when it suits their purpose of belittling a woman's achievement, as I discovered upon reading a negative review of one of my books in which a male reviewer referred to me as an *authoress*. The BNC has 22 instances of it.

The more general marking of women who occupy high status professions signals a deviation from some presumed norm. Namely, that a doctor is a man, so a woman who is a doctor must somehow be marked as such, either by derivation (*doctoress*), compounding (*woman doctor*) or adjectival modification (*female doctor*), which conveys the idea that she is not the "real" thing. This also works in opposite fashion, though rarely, as for example in the case of *male nurse* (or *male midwife*), where the male has to be marked because the norm is assumed to be female. The BNC has 20 instances of *male nurse* and only one of *female nurse*. The only other case I am aware of in English where the male term is the marked one is that of *bridegroom*, where *bride* is the basic term, and *widower*, where the male member is marked with the suffix *-er*.

Ms was in many respects the flagship of feminist reform initiatives in the English-speaking world. Pauwels (this volume) reports a significant increase in the self-reported use of *Ms* among Australian women between 1987 and 1996. Although usage nearly doubled from 20% to 37%, not all women shared an understanding of the term. Women who use *Ms* are likely to be younger, well educated, and urban. Women who live in heterosexual relationships but are not married are most likely to be *Ms* users, followed by separated/divorced women and women who describe themselves as single. Still, 31% of married women report using *Ms* as well.

Holmes (this volume) suggests that self-reported usage is even higher in New Zealand, though her results are from well educated women in the capital, Wellington. Holmes also examined the Wellington Corpus of Spoken New Zealand English, which contained only two instances of *Ms* in one million words! This indicates that although many young well educated women may be choosing the form for self-reference, it is still not a widely used form of address chosen by others in addressing women.

Table 1 shows comparable statistics from the BNC. Although the number of occurrences of *Ms* is obviously much larger due to the larger size of the corpus, usage of *Ms* is still marginal as an address title in the UK. It accounts for only 5% of the occurrences of the titled forms used for women.

This is, of course, only a very rough measure, and tells us nothing about the persons referred to as *Ms*; nor does it reveal instances where women are referred to without titles. However, it is of interest that many of the examples of *Ms* are taken from *The Independent*, a newspaper with liberal leanings.

Table 1. Titles in the British National Corpus

Miss	12,595	37%
Ms	1,687	5%
Mrs	19,845	58%
Mr	52,399	100%

In the early computer corpora such as the Brown Corpus of American English (the first computerized collection of texts compiled in the 1960s), or LOB (Lancaster-Oslo-Bergen corpus of British English) of the 1970s, there are no instances of *Ms* at all. The term *Ms* is still not as widely used in Britain as it is in the United States. An examination of practices at the University of Oxford, for example, reveals a system of address forms very much in flux with much variation in individual colleges, faculties and departments. In its list of students Merton College, for instance, still uses the conventional practice of using *Miss* or *Mrs* for females and no title for males, i.e. *Miss C. Smith*, but *P. Jones*. All three titles, *Ms*, *Miss*, and *Mrs* are in use for females in the internal telephone directory for the University of Oxford as a whole.

One reason for the lag of British English may be a more general concern with titles in a social system with a greater preoccupation with social status and correspondingly less social mobility. British English also has more gender-marked titles such as *manageress* (102 occurrences in the BNC) than American English, and it still preserves terms such as *spinster*, which has become archaic in the US. There are no instances of the word in the Brown Corpus, but there are still 156 occurrences in the BNC.

The word *spinster* is a good example of the tendency for the female member of pairs such as *master/mistress*, *Sir/Madam*, *baronet/dame*, *king/queen*, etc. to degenerate over time. The term *spinster* originally meant a woman engaged in spinning. Because these women spinners were often unmarried, this connotation eventually ousted the original meaning and became the primary sense of the word. In the 17th century *spinster* became the legal designation of an unmarried woman in Britain.

An examination of the terms with which *spinster* collocates are indicative of its largely negative meaning today (data are from the BNC). Although there are some neutral descriptive adjectives used with the word, such as *66 year old*, *disabled* or *American*, the majority of words collocating with *spinster* have negative connotations. They include: *gossipy, nervy, over-made up, ineffective, jealous, eccentric, love-/sex-starved, frustrated, whey-faced, dried-up old, repressed, lonely, prim, cold-hearted, plain Jane, atrocious, dreary old,* and *despised.* By comparison, the collocations of its male counterpart, *bachelor,* are largely descriptive or positive, with the exception of one occurrence of *bachelor wimp!* This example shows how the connotations of words do not arise from words themselves but from how they are used in context. The meanings of words are constructed and maintained by patterns of collocation. Collocations transmit cultural meanings and stereotypes which have built up over time. Although feminists such as Mary Daly (1987) have urged women to reclaim the use of *spinster* and other negative terms such as *crone, hag,* etc., so far this has not occurred in mainstream usage.

Schulz (1975) has shown how other female terms may start out on an equal footing, but become devalued over time. *Lord,* for instance preserves its original meaning, while *lady* is no longer used exclusively for women of high rank. This is especially true in the US, with the exception of the term *first lady* to refer to the President's wife. In the 17th century *lady* became a synonym for a prostitute. So did *courtesan,* which originally meant a female member of the court. *Baronet* still retains its original meaning, but *Dame* is used derogatorily, especially in American English. *Sir* is still used as a title and a form of respect, while a *Madam* is one who runs a brothel. Likewise, *master* has not lost its original meaning, but *mistress* has come to have sexual connotations and no longer refers to the woman who had control over a household.

The term *mistress* too, has a wider usage in Britain, where it serves as a title for a female head of school (e.g. *Headmistress, Vicemistress,* etc.), or female school teacher.[1] American feminists such as Robin Lakoff and Julia Penelope have paid much more attention to the term *lady* than their British counterparts. The fact that the use of *lady* as a polite euphemism for *woman* is far more common in Britain than in the US also reflects the different social histories of the two countries.

3.2 Androcentric generics

Prescriptive grammarians have long insisted that *everyone should get his hat when he leaves the room* is supposed to refer to both men and women, despite the use of the male pronoun *his.* In informal English, of course, the alternative exists of using the plural forms of the pronouns which are not gender-specific, *everybody should get their hat when they leave the room,* even though it has been condemned for some time as non-standard. Grammarians argue that the plural is ungrammatical because a singular antecedent such as *everyone, someone,* etc.

requires a singular pronoun to agree with it. However, many English-speakers have seen the plural forms as more elegant replacements for male pronouns than using both *he/him/his* and *she/her/hers*, i.e. *everyone should get his or her coat when he or she leaves the room.*

In a study of contemporary American English discourse from television interviews and talk shows, Michael Newman (1998) found that speakers used the plural forms *they/them* 60% of the time to refer to singular antecedents of indeterminate gender like *person, everyone, anyone,* etc. The male pronominal forms *he/him* were used in only 25% of such cases. The use of *he/him* occurs with items which are stereotypically associated with males, e.g. *lawyer, plumber,* etc. Newman also found, however, that reference to women in any fashion was much less frequent than reference to males, confirming a trend which other investigators have found; women are not often the subjects of discourse.

A very simple indication of this imbalance in reference to women and men can be found by doing a word search for the pronouns *he/she* in the many computer corpora available for English and other languages. One such count in the Brown corpus of American English containing just over one million words yielded a total of 9,543 occurrences of *he* compared to 2,859 of *she.* Generic usages do not account for the great discrepancy. Men are referred to three times as often as women. There were some interesting differences among the different text types included in the corpus. Romance and love stories, for instance, include a greater number of occurrences of female pronouns than does science fiction. Not surprisingly, women are seldom referred to in texts with religious subject matter. When the first allegedly non-sexist Bible published in Britain was launched, a press release said that "the revisers have systematically changed expressions such as *any man* to *anyone,* but have kept the masculine, especially for God, on the grounds that this is faithful to the original" (*Guardian,* October 4, 1985).

Generations of women have been expected to accept the use of *brother* in terms which served as symbols of universal human kinship. Even Germaine Greer (1971) urged women to cooperate with one another in "the matriarchal principle of fraternity", a seeming oxymoron better served by the simple term *sisterhood*! In 1992 a group of Catholic bishops objected to changes in the English mass which they said would diminish the Fatherhood of God (Ostling 1992). The proposed changes included eliminating *man* and male pronouns to refer to humanity as a whole, e.g. *Jesus Christ is the Son of Man.* Oxford University Press subtitled its 1995 edition of the *New Testament and Psalms* "an inclusive version". This version replaces *God the Father* with *Father-Mother* and *the Son of Man* with *the Human One.*

The BNC, however, may provide evidence of women getting more discourse time. A search of *he* and *she* in a three million word subcorpus revealed a total of 352,239 occurrences of *she* and 652,547 of *he*. If these rather gross statistics are indicative of changing usage over the past thirty years, then it appears that men are referred to only twice as much rather than three times as much as women.

Similar evidence of a lessening gap between reference to men and women has emerged from Cooper's (1984) survey of American English usage between 1971 and 1979. The frequency of reference to *he* and *man* fell from around 12 occurrences per 5,000 words to about 4. Women's magazines showed the steepest decline, followed by science magazines, with newspapers further behind, and the US Congressional Records last of all. However, such statistics reveal only a superficial view of language reform.

Some feminists have suggested new gender-neutral singular pronouns such as *tey* to replace *she* and *he*, or combining them as *s/he*, or using the feminine pronouns as new generics as a form of affirmative action. According to one count, at least 80 proposals have been made for replacement of singular pronouns in English, but none has caught on (see Baron 1986: 205–209 for a chronology of some of these proposals). This should not be surprising in view of the fact that the plural forms are already well established.

To complete the picture illustrated by Holmes in her Table 4 showing *chair/man/woman/person* and *spokes/man/woman/person*, I have compiled data from the BNC in Table 2.

Table 2. Occurrence of *chair/man/woman/person* and *spokes/man/woman/person* in the British National Corpus

chairman/men	12,052	spokesman/men	4,233
chairwoman/women	71	spokeswoman/women	618
chairperson/s	166	spokesperson/s	276
Madam chairman	37		
chairlady	1		

Although both Holmes's results and my own show that *chairman* and *spokesman* are still the prevailing titles, there is evidence of changing usage, by comparison with older corpora from the 1960s and 1970s which show no use of the gender-unmarked *chair/spokesperson*, or the female forms *chair/spokeswoman*, *chairlady* and *Madam Chairman*. Again, the results here are rather gross, as it is not always clear from the small amount of context in the citations whether a man or a woman occupies the position. A more careful analysis would need to examine the context.

Looking at the first 50 examples of *chairperson*, however, shows that nearly half the uses were generic; that is, they referred to the office rather than a particular person holding it. Gender-specific uses were roughly equal for men and women. Again, papers such as *The Independent* as well as *The Daily Telegraph* provided many of the examples of reformed usage such as *chairwoman* and *chairperson*. However, again it is reference to women which exhibits the greatest variability. Only women can be referred to with all 5 titles. Most of the instances of *Madam Chairman* were drawn from a meeting of the Highways Committee of West Sussex Council. I have not looked at *Chair*, a form often used in American universities for a department head, but which usually has a different meaning in Britain.

The fact that terms such as *chairman* still predominate partly reflects the fact that it is still men who occupy most of the discourse space. Most chairpersons are in fact chairmen. Given society's preference for gendered titles, this means that gross counts of terms will always favor the male one.

3.3 Reforming English

Nevertheless, the changes brought about in the pronoun system in response to feminist activism of a type many would prefer to ignore are actually remarkable, considering that there have been virtually no major changes in the English pronouns since the Middle English period (1100–1500). Nowadays, authors feel compelled either to use reformed language or to explain their choice of traditional wording. For instance, Rod Ellis (1985) explains in the preface to his book that he uses the male pronouns in reference to *learner* and *teacher* as a "stylistic convenience" rather than as "unmarked forms". He extends his apologies to those readers who may find this convention unacceptable. Likewise, Wolfgang Klein (1986) informs his readers in his preface that there are female and male researchers, but for "simplicity's sake" he refers to them as *he*.

Merton College at the University of Oxford, formerly all male, recently inserted into its by-laws a statement to the effect that male pronouns included the female. This harks back to the so-called Abbreviation Act of Parliament in 1850 proposed to clarify the generic *man* and *he* so that "words importing the Masculine Gender shall be deemed and taken to include Females". Declaring women's supposed inclusion in this way does about as much to combat sexism as a sign saying "Negroes admitted" would do to combat racism (see Miller and Swift 1991). Indeed, John Stuart argued for the repeal of Parliament's Abbreviation Act in the following year for fear that it might inadvertently give women rights they should not have, such as the right to vote!

In the 1990s it has become increasingly difficult for linguists to avoid confronting the problem, as can be seen from examining texts such as the second edition of Hudson (1996), who feels the need both to reform and apologize for sexist usage in the first edition, which he says is "a source of great embarrassment" to him now. He claims he has tried to ensure that his text is "bias-free". As a sociolinguist, Hudson is perhaps more aware of the social implications of sexism.

Others, however, continue to try to avoid reform with lengthy justifications, such as can be seen in a footnote in Lass (1997:368) commenting on his use of generic *he*:

> In my variety of English (and my wife's as well!) *he* is the only pronoun usable for unselfconscious generic reference. Using *s/he* (which of course can't be pronounced: does anybody say 'ess-stroke-he'?) or *he or she* or *they* or whatever would count as an 'act' (a deliberate flouting of grammatical convention in this case); but use of generic *he* is not, since it's simply historically given, and I can't not use it (without a conscious decision of a type not at all characteristic of 'normal' change) and still be speaking 'my own language'. Like all normal speakers, I am bound by the historically given.

This attempt to ridicule reform efforts by suggesting that reformers are not "normal" and reformed usages run counter to the "natural/normal" development of language has a long history. The very necessity for such a long comment is ironically testimony to the efficacy of feminist consciousness-raising which makes it increasingly difficult for authors such as Lass to hide behind a false illusion of neutrality, and to claim that one has no choice because he is bound by the "historically given".

Choices do exist, however, and they are symbolic of different beliefs and political positions. Compare *Ms Johnson is the chair(person)* with *Miss Johnson is the chairman*. While a narrow linguistic analysis would say they mean the same thing and refer to the same person who happens to hold a particular position, choosing one over the other reveals approval or disapproval of, for example, feminism, language reform, political conservatism or liberalism, etc. There is no way to maintain neutrality now because the existence of an alternative forces a reevaluation of the old one. With several alternatives available a woman can sometimes be referred to on the same occasion as *Madam Chairman*, *chairperson* and *chairwoman,* as I heard one male conference moderator do all in the space of a few minutes without evidently being aware of it.

It is this very impossibility of neutrality which annoys New Zealand literary critic, C.K. Stead (1989:279):

> My own response to feminist demands for 'non-sexist' language was at first to ignore them. I felt that as a writer I had to defend my own sense of style against any and every encroachment. But as time has gone by the complainants have brought about what they said was the case all along. By insisting that the generic 'he' is not neuter but masculine, they have made it so; and so for a male writer to go on using it becomes a defiant act which may seem to signal all kinds of irrelevant and untrue things about himself – that he doesn't care about rape, beats his wife, thinks women inferior, and so on. I have therefore struggled (shall I say) manfully to avoid saying "the writer will find that he ...". It continues to be difficult; and for reasons which are still not clear to me, but have everything to do with English grammar and nothing to do with gender, I found it impossible and gave up the attempt [...]

In Canada, the UK and the US, there are also multiple meanings of *Ms* and its use has diffused unevenly. *Ms* is now indexical of a number of meanings, such as feminist orientation, divorced/separated/ single, or in de facto relationships.

3.4 Language reform in public and private discourse

When evaluating the success or failure of language reform, we must distinguish between public and private usage. The examples I have cited have shown that reform has affected public usage unevenly and not always in the ways reformers intended. During the 1970s and 1980s many institutions and organizations made serious efforts to eliminate sexist language in their documents. Publications ranging from the Bible to dictionaries and newspapers have begun to reflect the new usage. The US Department of Labor's former Manpower Administration has been renamed the Employment and Training Administration. The Department of Labor revised the titles of almost 3,500 jobs so that they are unmarked for gender. Thus, *steward* and *stewardess* are officially "out" and *flight attendant* is in. A *hat check girl* has become a *hat check attendant,* a *repairman* a *repairer,* a *maid* a *houseworker,* etc. The Australian government even has a linguist who acts as an adviser on sexism in its publications. The city of Honolulu adopted a set of guidelines on non-sexist usage prepared by the Committee on the status of women.

The *New York Times* stopped using titles like *Mrs* and *Miss* with the names of women. At first, it resisted the adoption of the new title *Ms*, but eventually the editor acknowledged that the *Times* believed it was now part of the language. The London *Times*, however, still uses androcentric forms such as *spokesman* and the titles *Mrs* and *Miss*, unless a woman has asked to be referred to as *Ms*. The *Los Angeles Times* has adopted guidelines suggesting alternatives to language that may be offensive to ethnic, racial and sexual minorities. Such differences in policy are signals of the social and political outlook of editors, who play important roles as gatekeepers in determining which forms they will adopt and thereby help sanction and spread.

In 1978 the *Washington Post* decided to use last names alone on second reference to a person, e.g. *Ellen Smith, named to a new position on the Board of Directors of Exxon Corporation, will join the company next week. Smith was one of several contenders for the job.* Previously, the paper would have referred to women with titles. After the change in policy, titled forms of this kind disappeared altogether. Other more subtle aspects of discrimination against women, however, were not the subject of policy change. For example, it is much more common for men to be referred to on first reference with their first and last names together with middle initial. This is much less likely to be the case for women. The addition of the initial, e.g. *Ellen P. Smith*, apparently suggests a more important person.

Professional organizations such as the National Council of Teachers of English and the American Psychological Association, along with major publishing houses such as Macmillan, McGraw Hill, Holt, Rinehart and Winston have also adopted guidelines for non-sexist usage. The National Council of Teachers of English deals with sexist language by authorizing the editor to return manuscripts submitted to its journal with a copy of the guidelines and a letter encouraging the author to rewrite the article. If an author refuses to make changes, the article is still printed with a note saying that the sexist language appears at the author's express stipulation.

Linguists have generally avoided any involvement in what they call prescriptivism, i.e. prescribing norms of language use, insisting instead that linguistics is a descriptive science. Fearing that it would lose credibility as a professional organization if it endorsed prescriptivism, the Linguistics Association of Great Britain, for instance, rejected a proposal to amend its constitution, to remove generic masculine pronouns and to rename the office of chairman. The Linguistic Society of America, on the other hand, has embraced reform and issued a set of guidelines as well as established a Committee on the Status of Women in Linguistics. This is another indication of conservatism in the UK concerning gender reform.

Such guidelines, however, for the most part affect only written language. In everyday conversation things may be otherwise. For example, although most US airlines have publicly replaced the term *stewardess* with *flight attendant*, I routinely hear Americans using the older term *stewardess*. British usage, both public and private, lags behind American usage in this domain too. For example, in the BNC the female marked form *stewardess* occurred 92 times along with *air hostess* 51 times, while the neutral *flight attendant* occurred only 8 times and *cabin crew* 13 times. I have observed many flight attendants on British Airways flights wearing name tags identifying them as *stewardesses* or *stewards*.

Studies by Rubin & Greene & Schneider (1994) have also measured a decline in sexist language in public discourse of business leaders in the US between the 1960s and 1980s. Significantly, the biggest decline occurred between the 1960s and 1970s, which predated the widespread introduction of public guidelines for non-sexist usage. Yet, men still used three to four times more gender-exclusive language than women. The study also indicated another problem for reformers; namely, that attitudes toward gender equality did not match language usage. Those who had adopted more gender-inclusive language did not necessarily have a more liberal view of gender inequities in language. This means that superficial changes such as a decline in the use of generic *man* and *he* observed in some studies have to be seen in the larger context. If male generic terms are simply replaced by gender-specific male terms, then reform is not really successful. Men and women are often still referred to in stereotypical ways. I recall hearing a male colleague very carefully saying both *he and she* when making generic references, and on occasions even saying *she* first, but in the same breath referring to the secretarial staff in his departmental office as *girls*.

Fatemeh Khosroshahi (1989) has some experimental evidence to support my suspicion that his reference to *girls* indicates that he has not really changed his mental imagery of women despite having reformed his public use of androcentric generics. Those who appear more egalitarian in their language are not necessarily so in their thoughts. Groups of undergraduate students at Harvard University who either had or had not reformed their usage in their written work were asked to draw pictures to go with sentences such as *an unhappy person could still have a smile on his/her (or her/their) face*. The findings showed that there were still more male images than female ones, regardless of the pronoun used, and regardless of whether the subject had reformed his/her written usage. However, only women who had reformed their usage produced more female images, and they did so for all three pronouns. Thus, even the men who had ostensibly reformed their usage had done so only superficially and were still androcentric in their thought patterns.

In some respects, this shows too that language reforms have had only limited success. Proposed for the most part by women, not surprisingly, it is women for whom they seem to have the greatest effect. Men take more convincing, but then they stand to lose more, and women to gain more from such reform. This example shows again how meaning is socially constructed in line with particular ideologies.

4.   Reforming discourse and rhetoric

In order to contribute to a feminist theory, linguists must examine more critically how these gendered ways of speaking produce rhetorical resources for creating a social reality in which women are subordinate and marginal. Eliminating the negative connotations in women's semantic space does nothing to increase their space. Men and their activities still take up more space and time in discourse. Eliminating sexist language does nothing to address this discrepancy. The use of some of the titles and terms of address examined here do more than discriminate against women, particularly when we examine them in context. We can see the effects of what Julia Penelope (1990) called a "patriarchal universe of discourse" (PUD).

In order for linguistic parity to be achieved, it would be necessary to oust not only all or most words referring to women, but also most words referring to men too, since the enhanced positive image of men in relation to women would also have to be removed from the language or neutralized. Otherwise, how could linguistic reform deal with seemingly gender-neutral words such as *aggressive* and *professional*, which have different connotations when applied to men as opposed to women without a change in our beliefs about men's and women's roles in society? To call a man a professional is a compliment. To be an aggressive male is acceptable and expected in society, but to be a woman and a professional is perhaps to be a prostitute, in English as well as in other languages as diverse as Japanese and French, where *une professionelle* is a euphemism for a prostitute. To be an aggressive female is undesirable because such a woman would pose a threat to men. Feminist activism for language reform is perceived as an attack on the primarily male defined moral and social order.

At the moment, gender-neutrality is not a recognized category. We can see this reflected in other aspects of society. When we speak of "unisex" clothing or styles, for instance, what is happening is not really a neutralization of gender-specific styles of dressing, hairstyles, etc., but an erasing of the distinction in favor of the masculine form. Thus, unisex fashions have fostered greater acceptability for women to wear trousers, and other items of clothing once regarded as for men only. They have not created a social climate of tolerance for men to wear skirts or dresses. Where there is pressure leading to a blurring of gender roles or distinctions, usually women seek to adopt male prerogatives, as is the case with some English-speaking women who prefer to be called *chairman*, or the editor of a major news magazine in France who objected to being called *la rédactrice* instead of *le rédacteur* lest people assume she was the editor of a women's magazine.

As Deborah Cameron points out (1985:90), "In the mouths of sexists, language can always be sexist." When gender-neutral terms or positive feminine terms are introduced into a society still dominated by men, these words either lose their neutrality or are de- or re-politicized by sexist language practices of the dominant group. The reinterpretation of the feminist term *Ms* is a good example of how women's meanings can be appropriated and depoliticized within a sexist system. The title *Ms* is being used in ways its proposers never intended, to maintain the very distinctions it was supposed to replace. This indicates the high premium that dominant institutions still place on defining women in terms of their relationships with men. Thus, the category of gender gets reconstituted and implemented in a different way with a different set of terms.

In the same way the intended gender-neutral term *chair* or *chairperson* has become in effect a marked term in opposition to *chairman*, which still remains the neutral and unmarked term, an androcentric generic. It is the woman occupying the position referred to by the title who gets singled out by the new term. Like biological reproduction, meaning is sexually reproduced, and until women figure out a way of reproducing meaning more androgynously, their intended meanings will be reversed.

As noted in Section 3, collocations serve to gender the way we think about space, and to transmit culturally entrenched stereotypes; men's space is public, in the work place, while women's place is private and in the home. Expressions such as *working mother, businessman, housewife*, etc., reinforce these divisions in our thinking, making it easier to accept as "natural" the exclusion of women from public life. They reflect the traditional wisdom embodied in the English proverbs: *A man's home is his castle*, and *A woman's place is in the home*.

Traditional norms dictate that the husband is breadwinner, while the wife is the breadbaker. This is reflected historically in the Old English words *hlāfweard* 'loafkeeper' and *hlǣfdige* 'loafkneader', which became modern English *lord* and *lady*, respectively. Language plays an active role in the symbolic positioning of women as inferior to men. It both constructs and perpetuates that reality, often in obvious ways, but at other times in subtle and invisible ways.

Discrimination against women is built into such divisions between the work place and home, between production and reproduction, all of which are reinforced by the way we talk about them. Not only in western cultures, but in other parts of the world, there has been a persistent misrecognition of women's work as somehow less than work. Only work done to produce a profit in the public sector counts as work and goes by the name of *work*. The "work" women do at home is invisible (or what Ivan Illich (1982) calls "shadow work"), unpaid, not counted in Gross National Product, and goes by the special name of *housework*. These themes can be seen in English in such terms as *working mother, career girl/woman*. Men have control not only of the marketplace, where the "real" work gets done, but also control over women's sexuality and their labor in the home. In France, until quite recently bakers' wives who sold bread all day long were classified as unemployed and received no pension. Their labor was expected as part of their wifely duties and therefore did not officially count.

Similarly, we have the *career woman* (or even *career girl*, as I heard Sarah Ferguson, the Duchess of York, referred to on the BBC news in 1992), but not the *career man*. Men by definition have careers, but women who do so must be marked as deviant. A man can also be a *family man*, but it would be odd to call a woman a *family woman*. Women are by definition family women. Significantly, in the BNC the expression *family man* occurs 94 times, and the corresponding *family woman* 4 times. Similarly, *career woman* occurs 48 times, *career girl* 10 times, and *career lady* once, but *career man* only 6 times, and *career boy* or *career gentleman* not at all. Expressions such as *career woman/lady/girl* count as two strikes against women. On the one hand, they suggest that as women, females can't be real professionals, while on the other, they suggest that as professionals, females can't be real women, unless of course, they are prostitutes! Not surprisingly, the term *business girl* used to be a slang term for a prostitute.

The expression *Lady of the House* is not matched by *Gentleman of the House*, but contrasts instead with *Man of the World*, another indication of the linguistic mapping of the division between the public and private spheres onto male and female, respectively. Indeed, the French equivalent of 'woman of the world' (*femme du monde*) carries the meaning of 'prostitute'. Looking at the BNC, for instance, we find 25 cases of *lady of the house*, 3 of *woman of the house* and none of *gentleman of the house*, and only 8 of *man of the house*. By contrast, there are 29 occurrences of *man of the world*, but only 12 of *woman of the world*. There are no cases of *lady/girl/gentleman/boy of the world*.

In a 1982 speech about the economy, then president Ronald Reagan blamed the recession on the increase in women in the work force: "… it is the great increase of the people going into the job market, and – ladies, I'm not picking on anyone but … because of the increase in women who are working today". By pointing the finger at "ladies", while disclaiming that he was "picking on anyone", he drew attention away from his own economic policies. His use of the term *lady* is a double whammy here. It is polite, in keeping with his claim that he's not "picking on anyone", but it's also intended to suggest that ladies should be ladies of the house and have no place in the work force. Ladies don't work – unless of course they are doing housework, which is not "real" work. Thus, there are no working ladies, only working women. Julia Penelope (1990: 36) once told a telephone caller who asked her if she was the *Lady of the house* that no ladies lived in her house.

The idea that a real lady does nothing was part and parcel of the Victorian construction of ladyhood at a time when conduct books spelled out what it was proper for ladies and gentlemen to do. Gentlemen's wives were ladies of leisure, not to be engaged in baking, brewing, tending the chickens and garden. In commenting on the considerable waste of talent and energy directed towards becoming a lady in this constrained sense, Margaretta Grey noted that "A lady, to be such, must be a mere lady, and nothing else" (Butler 1894: 288). Many writers such as Sarah Ellis (1839: 71) observed how deficient was the education given to women with its concentration on manners rather than matter, in show rather than substance, as Lynda Mugglestone (1995: 177) puts it. Since a woman's object in life was to please men, skills such as dancing, singing, how to enter and leave a carriage or room, were supposed to add to her attractiveness.

In the Jamaican novel *Lionheart Gal* (1986: 180–81) we find the contrast between the meaning of *lady* and *woman* similarly distinguished when a child relates how she used to play at being a market woman with a basket on her head. She stood under her grandmother's window calling out "Lady, you want anything to buy, Maam?" Her grandmother told her to come inside at once, and asked what she was doing. Upon hearing that she was playing the role of market woman, her grandmother reprimanded her. The girl asked what was wrong with "market ladies". Her grandmother replied, "Ladies? They are not ladies. They are women. Go and take a seat in your room."

When the British nation as a whole became more affluent during the Victorian era, with the gap between rich and poor filled in by the middle classes, the term *gentleman* became a term of social approval and moral approbation; *ladies* were of the middle class and *women* of the working class. Female students at Owens College in Manchester, for instance, were divided between *ladies* (taking a single course, presumably for pleasure only, since ladies would not need to do real work) and *women*, who were registered for examinations, which they needed for career purposes. This suggests at least one reason for the finding that there are no *ladies of the world*, but only *women of the world*, and conversely that the woman who stays at home is overwhelmingly referred to as the *lady of the house* rather than the *woman of the house*.

The term *girl* was also used during the late Victorian period to refer to adult women, as is clear in the title of the "Hammersmith Sculling Club for Girls and Men", set up in 1896 and concerned only with "working girls". Without a father who could support her or a husband who could elevate her status to that of lady, a working woman had only domestic service, governessing or prostitution as a livelihood.

Not surprisingly, many women feel that *lady* cannot be reclaimed. Women are so degraded and demeaned that even the polite euphemism and aristocratic title of *Lady* does not confer dignity on women. Nessa Wolfson and Joan Manes, for instance, give examples to show why *lady* is not interchangeable with *ma'am* and is therefore not a term of respect in American English (though in South Africa it is, in interchanges between so-called "colored" and white, where it marks asymmetries of power grounded in racism). The term *lady* is often uttered sarcastically, as in this exchange they recorded on the telephone between a female caller and a male respondent (Wolfson & Manes 1980: 89):

> Mr Jones?
> Yes, Ma'am?
> I'm calling for Jim Smith, who's running in the Democratic primary next Tuesday.
> Yes, ma'am.
> May I ask what you think of Mr Smith?
> I'll tell you Lady. I'm voting for Jim Brown.
> Well, thank you very much.
> Yes, ma'am.

This contrast between *lady* and *ma'am* explains why many women, myself included, do not want to be called ladies. The historical association of the terms *woman* and *lady* with different social classes may be partly behind the greater and more positive use of the term *lady* today in British English. Deborah Cameron (1995:46), however, reports that *Today* newspaper, a downmarket publication, has now banned the word *lady*, designating it as a "coy genteelism".

5. Conclusions

One finding which emerges from my comparison of British and American English is that the British variety lags in the implementation of many reforms such as the use of new titles like *Ms*. This is interesting in view of the fact that historians of American English and other colonial varieties of English have documented a phenomenon termed "colonial lag" (see Marckwardt 1958:59–80 and Görlach 1987). This refers to the more conservative character of colonial Englishes with respect to certain linguistic features. American English, for example, retains *fall* instead of *autumn*, and *gotten* as the past participle of *get*, etc., which became obsolete in British English.

Of course, not all features of colonial Englishes are retentions. Moreover, the fact that the United States is notable for being the only former British colonial possession to supersede the mother country in terms of its importance on the world scene makes it hardly surprising that American English should lead British English in instances of planned reform. Interestingly, with respect to French language reform, Fleischman (1994) observes that France lags behind other countries such as Canada and Belgium where French is also spoken. French-speaking Canadians have more readily accepted terms such as *professeure* 'female professor'.

However, the success of reform cannot be measured by simply noting the frequency of occurrence of new titles such as *Ms* or gender-unmarked forms such as *chair(person)*. Studies have shown that some of the new neutral terms are used in such a way as to perpetuate the inequalities expressed by the old gender-marked terms they are supposed to replace. Thus, for example, women are much more likely than men to be referred to as a *chairperson* or *salesperson* or even *Madame Chairperson*, or *Madame Chairman*, which is similar to the French *madame le juge*.

Notes

1. It is the conventionalization of the terms *mistress* and *master* as titles in the British educational system which made Geoffrey Warnock's (former Vice-Chancellor of Oxford University) remark so witty (at least by male standards) when his wife, a philosopher who at the time also held the title Dame of the British Empire, became head of Girton College, Cambridge: "Once I was married to a Dame; now I have a Mistress." Due to differences in social structure between the US and Britain, terms like *dame, lady* and *mistress* have somewhat different connotations in the two countries. The remark sounds much less witty to American women for reasons I explain in Section 4.

References

Baker, Sidney J. 1945. *The Australian language.* Melbourne: Sun.

Baron, Dennis. 1986. *Grammar and gender.* New Haven: Yale University Press.

British National Corpus. 1995. Oxford: Oxford University Computing Services.

Butler, Josephine. 1894. *Memoir of John Gray of Dilston.* Edinburgh.

Cameron, Deborah. 1985. *Feminism and linguistic theory.* London: Macmillan.

Cameron, Deborah. 1995. *Verbal hygiene.* London: Routledge.

Clyne, Michael, ed. 1992. *Different norms in different languages.* Berlin: Mouton de Gruyter.

Cooper, Robert L. 1984. "The avoidance of androcentric generics." *International Journal of the Sociology of Language* 50: 5–20.

Daly, Mary. 1987. *Webster's first new intergalactic wickedary of the English language conjured by Mary Daly in cahoots with Jane Caputi.* Boston: Beacon.

Ellis, Rod. 1985. *Understanding second language acquisition.* Oxford: Oxford University Press.

Ellis, Sarah S. 1839. *The women of England, their social duties, and domestic habits.* 3rd ed. London.

Fleischman, Suzanne. 1994. "Eliminating gender bias in French: A case of language ideologies in conflict". In *Cultural performances: Proceedings of the Third Berkeley Women and Language Conference,* eds. Mary Bucholtz & Anita C. Liang & Laurel Sutton & Caitlin Hines. Berkeley: Berkeley Women and Language Group, 187–196.

Fowler, Henry W. 1927. *A dictionary of Modern English usage.* Oxford: Clarendon.

Görlach, Manfred. 1987. "The colonial lag? The alleged conservative character of American English and other 'colonial' varieties". *English World-Wide* 8: 41–60.

Greer, Germaine. 1971. *The female eunuch.* London: Paladin.

Haraway, Donna J. 1991. *Simians, cyborgs, and women. The reinvention of nature.* New York: Routledge.

Hellinger, Marlis. 1990. *Kontrastive feministische Linguistik. Mechanismen sprachlicher Diskriminierung im Englischen und Deutschen.* München: Hueber.

Hudson, Richard A. 1996. *Sociolinguistics.* 2nd ed. Cambridge: Cambridge University Press.

Illich, Ivan. 1982. *Gender.* New York: Pantheon.

Khosroshahi, Fatemeh. 1989. "Penguins don't care, but women do: A social identity analysis of a Whorfian problem." *Language in Society* 18: 505–526.

Klein, Wolfgang. 1986. *Second language acquisition.* Cambridge: Cambridge University Press.

Lass, Roger. 1997. *Historical linguistics and language change.* Cambridge: Cambridge University Press.

Lionheart gal: Life stories of Jamaican women. 1986. eds. Sistren with Honor Ford Smith. London: The Women's Press.

Marckwardt, Albert H. 1958. *American English.* New York: Oxford University Press.

McLuhan, Marshall. 1989. *The global village: Transformations in world life and media in the 21st century.* Oxford: Oxford University Press.

Mencken, Henry L. 1919. *The American language.* New York: Knopf.

Miller, Casey & Kate Swift. 1991. *Words and women: New language in new times.* 2nd ed. New York: Harper Collins.

Mugglestone, Lynda. 1995. *'Talking proper'. The rise of accent as a social symbol.* Oxford: Oxford University Press.

Newman, Michael. 1998. "What can pronouns tell us? A case study of English epicenes." *Studies in Language* 22: 353–389.

Ostling, Richard N. 1992. "A somewhat less fatherly God." *Time.* Oct. 26:72.

Penelope, Julia. 1990. *Speaking freely: Unlearning the lies of the fathers' tongues.* New York: Pergamon.

Pusch, Luise F. 1984. *Das Deutsche als Männersprache.* Frankfurt am Main: Suhrkamp.

Quirk, Randolph & Sidney Greenbaum & Geoffrey Leech & Jan Svartvik. 1985. *A comprehensive grammar of the English language.* London: Longman.

Ramson, William S., ed. 1988. *The Australian national dictionary: A dictionary of Australianisms in historical perspective.* Melbourne: Oxford University Press.

Romaine, Suzanne. 1997. "Grammar, gender and the space in between." In *Communicating gender in context,* eds. Helga Kotthoff & Ruth Wodak. Amsterdam: Benjamins, 51–76.

Romaine, Suzanne. 1998. "Introduction". In *Cambridge history of the English language.* Vol. 4: *1776 to 1997,* ed. Suzanne Romaine. Cambridge: Cambridge University Press, 1–56.

Romaine, Suzanne. 1999. *Communicating gender.* Mahwah: Erlbaum.

Rubin, Donald L. & Kathryn Greene & Deirdra Schneider. 1994. "Adopting gender-inclusive language reforms. Diachronic and synchronic variation." *Journal of Language and Social Psychology* 13: 91–114.

Schulz, Muriel. 1975. "The semantic derogation of women." In *Language and sex: Difference and dominance,* eds. Barrie Thorne & Nancy Henley. Rowley, MA: Newbury House, 64–75.

Spender, Dale. 1980. *Man made language.* London: Routledge.

Stead, Christian K. 1989. *Answering to the language. Essays on modern writers.* Auckland, NZ: Auckland University Press.

Webster, Noah. 1828. *An American dictionary of the English language.* New York: Converse.

Wolfson, Nessa & Joan Manes. 1980. "Don't 'dear' me!" In *Women and language in literature and society,* eds. Sally McConnell-Ginet & Ruth Borker & Nelly Furman. New York: Praeger, 79–93.

Gender switch in Modern Hebrew

Yishai Tobin
Ben-Gurion University of the Negev, Israel

1. Introduction: Historical and sociolinguistic background

Modern Hebrew is also known as Israeli Hebrew, Contemporary Hebrew, and *Ivrit*.[1] It is the national language of the Jewish majority of the State of Israel and a second language for the Jews of the world (as well as the Arab minority residing in Israel). There are approximately 5 million speakers including about half a million who use Hebrew as a second language. The Hebrew language is usually divided into four major historical periods: (1) Classical or Biblical Hebrew (ca. 1200 B.C. – 200–300 B.C.); (2) Mishnaic or Rabbinical Hebrew (ca. 300 B.C. – A.D. 400–500); (3) Medieval Hebrew (ca. A.D. 500 – A.D. 1700); (4) Modern Hebrew (including the period of the Enlightenment and the revival of Hebrew in Israel (ca. A.D. 1700 to the present).[2]

Despite the wide spread of Jews throughout the world and the ingathering of the exiles in Israel with the multitude of mother tongues that they speak, Modern Hebrew is strikingly uniform in its dialects and varieties of usage, including both ethnic dialects used by Jews of African-Asian origin (known as Sepharadim) and European-American origin (known as Ashkenazim) as well as sociolinguistic and regional dialects. The cover term *Hebrew* includes all the historical varieties of the language, which form a fairly comprehensive continuum of a single, basically synthetic language, rather than what might be considered to be different languages, such as more synthetic Old English, opposed to a more analytic Modern English, a fact with significant implications for translation and crosslinguistic analysis (e.g. Aphek & Tobin 1988; Tobin 1989, 1990, 1994).

Like other Semitic languages, Hebrew has a structure fundamentally different from the Indo-European languages. In the Semitic languages, the isomorphic connections between phonology, morphology, syntax, and semantics are much more overt. The vast majority of the words of the language can be analyzed into consonantal roots signaling broad semantic fields; these roots are combined with fixed morphophonemic patterns for what are traditionally called nominal, verbal, and adjectival forms. More often than not, the connection and relations between the roots and these fixed morphophonemic patterns are transparent – certainly much more so than in English (Tobin 1994: chaps. 2–8).

Modern Hebrew is unique in that it is a language that has been successfully revived as a national vernacular, although most scholars agree that, as a language of scholarship, liturgy, business, correspondence, and other needs, it never suffered a real demise.[3] As may be expected with a language that – whether revived or not – is under constant linguistic scrutiny regarding its rich written legacy and its concurrent use as an everyday vernacular for a vibrant, multiethnic society, standardization, in the form of normative prescriptivism advocated by the powerful Hebrew Language Academy, is rampant.

Modern Hebrew has been referred to as a fusion language because it draws simultaneously on a number of linguistic sources, including Biblical, Mishnaic, Medieval and later literary sources, each of which contributed individually to the language prior to its revival. The strongest or most obvious influence the above facts have had on the language is in the lexicon, a phenomenon that has been referred to as the large-scale relexification of the language through extensive borrowing from both Jewish and contemporary European and other languages as well as from earlier Hebrew and Aramaic sources. Modern Hebrew has also been referred to as an immigrants' language because it was revived in the context of intense exposure to other languages that were spoken by Jewish immigrants who originally returned to prestate Israel. This original immigrants' language became the source for the language acquisition of subsequent generations born in Israel, whose own language has subsequently become a standard for new waves of massive immigration to the State of Israel up to and even today. Modern Hebrew, therefore, has contributed to the sociological complexity of what has been called the languages in contact situation, which is simultaneously accompanied by the prescriptive process of consolidating the norms of a revival language that is serving as a colloquial everyday vernacular. Thus it may be inferred that Modern Hebrew has been revived in extralinguistic circumstances resembling the birth of a creole language: i.e. one can identify the first generation of native speakers who had no other native speakers from whom to acquire their language. The revival of the Hebrew language has been considered both a great achievement and a strong necessity in Israeli society, which has great implications for the study of gender in general and gender switch or gender reversal in particular.

2. Grammatical gender in Modern Hebrew

Gender is inherent, integral, and ubiquitous in the structure of Hebrew. All Hebrew nouns have grammatical gender; they are either masculine or feminine. Adjectives, verbs, pronouns, inflected prepositions, and other word classes show agreement with the gender of the noun. It is generally considered that masculine morphology is unmarked and feminine morphology is marked.[4] Nouns and adjectives are inflected for gender (m/f) as well as number (sg/pl) with the suffixless (*zero*) masculine singular morphology as the unmarked base form. In addition to singular and plural nominal morphology, there is also a dual form which lacks gender distinctions.[5] Verbs and pronouns are inflected for gender, number and person (1st, 2nd, 3rd), although gender is not distributed symmetrically in the pronoun system: 1st person pronouns (both singular *ani* 'I' and plural *anaxnu* 'we') are not differentiated for gender while both 2nd person (*atah/at*) 'you' (m.sg/f.sg), *atem/aten* 'you' (m.pl/f.pl) and 3rd person (*hu/hi*) 'he/she', (*hem/hen*) 'they' (m.pl/f.pl) pronouns are differentiated for gender. Glinert (1994:5) adds: "The feminine plural pronouns *aten* [2nd person] and *hen* [3rd person] are rather formal and typical of newscasters, newspapers, books and so on. In casual usage, their masculine counterparts *atem* and *hem* are used instead" – an additional argument for the classification of the masculine forms as unmarked.

Compound nominal forms, numerals, and certain determiners and quantifiers are also inflected for gender and number. Even certain particles and prepositions are inflected for gender, number and person: e.g., *ein* 'there is not', a negative existential particle, is fully inflected: *eineni* 'I am not', *einxa* 'you (m.sg) are not', *einex* 'you (f.sg) are not', *eino/einenu* 'he is not', *eina/einena* 'she is not', *einenu* 'we are not', *einxem* 'you (m.pl) are not', *einxen* 'you (f.pl) are not', *einam* 'they (m.pl) are not', *einan* 'they (f.pl) are not'. Additional existential particles and prepositions that are inflected for number, gender, and person are discussed in Tobin (1982, 1991b). Both singular and plural feminine adjectival inflectional suffixes are also used as adverb forming devices (Ravid & Shlesinger 2000).

2.1 Masculine and feminine nouns

As was stated above, all nouns in Hebrew belong to one of two gender classes, masculine and feminine. The gender of animate and human nouns corresponds to "biological" gender while the gender assigned to inanimate nouns is considered to be arbitrary. According to Glinert (1994:6):

> "Every noun is either masculine or feminine. Such gender does not have very much to do with maleness and femaleness: although most nouns denoting a male or female are indeed masculine or feminine, respectively, nouns denoting *objects* are masculine or feminine without any apparent rhyme or reason."

The general and accepted productive rule is that singular masculine nouns lack a suffix or have a *zero* suffix – a reason why the masculine form is considered to be the base or the unmarked form – while feminine nouns add the suffix -*ah* or -*(i)t*: e.g. *sus* 'horse, stallion'/*sus-ah* 'mare', *saxkan* 'actor'/*saxkan-it* 'actress', *sheled* (m) 'skeleton (in all its senses), outline, framework, frame'/*shild-ah* (f) 'skeleton' (although obviously only a small number of inanimate nouns appear in gender-differentiated pairs). In the plural, the suffixes -*im* (m) and -*ot* (f) are added to the singular stem or slightly phonetically altered singular forms: e.g. *sus-im* 'horses, stallions'/*sus-ot* 'mares', *saxkan-im* 'actors'/*saxkan-iot* 'actresses', *shlad-im* 'skeletons, outlines, frameworks, frames'/*shild-ot* 'skeletons'.

I would like to take issue with the claim that grammatical gender assignment is arbitrary. There is a rapidly developing literature in sign-oriented and cognitive linguistics that seeks to "make sense" of, or to find a motivation for, what is generally considered to be the arbitrariness of gender assignment and noun classification (e.g. Contini-Morava 1996, in press; Jakobson 1963; Morris 1991; Otheguy 1977; van Schooneveld 1977; Zubin 1984; Zubin & Köpcke 1981, 1984, 1986a, b). Furthermore there is a limited number of "bi-gender" or common gender nouns (epicene nouns) which are both masculine and feminine: e.g. *derex* 'way, road', *ruax* 'wind, spirit', *shemesh* 'sun', *etsem* 'bone, substance, essence'. In addition, there are some exceptions, such as singular feminine nouns having a *zero* suffix: e.g. *yad* 'hand, arm', *ez* 'ewe'; and singular masculine nouns ending in *-ah* or *-(i)t*, e.g. *sherut* 'service'. There are many exceptions in the plural forms as well: e.g. the plural of the masculine *shulxan* 'table' is *shulxanot* 'tables'; the plural for the feminine *shanah* 'year' is *shanim* 'years'. However, the intrinsic gender of the noun with the corresponding agreement is maintained, and *shulxanot* remains masculine and *shanim* remains feminine, despite their irregular endings. The question remains whether these "exceptions" are arbitrary or not. Just like gender assignment may not be arbitrary, it may very well be that this "irregular" plural gender switch may have some semantic, cognitive, or other motivation. These gender-reversed plural forms in the Hebrew lexicon have been dealt with descriptively by Schwarzwald (1991) and still remain an open question worthy of future research.

2.2 Gender agreement

There is obligatory gender and number agreement between nouns and the adjectives, verbs and certain other forms that relate to them. Gender agreement for nouns, adjectives, and ("present tense") verbs is illustrated using the lexical items for 'horse', 'good', and 'gallop' in examples (1 a–d):

(1) a. *ha-sus*　　　　　*ha-tov*　　　　　*doher.*
　　　　DET-horse.MASC.SG DET-good.MASC.SG gallops.MASC.SG
　　　　'The good horse gallops.'

　　b. *ha-sus-ah*　　　*ha-tov-ah*　　　*doher-et.*
　　　　DET-horse-FEM.SG DET-good-FEM.SG gallops-FEM.SG
　　　　'The good mare gallops.'

　　c. *ha-sus-im*　　　*ha-tov-im*　　　*dohar-im.*
　　　　DET-horse-MASC.PL DET-good-MASC.PL gallop-MASC.PL
　　　　'The good horses gallop.'

　　d. *ha-sus-ot*　　　*ha-tov-ot*　　　*dohar-ot.*
　　　　DET-horse-FEM.PL DET-good-FEM.PL gallop-FEM.PL
　　　　'The good mares gallop.'

As may be seen in these examples, the gender and number suffixes for nouns and adjectives are generally the same and reflect the same markedness relationship: *zero* (m.sg), *-ah* (or *-(i)t*) (f.sg), *-im* (m.pl), *-ot* (f.pl); for the feminine singular present tense verb the suffix is *-et*.

Verbs generally agree with their subject in gender, number, and person. The "present tense" forms (which are historically participle/adjectival forms) distinguish masculine from feminine and singular from plural but are neutral to person like nominal and adjectival forms:

(2) *ani/atah/hu*   *kam*   'I/you/he get(s) up'   (MASC.SG)
     ani/at/hi   *kamah* 'I/you/she get(s) up'   (FEM.SG)
     anaxnu/atem/hem   *kamim* 'We/you/they get up'   (MASC.PL)
     anaxnu/aten/hen   *kamot* 'We/you/they get up'   (FEM.PL)

Note that in the 2nd person singular it is the feminine which is unmarked (*at* 'you') while the masculine is marked (*atah* 'you'). The "past"[6] and "future"[7] tenses (originally perfective and imperfective aspects also called "prefix" and "suffix tenses") do distinguish 1st, 2nd, and 3rd person:

Table 1. Past tense forms in Modern Hebrew

Person	Singular	Plural
1 masc/fem	*ani kamti*	*anaxnu kamnu*
	'I got up'	'we got up'
2 masculine	*atah kamta*	*atem kamtem*
	'you got up'	'you got up'
2 feminine	*at kamt*	*aten kamten*
	'you got up'	'you got up'
3 masculine	*hu kam*	*hem kamu*
	'he got up'	'they got up'
3 feminine	*hi kamah*	*hen kamu*
	'she got up'	'they got up'

The imperative has three (or four) suffixes, i.e. the same suffixes as the 2nd person future tense, but without its prefixes for gender and number:

Table 2. Future tense forms in Modern Hebrew

Person	Singular	Plural
1 masc/fem	*ani akum*	*anaxnu nakum*
	'I'll get up'	'we'll get up'
2 masculine	*atah takum*	*atem takumu*
	'you'll get up'	'you'll get up'
2 feminine	*at takumi*	*aten takumu*
	'you'll get up'	(*aten takomna*)
		'you'll get up'
3 masculine	*hu yakum*	*hem yakumu*
	'he'll get up'	'they'll get up'
3 feminine	*hi takum*	*hen yakumu*
	'she'll get up'	(*hen takomna*)
		'they'll get up'

Table 3. Imperative forms in Modern Hebrew

Gender	Singular	Plural
masculine	*kum*	kumu
	'get up!'	'get up!'
feminine	*kumi*	*kumu* (*komna*)
	'get up!'	'get up!'

As may be seen in Tables 1–3, the markedness relationship between unmarked singular masculine forms and marked feminine and plural forms holds for verb morphology as well.

2.3 Generic masculines

Masculine plural forms are used generically for inanimate, animate, and human plural subjects, i.e. a sentence with a complex subject containing nouns of both genders will have masculine plural agreement throughout. Thus, for humans and animates in general, the masculine plural forms indicate groups of males and females as well as all-male groups, while feminine plural forms are restricted to all-female groups – another argument for the unmarked status of the masculine forms. Example (3) illustrates the use of the masculine plural generic for inanimate nouns:

(3) *ha-sefer*   *ve-ha-maxberet*
DET-book.MASC.SG and-DET-notebook.FEM.SG
nimtsaim   *kan.*
are.found.MASC.PL here
'The book and the notebook are here.'

The use of the masculine generic for non-human animates is found in example (1c) where *susim* could refer to either 'horses' in general or to 'stallions' only, while example (1d) *susot* can only refer to 'mares'. Example (4) illustrates the masculine generic for humans using the masculine plural pronoun *hem* 'they' as a "present tense copula", the masculine plural noun *yeladim* 'boys, children', and a masculine plural adjective *tovim* 'good', to refer to a girl and a boy:

(4) *yael*   *ve-xaim*   *hem*
yael.FEM.SG and-haim.MASC.SG they.MASC.PL
yelad-im   *tov-im.*
child-MASC.PL. good-MASC.PL
'Yael and Haim are good children.'

In all-female groups, a choice between the marked feminine plural forms or the masculine generic has to be made. The author, for example, teaches a university course for speech pathologists which is usually composed exclusively of women (although there were two or three classes with one or two male students in attendance). The presence of only one male student facilitated the consistent use of the unmarked masculine generic, while in all-female classes, the author finds that both he and the female students alternate marked feminine plural forms with the unmarked masculine generic plural when referring to the all-female class. Marked feminine plural forms are used more consistently in non-coeducational religious schools and in army basic training courses for women soldiers where a separate and exclusively all-female population is a mandatory prerequisite. Singular generics for unknown or unspecified gender are usually masculine but can also be marked for gender depending on the speaker or context: (e.g., both *mishehu* 'someone, somebody', m.sg, versus *mishehi* 'someone, somebody', f.sg, can be used for singular generics for an unknown or unspecified person, but the masculine form is the more familiar or unmarked one).

According to Mira Ariel (p.c.), the question of how masculine generics are interpreted and accepted has not really been examined for Hebrew. Published and unpublished psycholinguistic studies are conflicting. Advertisements for student jobs written with feminine forms had no male responses and fewer women responded to ads written with masculine forms in a study by Ariela

Friedman. On the other hand, studies by Shoshana Ben Zvi-Mayer and others found that children interpret masculine forms both generically as well as male-only. The literature on masculine generics, female/male discourse and other feminist and gender issues in Hebrew is rather meager (e.g. Ariel 1986, 1988, 1990: chap. 9.2; Ariel & Giora 1998a, 1998b; Muchnik 1992) and there is very little written in English.

This brief description of the distribution of gender forms in the major parts of speech in Hebrew should suffice to show that Hebrew is a highly synthetic language richly inflected for gender. In this respect, it resembles Arabic (cf. Hachimi, this vol.). I have limited this survey to the major parts of speech only: nouns (pronouns), adjectives, and verbs. I have omitted the nominal construct forms (*smixut*), the determiners and quantifiers, the prepositions and particles, and the numerals which are also inflected for gender, some of which I have discussed elsewhere (Tobin 1982, 1991b, 1995, 2000). The existential particles, because of their alternative inflectional paradigms (one for number and gender only and one for number, gender and person), and the numerals, because of their irregular reversed-gender inflectional morphology, (the feminine numerals are the base or unmarked forms without suffix or with *zero* suffix and the masculine numerals receive the *-ah* suffix) are not only of particular interest linguistically, but also for their longrange sociolinguistic implications concerning actual language use versus prescriptive norms (Glinert 1994: 16–17, Tobin 1997: chap. 5).

3. "Call me Yigal": Gender switch, gender reversal, cross addressing[8]

A particularly interesting aspect of what I refer to with the interchangeable terms *gender switch, gender reversal,* and/or *cross addressing* in Israeli Hebrew is the following phenomenon: males will address close female friends, relatives, associates, and partners using masculine pronouns and verb morphology as a sign of affection, intimacy, and solidarity. Furthermore, close female friends, relatives, and associates will also refer to themselves and others, and address each other, using masculine forms in a similar manner. More often than not, these instances of gender reversal are accompanied by a rise in pitch and/or an intonation pattern associated with "baby talk" or other instances of affection-ate and intimate speech. This use of masculine forms as a sign of affection, intimacy, and solidarity has been recorded in literary (both contemporary prose and poetry) as well as spoken Hebrew. Example (5) is taken from a contemporary novel, *xayei ahava* 'Love Life' (Shalev 1997), where the female narrator employs and describes gender reversal as it takes place. The scene is a couple in bed, and presents and defines her reflexive, gender-switched self-reference, and his gender-switched, cross-addressing pillow talk to her during special, intimate moments:

(5) [...] *ve-hu nitsmad   elai   me-axor*
     [...] and-he joined.MASC.SG to.me from-behind
     ve-sha'al: mah amarta,   be-rega'im
     and-asked.MASC.SG what you.said.MASC.SG in-moments
     ka-eileh   hayinu shneinu   ovrim
     like-these we.were two.us.MASC.PL pass.MASC.PL
     le-lashon   zaxar, ve-ani amarti ani ayef,
     to-language male   and-I said.I I   tired.MASC.SG
     axbarosh, ve-hu   amar,   az   tishan,
     rat   and-he said.MASC.SG then you.will.sleep.MASC.SG
     xafarpur, maxar   atah   maflig   el
     little.mole tomorrow you.MASC.SG sail.MASC.SG toward
     ever   ha-nahar.
     across DET-river
     (Shalev 1997: 175)
     '[...] and he clung to me from behind and asked: what **did you say** (m.sg), **at moments like these we would both** (m.pl) **switch over** (m.pl) **to masculine forms (male language)**, and I said I'm **tired**, (m.sg) rat, and he said, then **sleep**, (m.sg) **little mole** (m.sg), tomorrow **you** (m.sg) **are sailing** (m.sg) across the river.'

Gender reversal of this type has been recognized across many diverse languages: certain lexical items originally used to address males only have extended their use to designate both mixed groups as well as females, by both male and female speakers: e.g. *guys/man* (American English); *hombre* (Spanish); *jongens* 'boys, kids, guys' (Dutch); *mecs* 'boys, kids, guys' (French); *gē* 'older brother', *gē merr* 'you guys' (Mandarin Chinese). In Swahili, a woman may call another woman (of the same age or younger) *bwana* 'sir', *baba* 'father' or *babu* 'grandfather' as a term of endearment. The opposite never happens, you may not call a boy *mama* 'mother' or *bibi* 'madam' (Ellen Contini-Morava and Elena Bertoncini, p.c.). The fact that this kind of gender reversal, or the extension of male forms to the realm of females, has a positive connotation but the extension of female forms to males may often have the opposite effect, has also been attested to in Hebrew, Arabic (Wilmsen in press), Japanese (Jugaku 1979, Reynolds 1997), and Russian (Yokoyama 1999) both in the lexicon and in grammar. Crossing gender lines in both directions for various communicative and pragmatic purposes with both positive and negative connotations has been documented for Polish, Tsova-Tush, and Grebo (Corbett 1991:322–323), Brazilian Portuguese (Kulick 1998); Hindi (Hall & O'Donovan 1996), and Lakhota (Trechter 1995), and has been reported for Romanian, Amharic, Serbian and other languages by native speakers.

Wilmsen (in press) supports Ferguson's (1964:106) claim that gender reversal may have originated, and commonly occurs in Arabic baby talk as a mark of affection; and then lists some of its major uses: (1) to establish, maintain, and express intimacy, (2) to protect or conceal the reputation of the referee or the referent, (3) to banter with same-sex cohorts, (4) to coarsely joke about the opposite sex. Wilmsen further states that gender switch may exemplify a conscious attempt to obliterate status differences: i.e. a deliberate manipulation of the gender capacity of Arabic for the purpose of dissimulation. Some women informants maintain that they use it amongst themselves deliberately to level the status differences between men and women. There is a similar use of gender switch in Japanese: Reynolds (1997) and Jugaku (1979) elaborate on the conscious use of *boku* 'I' (male) by female Japanese junior high school students rather than *watasi* 'I' (female) as a means to successfully compete with boys in class, in games, or in fights. According to Corbett (1991:322–323) gender switch is a common secondary function in a wide range of languages: (1) to show the attitude of the speaker, (2) to mark status, (3) to show respect or a lack of it, and (4) to display affection.

The following instances of gender reversal are taken from informal conversations in a family composed of native Israeli Hebrew-speaking parents, a 14-year-old son, and two non-identical twin sisters aged 8.5 years who are clearly distinguished in size as the "bigger" and "smaller" twin. It is the "smaller" twin who is referred to most often with gender switch both reflexively and reciprocally, both by herself and others. The following examples illustrate the use of cross addressing accompanied by a rise in pitch and/or an appropriate familiar intonation pattern as a sign of affection, intimacy, and solidarity within the family interaction.

Example (6) presents the "smaller" twin referring to herself with a masculine form while asking her grandmother to take care of her before her "bigger" sister whom she refers to with the feminine form, thus trying to focus on herself and create an intimate and affectionate solidarity with her grandmother in order to get her own way:

(6) *ki   hi gdolah   ve-ani katan.*
     because she big.FEM.SG and-I little.MASC.SG
     'because she's big and I'm **little**.'

Example (7) is taken from a conversation between the twin sisters, who were sent to their rooms as punishment. They both switch gender while addressing each other as a sign of camaraderie or solidarity as they negotiate how to deal with their uncomfortable situation:

(7) a. *rotseh   lesaxek?*
         want.MASC.SG to.play
         '**Ya wanna** play?'

     b. *lo, aval tixtov   mixtav le-aba*
         no but write.MASC.SG letter   to-daddy
         ve-tivakesh   slixa
         and-ask.MASC.SG sorry
         'No, but **write** a letter to Daddy and **apologize**.'

Example (8) shows how the twin sisters cross address each other when they want to trade two different presents they have just received. Neither of them wants to openly admit that she prefers the other's gift, but this covert element in the message is accomplished by their switching to the more intimate, affectionate, and conspiratorial masculine forms:

(8) a. *rotseh   lehitxalef?*
         want.MASC.SG to.trade
         '**Ya wanna** trade?'

     b. *lo ixpat li,   ata   rotseh?*
         no care to.me you.MASC.SG want.MASC.SG
         'I don't care, do **you want to**?'

On the opposite pole of intimacy, affection, and solidarity, even when the twins argue, they employ gender reversal when directing insults at each other:

(9) *metumtam!   mefager!   tafsik!*
     moron.MASC.SG retard.MASC.SG stop.MASC.SG
     bo   kvar!
     come.MASC.SG already
     'Moron! Retarded! Stop it! Come on already!'

In example (10), the twins are taking a shower together, and the mother announces that she is leaving. The smaller twin calls her sister *Tutu*, a pet name,

and cross addresses her when requesting her protection. When the mother
announces that she is still in the room, the smaller twin replies that she just asked
'him' (a 3rd person masculine reference to the bigger sister!) to take care of her:

(10) a. *tutu, **tishmor**   alai!*
          tutu take.care.MASC.SG on.me
          'Tutu, **take care** of me!'

      b. *ani od kan.*
          I   still here
          'I'm still here.' (the mother)

      c. *rak amarti **lo***
          only told.I to.him.MASC.SG
          *she-**yishmor**   alai.*
          that-he.will.take.care.MASC.SG of.me
          'I only told **him** that **he take care** of me.'

Example (11) illustrates the father's use of gender reversal when affectionately
chiding his smaller twin daughter for being too slow, and then he returns to the
feminine imperative form to urge her on.

(11) *mah karah   she-**atah**   iti   kol-kax*
      what happened that-you.MASC.SG slow.MASC.SG all-such
      ha-yom? nu tizdarzi   kvar!
      DET-day well hurry.up.FEM.SG already
      'What happened that **you** are so **slow** today? Well hurry up already!'

Examples (12a, b) also illustrate instances of cross addressing in the context of
the smaller twin entreating her bigger sister to accompany, or protect her when
she is wary of doing something alone. In (12a) the entire family is on the second
floor of the house; it is already evening and the house is dark; and she wants to
go downstairs but is afraid. Once again, we have the use of the pet name, *Tutu*,
plus gender reversal. It is also interesting to note that she uses the same idiom
bo kvar! 'come on already' that was used in example (9) during their argument,
thus lending further support to the inherent intimacy of both these interactions.
In (12b), the entire family is downstairs and have asked the smaller twin to go
upstairs alone. She switches to the masculine form when proposing that her
bigger sister join her:

(12) a. *tutu, **bo**   iti   kvar.*
          tutu come.MASC.SG with.me already
          'Tutu, come with me already.'

b.   *tutu, atah*   *maskim*   *lavo*
tutu you.MASC.SG agree.MASC.SG to.come
iti   *le-ma'alah*
with.me to-above
'Tutu, **do you agree** to come upstairs with me?'

In example (13) the father is telling the smaller twin what she was like as a baby. During the entire conversation he addresses her with feminine forms save for one instance of gender switch when he tells her that she had to remain in the hospital alone (a very emotionally charged topic!) in order to become stronger before they could take her home:

(13)   *ki*   *hayita*   *tsarix*
because you.were.MASC.SG necessary.MASC.SG
lehitxazek   *ktsat*
to.become.strong little
'Because **you had to** become a little stronger.'

The older brother, when he was younger, would use gender reversal almost exclusively with the smaller twin (who was less of a threat to him than her bigger sister). He would only use it for the bigger twin when he needed her to further his own interests: e.g. to get her to play, or to get her involved with, or to participate in, something that would also include the smaller twin. The following exchange between the older brother and the smaller twin exemplifies an instance of affectionate gender switch. The brother has prepared her dinner and is watching her eat, and in an extended moment of quiet and total concentration on the food, the brother (in a very gentle and soft tone) says:

(14)   *ta'im*   *lexa?*
delicious.MASC.SG to.you.MASC.SG
'**Do you like** it?'

Example (15) is an instance of self-referential gender reversal by the bigger twin who generally uses it much less. The context: a Friday night when she is the only child in the house (a rare occurrence in a family with three children, two of whom are twins). She utters the following with a "baby talk" intonation pattern when her parents ask her to go to bed:

(15)   *aval ani lo* **ayef,**   *ani rotseh*
but I   no tired.MASC.SG I   want.MASC.SG

lehishaer itxem.
to.stay   with.you
'But I'm not **tired**, I **want** to stay with you.'

There are several unanswered questions concerning the choice of *masculine* forms to correlate with affection, intimacy, and solidarity which probably are not related to the unmarked grammatical status of masculine morphology. It is well-known that in certain languages "formal", "deferential", or "polite" 2nd person singular (and plural) forms of address are synchronically identical with singular 3rd person feminine forms: e.g. *lei* 'she/her', (formal) 'you' in Italian (Joseph Davis, p.c.) or *sie* 'she/her', *Sie* '(formal) you' in German. In the case of Italian and German, as well as in the cases of gender reversal cited in this chapter, it is the *feminine* form that correlates with a lack of openness and familiarity, or (what is referred to as male!) bonding. Hofstadter (1997) credits this to societies in which boys enjoy more freedom than girls and may therefore constitute a privileged class, while girls may be more restricted. Thus, masculine forms associated with closeness and camaraderie, when extended to females, may reflect what he calls "freeness envy". This concept of "freeness envy" supports the inherent desirability of masculine attributes which also bestows them with a positive connotation. Therefore, it is not by chance that Golda Meir, while serving in various governments and as Prime Minister of Israel, was constantly complimented with familiar gender reversal idioms like: *yesh lah beitsim* 'she has balls', and was lauded as *ha-gever ha-yexid ba-memshala* 'the only man in the government'. By the same token, the reverse direction of cross addressing, referring to males with feminine forms, has been reported to be either non-existent, or less frequent, and oftentimes pejorative in many of the languages previously discussed (cf. Yokoyama 1999).

Morris (1991, 2000) in her studies of non-sexually motivated usage of animate pronouns for inanimates in English, i.e. the use of *she* or *he* for inanimate referents, discovered a clear-cut pattern that may have implications for the phenomenon of gender switch, gender reversal, or cross addressing:

> "The feminine pronoun is used when the referent being evoked is behaving in a manner which is salient but which falls within the realm of what might be expected or predicted. The masculine is used for referents whose behaviour is also salient, standing out from the speaker's experience of that type of referent, but in an essentially unpredictable manner. Thus we find ourselves with two different forms of otherness, one predictable and one unpredictable. If this opposition is expressed in spatial terms, it could be said that the feminine gender is perceived to occupy a space whose limits can be clearly

defined. The masculine, on the other hand, occupies a space whose limits cannot be clearly defined.

The next step is to see how this explanation fits with the numerous cases in which sex seems to play a deciding role in pronominal gender attribution. It could be argued that there is a reasonable match. In purely spatial terms, the male sex is the greater force of the two and therefore the less controllable and the less likely to be contained in a clearly defined sphere of influence or activity. Given that the roots of the system of gender are lost in time, no further proof can be offered that this is indeed the case. However, it can be argued that this view of gender has a great deal of explanatory power as far as pronominal gender use is concerned since it accounts for all of the examples studied, including more than 1500 "exceptions" to the natural gender hypothesis." (Morris 2000: 12)

If we view gender switch, gender reversal, and cross-addressing as another "exception" to the normal use of gender forms, Morris's spatial perception of the greater force of male gender, its being less controllable and less likely to be contained, etc. – which can be linked to Hofstadter's concept of "freeness envy" – may serve as a basis for the extension of masculine forms for intimacy, affection, and solidarity in Modern Hebrew as well as in other languages.

4.   The implications of grammatical gender for language use

It should be clear that, structurally speaking, gender (biological and grammatical) is almost always present at all levels of word and utterance formation in Modern Hebrew. For example: encoders (speakers/writers) of Hebrew must always choose appropriate gender and number verb forms to refer to themselves and others. Simultaneously, they must also be aware of, or at least make conscious or unconscious decisions concerning the gender (and the number and person) of the real and/or potential decoders (hearers/readers/addressees), i.e. the audience to whom their communication is directed also by having to choose appropriate forms of verb morphology for all the tenses, aspects and moods. Not only is referential gender expressed by grammatical gender, but this grammatical category is also extended to all inanimate nouns and is thus part and parcel of the language structure. Therefore, the structure of Hebrew, potentially and almost invariably, requires gender categorization on all levels of language at all times and under all circumstances, and thus, inherently, most discourse is gendered.

However, in practice, not all social discourse is gender-specific and various attempts are made to neutralize gender as well. The unmarked status of the masculine forms reflected in the *zero* morphology of the masculine singular morphology across most, if not all categories and parts of speech (save for the numerals and second person singular pronouns), the generic use of masculine plural forms for mixed groups, and the total (or partial) syncretism of plural 2nd and/or 3rd person gender morphology in the past and future tenses and imperatives makes these masculine forms the most efficient and frequent way of "neutralizing" gender.

A similar (or opposite) phenomenon may be found in choosing gender forms to designate professions which are stereotypically gender-favored: e.g., *axot* 'nurse', literally 'sister', where a male nurse will be called an *ax* 'brother', but that same male nurse, or *ax*, may take his break in the *xadar axayot* 'nurses' room' (f.pl); a *ganenet* 'kindergarten teacher' (f.sg) versus *ganan* 'gardener' (m.sg) potentially leaves the issue of what to call a 'male kindergarten teacher' (*ganenet/ganan*?) or a 'female gardener' (*ganan/ganenet*?) open, etc. One of the ways of solving the problem is to use both forms in the plural: *xadar axim ve-axayot* 'nurses (m.pl) and (f.pl) room' which could be considered to be quite a mouthful; and for most professions, there are distinct gender-specific forms: e.g. *moreh/morah* 'teacher' (m/f), *rofe/rofah* 'doctor' (m/f), *orex/orexet din* 'lawyer' (literally a nominal construct meaning 'arranger-law') (m/f), with masculine generic plurals: *morim/rofim/orxei din* 'teachers'/'doctors'/'lawyers'. It should also be noted, that according to Connors (1971:598), there is generally no facetious or derogatory connotation for the Hebrew (and Russian) words designating female occupations (except when referring to males facetiously, Y. T.) which she credits to the structure of Israeli (and former Soviet) society.

The orthographic system of Modern Hebrew has also been used in attempts to avoid the neutralization of gender through the use of the unmarked masculine singular *zero* form. The Hebrew writing system, a syllabary based on consonants only, requires the reader to actively fill in the missing vowels of words according to context. Thus, the English sentences *The man/men/moon went home* or *The men want home/ham/him* would all be rendered in an English version of this syllabic consonantal orthography as: *TH MN WNT HM*. In many official government or other documents, sets of instructions, etc., the feminine singular imperative suffix (*-i*) (written with the consonant /y/) is added (after a slash or within parentheses) to the suffixless/ *zero* masculine singular imperative in order to include both male and female addressees equally. Due to the fact that the internal vowel variation distinguishing these gender specific imperatives is not captured by the Hebrew consonant-only syllabic writing system, one can therefore read the tri-consonantal root *KTV* 'write' in these alternative gender (m.sg vs. f.sg) imperative forms written on the documents *KTV/Y* as both *KToV/KiTVi* 'write!' (m.sg/f.sg), according to whether the reader is male or female. In short, the unmarked status of the masculine singular form (without suffix or with *zero* suffix) and the syncretized masculine plural forms make them suitable iconically for neutralizing gender, but their inherent masculine meaning has also inspired the inclusion of marked feminine forms in written and spoken discourse to give females equal status socially and linguistically.

Notes

1. Cf. Berman (1978: 1–4); Glinert (1989: 1–5); Rosén (1977: 15–24), reviewed in Tobin (1998).

2. On the history of Hebrew cf. Harshav (1993), Kutscher (1982), Sáenz-Badillos (1993); English-Hebrew dictionaries are The Oxford English-Hebrew dictionary (1996), Ben-Abba (1994); the standard grammar of Hebrew is Glinert (1994).

3. The so-called revival of Modern Hebrew has been the subject of much research; the "revival" itself and its implications for the highly prescriptive attitudes towards language prevalent in Israel are discussed in Tobin (1997: chap. 5).

4. The term markedness is used in the structural, sign-oriented sense of Roman Jakobson and the Prague School (e.g. Andrews & Tobin 1996; Battistella 1996 (reviewed in Tobin 1998); Tobin 1988, 1989, 1993) regarding both the iconicity of the marked and unmarked forms as well as the asymmetrical relationship found in their invariant meanings.

5. Unlike the morphemes for singular and plural, which are differentiated for gender, there is only one dual suffix *-ayim* which is neutral to gender, one of the descriptive facts which has led scholars to consider it to be an historical lexical remnant of the language rather than a full-fledged member of the grammatical system of number (Glinert 1989: 450–456, Rosén 1977: 165); a hypothesis disputed in Tobin (1990: chap. 5, Tobin 1994: 45–66, Tobin 2000) who views the dual number as a part of a continuum spanning the opposition between lexicon and grammar.

6. The reader will note that the third person plural forms are syncretized for gender in the past tense (the *-u* suffix is a masculine (or common gender) suffix, as may be seen later in the future and imperative forms, thus providing an additional argument for the unmarked status of masculine morphology).

7. The reader will also note that there is a syncretization in the plural of 2nd and 3rd person masculine and feminine forms in the future, both taking the unmarked masculine inflected forms. I have included the feminine plural inflected forms (which are considered to be "formal") in square brackets to the paradigm. Glinert (1994: 25) says: "Note: In elevated style, a special form may be used for the feminine 2nd and 3rd person plural (one form for both):

t...nah, e.g. *takomna* 'they will arise'. We disregard it here. It is listed in traditional grammars". The use of these forms will be discussed in Section 2.3 on masculine generics.

8. *Yigal* is a boy's name in Hebrew. The phrase "Call me Yigal" is taken from the conversation of one of two non-identical female twins from whom our data on gender switch, gender reversal, or cross addressing were taken. I would like to thank my graduate student, Hadas Aniv, the mother of the twins, who provided the examples in this section. The term "Cross Addressing" is a deliberate pun (based on the term "cross dressing") for the phenomenon of gender switch or gender reversal employed by David Wilmsen (in press). It should be remembered that we are not including gender reversal in the speech of the gay community (which is used both with positive-endearing and negative-pejorative connotations) (cf. Rudes & Healy 1979) in the present paper. Nor are we discussing the common cross-cultural and cross-linguistic phenomenon of biological males engaging in "feminine" behaviors of various kinds to regularly address one another using feminine forms, for example transvestites or drag queens (Barrett 1995). Gender switch in Hebrew for speakers of various generations has been attested to and verified in personal and e-mail communications by Hadass Sheffer (University of Pennsylvania), Rutie Adler (Berkeley), Shlomo Izre'el (Tel-Aviv University), Nilli Mandelblatt, and Benjamin Hary (Emory University). I must mention, however, that not all Israelis are familiar with gender reversal, and some academics I have presented it to have even questioned its existence. I also have encountered several cases of mothers and daughters, and siblings (both male and female and female only) of various ages, who thought that their cross addressing within the confines of their own families was unique and idiosyncratic. This lack of recognition of gender reversal as a common phenomenon may be attributed to the strong prescriptive ideology advocated by the Hebrew Language Academy that is prevalent in Israel. I would like to thank Ellen Contini-Morava for her comments and suggestions on these and other issues appearing in this paper.

References

Andrews, Edna & Yishai Tobin, eds. 1996. *Towards a calculus of meaning: Studies in markedness, distinctive features and deixis.* Amsterdam: Benjamins.

Aphek, Edna & Yishai Tobin. 1988. *Word systems in modern Hebrew: Implications and applications.* Leiden: Brill.

Ariel, Mira. 1986. *Women, men and language.* Haifa: Haifa University Press.

Ariel, Mira. 1988. "Female and male stereotypes in Israeli literature and media: Evidence from introductory patterns." *Language and Communication* 8: 43–68.

Ariel, Mira. 1990. *Accessing NP antecedents.* London: Routledge.

Ariel, Mira & Rachel Giora. 1998a. "A self versus other point of view in language: Redefining femininity and masculinity." *International Journal of the Sociology of Language* 129: 59–86.

Ariel, Mira & Rachel Giora. 1998b. "Power and cooperation in new Israeli film discourse. An analysis of impositive speech acts." In *A critique of new Israeli films*, eds. Nurit Gertz & Orly Lubin & Judd Ne'eman. Tel-Aviv: Open University, 179–204.

Barrett, Rusty. 1995. "Supermodels of the world unite! Political economy and the language of performance among African-American drag queens." In *Beyond the lavendar lexicon,* ed. William Leach. Amsterdam: Overseas Publishers Association – Gordon and Breach, 202–226.

Battistella, Edwin. 1996. *The logic of markedness.* Oxford: Oxford University Press.

Ben-Abba, Dov, ed. 1994. *The Meridian Hebrew-English, English-Hebrew dictionary.* New York: Washington Square Press.

Berman, Ruth A. 1978. *Modern Hebrew structure.* Tel-Aviv: University Publishing Projects.

Connors, Kathleen. 1971. "Studies in feminine agentives in selected European languages." *Romance Philology* 24: 573–598.

Contini-Morava, Ellen. 1996. " 'Things' in a noun class language: Semantic functions of grammatical agreement in Swahili." In *Towards a calculus of meaning: Studies in markedness, distinctive features and deixis,* eds. Edna Andrews & Yishai Tobin. Amsterdam: Benjamins, 251–290.

Contini-Morava, Ellen. In press. "(What) do noun classes mean?" In *Signal, meaning and message: Perspectives on sign-based linguistics,* eds. Wallis Reid & Ricardo Otheguy. Amsterdam: Benjamins.

Contini-Morava, Ellen. 2000. "Noun class as number in Swahili." In *Between grammar and lexicon,* eds. Ellen Contini-Morava & Yishai Tobin. Amsterdam: Benjamins, 3–30.

Contini-Morava, Ellen & Yishai Tobin, eds. 1998. *Between grammar and lexicon.* Amsterdam: Benjamins.

Corbett, Greville. 1991. *Gender.* Cambridge: Cambridge University Press.

Ferguson, Charles. 1964. "Baby talk in six languages." *Language* 66: 103–114.

Glinert, Lewis. 1989. *The grammar of modern Hebrew.* Cambridge: Cambridge University Press.

Glinert, Lewis. 1994. *Modern Hebrew: An essential grammar.* London: Routledge.

Hall, Kira & Veronica O'Donovan. 1996. "Shifting gender positions among Hindi-speaking hijras." In *Rethinking language and gender research,* eds. Victoria L. Bergvall & Janet M. Bing & Alice F. Freed. London: Longman, 228–266.

Harshav, Benjamin. 1993. *Language in time of revolution.* Berkeley: University of California Press.

Hofstadter, Douglas. 1997. *I'm a guy; you're a guy; he's a guy; but is she one? We are guys; you guys are guys; but she would like to be one.* Paper read at the Fifth International Cognitive Linguistics Conference, Amsterdam.

Jakobson, Roman. 1963. *Essais de linguistique générale. Les fondations du langage.* Paris: Editions de Minuit.

Jugaku, A. 1979. *Nihongo to Omna.* [Japanese and Women]. Tokyo: Iwanami-syoten.

Kulick, Don. 1998. *Sex, gender, and culture among Brazilian transgendered prostitutes.* Chicago: University of Chicago Press.

Kutscher, Edward Yechezkel. 1982. *A history of the Hebrew language.* Jerusalem: Magnes Press.

Morris, Lori. 1991. *Gender in modern English: The system and its uses.* Ph.D. dissertation, Université Laval, Québec.

Morris, Lori. 2000. "The grammar of English gender." In *Between grammar and lexicon,* eds. Ellen Contini-Morava & Yishai Tobin. Amsterdam: Benjamins, 185–203.

Muchnik, Malka. 1992. *Differences in the language of men and women in the Israeli press.* Ph.D. dissertation, Bar-Ilan University Ramat-Gan, Israel.

Otheguy, Ricardo. 1977. "A semantic analysis of the difference between *el/la* and *lo.*" In *Contemporary studies in Romance linguistics,* ed. Margarita Suñer. Washington, DC: Georgetown University Press, 241–257.

Oxford English-Hebrew dictionary. 1996. Oxford: Oxford University Press.

Ravid, Dorit & Yitzhak Shlesinger, eds. 2000. *Modern Hebrew adverbs: Between syntactic class and lexical category.* Amsterdam: Benjamins, 333–351.

Reynolds, Katsue Akiba. 1997. "Female speakers of Japanese in transition." In *Language and gender,* ed. Jennifer Coates. Oxford: Blackwell, 299–308.

Rosén, Haiim. 1977. *Contemporary Hebrew.* The Hague: Mouton.

Rudes, Blair A. & Bernard Healy. 1979. "Is she for real? The concept of femaleness and maleness in the gay world." In *Ethnolinguistics: Boas, Sapir and Whorf revisited,* ed. Madeline Mathiot. The Hague: Mouton, 49–61.

Sáenz-Badillos, Angel. 1993. *A history of the Hebrew language.* Cambridge: Cambridge University Press.

Schwarzwald, Ora. 1991. "Grammatical vs. lexical plural formation in Hebrew." *Folia Linguistica* 25: 577–608.

Shalev, Tsruya. 1997. *xayei ahava* [Love life]. Jerusalem: Keter.

Tobin, Yishai. 1982. "Asserting one's existence in modern Hebrew: A Saussurian based analysis of the domain of attention in selected 'existentials'." *Lingua* 58: 341–368.

Tobin, Yishai, ed. 1988. *The Prague School and its legacy.* Amsterdam: Benjamins.

Tobin, Yishai, ed. 1989. *From sign to text: A semiotic view of communication.* Amsterdam: Benjamins.

Tobin, Yishai. 1990. *Semiotics and linguistics.* London: Longman.

Tobin, Yishai. 1991a. "Review article: Comparing and contrasting grammars." *Studies in Language* 15: 423–452.

Tobin, Yishai. 1991b. "Existential particles and paradigms in modern Hebrew." *Multilingua* 10: 93–108.

Tobin, Yishai. 1993. *Aspect in the English verb: Process and result in language.* London: Longman.

Tobin, Yishai. 1994. *Invariance, markedness and distinctive feature analysis: A contrastive study of sign systems in English and Hebrew.* Amsterdam: Benjamins.

Tobin, Yishai. 1995. "The iconicity of focus and existence in modern Hebrew." In *Syntactic iconicity and linguistic freezes,* ed. Marge E. Landsberg. Berlin: de Gruyter, 177–188.

Tobin, Yishai. 1997. *Phonology as human behavior: Theoretical implications and clinical applications.* Durham, NC: Duke University Press.

Tobin, Yishai. 1998. "Review: The logic of markedness by Edwin Battistella." *Language* 74: 832–834.

Tobin, Yishai. 2000. "The dual number in Hebrew: Grammar or lexicon, or both?" In *Between grammar and lexicon,* eds. Ellen Contini-Morava & Yishai Tobin. Amsterdam: Benjamins, 87–119.

Trechter, Sara. 1995. "Categorical gender myths in native America: Gender deictics in Lakhota." *Issues in Applied Linguistics* 6: 5–22.

van Schooneveld, Cornelis H. 1977. "The place of gender in the semantic structure of the Russian language." *Scando-Slavica* 23: 129–138.

van Schooneveld, Cornelis H. 1988. "Paradigmatic structure and syntactic relations." In *The Prague School and its legacy,* ed. Yishai Tobin. Amsterdam: Benjamins, 109–122.

Wilmsen, David. in press. "Cross addressing: Reverse gender reference in Cairene Arabic." In *Proceedings of the Symposium on Arabic grammar and linguistics*, ed. Yasir Suleiman. London: Curzon.

Yokoyama, Olga T. 1999. "Russian genderlects and the gender linguistics of Russian referential expressions." *Language in Society* 28: 401–429.

Zubin, David. 1984. "Superordinates and basic level terms in the German gender system." Ms. Department of Linguistics. Buffalo: SUNY. [publ. 1986 as "Superordinates and basic level terms in the German gender system." In *Categorization and noun classification*, ed. Colette S. Craig. Amsterdam, Benjamins.]

Zubin, David & Klaus-Michael Köpcke. 1981. "Gender: A less than arbitrary category." *Chicago Linguistic Society* 17: 439–449.

Zubin, David & Klaus-Michael Köpcke. 1984. "Affect classification in the German gender system." *Lingua* 63: 41–96.

Zubin, David & Klaus-Michael Köpcke. 1986a. "Gender and folk taxonomy: The indexical relation between grammatical and lexical classification." In *Noun classes and categorization*, ed. Colette Craig. Amsterdam: Benjamins, 139–180.

Zubin, David & Klaus-Michael Köpcke. 1986b. "Natural classification in language: A study of the German gender system". In *Buffalo Cognitive Science Report No. 2*. Buffalo: SUNY.

Gender in Javanese Indonesian[*]

Esther Kuntjara

Petra Christian University, Surabaya, Indonesia

1. Introduction: Sociolinguistic background

It is impossible to talk about Indonesia and the Indonesian language (*Bahasa Indonesia*) without taking into account the different ethnic groups with 669 languages that are spoken partly or entirely within the Republic of Indonesia (cf. Jones 1994). The largest ethnic group, which comprises about 40 percent of the Indonesian population, are the Javanese, who live primarily on the island of Java, which is the fifth largest island in the Indonesian archipelago. In Java alone, there are approximately 170 related but mutually unintelligible languages. Javanese belongs to the western (Indonesian) branch of the Austronesian language family, related languages being Sundanese and Madurese.

Javanese is spoken by some 80 million people. However, *Bahasa Indonesia* was declared the national language of Indonesia by young nationalists as early as 1928, long before Indonesia gained independence from the Netherlands in 1945.[1] *Bahasa Indonesia* became established as the new name for Malay, the most widespread *lingua franca* in Indonesia (the native language of only ca. 5% of the population), which – even during Dutch colonial rule when Dutch was the official language – had confirmed its status as administrative language and the medium of instruction in education. This was due to the fact that the colonial government of Netherlands East Indies considered language issues increasingly important for gaining knowledge of and control over the local affairs. Ch. A. Van Ophuysen was noted as the first person who founded rules for spelling Malay with Latin characters in 1901 (Errington 1998: 52–53). The fact that Malay was preferred to Javanese by the Dutch might be related to the complicated Javanese script and speech style. The Indonesian language uses a Latin alphabetic writing system, while Javanese is written in a script derived from a Sanskrit writing system.[2]

The choice of Indonesian (*Bahasa Indonesia*) as a national language is remarkable. It was a politically fortuitous choice because it was so strongly associated with nationalism (Jones 1994: 1668). Today, *Bahasa Indonesia* enjoys high prestige in a linguistically extremely diverse country as the official language of government, education and mass communication, while Javanese is still spoken at home, at school, in offices, in local gatherings and traditional rituals (Horne 1992: 254).

Embedded in Javanese is the social stratification in a rather strict system of speech levels based on genealogy, kinship ties, wealth, education, age and gender. The chief markers of the speech levels are differences in vocabulary and tone of voice as well as paralinguistic features. Every speaker of Javanese, regardless of his/her social status or geographical origin, uses all of the speech levels, each in the appropriate situation depending upon whom he/she is addressing (Poedjosoedarmo 1968: 57). Hence, it is impossible to speak Javanese without explicitly taking into account the relative status of the people involved. Two major distinctions of the Javanese speech levels are called *ngoko*, the familiar level, and *krama*, the respect level. *Ngoko* is learned by a child from peers and siblings and is used throughout his/her life with close friends, younger persons, or people of a lower social status. *Krama* can be modulated into *krama inggil*, or 'High Krama', and *krama andhap*, or 'Humble Krama'. These are applied to persons, actions and possessions of those to whom one shows particular deference. *Krama* is learned rather than acquired through a more conscious process, often through explicit instruction by parents and teachers.

Bahasa Indonesia (henceforth Indonesian), which is spoken by most urban people, can be regarded as a less traditional and more democratic language than Javanese. For Javanese speakers, Indonesian is a relatively flexible means of communication that does not indicate levels of formality and lacks ethnic identification (Errington 1988:8). It allows people to avoid the choice of speech style that reveals a person's status as is obligatory in Javanese. Hence, people have more freedom in expressing themselves in Indonesian than when they have to use Javanese. However, the daily interaction is more often conducted in a mixture of Indonesian and Javanese, with Indonesian being used on more formal occasions such as in classrooms, conferences, national ceremonies, offices, and when talking to strangers or other Indonesians who are not close. This offers an opportunity for people to switch and/or mix their language use from Indonesian to Javanese and its appropriate speech level. Thus the hierarchical social level can still be revealed through the choice of words, phrases, or sentences used when people talk. A recent example that illustrates this practice is the use of the Javanese phrase *"lengser keprabon"* by the former President of Indonesia, Soeharto, approaching his downfall in 1998. The phrase itself means 'stepping down from the throne' and was traditionally used by the king of Java. As a Javanese, Soeharto felt that it was the appropriate phrase to describe his willingness to step down from the 'throne', as he regarded himself as one of the Javanese kings.

2. Structural properties of *Bahasa Indonesia* and Javanese

Unlike Javanese, which has a complex system of speech levels and structural properties, especially in its morphology with many prefixes, suffixes, and infixes, Indonesian is relatively simpler with no comparable speech levels.[3] The egalitarian spirit and the relative simplicity of Indonesian is expected to neutralize the hierarchical structure of Javanese, although many lexical items in Indonesian are similar to Javanese. In his study of Javanese Indonesian language contact in Central Java, Errington (1998) found that many Javanese used a lot of Indonesian, but in a very Javanese sense. He maintains that "bilingual usage like this can be seen as binding Javanese and Indonesian material in a kind of figure-ground relation of simultaneity, as an Indonesian vehicle of reference enters into the linguistic modes of Javanese social biographies" (1988:113).

Not only has Javanese been used in Indonesian, but its usage has also influenced other regional languages. Smith-Hefner's (1989) study on the language of the Tengger people in East Java, who commonly use *ngoko* as the affirmation of group membership regardless of a person's status in the community, suggests that many Tengger people have had to adopt Javanese *krama* as it was increasingly identified as a prestigious code spoken by high-status outsiders who are mostly Central Javanese Moslem. The ability to speak *krama* became an important requirement of Tengger officials' roles and set them apart from their fellow villagers (cf. Smith-Hefner 1989:264).

Neither Javanese nor Indonesian have grammatical gender, not even pronominal gender distinctions like English *he* or *she*. The word *dia* or *ia* in Indonesian is the third person singular personal pronoun, which is used to refer to both males and females; this is also the case for the possessive suffix -*nya* 'him/his' or 'her/hers'. In Javanese, the third person singular pronouns *panje-nenganipun* (in *krama inggil*), *piyambakipun* (in *krama andhap*) or *dhéwéké* (in *ngoko*) also refer to both females and males. It is interesting to note that these pronouns are derived from the Javanese terms *panjenengan,* meaning 'you', and *piyambak* and *dhéwék* meaning 'self', respectively. The suffixes -*ipun* (*krama*) and -*é* (*ngoko*) are the possessive forms corresponding to Indonesian -*nya*.

3. Showing respect in Javanese

When the anthropologist Hildred Geertz came to Indonesia during the late 1950s to study kinship and socialization in the Javanese family in the small town of Modjokuto (a fake name) in Central Java, she noticed that *hormat* 'respect' was an element of every social interaction in Java. She argued that perhaps the first thought a Javanese had when meeting a stranger was "What degree of respect should I show him?" (Geertz 1961:19). Once the degree of respect has been established and expressed verbally, further interaction can take place in a controlled and orderly way. Anderson (1990:131) maintains that Javanese "krama is essentially an honorific language [...] social prestige among the Javanese is indicated most clearly by an individual's mastery of the finer forms of this langage de politesse." Smith-Hefner (1988:537) in her study of Javanese women's language of politeness acknowledged that language practices in Javanese, which have been referred to as "vocabularies of courtesy or levels of respect", belong to the world's most elaborate systems. Irvine (1992:255) also maintains that "the Javanese system's complexity and subtlety are evidently recognized by the speakers themselves as characterizing both the system and its highest-ranking use".

Being polite and showing respect are indeed the essence of the Javanese communication. Although Indonesian is more democratic and has been declared the national language, Javanese is still spoken by the majority of Indonesians living in Java. Concerning the expectation that Javanese language and literature might gradually be disappearing, Anderson (1990: 235) maintains that the "ghost" of Javanese is still powerful:

> If we ask ourselves why in the Indonesian context the language and culture of Java are sui generis, I do not believe that the answer is simply that the Javanese are by far the largest ethnic group, that Javanese culture is somehow "superior" to its competitors, or that the Javanese run the country – though all these propositions have some elements of truth. For the fact is that the Javanese language and Javanese culture have for almost a century now been much more a problem to the Javanese themselves than to anyone else: a problem that cannot be resolved by any obvious or easy means, since it involves and implicates almost all sectors of Javanese society.

Well before Anderson, Clifford Geertz (1960: 259) had also acknowledged that Indonesian seems destined to become one among other systems available to be selected for use in special contexts and for special purposes. This was supported by Smith-Hefner (1989: 259) who maintained that the use of Indonesian does not appear to have impaired the use of Javanese with its polite speech forms. Hence I believe that even though Indonesian has been emerging as the language of the educated, the spirit of Javanese continues to permeate the life of Javanese Indonesians.

People's practice of switching to Javanese while conversing in Indonesian is analyzed by the Indonesian scholar Leo Indra Ardiana as evidence of the *krama*-nization (the process of making into *krama*) of Indonesian (*Surabaya Post*, May 25, 1998), as is also suggested by Anderson. Anderson (1990: 145) argues that the *krama*-nization of Indonesian is meant to glorify the present through a heroic past. Hence, the egalitarian spirit in Indonesian may be manipulated by the use of Javanese to assert the speaker's dominance in terms of power and the demand for *hormat* 'respect'.

Code-switching from Indonesian to Javanese can be observed especially in asymmetrical relationships. Given the low status of women in Javanese society (apparently also found in many other ethnic groups in Indonesia besides the Javanese), female-male interaction in particular demonstrates hierarchical patterns. In the interaction between husband and wife, for instance, a traditional Javanese woman is supposed to use a more deferential speech style (*krama*) when talking to her husband, while a husband may use the casual *ngoko* style to his wife. However, it is difficult for a person to be harsh and rude when speaking in *krama*, since it is a refined language. By contrast, one can express anger only in *ngoko* (Poedjosoedarmo 1968:77), for the use of the casual *ngoko* form is more open and expressive, which tends to be considered as rude in many ways. In other words, when there is an asymmetrical relationship between a Javanese husband and wife, the wife should use deferential speech style to her husband; a husband can talk rudely to his wife, while a wife cannot do the same to her husband by using the same linguistic strategies. The use of Indonesian, which is widespread in the more urban families, may mitigate such asymmetries, but when status and power are to be asserted, people may switch to Javanese, whereas the switching from Javanese to Indonesian may indicate a desire to establish a more symmetrical relationship. Hence, a man may initiate the use of Javanese to assert his status and power when talking to a woman. In this case, a woman is expected to reply in a more deferential style to show *hormat* or respect; but she could also initiate the use of Indonesian to signal equal status. The choice of the same *ngoko* style would be regarded as rude, uneducated or impolite, although on certain occasions it shows intimacy or solidarity.

In the following, the discussion of language and gender will be restricted to Indonesian as spoken in Javanese society with its different ethnic and language backgrounds, and no claim is made that the analysis will be relevant for other groups also.

4. The lexical representation of women and men in Indonesian

4.1 Generic nouns and the exclusion of women

Indonesian has many terms for human referents which are supposed to be gender-neutral, such as *manusia* 'human' or *orang* 'person'. Kinship terms have lexical gender, like *ibu* 'mother', *paman* 'uncle', *nénék* 'grandmother', etc. Some kinship terms, however, are specified according to age rather than gender, such as *kakak* 'older brother/sister', *adik* 'younger brother/sister', etc. Personal nouns which are in principle generic can nevertheless cause confusion and may reveal a gender bias. Consider the following examples:

(1) *Ada berapa   mahasiswa di universitas itu?*
      are how.many student   in university that
      'How many students are there in the university?'

(2) *Susan bekerja sebagai karyawan di Bank Indonesia.*
    Susan works as   clerk   in Bank Indonesia
    'Susan works as a clerk in the Bank of Indonesia.'

Although the words *mahasiswa* and *karyawan* are used generically, Indonesian has female parallel forms for those words:

(3) Male-specific/Generic Female-specific
    mahasiswa   *mahasiswi*   'student'
    karyawan   *karyawati*   'clerk'

The female forms, however, are not frequently used, which leads to a fusion of the male-specific and the generic meaning in *mahasiswa* and *karyawan*. There are many other, allegedly generic terms, for which Indonesian provides specifically female counterparts. The following are other personal nouns which have morphologically related female forms:

(4) *saudara*   'brother/sister'   *saudari*   'sister'
    putra   'son/daughter, boy' *putri*   'daughter, girl'
    sukarelawan 'volunteer'   *sukarelawati* 'woman volunteer'
    seniman   'artist'   *seniwati*   'woman artist'

There are also unmarked words which can be marked as female by adding the word *wanita* or *perempuan* 'woman', cf. the following compounds:

(5) *dokter*   'doctor'   *dokter perempuan*   'woman doctor'
    polisi   'police officer' *polisi wanita*   'woman police officer'
    pengemudi 'driver'   *pengemudi perempuan* 'woman driver'

The words *wanita* and *perempuan* have undergone a shift in meaning, although both are often used interchangeably to refer to women. *Wanita* is often regarded as a more graceful word for a woman and has been widely used for many names of women's organizations, such as *Dharma Wanita* 'the mission of women' and *Ikatan Wanita Karya* 'working women's union', while *perempuan* is often used with a pejorative meaning. Recently, however, the word *perempuan* has been used more frequently, especially by women's movement activists. It refers to 'one who can menstruate, become pregnant, bear children, and breastfeed' (cf. Pusat pembinaan 1997). The preference for the word *perempuan* over *wanita*, according to Budiman (1992:72), may have been motivated by the common knowledge of the basic meaning of *wanita*, which is *wani ditata* 'dare to be ordered' in Javanese, while *perempuan* contains an element *empu* which denotes an 'expert in crafts'.

The suffixes -*wan*/-*man* or -*wati* indicate male or female reference. However, the suffix -*wati* 'female' cannot be attached to all professional or occupational titles, cf. the following examples:

(6)   *Ibu   Susi seorang jutawan   yang dermawan.*
      mother Susi a   millionnaire who generous.person
      'Mrs Susi is a millionaire who is a generous person.'

(7)   *Ibu   Kartini adalah pahlawan emansipasi   wanita.*
      mother Kartini is   hero   emancipation woman
      'Mrs Kartini is a heroine of women's emancipation.'

The words *jutawan* 'millionaire', *pahlawan* 'hero' and *dermawan* 'generous person' have no female form, and (8) and (9) are unacceptable (cf. Budiman 1992:77):

(8)   *Ibu Susi seorang *jutawati yang *dermawati.*
      'Mrs Susi is a female millionaire who is a generous female person.'

(9)   *Ibu Kartini adalah *pahlawati emansipasi wanita.*
      'Mrs Kartini is a female emancipation hero.'

Other nouns with the agent suffix -*wan* that have no female -*wati* parallel are:

(10)   *bendaharawan*   'treasurer'
       sastrawan   'person of letters'
       usahawan   'businessperson'
       ilmuwan   'scientist'
       purnawirawan   'veteran'
       wisudawan   'graduate'
       pustakawan   'librarian'
       cendekiawan   'intellectual'

While these words can be used as generics, corresponding female parallels do not exist. It can perhaps be assumed that the professions or activities indicated by these nouns have mostly been performed by men, and that generally it is not considered to be important to name women. Budiman (1992:77) maintains that this evidence reflects the subordination of women; in addition, designations for women are merely derived from designations for men. This issue has so far not been discussed in public.

Terms for women may be more various, usually in cases where reference is made to stereotypical female roles. The word *suami* 'husband' refers to a man who has a wife or *istri*. However, there are several names for a wife besides *istri*:

(11) *bini*   'wife', more often used by the Jakartanese
      nyonya   'Mrs', but also 'wife'
      ibunya anak-anak   'mother of the children'
      garwa / sémah   from Javanese, *garwa,* often translated as 'half of
                                the soul'; a generic word, but more often used to
                                refer to wife than to husband
      kanca wingking /   from Javanese, meaning 'rear friend / girl friend'
      kanca estri

The Indonesian term *nyonya* actually has a male parallel, i.e. *tuan.* However, *tuan* is used only in the meaning of 'Mr' or 'Master', while *nyonya* can mean both 'Mrs' and 'wife'. A wife will usually not say *tuan saya* to refer to her husband, as it may mean 'my Master', while a husband can say *nyonya saya,* which means 'my wife'. Thus, the two terms are parallel only in those contexts in which they mean 'Mrs' and 'Mr'. The Javanese terms *garwa* and *kanca estri* are used to refer to a wife and often replace the Indonesian term *istri.* However, there is no parallel term for the husband. The function of the female terms is to show the position of the wife, that is, the husband's friend whose place is at the back of the house or merely half of the husband's soul. This is in line with the portrayal of the ideal Javanese woman and wife who should be loyal to her husband, able to do women's chores, and take care of her physical beauty, be good at serving her husband, and care for her in-laws (Mulder 1996:85). A common expression in Javanese is:

(12) *swarga nunut neraka katut*
      heaven follows hell   included
      'in heaven she follows, in hell she is included'

These Javanese terms for 'wife' are used even when people speak in Indonesian in order to emphasize the role of women as wives in the Javanese society.

The English terms *master bedroom* and *master key,* which may be considered to express a male bias, have the following Indonesian equivalents: *kamar induk* 'mother room' and *kunci induk* 'mother key'. *Induk* is an Indonesian term for a mother used mainly for animals. Other Indonesian expressions using *induk* that convey a meaning similar to 'master' in English 'master bedroom' are: *buku induk* 'mother book', i.e. a book that contains all the names of the members of an organization or the students in a school, *rumah induk* 'mother house/main building', *kalimat induk* 'main clause', *nomor induk* 'base number', *induk karangan* 'editorial', *induk semang* 'landlady' (which can also be used as a generic term meaning the manager of a rented house), etc. These terms seem to indicate the value of women in Indonesian.

Another Indonesian word with a generic function (but basically a female meaning) is *ratu*. The word literally means 'queen', but when it is used in the Javanese context it can mean either 'king' or 'queen'. It is used, for instance, in the phrase *Ratu adil* meaning 'a just King' or 'a just Queen'; *Petruk dadi ratu* 'Petruk becomes King', a title in a famous Javanese *wayang* play, when translated into Indonesian becomes *Petruk jadi raja* meaning 'Petruk becomes King'.[3] The word *keraton*, which means 'the palace of a King', comes from the head word *ratu* plus the *ke-* prefix and the *-an* suffix to mean the place where the *ratu* lives, i.e. *keraton*. However, when people say *Ratu Kidul* in Javanese, it refers to the South Queen, a goddess who people believe rules the South Sea of Java. *Sri*, which is a common name in Indonesian for a girl, may be used to refer to a man of noble status in Javanese society.

4.2 Terms of address, reference to self and others

4.2.1 *Pronominal forms*

The choice of Indonesian intimate and polite address forms is much more complicated than the corresponding *Tu/Vous* forms in some European languages (cf., e.g., Brown & Gilman 1960), and perhaps one of the most complicated among Asian languages. Even a list of selected terms for 'I', 'you' or 'he/she' used among Indonesian speakers in the Javanese society can be of considerable length. Below are some pronouns used for 'I', 'you' and 'he/she' in several major languages used by people in Java who also speak Indonesian:

(13) a.   First Person Singular 'I'

saya, aku	*/Indonesian/*
kula, dalem	*/Javanese/*
urang, abdi	*/Sundanese/*
gua / gué	*/Jakartanese/*
nyong	*/Tegalese/*
isun	*/Cirebonese/*
(s)engko, gulah, abdinah	*/Madurese/*
wo	*/Mandarin Chinese/*
ik	*/Dutch/*

b. Second Person Singular 'you'

kamu, engkau, anda	/Indonesian/
kowé, sampéyan, panjenengan	/Javanese/
lu	/Jakartanese/
kon	/Surabayanese/
manéh, anjeun	/Sundanese/
ba'é, ba'na	/Madurese/
sira	/Cirebonese/
ni	/Mandarin Chinese/
jij	/Dutch/
you	/English/
enté	/Arabic/

c. Third Person Singular 'he/she'

dia, ia, beliau	/Indonesian/
déwéké, piyambakipun, panjenenganipun	/Javanese/
manéhna	/Sundanese/
hij, zij	/Dutch/

4.2.2 *Kinship terms*

In addressing, personal pronouns can be replaced by kinship terms, names or nicknames. Some kin terms are:

(14) a. Indonesian

kakak	'older brother/sister'
adik	'younger brother/sister'
bapak	'father'
ibu	'mother'
kakék	'grandfather'
nénék	'grandmother'
cucu	'grandchild'

b. Javanese

éyang	'grandfather/grandmother'
mak/mbok	'mother'
mas	'older brother'
mbak	'older sister'
jeng	'younger sister'
budé/bullik	'aunt older/younger than one's parent'
pakdé/pakllik	'uncle older/younger than one's parent'

    c. Dutch

oom	'uncle'
tante	'aunt'
oma	'grandmother'
opa	'grandfather

    d. Jakartanese

babé	'father'

    e. Chinese

susuk	'uncle'
aai	'aunt'

4.3 The communication of respect in Indonesian

The most important extra-linguistic factors that determine the choice of terms of address are a person's gender, age, ethnic background, wealth, occupation, and his/her status in society. Sometimes there may be some conflict, such as that between age and status, or gender and status, wealth and occupation etc., in which people need to choose the most appropriate term or switch to a more neutral term to avoid the conflict. Very often, a person's interpersonal sensitivity is required in order to select the proper term by observing the reaction of the addressee. In this case, it is difficult to make any general statements about the selection of the kind that Errington observed in one of his Javanese informants:

> Take a look, see what the situation is first. If you are dealing with an older person who is of the nobility, *dalem* is fine. But if you are dealing with an ordinary person …[such as] two mutual acquaintances of low to middling noble descent, you should use *kula*. They are nobles, but only low nobles. (Errington 1988:122)

Indonesian people usually respect older people. A person's age should be considered before the correct term of address is chosen. Two women, especially older women, of about the same age on meeting for the first time may need to ask each other's age before they start to address each other. Nevertheless people could sometimes speak to each other without using any term of address, such as between two strangers. For a man who looks older than or about the same age as the speaker, the safe Indonesian terms commonly used would be *bapak/ pak* 'father', and *ibu/bu* 'mother' for a woman. If the addressee looks a bit younger, he or she can be addressed as *mas, mbak, dik* or *jeng*, which are the Javanese terms for a young man, a young woman, a much younger man, and a much younger woman. However, it is sometimes difficult for a person to decide whether the other person is younger or older. In that case, *mas* or *mbak* is commonly used to show respect to the addressee.

Although most people in Java are familiar with both the Indonesian and the Javanese terms of address, there are people from different ethnic backgrounds who may still use their own terms of address. The Sundanese in West Java, for instance, will either use the Indonesian terms or their own western Javanese terms, such as *Akang* or *Bang* 'older brother' for men and *mpok* or *nyai* 'older sister (usually married)' for women. Chinese Indonesians in Java are often addressed as *oom* for men, and *tante* for women (terms derived from Dutch), even if there is no kinship relation. While in the Chinese Indonesian community such terms may be well accepted, many Chinese Indonesians prefer the Indonesian terms of address to be used in the work place and in public. Many educated Chinese Indonesians prefer to be addressed as *bapak/pak* or *ibu/bu*, since outside the family the Dutch terms may also have derogatory connotations.

It seems that the Indonesian terms may sound more prestigious than the Javanese. A colleague of mine who once taught at the same university with me was once addressed with *mbak* 'older sister' by a new employee in the administration office who mistook her for another clerk. She immediately instructed her to call her *ibu* 'mother/Mam' instead of *mbak*, for professors are normally addressed as *Ibu/Bu*, while *Mbak* is more often used among common people. Other terms may also convey different shades of meaning. An old Javanese woman vendor who was once addressed with *embok* 'old woman' or 'mother' (when used by rural Javanese) by a boy objected to the term and asked him to call her *bu* instead. The Javanese term *embok* is usually employed to address an old woman servant. An adult woman who is addressed as *tante* by a stranger could be considered as a "bad" woman. The late first lady of Indonesia, Tien, used to be nicknamed *Madame Tien,* which carries a derogatory meaning and is often ridiculed as *Madame Tien percent,* referring to her assumed practice of asking for a ten percent commission of any business deal made in Indonesia.

A conflict of status can arise when two Javanese men have different social status in the community and in the office. A good example of this is the relationship of the former President Soeharto and the late Sri Sultan Hamengku Buwono IX when he was Vice President of Indonesia. In Yogyakarta, where Sri Sultan Hamengku Buwono IX came from, he was the king of the *Keraton* Yogyakarta. As a king, he was highly respected by the people in Yogyakarta, who still spoke to him in highly formal Javanese *krama*. In fact, many Javanese people who still speak Javanese would talk to a king in Javanese *krama inggil.*

Hence, Soeharto, who is also a Javanese, should, as a matter of fact, talk to Sri Sultan in polite Javanese, since Sri Sultan was a king. However, within the government, Soeharto's status was higher than Sri Sultan's. This means that Sri Sultan owed respect to him. This conflict was almost impossible to solve when they had to talk to each other in Javanese. So, to avoid the complication of who had to use *sampéyan* (a less refined Javanese term for 'you') and who had to use *panjenengan* (a more polite and refined Javanese term for 'you') when addressing each other, it is likely that the Indonesian terms of address *bapak/pak* would have been preferred.

4.4 Addressing women and men

The use of terms of address by Indonesian speakers with Javanese ethnic background shows a general preference for Javanese terms of address over Indonesian terms. Even when people are talking in Indonesian, many Javanese are more comfortable with using the Javanese terms of address. Since Javanese is highly hierarchical and structured, the use of these terms therefore strengthens the hierarchical relationship of the interlocutors, even though they are conversing in the more egalitarian Indonesian.

The Indonesian terms of address for men and women are less complicated and more egalitarian than the Javanese terms. The words *bapak* (abbreviated as *pak*) for a man and *ibu* (abbreviated as *bu*) for a woman are similar to English *Mr* and *Mrs*, but they literally mean 'father' and 'mother'. In fact, regardless of their marital status a man or a woman can be addressed with *bapak/pak* and *ibu/bu*, such as when students have to address their teachers. Although the teachers may still be single, they are addressed as *bapak/pak* or *ibu/bu* by the students. This suggests that the relationship between teachers and students is considered to be similar to that of parent and child. A man of high status can be addressed with *bapak/pak*, while a man of lower status is commonly addressed only with *pak*. Meanwhile, only women of high social status are addressed with *ibu/bu* (Errington 1998:83–88).

Some Indonesian kinship terms are differentiated according to age and position or status relationship in the family rather than gender. In this case, problems usually arise in translation from Indonesian to English. Such terms are, for instance:

(15) *kakak*   'older brother or sister'
      adik   'younger brother or sister'
      saudara   'brother or sister'

Other Indonesian kinship terms of address have lexical gender; in addition to *bapak* and *ibu* these are:

(16) *paman / bibi*   'uncle' / 'aunt'
      kakek / nenek   'grandfather' / 'grandmother'

While Indonesian terms of address for men and women are quite simple and more egalitarian, very often people still use the Javanese terms, or other regional and foreign terms of address which are more differentiated. Because of the asymmetrical social status of men and women, a traditional Javanese husband will call his wife by her first name or by the term *dik* 'younger sibling', while his wife will address him as *mas* 'older brother' even though she might be older than her husband. The expression of intimacy and respect is distributed asymmetrically between women and men. Young Javanese couples who call each other by family names before they get married will often return to traditional practice in Javanese after they get married. Another change that may occur with many Javanese women is the loss of their own names once they get married. Many Javanese men have only one name. For instance, when a man named *Parman* gets married to a woman named *Siti*, people will call them *Bapak Parman* and *Ibu Parman* 'Mr and Mrs Parman' instead of *Bapak Parman* and *Ibu Siti*. The wife of a man named *Joko Dolok* will be called *Ibu Joko* or *Ibu Joko Dolok*.

Terms of address for a Javanese couple can be more complex in the case of a conflicting social status of both partners. This can be illustrated by the example of former President Soeharto and his late wife Tien. Tien came from the royal family in Surakarta, Central Java, while Soeharto is the son of a Javanese peasant. This means that he has lower social status than Tien. However, since Soeharto is Tien's husband, she has to show respect to him. Tien would address Soeharto with the deferential term *panjenengan* (the refined Javanese term for 'you') and use *dalem*, which are refined forms of self-reference in Javanese, while Soeharto might address Tien with a less refined form for 'you' *sampéyan*, and use *aku* for 'I'. Taking social status as a basis, however, it is Soeharto who would have to use the deferential form to Tien. Yet no one ever reported on how they addressed each other at home. The terms *pak* and *bu* could have been used in a more public and formal situation, or the Javanese terms *mas* and *jeng* (an honorific Javanese term for a younger sister) among the family members where both would respect each other, instead of *panjenengan* or *sampéyan.*

In many Javanese families, mothers take the responsibility of telling their children how to use the proper terms of address for their close family and extended family. Mothers have often been the ones to preserve the use of Javanese address terms in their families, and consequently have become the preservers of hierarchical structures in both the family and community. On the other hand, as many urban people do not use Javanese anymore, urban women or mothers also seem to be the ones who initiate the use of the more democratic Indonesian.

4.5 Terms of endearment

Concerning terms of endearment, Wolfson (1989) maintains that in English, women are often addressed with endearment terms like *dear, hon, sweetheart,* or *doll* by men, irrespective of age and social status. At the same time, the use of terms of endearment is often non-reciprocal, which can be interpreted as a sign that females are generally held in less respect than males. The person who receives such a term in an unequal encounter cannot return it unless she or he intentionally breaks social conventions. Thus the fact that many males use terms of endearment to females is a clear message of dominance and power.

Terms of endearment are hardly used among adults in Javanese society. This is partly due to the fact that people are expected to restrain their emotional feelings in public places. An outburst of emotion can be considered as quite rude or a sign of showing off (Suseno 1984:53). Some terms of endearment in Indonesian and Javanese, like *sayang* 'dear', *manis* 'sweetie', *cah bagus* 'hand-some young man', *den bagus* 'handsome young man of high nobility', *cah ayu* 'pretty young girl', *den ayu* 'pretty young girl of high nobility', are often used to address children. They are usually used non-reciprocally. The use of such terms by an adult to another adult often has the implication of teasing the addressee instead of being serious. Some terms of address for adults reflect age difference rather than gender, such as *ananda* 'dear son/daughter', *adinda* 'dear younger peer or sibling', *kakanda* 'dear older peer or sibling'. Significantly though, *adinda* is more often used from a man to a woman, while *kakanda* is used from a woman to a man. Gender-differentiated terms of address are *ibunda* 'mother dear' and *ayahanda* 'father dear'. However, terms of endearment for adults are more often used in written than in oral communication.

When an adult term of endearment is used orally, it usually contains additional shades of meaning besides signalling intimacy. One example is the use of *adinda* by a man to another man younger than himself. During the Indonesian riots that took place in Jakarta in May 1998, Adnan, a lawyer and human rights activist, hurriedly came to the House of Representatives where the Chairperson was having a meeting with his staff. Adnan immediately addressed the Chairperson, whose social status was undoubtedly higher than Adnan's, with *adinda*. At that time he seemed unable to control his anger and emotion about the government's passive reaction (*Jawa Pos*, May 15, 1998). The address term used by Adnan was indeed an unusual event, and can be interpreted in the following way. First, Adnan wanted to communicate to the addressee as well as to bystanders that the addressee was a person dear to him and that he wanted to regard him like his own younger brother. Second, as a younger brother, the addressee was expected to listen, pay attention, and respect his older brother as he spoke. Third, the way in which the term was uttered, which was loud, stern, and full of anger instead of using it affectionately as the term is supposed to be used, signalled an attempt to humiliate the addressee and criticize his inability to respond promptly to the emergency situation. Finally, since the term *adinda* is most often used by a man to a younger woman, Adnan's use of the term may convey an impression that the addressee was acting more like a woman who was incapable of solving a problem. Hence the deliberate misuse of a term of endearment implicitly conveys a derogatory perception of women.

5.   Code-switching: The use of Javanese in Indonesian female/male discourse

Research in the study of gender and politeness in conversational interaction suggests that women's language is more indirect, oriented more towards affective and interpersonal relationships, e.g. by interrupting others less often and asking more questions that help maintain the conversation. Men, on the other hand, are more direct and confrontational, more concerned with the referential function of their talk. Women's language has been described as powerless and men's as powerful (Holmes 1995). Tannen (1993: 175) argues that "the interpretation of a given utterance and the likely response to it depend on the setting, on individuals' status and their relationship to each other, and also on the linguistic conventions that are ritualized in the cultural context". Bergvall (1999) also maintains that "with so many of our notions of gender arising from studies of western cultures, we risk saturating L&G [language and gender] interpretations with middle-class-white-Anglo-American attributes".

Many Javanese Indonesians describe mixed Javanese-Indonesian usage as *bahasa gadho-gadho* 'language salad' or 'hybrid language' (Errington 1998:98). Indeed it is difficult to find any Javanese Indonesians who speak pure standard Indonesian in their daily communication. Errington maintains that "Indonesian counts more as what DeVries calls the 'vague ideal norm' of a national language, which is always tacitly in need of practical native-speaking supplement" (1998:99). In my own research of Chinese Indonesian women's language of politeness (Kuntjara 2001), one Chinese Indonesian woman was able to switch using five different languages (Indonesian, Javanese including Central and Eastern Javanese, Chinese, Dutch and English). This kind of hybrid, syncretic usage seems to be "less conflictual than complementary" (Errington 1998:115). Javanese Indonesian code-switching can be counted as "among the most intimate points of entry for Indonesian-ness, via Indonesian, into everyday Javanese life" (Errington 1998:155). Hence, it can be said that Indonesian use is often shaped by Javanese senses of conversational practice.

Below I will discuss some Indonesian conversational interactions of men and women in the Javanese context. The examples are taken from telephone dialogues recorded with the consent of the participants by Indrati (1996).

One male caller and one female caller took part in the research study. Each talked to three male and three female informants. They were all undergraduate students from different departments. Indrati herself used the samples to study verbosity between males and females in the telephone dialogues, but the data are of wider interest in that they illustrate the influence of Javanese in an Indonesian conversational interaction, and in particular, how concepts of politeness are employed in such a situation.

Lakoff (1990:45) suggests that "ordinary conversations are more heavily ritualized at their beginnings and ends than in the middle". She maintains that these are the times when both speakers wish to establish a relationship besides finding out whether to continue the conversation and when to end it. Below are some sections from the conversation of the female caller (FC) with one of the female respondents (FR). The language of the conversation is Indonesian; the underlined words are from Javanese or other regional languages (Jakartanese and Surabayanese); the bold italics are foreign terms (in this case Dutch):

TEXT 1

FC: *Halo? Oli ya?*
  hello Oli yes
  'Hello, is it Oli?'

FR: *He eh.*
  'Yes.'

FC: *Kamu habis* dari Jakarta ya?*
  you   finish from Jakarta yes
  'Haven't you been from Jakarta?'

FR: *Iya.*
  'Yeap.'

FC: *Oo mbolosan   iki.*
  oo habit.of.cutting.class this.is
  'Always cutting class, heh.'

FR: *Lho** dua minggu tok   kok** Apa? Ada kabar apa?*
  oh   two weeks only   what was news what
  'Oh, two weeks only. What? What's the news?'

FC: *Heh?*
  'What?'

  Apa?
  'What?'

FR: *Ada kabar apa?*
  was news what
  'What was the news?'

FC: *Ndak, aku kapan tuh nyari   kamu, ada perlu.*
  no   I   when that looking.for you   was need
  Cuman wis   telat***.
  but   already late
  'Nothing, I was looking for you last time. I need something.
  But it's too late now.'

  Mmm kamu ngapain   di Jakarta?
  mmm you   doing.what in Jakarta
  'Mmm, what were you doing in Jakarta?'

FR: *Main ke rumah saudaraku.*
  play to home my.sibling
  'Visiting my sister's/brother's home.'

FC: *Oh sama* saudaramu?*
      oh with   your.sibling
      'Oh, with your brother/sister?'

FR: *Iya.*
      'Right.'

FC: *Terus?*
      continue
      'Then?'

FR: *Ya udah.*
      OK already
      'Ok, that's all.'
      [...]

FR: *Makasih ya udah telepon.*
      thank.you OK already call
      'Thank you for calling, ok.'

FC: *Ya, daag.*
      'Ok, bye.'

FR: *Daag.*
      'Bye.'

*   Indonesian word but used in a Javanese sense.
**   *lho:* a particle that marks speaker's surprise or doubt.
      kok: a particle at the end of a phrase denying a presumption or statement of
      the interlocutor.
*** This word is used in both Javanese and Indonesian.

The following is a call from the male caller (MC) to one of the male respondents (MR):

TEXT 2

MC: *Selamat malam.*
      safe   evening
      'Good evening.'

MR: *David ya? Ono opo?*
      David right is   what
      'Is it David? What's up?'

MC: *Awakmu gak nang   kampus?*
      you   not going.to campus
      'Aren't you going to campus?'

MR: *Iyo, mari iki.*
yes after this
'Yes, after this.'

MC: *Arep   budhala?*
going.to leave
'Are you leaving now?'

MR: *Iyo.*
'Yes.'

MC: *Kesusua?*
hurry
'Are you in a hurry?'

MR: *Nggak, opo'o?*
no   what
'No, what is it?'

MC: *Aku sakjané kepingin nang kampus, weteng-ku   lara.*
I   actually want.to go.to campus stomach-my ache
'Actually I wanted to go to campus, but my stomach aches.'

MR: *Opo'o weteng-mu?*
what stomach-your
'What's wrong with your stomach?'

MC: *Iyo. Weteng-ku   nggak énak*.   Kayak masuk angin*
yes stomach-my not   comfortable like   enter   wind
wis.
already
Yokopo awakmu nggak sempat omong-omong* ambik
how   you   no   chance chat   with
pak* Frans ambik Iwan?
Mr Frans with Iwan
'Yes, my stomach does not feel very well. It's like catching a cold.
How about your chance for talking with Mr Frans and Iwan?'

MR: *Ngomong opo?*
talk   what
'Talk about what?'

MC: *Masalah Mang ditolak ambik pak Wasis itu.*
problem Mang refused with   Mr Wasis that
'The problem of Mang being refused by Mr Wasis.'

MR: *Nggak, nggak omong. Disalahno aé.*
no   no   talk   blamed   only
'No, no such talk. Only being blamed.'

> [...]
>
> MR: *Yo wis   nék ngono Ndan. Nék ono opo-opo   telpon*
>   OK already if so   Ndan if   exist something call
>   *yo.*
>   OK.
>   'Ok then, Ndan. Just call when something comes up.'
> MC: *Yo, yuk. Selamat malam.*
>   OK come safe   night
>   'Ok then. Good night.'
> MR: *Malam.*
>   'Night.'

* These words are used in both Indonesian and Javanese.

The greetings and farewells used in both dyads are in Indonesian. Indonesian can be considered an appropriate language to use when both conversational partners do not know whether the other person is the one he or she is looking for. It is a more formal language to use. However, once the relationship is established, the male speakers feel more comfortable in using Javanese than Indonesian, unlike the female speakers.

The Javanese used here is the casual Javanese *ngoko* mixed with a regional eastern Javanese accent. When *ngoko* is used reciprocally, it is in fact a more casual language and it shows intimacy and solidarity between the speakers. When Indonesian is used reciprocally, it may also show a symmetrical relationship, but on a more formal level. This may be parallel to the finding by Coates (1993) that non-standard, non-prestige forms seem to be associated with male speakers, while women are more sensitive to prestige forms. *Ngoko* can be considered as a non-prestige form; also, the mixture of *ngoko* with the regional language and accent can be considered as non-standard. In the Javanese context, however, when *ngoko* is used non-reciprocally by a male to another male or female, it can signal the assertion of dominance over the addressee, for only if he knows that he is more powerful or has equal status with the addressee who is his close friend, will he confidently use Javanese *ngoko*. The female dyad, however, prefers the use of Indonesian, which is more egalitarian. Only if they are very close, like the two females in TEXT 1 above, will they later switch to Javanese *ngoko*. Meanwhile, the male dyad continues in Javanese. When the topic turns to something more serious, there is a switch to Indonesian. The following is used in the midst of the male conversational dyad when discussing what to talk about to their superior:

TEXT 3

MC: *Lha nyampiknoné piyé? Nyampiknoné piyé?*
so to.say.it how to.say.it how?
'So how should I say it? How should I say it?'

MR: *Ya berdasarkan karena apa dengan adanya permasalahan*
well based.on because what with there.is problem
yang ada di satuan, dan untuk mendinginkan keadaan
which exist in unit and to cool.down situation
ya kita ya mengadakan apa itu pemilihan lagi
well we PRT conduct what that election again
untuk melihat apa itu kandidat komandan.
to see what that candidate commander
'Well, just based on the problem we have in the unit, and to cool down the situation we can conduct the election again to see if he is the candidate for a commander.'

MC: *Lha mosok kéné sing ngomong ambik Bernard?*
so should here who say with Bernard
'So should I be the one who talk to Bernard?'

MR: *Opo'o?*
'Why?'

Here, Indonesian is considered as more appropriate for a more formal and serious conversation. The use of Indonesian rather than Javanese here also makes the utterance less private and helps "to effect a minor shift in inter-subjective relations" (Errington 1998: 177). Text 4 is the dyad of a female caller (FC) and a male respondent (MR):

TEXT 4

FC: *Halo.*
MR: *Halo.*
FC: *Mas Bambang ya?*
brother Bambang yes
'Is it brother Bambang?'

MR: *Iya, ini siapa?*
yes this who
'Yes, who is it?'

FC: *Ini Retno. Gimana habis nyelam kemarin?*
this Retno how   after diving yesterday
'This is Retno. How were you after your diving yesterday?'

MR: *Ya   capék.*
'Yea, tired.'

FC: *Gitu ya? Kemarin Mas   Bambang sampai rumah jam*
that so yesterday brother Bambang arrived home   hour
berapa?
what
'Is that so? …What time did you arrive home yesterday?'

MR: *He eh*
'Yeah.'

      Apaé?
'What?'

FC: *Sampai rumah jam berapa?*
arrive   home hour what
'What time did you arrive home?'

MR: *Siapa?*
'Who?'

FC: *Ya Mas   Bambang.*
yeah brother Bambang
'Yeah, brother Bambang.'

The FC and the MR start with Indonesian even though she is using the Javanese address term *mas* that shows respect. Even when MR starts to ask in Javanese, FC keeps using *Bahasa Indonesia* in answering him except for the address term. It would sound awkward for FC to address MR only with his first name *Bambang* if she knows that he is older than herself. On another occasion, when FC calls another male respondent who is her close friend and about the same age, she prefers *ngoko* and calls him by his first name:

TEXT 5

FC: *Halo Eri?*

MR: *Iya*
'Yes.'

FC: *Bener?*
right
'Is that right?'

MR: *Sopo iki?*
    who this
    'Who is this?'

FC: *Ini Retno.*
    this Retno
    'This is Retno.'

MR: *O yo. Opo Ret?*
    o yeah what Ret
    'Oh ... what's up Ret?'

FC: *Kon mélok panitiané Pesparawi?*
    you join   committee Pesparawi
    'Do you join the committee of Pesparawi?'

MR: *Nggak mélok. Mau   bengi telpon nggak?*
    not   join   immediate night call   not
    'No, I don't. Did you call last night?'

FC: *Bengi? Aku wingi   telpon tapi wis   anu kon*
    night I   yesterday call   but already eh you
    nggak ono. La opo kon?
    not   exist doing what
    'Last night? I did call but you were not there. What were you doing?'

MR: *Metu. Oh jam setengah wolu yo?*
    out   oh hour half   eight right
    'Out. Oh, was it at half past seven?'

The above examples illustrate the common daily conversation among young people. Both males and females use a mixture of Javanese, local language and Indonesian. Males tend to use Javanese *ngoko* more often than females. A male who knows that he is in a lower social status will prefer the use of Indonesian rather than using Javanese *krama*. Several students from the urban city of Surabaya whom I asked whether they still conversed with their families in Javanese, either *krama* or *ngoko*, often felt embarrassed to say that they did not converse in Javanese any more. The Javanese *ngoko* that they use as they grow up is usually learnt from their peers outside their homes. They admit that their parents, especially mothers, have always talked to them in Indonesian since they learned to talk. Only on special occasions, such as when asking children to deliver a message to their grandparents, a mother would model the appropriate *krama* in an Indonesian sentence for her child instead of using an all-Indonesian sentence (*Sana beritahu kakek untuk makan dulu*).

(17) *Sana* <u>*matur eyang*</u>   *supaya* <u>*dahar*</u> *dulu.*
      there tell   grandparent to   dine first
      'Go tell grandfather/mother to dine now.'

The insertion of Javanese *krama* (*matur eyang* and *dahar*) is intentionally done by the mother to indicate the necessity for the children to respect their elders with their language. Thus they will know what to say to their grandparents and not slip into the low-level Javanese that would be inappropriate and would possibly embarrass the mother as well, as she would be considered to be ignorant with regard to educating her children properly.

While boys may pick up quickly the Javanese *ngoko* and use it among their peers as a language of friendship, girls may consider Javanese *ngoko* as harsh and often impolite, preferring the more formal Indonesian, unless they are talking to very close friends or siblings. The above examples suggest that female speakers are the ones who often start and maintain the use of Indonesian when conversing with both males and females.

6. Conclusion

It is almost impossible to discuss the use of Indonesian without discussing the influence of Javanese in its usage, for it is difficult to find people in Java who really talk in pure Indonesian. When looking at gender issues in Indonesian we can see the exclusion of women in many "generic" words. However, it can also be noted that, surprisingly, some generic words in fact seem to exclude men, such as the word *ratu*, whose meaning is 'king' or 'queen' in Javanese, but only 'queen' in Indonesian.

One thing that is difficult to eliminate when talking in Indonesian is the use of Javanese address terms. Apparently, Javanese terms of address express the hierarchical relationship of the speakers. Javanese women are traditionally considered to have lower social status than men. They have to use the deferential style when addressing men. A wife has to address her husband in the refined form when they converse in Javanese, while a husband would often use the casual form. Smith-Hefner (1988:540) found, however, that "Javanese women generally insist that their use of a polite speech form to their husbands is not a sign of their lower social status or social inferiority". In speaking politely, Javanese women are not being subservient, as this is the proper conduct of a mature woman. This may be partly true, since many traditional Javanese women will acknowledge that people who speak refined Javanese are considered to have higher social status. Those who belong to the *priyayi*, the elite Javanese group, have to talk in the refined form. Talking in casual Javanese, which can often sound rude and impolite, may indicate that the person is uneducated. However, Javanese women may also be reluctant to admit that asymmetrical language use between husband and wife is a sign of inferiority of women.

The reluctance of women to use Javanese in conversational interaction may reflect women's preference of a more egalitarian language. This is supported by the fact that many Indonesian mothers who live in urban areas have gradually abandoned using Javanese with their children. However, when a power differential is to be asserted, people would tend to initiate the use of Javanese terms and *ngoko*. Meanwhile, terms in Javanese that are inserted in Indonesian are often loaded with the assertion of an asymmetrical power relationship. Hence, the "ghost" is still roaming around, and is used either consciously or inadvertently to confirm that Indonesian people are not quite egalitarian, that men still constitute the powerful group and women the powerless.

Notes

* I would like to thank the editors of this volume for their help in the preparation of the manuscript.

1. Bahasa Indonesia has some 140 million speakers, of whom approximately 20–30 million are native speakers.

2. However, today many people in Java do not use this script for daily use. Rather, Javanese is also written in the Latin script, e.g., in books or newspapers. Elementary school children in Central and East Java still learn the traditional script, but hardly use it once they leave school.

3. For a more complete description of Javanese structure, see Sudaryanto (1991), Uhlenbeck (1970) and Poedjosoedarmo (1968).

References

Anderson, Benedict R. O'G. 1990. *Language and power. Exploring political cultures in Indonesia.* Ithaca: Cornell University Press.
Ardiana, Leo Indra. 1998. "Lengser keprabon [Stepping down from the throne]." *Surabaya Post*, May 25.

Bergvall, Victoria. 1999. "An agenda for language and gender research for the start of the new millennium." *Linguistik Online*: http://viadrina.euv-frankfurt-o.de/~wjournal/1_99/bergvall.htm.

Brown, Roger & Albert Gilman. 1960. "The pronouns of power and solidarity." In *Style in language*, ed. Thomas A. Sebeok. Cambridge, MA: MIT Press, 253–276.

Budiman, Kris. 1992. "Subordinasi perempuan dalam bahasa Indonesia [Women's subordination in Bahasa Indonesia]." In *Citra wanita dan kekuasaan (Java)* [Image of women and (Javanese) power], eds. Budi Susanto & Sudiarja & Praptadiharja. Yogyakarta: Penerbit Kanisius, 72–80.

Coates, Jennifer. 1993. *Women, men and language*. London: Longman.

Errington, J. Joseph. 1988. *Structure and style in Javanese: A semiotic view of linguistic etiquette*. Philadelphia: University of Pennsylvania Press.

Errington, J. Joseph. 1998. *Shifting languages: Interaction and identity in Javanese Indonesia*. Cambridge: Cambridge University Press.

Geertz, Clifford. 1960. *The religion of Java*. New York: The Free Press of Glencoe.

Geertz, Hildred. 1961. *The Javanese family: A study of kinship and socialization*. New York: The Free Press of Glencoe.

Holmes, Janet. 1995. *Women, men, and politeness*. London: Longman.

Horne, Elinor Clark. 1992. "Javanese." In *International encyclopaedia of linguistics*, ed. William Bright. New York: Oxford University Press, 254–258.

Indrati, Retno. 1996. *A study of verbosity between male and female in a telephone dialogue*. A final linguistic research project report. Surabaya: Petra Christian University.

Irvine, Judith T. 1992. "Ideologies of honorific language." *Pragmatics* 2: 251–262.

Jawa Pos. 1998. *Cari jalan pintas! Panas. Pertemuan Buyung-Harmoko* [Looking for a by-pass! Hot. Buyung-Harmoko's meeting]. May 15.

Jones, L. K. 1994. "Indonesia: Language situation." In *The encyclopedia of languages and linguistics*, vol. 3, eds. R. E. Asher & J. M. Y. Simpson. Oxford: Pergamon Press, 1667–1669.

Kuntjara, Esther. 2001. *Women and politeness: A sociolinguistic study of two Chinese Indonesian mother-daughter pairs in Surabaya*. Ph.D. dissertation, University of Toronto.

Lakoff, Robin T. 1990. *Talking power*. New York: Basic Books.

Mulder, Niels. 1996. *Inside Indonesian society: Cultural change in Java*. Amsterdam: Pepin.

Poedjosoedarmo, Soepomo. 1968. "Javanese speech levels." *Indonesia* 6: 54–81.

Pusat pembinaan. 1997. = Pusat pembinaan dan pengembangan bahasa [Center for guidance in language development]. 1997. *Kamus besar bahasa Indonesia* [Great Dictionary of Bahasa Indonesia]. Balai Pustaka: Departemen Pendidikan dan kebudayaan [Department of Education and Culture].

Smith-Hefner, Nancy J. 1988. "Women and politeness: The Javanese example." *Language in Society* 17: 535–554.

Smith-Hefner, Nancy J. 1989. "A social history of language change in highland East Java." *The Journal of Asian Studies* 48: 257–271.

Sudaryanto. 1991. *Tata bahasa baku bahasa Indonesia* [Standard grammar of Javanese]. Yogyakarta: Duta Wacana University Press.

Suseno, Franz Magnis. 1984. *Etika Jawa: Sebuah analisa falsafi tentang kebijaksanaan hidup Jawa* [Javanese ethics: A philosophical analysis of Javanese ways of life]. Translated into

Indonesian with revision from the original version: Javanische Weisheit und Ethik, Studien zu einer östlichen Moral. Jakarta: PT Gramedia.

Tannen, Deborah. 1993. "The relativity of linguistic strategies: Rethinking power and solidarity in gender and dominance." In *Gender and conversational interaction,* ed. Deborah Tannen. Oxford: Oxford University Press, 165–188.

Uhlenbeck, Eugenius M. 1970. "The use of respect forms in Javanese." In *Pacific linguistic studies in honour of Arthur Capell,* eds. Stephen A. Wurm & Donald C. Laycock. Canberra: Linguistic Circle, 441–466.

Wolfson, Nessa. 1989. *Perspectives: Sociolinguistics and TESOL.* Cambridge: Newbury House.

Deconstructing gender – The case of Romanian*

Florence Maurice
Munich, Germany

1. Introduction

Romanian[1] (*Limba română*) is the official language of Romania and is also called Daco-Romanian. Besides the Daco-Romanian language there are three other minor Romance dialects spoken in the Balkans, Arumanian, Megleno-Romanian, and Istro-Romanian. Romania has approximately 22 million inhabitants; 90 percent of these have Romanian as their first language. The largest minority are Hungarians (8.9%), but there are also German-speaking inhabitants (0.4%) and Ukrainian, Serbian, Croatian, Russian, Turkish, and Gypsy minorities. Romanian is also spoken in the adjacent Republic of Moldova, with 4.4 million inhabitants and important Slavic minorities (Russian: 13%,

Ukrainian: 13.8%).[2]

Romanian minorities live in the neighboring countries of Ukraine, Yugoslavia and Hungary. In total there are some 26 million speakers of Romanian (World Almanac 1995, cited in Grimes 1996–1999). The Daco-Romanian language is itself divided into dialects. The exact number is open to discussion; generally there are considered to be five dialects: Muntenian, Moldovian, Banatian, Crişean and the dialect of Maramureş (Caragiu Manoţeanu 1989:415).

Romanian is a Romance language and forms the East Romance branch together with Italian and Dalmatian; its historical basis is Balkan Latin, the Latin language which was formerly spoken in the Balkans. The first written documents in Romanian date back to the 16th century (the first being the letter from the nobleman Neacşu to the mayor of Braşov in 1521, written in Cyrillic). In the 19th century the Latin alphabet was introduced.

One can account for the peculiar nature of Romanian if one considers that it became isolated from the other Romance languages very early on and was subjected to strong influences from non-Romance languages. This can not only be seen in the vocabulary (with Slavic, Hungarian, Turkish and Greek elements), but also in the language's morphology and syntax. Romanian shares the so-called "Balkanisms" with Albanian and Macedonian: for example, the postposition of the definite article (*hotel-ul* 'hotel-DET'), the replacement of the infinitive by a subjunctive construction (*vreau să plec* 'I want that I go') and a periphrastic future form with the modal verb 'to want'.[3]

It could prove useful to carry out a more detailed examination of the Romanian language and its gender system by considering separately linguistic and non-linguistic differences in the different regions of Romania. Of particular interest is the role of women in Banat and Transylvania, which for a long time belonged to the Austro-Hungarian empire, as opposed to their role in the East, where the oriental or Ottoman influence was strong. However, this article concentrates on the general features of Romanian.

2.   The structural properties of Romanian

2.1   Grammatical gender

In contrast to the other Romance languages Romanian has a complex synthetic inflectional nominal system. There are five cases: nominative/accusative, dative/genitive, vocative[4] and two numbers: singular and plural. The definite article appears in postposition as in Bulgarian, Macedonian and Albanian:

(1) *pom*   *pomul*
  fruit-tree.MASC fruit-tree.MASC.DET
  'fruit-tree' 'the fruit-tree'

With feminine nouns the postponed article is *-a* which forms a single phonological entity with the noun or adjective (for details cf. Tasmowski 1989):

(2) *casă* *casa*   *femeie* *femeia*
  house.FEM house.FEM.DET woman.FEM woman.FEM.DET
  'house' 'the house'   'woman' 'the woman'

There are three genders: feminine, masculine and neuter.[5] The existence of the latter has been disputed for a long time and remains disputed[6] as the neuter nouns show masculine agreement in the singular and feminine agreement in the plural.[7] That means that in Romanian gender is not neutralized in the plural as in other languages, e.g. German or Russian. In the following example the nouns are combined with the word 'one/a' and 'two', which have different forms for each gender.

(3) *o*   *femeie*   *două*   *femei*
  a.FEM.SG woman.FEM   two.FEM.PL woman.FEM.PL
  'a woman'   'two women'

(4) *un*   *bărbat*   *doi*   *bărbați*
  a.MASC.SG man.MASC   two.MASC.PL man.MASC.PL
  'a man'   'two men'

(5) *un*   *glas*   *două*   *glasuri*
  a.NEUT.SG=MASC.SG voice.NEUT two.NEUT.PL=FEM.PL voice.NEUT.PL
  'a voice'   'two voices'

The neuter has vanished in the other Romance languages. There are remnants in the pronominal forms; for example in French: *ce, cela* and *ceci* 'that', or in Spanish *ello, esto* and *aquello* 'it/that'.[8] In Italian there is a group of words which shows the same agreement pattern as Romanian neuter words. It is not yet resolved whether the Romanian neuter should be considered as a deviation from the Latin neuter (Priestly 1983: 348) or whether it is a new invention. The Slavic languages in the adjacent areas – Ukrainian, Bulgarian, Macedonian, and Serbian – also have a neuter form, but there seems to be no connection to the Romanian example, as many neuter words which Romanian borrowed from these languages are feminine in Romanian (Rosetti 1965: 88).[9]

As a rule, human nouns do not have neuter gender; words such as *popor* 'people' or *mamifer* 'mammal' are not really contradictory examples, as they are either collective or generic nouns. However, neuter cannot be used for gender-inclusive or unspecific reference. Besides, feminine and masculine nouns also include common nouns.

Corbett (1991: 151) differentiates between "target gender" and "controller gender": "We should therefore differentiate *controller genders*, the genders into which nouns are divided, from *target genders*, the genders which are marked on adjectives, verbs and so on". Applying this distinction to Romanian, he suggests that: "It can be seen that Rumanian has two target genders in both singular and plural; it has three controller genders [...]" (Corbett 1991: 151).

In most Romanian grammar books the term "neuter" is used (e.g. GLR 1966, Vol. 1: 57, Avram 1997: 47); thus the term "neuter" will be used in the following (including interlinear glosses),[10] but it should be kept in mind that the Romanian neuters receive their inflections from both the feminine and masculine paradigms, and thus are often not comparable to neuter forms in other languages.

Grammatical gender is an inherent and invariant property of nouns. Adjectives, articles and to some extent pronouns show morphological variation according to the noun's grammatical gender. Adjectives can have four different forms for number and gender and show agreement as demonstrated in (6); there are also adjectives with only one form, for example *gri* 'grey'.

(6) *bun*   *profesor*   *buni*   *profesori*
     good.MASC.SG (male) professor   good.MASC.PL (male) professors

     bună   *profesoară*   *bune*   *profesoare*
     good.FEM.SG (female) professor   good.FEM.PL (female) professors

Some of the pronouns have separate forms for masculine and feminine, but often only in the nominative. The personal pronouns have gender-specific forms for the third person singular (*ea* 'she' and *el* 'he') and plural (*ele* f.pl 'they' and *ei* m.pl 'they'). The situation remains the same in the oblique cases but in the plural, only for the nominative and accusative; the genitive and dative are identical.

The interrogative pronoun *cine* 'who/which' has only one form, but it can be used with adjectives which show feminine or masculine inflection:

(7)   *Cine e bolnav?*   *Cine e bolnavă?*
      who is ill.MASC.SG   who is ill.FEM.SG
      'who is ill?'

However, with feminine adjectives the pronoun *care* 'who' is preferred, because it has different gender forms at least in the genitive and dative: *cărui* 'which/who.GEN.SG.MASC' and *cărei* 'which/who.GEN.SG.FEM'.

The only verbal form which shows gender agreement is the past participle:

(8)   *o*   *femeie,*   *care e născută*   *în Timişoara*
      a.FEM.SG woman.FEM.SG who is born.FEM.SG in Temeswar
      'a woman born in Temeswar'

(9)   *un*   *om,*   *care e născut*   *în Timişoara*
      a.MASC.SG man.MASC.SG who is born.MASC.SG in Temeswar
      'a man born in Temeswar'

It is important to differentiate between inflectional classes and genders. Gender implies an agreement property. To assign a noun to one or another gender is to indicate how other elements will agree with it. Inflectional categories, however, relate to morphological variations of nouns in different cases and numbers (cf. Bernstein 1993).

2.2 Word-formation

Typically, in kinship terms there is a correlation between grammatical gender, lexical gender and referential gender.[11] Male and female forms are formed from different stems:

(10)   *soră* (f)   'sister'   *frate* (m)   'brother'
       mamă (f)   'mummy'   *tată* (m)   'daddy'
       mătuşă (f) 'aunt'   *unchi* (m)   'uncle'
       femeie (f) 'woman, wife'   *bărbat* (m)   'man, husband'[12]

Some nouns denoting animals show the same patterns:

(11)   *găină* (f)   'hen'   *cocoş* (m)   'cock'
       vacă (f)   'cow'   *taur* (m)   'bull'

For most nouns denoting people the different forms are derived morphologically. For the most part feminine nouns are derived from existing masculine terms, the opposite case (derivation of masculine nouns from existing feminine terms) is extremely rare.

There are three possibilities for the formation of feminine nouns: conversion, derivation and compounding.

2.2.1   *Conversion*

Conversion means the change of declensional classes; the feminine nouns then have an *-ă* or an *-e*: *funcţionar/funcţionară* (m/f) 'civil-servant', *ziarist/ziaristă* (m/f) 'journalist', *muncitor/muncitoare* (m/f) 'worker' (the diphthongization is due to internal phonological rules). Sometimes these examples are categorized under the label "suffixation": e.g., the contrastive grammar by Engel & Isbăşescu & Stănescu (1993:480) counts *-ă* among the suffixes used for derivation. But if we look at *ziarist/ziaristă* we find an identical stem, the masculine has the typical zero ending, the feminine the typical *-ă* in the nominative. The same holds for most adjectives, for example *bun–bună* 'good (m–f)'. Neither does Dimitriu (1994:62–63) regard them as examples of suffixation because *-ist/istă* and *-tor/toare* are typical suffixes for nomina agentis, but *-ă* and *-e* are not suffixes.[13]

The suffix *-toare* (a conversion from the masculine *-tor*) can be used to derive feminine nouns which refer either to the person engaged in a certain action or to the tool used for this action; thus *seceră-toare* means 'a person who mows' or 'the instrument used for mowing'; *apărătoare* '(female) defendant' or 'instrument used to defend something', as in *apărătoarea roţilor* 'mudguard'; *măturătoare* '(female) sweeper' or 'the instrument used for sweeping'. However, the different meanings each have different plural forms.

Considering *ziarist* and *ziaristă* from a formal point of view, we could say that the masculine is unmarked because of the zero ending. But this is only the case in the singular when no determining article is used. The genitive case with a determining article appears as follows for the two genders: *ziarist-ului* (gen.sg.m) – *ziarist-ei* (gen.sg.f).

2.2.2   *Derivation*

A very productive word-formation process for the formation of feminine nouns is derivation:

(12) *-iţă*:[14]   *pictor/pictoriţă*   'painter, m/f'
                    doctor/doctoriţă   'medical doctor, m/f'
                    casier/casieriţă   'cashier, m/f'

-e(a)să:	*bucătar/bucătăreasă*	'cook, m/f'
	mire/mireasă	'groom/bride'
	poet/poetesă	'poet, m/f'(the feminine has a derogatory connotation)
-că:	*țăran/țărancă*	'peasant, m/f'
	român/româncă	'Romanian, m/f'
	bucureștean/bucureșteancă	'inhabitant of Bucarest, m/f'
-oiacă:	*turc/turcoaică*	'Turk, m/f'

If we compare these examples with those in 2.2.1, it is evident that here the stem is different *pictor-Ø – pictoriț-ă*.

There are a few cases in which masculine nouns are derived from the feminine. Two suffixes are used for this, *-an* and *-oi*: *curcă/curcan* 'turkey hen'/'turkey cock', *cioară/cioroi* 'female crow'/'male crow'. The suffix *-oi* can also be used to derive masculine nouns with female referents: *babă* (f) 'woman' – *băboi* (m) 'heavily built woman', *fată* (f) 'girl' – *fătoi* (m) 'heavily built girl'. *Curvar* 'rake' is derived from *curvă* 'whore', but this is not a productive type of word-formation. What is remarkable is the clear pejorative connotation of the feminine, which the masculine lacks.

Some of the suffixes used for the derivation of feminine nouns are at the same time used to form diminutives: e.g. *-iță: grădină* 'garden' – *grădiniță* 'little garden'.[15] On the other hand, suffixes deriving masculine nouns are also used for the formation of augmentatives: *-an: bețiv* 'drinker' – *bețivan* 'drunkard'. Thus we can see that suffixation reflects stereotypical gender properties.

2.2.3 Compounding

The third possibility for the formation of feminine nouns is compounding with the word *femeie* 'woman': *femeie-pilot* 'woman-pilot', *femeie-marinar* 'woman-sailor', *femeie-medic* 'woman-doctor'. Interestingly, *femeie* determines the grammatical gender of the compound. For these particular words, derived feminine nouns do not exist; however there are examples of compounding in two other cases (Dimitrescu 1982: 201–205): on the one hand compounds with masculine nouns from which feminine nouns have already been derived: *femeie-pictor* 'woman-painter', but note also the derived *pictoriță* 'painter-FEM'. On the other hand, there are examples of compounding with feminine nouns: *femeie-autoare* 'woman author-FEM', even with the nouns *mamă* 'mother' and *soție* 'wife' (cf. Dimitrescu 1982: 201–205). These forms focus specifically on the role of mother and wife. There is no such use of the noun 'man'. The following example goes back to communist times.

(13)   *Destoinică muncitoare, harnică țărancă, iscusită cercetătoare, femeia-ingi-*
       ner, femeia-medic, femeia-profesor și în același timp femeia-soție și mamă,
       în toate aceste ipostaze, femeia din țara noastră se face prețuită și respectată.
       'The efficient worker (f), the hard-working peasant (f), the skillful re-
       searcher (f), the woman-engineer, the woman-doctor, the woman-pro-
       fessor, and at the same time the woman-wife and mother, in all these
       roles the woman in our country is esteemed and respected.'
       (Dimitrescu 1982:203, transl. F. M.).

Avram (1997:54) rightly considers these formations to be superfluous, but they
demonstrate the productivity of this pattern of compounding in the eighties
and are presumably only used in specific contexts.

2.2.4   *Generic nouns and neutralization of referential gender*

There are some masculine nouns denoting white collar professions or professions which are typically associated with male agents, for which no feminine
nouns can be derived; for example, *ministru* 'minister', *decan* 'dean', *rector*
'rector', *mecanic* 'mechanic', *chirurg* 'surgeon'. These nouns are therefore
considered as generics. The masculine epicene *membru* 'member' is rather
neutral concerning referential gender.

A small number of feminine nouns are epicenes. Some of them are rather
out of use, e.g. *beizadea* 'heir to the throne', but others are very common, such
as the word *călăuză* 'guide'. Both nouns typically have male referents. A few
nouns which are related to the semantic field of domestic relations are also
epicenes and can be used with male and female referents: *gazdă* 'host/hostess',
rudă 'relatives'. The feminine nouns *persoană* 'person' and *victimă* 'victim' are
equally applicable to females and males.

One particular group of feminine nouns is markedly derogatory and
demonstrates negative characteristics of a person: e.g., *cutră* 'hypocritical
person'. This group was expanded by the addition of nouns which had the
ending *-ă* but were originally masculine; now they are feminine: e.g. *iudă*
'traitor'. Byck (1933:108–110) states that masculine nouns became feminine
when they acquired the semantic feature "negative characterization" and uses
the term "pejorative feminine".

Nouns such as *complice* (m/f) 'accomplice' are double-gendered. They have
masculine or feminine gender agreement according to their reference.
Complice is semantically rather neutral, but in this group there are also some
words denoting more explicitly negative personal characteristics: *gură-cască*

(m/f) 'gaper', *încurcă-lume* (m/f) 'muddle-headed thinker', *terchea-berchea* (m/f) 'good-for-nothing'.

2.3 Agreement

In complex (subject) noun phrases agreement is determined on the basis of whether the nouns are human/animate or inanimate.

When an attributive adjective modifies both a masculine and a feminine noun it shows masculine agreement:

(14)   *un vizitator   şi   o turistă   mult interesaţi*
a   visitor.MASC and a tourist.FEM very interested.MASC.PL
'a very interested (male) visitor and a very interested (female) tourist'

A different agreement pattern can be seen in example (15). Here we have two feminine nouns, but one of them, *persoană* 'person', is a feminine epicene, and in this sentence it has a male referent: *persoana cu barbă* 'person with a beard' (if we consider stereotypical situations), and thus the adjective shows plural masculine agreement:

(15)   *Maria şi   persoana   cu   barbă au   fost văzuţi.*
Maria and person.DET.FEM.SG with beard have been seen.MASC.PL
'Maria and the person with a beard have been seen.'
(example taken from Farkaş & Zec 1995: 95)

On the other hand, the agreement in (16) is feminine because *persoana cu rochie* 'the person with a dress' refers to a female person:

(16)   *Maria şi   persoana   cu   rochie au   fost văzute.*
Maria and person.DET.FEM.SG with dress have been seen.FEM.PL
'Maria and the person with a dress have been seen.'

In the singular it is grammatical gender which overrides referential gender, *persoana cu barbă* 'person with a beard' triggers feminine agreement:

(17)   *Persoana   cu   barbă a   fost văzută.*
person.DET.FEM.SG with beard has been seen.FEM.SG
'The person with a beard has been seen.'

Examples of this kind suggest that with simple animate subjects, grammatical gender determines agreement while in coordinated mixed subjects referential gender overrides grammatical gender.

With inanimate coordinated subjects the situation is different: If the coordinated subjects are singular and plural, it is the noun in the plural form that determines the agreement.

(18)   *Satelitul*   *şi   avioanele*   *au   fost*
       satellite.DET.MASC.SG and airplane.DET.NEUT.PL have been
       doborîte.
       shot.down.NEUT.PL
       'The satellite and the airplanes have been shot down.'

(19)   *Sateliţii*   *şi   avionul*   *au   fost*
       satellite.DET.MASC.PL and airplane.DET.NEUT.SG have been
       doborîţi.
       shot.down.MASC.PL
       'The satellites and the airplane have been shot down.'

When two plural nouns are of different gender, the predicate agrees with the closer antecedent (cf. Corbett 1991: 265f):

(20)   *Sateliţii*   *şi   avioanele*   *au   fost*
       satellite.DET.MASC.PL and airplane.DET.NEUT.PL have been
       doborîte.
       shot.down.NEUT.PL
       'The satellites and the airplanes have been shot down.'

(21)   *Avioanele*   *şi   sateliţii*   *au   fost*
       airplane.DET.NEUT.PL and satellite.DET.MASC.PL have been
       doborîţi.
       shot.down.MASC.PL
       'The airplanes and the satellites have been shot down.'[16]

As mentioned above, this kind of agreement only applies to inanimate coordinated subjects, while in other cases masculine agreement predominates. These rules of agreement are rather complex, and Mallinson (1984: 448) claims that "the position adopted by the Romanian Academy was highly prescriptive and that in actual usage the facts might not be as straightforward as claimed". Avram (1997: 345) notices that the complex cases tend to be avoided in everyday speech.

What is remarkable is the behavior of demonstrative pronouns when they replace a clause:

(22)   *Ai   plecat   fără   să-mi   spui şi   asta   e   rău.*
       you have gone without telling me   and this.FEM.SG is bad.MASC.SG
       'You have gone without telling me and this is bad.'[17]

In (22) *asta* is formally a homonym of the feminine form of the demonstrative pronoun, but controls masculine predicate agreement. If *asta* did not have a clause as an antecedent it would trigger feminine agreement: *asta e rea* 'this.FEM.SG is bad.FEM.SG'.

Grammatical gender can conflict with referential gender. I will demonstrate this with the feminine epicene *călăuză* 'guide'. Twenty-seven persons, who had crossed over the border illegally, were arrested on a Saturday night by the Austrian police at the Slovakian border:

(23) *Călăuza   ce   însoţea   grupul,   a.fost şi   ea*
      guide.DET.FEM.SG who had.accompanied group.DET was   even she
      arestată.
      arrested.FEM.SG
      'The guide who was accompanying the group was arrested, too.'
      (*Monitorul*, 5 August 1997)

In example (23) the feminine noun *călăuză* is used, and the anaphoric pronoun used, *ea* 'she', is feminine, too, but the referent could be either male or female. If we wanted to provide further information about the person, in the case that it was a man, the masculine pronoun would be used:

(24) *El era de origine română.*
      'He was of Romanian origin.'

If we were speaking of a man in example (23) the masculine pronoun could also be used:

(25) *Călăuza   ce   însoţea   grupul,   a.fost şi   el*
      guide.DET.FEM.SG who had.accompanied group.DET was   even he
      arestat.
      arrested.MASC.SG
      'The guide, who was accompanying the group, was arrested too.'

That means that the feminine noun *călăuză* has two referential potentials: generic and gender-specific. If the grammatically correct feminine pronoun is used, no information about the referential gender is given, only the use of the masculine pronoun would be an indication of a male referent.

For gender conflicts of this kind an Agreement Hierarchy was developed by Corbett (1991:226):

> attributive < predicate < relative pronoun < personal pronoun [...]
> Possible agreement patterns are constrained as follows: As we move rightwards
> along the hierarchy, the likelihood of semantic agreement will increase mono-
> tonically [...]

Our examples support this hierarchy, as they show that the likelihood of semantic agreement of pronouns is greater than the likelihood of semantic agreement
of predicates. However, it should be noted that the use of masculine nouns for
female referents is more frequent than the use of feminine nouns for males.

Agreement patterns in Romanian are complex. When coordinated human
nouns are of different genders, it is the masculine which overrides the feminine.
Otherwise the number – singular or plural – and the position of the nouns
relative to the words showing agreement have to be taken into account.

The fact that the agreement patterns in Romanian are more complex than,
for example, in French, where the masculine always overrides the feminine, may
be explained by the existence of neuter nouns in Romanian, which trigger
masculine inflections in the singular and feminine in the plural.

3. The use of human nouns

As we have seen, there are different possibilities to indicate referential gender in
Romanian. Now we will turn to the question of the forms used. It is important
to differentiate between cases where feminine forms can be derived – e.g.
profesor/profesoară 'male/female professor' – and cases where no feminine forms
exist, such as *decan* 'dean'.

If feminine forms exist, predicative use has to be differentiated from
referential use. In the predicate, masculine forms can be used for female
referents without this leading to misunderstandings, as the information about
the referential gender can be encoded in the subject.

A statement like *profesorul* (m) *lucrează* 'the professor works' will normally
be interpreted as referring to a male individual. The same interpretation of the
masculine noun *profesor*, however, is not possible in the following example
which refers to a female individual:

(26)   *Maria a.devenit profesor*
       Maria became   professor.MASC.SG

Besides the predicate, the apposition is a function where the human noun need
not provide information about referential gender, as this is already encoded in

the nominal head and therefore contextually retrievable. The journal *Dilema* 'Dilemma' interviewed persons about the subject of what it is like to be a woman, the disadvantages and the advantages. After every statement, the name and the profession of the person interviewed was given. Of the nine women interviewed the professions of five were given in the masculine form:

(27) *Doina Popescu, ziarist,*　　　　*45 de ani*
　　　Doina Popescu journalist.MASC.SG 45 of years
　　　'Doina Popescu, journalist, 45 years old'

(28) *Manuela Bricman, inginer,*　　　*32 de ani*
　　　Manuela Bricman engineer.MASC.SG 32 of years
　　　'Manuela Bricman, engineer, 32 years old'
　　　(*Dilema* 5 (226), 23–29 May 1997: 9)

The use of generic masculines is also illustrated in the following excerpt from a short biography of the Romanian linguist, Maria Manoliu-Manea, who lives in the United States. Here eight masculine human nouns are used with reference to a specific, female individual:

(29) *Maria M.-Manea, profesor*　　　　　*universitar, specialist*　　　*în*
　　　Maria M.-Manea professor.MASC.SG of.university specialist.MASC.SG in
　　　lingvistică între　　*1968 şi*　*1977 este conferenţiar*　　[...] *este*
　　　linguistics between 1968 and 1977 is　lecturer.MASC.SG　　is
　　　numită　　　　*profesor*
　　　appointed.FEM.SG professor.MASC.SG
　　　'Maria M.-Manea, university professor and a specialist in linguistics,
　　　from 1968 to 1977 she was a lecturer and [...] was appointed professor'
　　　(RLŞL 1994: 95)

A predicatively used participle shows agreement with its subject, and thus *numit-ă* 'appointed-FEM.SG' has feminine inflection; the nouns, however, are all masculine. Here the feminine forms would be possible, too. Avram (1997: 55) reports that: "in the language of today a strong tendency can be seen not to specify the sex of referent for people with certain professions or titles here, masculine forms are also used with reference to women, even when feminine forms exist" (transl. F.M.).[18]

In the function of predicate and apposition, feminine and masculine forms can be used to refer to women. Since grammar allows for both forms with titles and white-collar professions, the choice is determined in a different manner: In Romanian, choosing the masculine form with reference to women is typical of official language. This use, however, is asymmetrical, as a feminine occupational term could not be used with reference to men.

The official form of address for a female professor is: *doamnă profesor* (m) 'Mrs Professor', but in informal situations the feminine form is preferred *doamnă profesoară* (f) 'Mrs (female) Professor', e.g. by students. The masculine form can be interpreted in two ways: It can refer to: (a) the woman whose profession it is; (b) the wife of the man whose profession it is. In communist times, *tovarășă* 'comrade' was used instead of *doamnă*.

On the other hand, with titles designating low-status occupations or professions stereotypically associated with women, it is not possible to use masculine nouns to refer to women. In the article in *Dilema* quoted above, three feminine forms are used in the apposition: *țărancă* (f) 'female peasant', *casnică* (f) 'housewife', and *ospătăriță* (f) 'waitress'. So (30) is unacceptable; feminine forms as in (31) must be chosen:

(30) **Ea este educator   / infirmier   / casnic.*
     *she is   teacher.MASC / nurse.MASC / home.loving.MASC

(31) *Ea este educatoare   / infirmieră / casnică.*
     she is   teacher.FEM / nurse.FEM / home.loving.FEM
     'She is a teacher/nurse/housewife.'

Casnic is an adjective and so, of course, is expected to show agreement. But another asymmetry can be observed: *Ea este casnică* means 'she is a housewife', but when referring to a man *el este casnic* means 'he is house-loving', i.e. in addition to anaphoric agreement there is a change in denotative meaning.

With nouns indicating the geographical origin of a person, the feminine form has to be used with reference to women:

(32) *Ea est româncă.*   **Ea este român.*
     she is Romanian.FEM   *she is   Romanian.MASC
     'She is Romanian.'

The Romanian grammar book LRC (1985: 12) gives the following explanation: "This shows that it is less important to specify the sex of the referent if we are dealing with professional terms" (transl. F. M.), but this is only partly true, for the feminine form is obligatory with low-status professions and typically female professions.[19]

There are masculine human nouns, from which no feminine form can be derived, e.g. *decan* 'dean' or *chirurg* 'surgeon'. Here the masculine forms are used with reference to women. But in certain cases it is not always evident that they actually do refer to women. The following story has been used in other languages to show that the use of generic masculines may lead to comprehension problems. The story has also been translated into Romanian:[20]

(33) *Un om merge cu maşina cu fiul la un meci de fotbal. Deodată se întâmplă un accident. Tata este mort, dar fiul rănit este condus la spital. Chirurgul* (m.sg) *care îl primeşte spune: nu-l pot opera. Este fiul meu.*
'A man drives to a football match with his son. Suddenly there is an accident. The father dies and the son is taken to hospital. The surgeon (m.sg) who receives the child says: I cannot operate on him. It is my son.'

The story was shown to Romanians who were asked to explain the situation. They began to speculate and invented incredible solutions. But the correct – and simple – solution that the surgeon (*chirurgul*) is a woman and, hence, the mother of the child did not occur to them.

So in Romanian there is a tendency – which could be called iconic – that the higher the prestige of an occupation, the greater is the likelihood that there is no feminine derived noun. And the higher the level of language, the greater is the likelihood that even if there is a feminine noun, it is not used. So we can discern a discriminatory tendency towards women at high levels of language use and occupational prestige.

For generic reference masculine nouns are used which are intended to include women; this, however, may be ambiguous, as they can also be used in reference to men alone. In the language of the press, some epicene forms are used that do not express the gender of the referent, e.g. *persoană* (f) 'person', or *membru* (m) 'member'.

(34) *Persoanele   urmărite   de fosta   Securitate au*
     person.DET.FEM.PL persecuted.FEM.PL by former.DET Securitate have
     dreptul   [...]
     right.DET
     'The persons persecuted by the former Securitate have the right to [...]'
     (*România liberă*, 24 September 1998: 2)

Another gender-neutral form is the second person in generalized use; adjectival attributes can show feminine or masculine inflection:

(35) *Când eşti   inteligentă   nu e nici o problemă.*
     when you.are intelligent.FEM.SG NEG is NEG a problem
     'When you are intelligent, it's not a problem.'

Mixed groups are normally denoted by a masculine noun in the plural. Sometimes, nouns which do not express gender differences are used. There are hardly any cases of splitting, i.e. the explicit use of both masculine and feminine nouns in neutral contexts.

4. The lexicon, idiomatic expressions and proverbs

Even the treatment of women and men in the dictionary is asymmetrical: For *bărbat* 'man' there are two definitions: "1. male person, brave, courageous person, 2. husband"; for *femeie* 'woman' there are three definitions: "1. female person; 2. married female person; 3. wife" (Breban 1992:96, 357).

Besides 'male person', *bărbat* 'man' denotes a person with positive characteristics – 'courageous person' (for a similar phenomenon in Turkish cf. Braun, this vol.). The equivalent does not exist in the case of *femeie* 'woman', but there is an additional meaning – 'married female person'.

The positive meaning of the noun *bărbat* 'man' can be seen in the morphologically related words, which can be attributed to women, too.

(36) *bărbătesc*   lit. 'of male gender'   'courageous'
      a lupta bărbăteşte   lit. 'to fight like a man' 'to fight courageously'
      femeia bărbată   lit. 'a male woman'   'an energetic woman'
      a îmbărbăta   lit. 'to make male'   'to encourage'
      bărbăţie   lit. 'maleness'   'courage'

Physical attributes of men can be metaphorically attributed to women and then have a positive meaning:

(37) *Tansu Ciller [...] a reuşit în politică pentru că are coaie.*
      'Tansu Ciller [...] succeeded in politics, because she has balls.'
      (*Sfera Politicii* 47, 1997:10)

The above example suggests that Tansu Ciller is an energetic woman, who gets her own way. Of course, this is not a formal expression. In contrast, "feminine" characteristics attributed to men carry negative connotations:

(38) *El este muiere.*
      he is   woman
      'He is a cry-baby.'

In idiomatic expressions and proverbs the woman is stereotypically characterized as stupid (39–40), talkative (41) and fickle (42):

(39)   *a şti cât baba mea*
       lit. 'to know as my wife'
       'to know very little'

(40)   *socoteală băbească*
       lit. 'feminine calculation'
       'oversimplified calculation'

(41)   *Vorbele sunt femei, faptele sunt bărbaţi.*
       'Words are women, facts are men.'

(42)   *Nimic mai schimbător ca vremea şi ca muierile.*
       'Nothing changes more quickly than the weather and women.'

The hierarchy of gender roles is a given and unchangeable:

(43)   *Bărbatul este capul femeii.*
       'The man is the head of the woman.'

(44)   *Vai de casa unde bărbatul e muiere*
       'Woe betide the house, where the man is the woman.'

The proverb in (43) is a translation from Latin and means: 'the man is the head
of the family.' In Romanian the Latin word *familia* developed into the word
'woman', and this sentence is now interpreted as 'the man is the head (the one
who does the thinking) of the woman'.

For general reference in proverbs, either the verb form of the second person
'you' is used, or the word *om* (m) which means 'human being' or 'man'. Both
expressions can exclude (45) or include (46) women.

(45)   *Este bine să   asculţi   şi   sfatul unei neveste.*
       it.is good that you.listen also advice of.a wife
       'It is good to listen (even) to the advice of your wife.'

(46)   *Norocul este.după cum şi-l   face   omul.*
       luck.DET depends how self.it-ACC makes man
       'Luck depends on oneself.' (*om* 'human being')

In many proverbs, women are treated like inanimate objects or animals. In the
following examples, one of the *trei lucruri* 'three things', is a woman:

(47)   *Trei lucruri nu se împrumută: calul, nevasta şi puşca.*
       'Three things you don't lend to others: your horse, your wife and your gun.'

(48)   *Trei lucruri nu lasă în pace pe om: vinul, femeia și banul.*
'Three things that don't leave men in peace: wine, women and money.'

In the following proverb a woman is also compared to a thing; this saying is especially shocking, as it recommends the beating of a woman (today it is little used):

(49)   *Femeia nebătută e ca moara neferecată.*
'A woman who is not beaten is like a mill without an owner.'

Of course, these sayings were coined a long time ago: the metaphors are agricultural in origin. And the same is true for the Romanian language as for many other modern languages: proverbs are rarely used literally and in their full version; they are more often ironically transformed. Many of them are only part of the passive vocabulary of younger speakers. On the other hand, a transformed example may not necessarily be less sexist (cf. Hufeisen 1993:158). The fact that many of the proverbs are agricultural in origin is not an argument against their use today: the knowledge that the earth moves around the sun has not changed our referring to the sun as a moving body: *soarele răsare* 'the sun rises' (the sun is moving).

5.   Beginning the discourse on language and gender

In Romania the subject of language and gender is not much discussed (cf. also Brumme 1997:95).[21] However, the question of whether women speak a different language was treated in some articles devoted to folklore and dialectal usage. Lüder (1989) provides an overview of the publications on this subject, and she cites a distinguishing phonetic feature: women tend to use more palatalized consonants than men. Another distinguishing feature is the use of diminutive suffixes: Lüder (1989:210f) compared 695 variants of the ballad *Miorița* and found out that women use significantly more diminutives than men.[22]

Feminist discourse on the question of language and gender is nearly non-existent. In *România literară* 'Literary Romania', the most important literary journal in Romania, Rodica Zafiu describes new tendencies and noteworthy mistakes in the language of the newspapers in the rubric *Păcatele limbii* 'linguistic errors'. It is of interest, that, for example, in 1998 there was no discussion about the treatment of women in the newspapers or in everyday speech; but Zafiu wrote about taboo subjects like the impact of the Romani language on

Romanian (8 July 1998). This implies that "gender and language" is not a taboo subject; rather for most people it is simply not a subject for discussion. An exception is Mihalea Miroiu, who fights for the equal rights of women in Romanian society. In her article *Dimensiunea de gen a educaţiei* 'The role of gender in education' she demands that a non-sexist language should be used in textbooks, and she criticises the fact that women in higher-status occupations are invisible in the language. However, she does not discuss these ideas in detail and does not provide any examples (Miroiu 1998b).

To explain the fact that there is so little discussion about this subject in Romania, one has to consider the specific political situation of post-communist countries.[23] Officially, under communism women had the same rights as men, which meant that they had to work as men did. At the same time there was no sharing of house work: "[...] this led to the double or triple burden – work, housework, and children" (Harsanyi 1993:44). Women experienced the so-called equality of the regime negatively, and thus feminism is frowned upon. "Women pay the price for the former dubious politics of equality by a double and triple burden and an anti-feminism which had already started before the transformation" (Nève 1998:75, transl. F.M.).

Western women also fought against the commercialization of women. But one can only fight against the commercialization of women and their beauty and against reducing them to mere external appearance, if such commercialization exists. In the Eastern European countries, such commercialization did not exist. Beauty competitions have appeared in recent times and enjoy great success.

> Western feminists' concern regarding the commercialization of women's bodies and the pressure exerted on women by the "beauty myth" have no place in today's Romania, for both commerce and beauty were clandestine for more than half a century. (Harsanyi 1993:49)

An example of the general mentality is provided in the article by Tudor Popescu from the March 10, 1998 issue of the journal *Adevărul* 'Truth', entitled *Femeia nu e om* 'the woman is not a human being/not a man'. Here the author claims, for instance, that women are different because they cannot think. This article, of course, provoked sharp reactions. The low level of the discussion on this subject is reflected in the following remark by Mihaela Miroiu:

> A student told me that we should feel privileged that we can read an article like that at the end of the 20th century. He is right. It seems unreal that there are still journalists with an opinion about the gender subject which is typical of the 18th century. (Miroiu 1998a:7, transl. F.M.).

Still, there are indications of an emerging debate of feminist issues in the press. For example, in 1997 the journal *Sfera politicii* 'World of Politics' published an issue with the title "Gender" (No. 47), and the journal *Dilema* an issue on "female types, archetypes and stereotypes" (No. 226).[24] In the field of linguistics things are changing, too: In 1991 in Romania the organization ANA was founded. The name ANA was not chosen by chance: Ana is a person from the Romanian legend about the monastery of Arges; she was sacrificed so that the walls of the monastery could be built. The organization is working on linguistic guidelines for the equal treatment of men and women, which were to be published at the end of 1998. (As of November 2000, they have not been released.)[25]

I believe recommendations should cover the following: any reference to individual women should favor the feminine form, i.e. *ea este profesoară* (f) 'she is a (female) professor' should be preferred to *ea este profesor* (m) 'she is a professor'. Where no feminine noun exists, an attempt should be made to derive a new term using a productive suffix. For generic reference the use of forms that are not differentiated for gender should be suggested wherever possible. In some cases the identification of women could be ensured by applying split forms. One should hope that the guidelines by ANA will launch a broad discussion and a sensibility towards the issue of language and gender, so that the contribution of women to society is reflected in the language as well.

Notes

* I wish to express my deep gratitude towards the editors for their immeasurable support and assistance in the process of writing this chapter.

1. Besides *Romanian* the name *Rumanian* is used. The former emphasizes the Latin origin of the word.

2. The statistical data is taken from Brunner (1998:300). The Moldovian Republic formed part of the Soviet Union until it declared its independence in 1991. When it was a Soviet Republic the language spoken there was considered to be a language of its own and was written with Cyrillic letters. Nowadays the Latin alphabet is used.

3. Standard reference works on Romanian are: Mallinson (1986), Rosetti (1986), and Daniliuc & Daniliuc (2000); Niculescu (1990/1981); Habian (1979).

4. The traditional grammar books (e.g. GLR 1966, vol.1: 74) always speak of five cases, even if there are only three distinct case forms.

5. Some grammar books identify a fourth gender, the "genul personal" (personal gender). But this is not a gender of its own. Some feminine and masculine nouns show special features, when they are used with reference to persons and these peculiarities are categorized under the

label of personal gender. For further details see GLR (1966, vol. I: 59f), Beyrer & Bochmann & Bronsert (1987:67); Avram (1997:55) rejects this notion and speaks of a "subgenus".

6. A detailed bibliography on this subject can be found in Marcus (1967:153–154), Hall (1965) and Mallinson (1984); cf. also Manoliu-Manea (1989:102f).

7. This is not surprising for Indo-European languages, e.g. Tokharian shows the same agreement patterns (Priestly 1983:349). Other Indo-European languages, when syncretism of cases is observed, often have identical forms for the masculine and the neuter in the singular (for example, in German), and for neuter and feminine in the plural (for example, the genitive plural form in Russian).

8. According to Priestly (1983:340–341), "[…] the normal order of categories to lose formal gender-opposition is noun, adjective, pronoun".

9. Mallinson (1988:401) has a different view: "[…] also doubtless a result of Slavic contact is the existence of a so-called neuter gender in Rumanian".

10. Another term found is "ambigeneric", e.g. Mallinson (1987:312).

11. On the correlation between grammatical gender and semantic specification in Spanish, cf. Harris (1991).

12. The etymology of the latter two examples is interesting to note: *femeie* developed from the Latin *familia* 'family', *bărbat* from *barbatus* 'bearded'.

13. Beyrer et al. (1987:46) are not consistent in their treatment of feminine nouns either. They describe the suffixes -*ist/istă* together, but only speak about masculine nouns. With the suffixes -*tor/toare* they mention feminine nouns, but no examples are given.

14. In these examples, *ă* is not part of the suffix, but constitutes the ending of the nominative singular.

15. In contrast to the suffixation described above, typical suffixation in Romanian does not involve a change in nominal gender.

16. Examples (18–21) are taken from Engel et al. (1993:1040).

17. Example taken from Manoliu-Manea (1993:28).

18. A throwback to the official communist politics under Ceauşescu can be discerned: "Ceauşescu militated against gender discrimination, demanding that persons be treated not as men and women, but in terms of their qualities as members of the Party, and as citizens" (Kligman 1992:378).

19. Cf. Brumme (1997:90–95) for an analysis of the use of personal nouns in job advertisements. She shows that in job advertisements feminine nouns are used only with low-status professions or typically female professions.

20. Translated from "La féminisation des noms de métier, fonction, grade ou titre", an article written by the Government of the French Community, the minister of culture, Eric Tomas, published in the Internet: http://www.cfwb.ge/franca/publicat/pg006.htm.

21. Lüder states the same and wonders whether this contradicts the fact that in Romania there are many more female linguists than in Germany or whether this is a consequence of this fact (1989:209).

22. Cf. Brumme (1997) for a survey of other articles in the area of folklore on this subject.

23. On this subject cf., e.g., Buckley (1997) (with no reference to Romania), Moghdan (1993), Nève (1998); cf. Funk & Mueller (1993) for communication problems between Western feminists and Eastern women.

24. Other publications on this subject are for example: *Dilema* 1993 (47): "The Voices of Women in Times of Transition"; *Revista 22*, 1999 (supplement No. 84): "De la traumă la integritate" 'From trauma to integrity'; *Sfera Politicii*, 1999 (71/72): "Feminism".

25. For information (English version), cf. www.anasaf.ro.

References

Avram, Mioara. 1997. *Gramatica pentru toți. Ediția a II-a revăzută și adăugită*. [Grammar book for everybody. Second corrected and updated edition]. București: Humanitas.

Bernstein, Judy B. 1993. *Topics in the syntax of nominal structure across Romance*. Ph.D. dissertation, CUNY, New York, NJ.

Beyrer, Arthur & Klaus Bochmann & Siegfried Bronsert. 1987. *Grammatik der rumänischen Sprache der Gegenwart*. Leipzig: Enzyklopädie.

Breban, Vasile. 1992. *Dicționar general al limbii române* [General dictionary of the Romanian language]. Bucharest: Editura enciclopedică.

Brumme, Jenny. 1997. "'Inginer și femeie de serviciu' [Engineer and woman of service] – Die rumänische Sprache zwischen patriarchalischer Tradition and postkommunistischem Sexismus." In *Sprache und Geschlecht in der Romania*, eds. Wolfgang Dahmen & Günther Holtus & Johannes Kramer. Tübingen: Narr, 63-101.

Brunner, Borgna, ed. 1998. *Information Please Almanac*. Boston: Information Please LLC.

Buckley, Mary, ed. 1997. *Post-Soviet women: From the Baltic to Central Asia*. Cambridge: Cambridge University Press.

Bulgăr, Gheorge. 1995. *Limba română* [The Romanian language]. București: Vox.

Byck, Jacques. 1933: "Le féminin péjorative." *Bulletin linguistique* 1: 108–110.

Caragiu Manoțeanu, Matilda. 1989. "Areallinguistik." In *Lexikon der Romanistischen Linguistik*, III, eds. Günter Holtus & Michael Metzeltin & Christian Schmitt. Tübingen: Niemeyer, 405–422.

Chițoran, Ioana. 1992. "The Romanian gender system in the framework of markedness theory." *Revue roumaine de linguistique* 37: 177–190.

Corbett, Greville G. 1991. *Gender*. Cambridge: Cambridge University Press.

Daniliuc, Laura & Radu Daniliuc. 2000. *Descriptive Romanian grammar: An outline*. Munich: LINCOM.

DEX. 1975 = *Dicționar explicativ al limbii române* [Explanatory dictionary of the Romanian language]. Bucharest: Editura Academiei Republicii Socialiste România.

Dimitrescu, Florica. 1982. *Dicționar de cuvinte recente* [Dictionary of new words]. Bucharest: Dicționarele Albatros.

Dimitriu, Călin. 1994. *Gramatica limbii române explicată* [Romanian grammar explained]. Iași: Virgina.

Engel, Ulrich & Mihai Isbăşescu & Speranţa Stănescu & Octavian Nicolae. 1993. *Kontrastive Grammatik deutsch-rumänisch*. Heidelberg: Groos.

Farkaş, Donka F. & Draga Zec. 1995. "Agreement and pronominal reference." In *Advances in Roumanian Linguistics*, eds. Guglielmo Cinque & Ciuliana Giusti. Amsterdam: Benjamins, 83–101.

Funk, Nanette & Magda Mueller, eds. 1993. *Gender politics and post-communism. Reflections from Eastern Europe and the former Soviet Union*. London: Routledge.

GLR. 1966 = *Gramatica limbii române* [Grammar of the Romanian language]. 2 vols. Bucharest: Editura Academiei Republicii Socialiste România.

Grimes, Barbara F., ed. 1996–1999. *Ethnologue: Languages of the World*, 13th edition (electronic version). SIL International.

Habian, George. 1979. *English-Romanian, Romanian-English dictionary*. Cleveland, OH.

Hall, Robert A. 1965. "The 'neuter' in Romance: A pseudo-problem." *Word* 21: 421–427.

Harris, James W.1991. "The exponence of gender in Spanish." *Linguistic Inquiry* 22: 27–67.

Harsanyi, Doina Pasca. 1993. "Women in Romania." In *Gender politics and post-communism*, eds. Nanette Funk & Magda Mueller. London: Routledge, 39–52.

Hufeisen, Britta. 1993. "Frauen und Pelze wollen oft geklopft sein: Zur Darstellung der Frau in Sprichwörtern, Redewendungen und sonstigen feststehenden Ausdrücken." In *Das Weib soll schweigen ...* " (I. Kor. 14, 34): Beiträge zur linguistischen Frauenforschung, ed. Britta Hufeisen. Frankfurt am Main: Lang, 153–171.

Kligman, Gail. 1992. "The politics of reproduction in Ceauşescus's Romania." *East European Politics and Societies* 6: 364–418.

LRC. 1985 = *Limba română contemporană* [The Romanian language today]. Bucharest: Editura didactică şi pedagogică.

Lüder, Elsa. 1989. "Rumänisch: Sprache und Geschlecht." In *Lexikon der Romanistischen Linguistik III*, eds. Günter Holtus & Michael Metzeltin & Christian Schmitt. Tübingen: Niemeyer, 209–216.

Mallinson, Graham. 1984. "Problems, pseudoproblems and hard evidence – another look at the Rumanian neuter." *Folia Linguistica* 18: 439–451.

Mallinson, Graham. 1986. *Rumanian*. London: Croom Helm.

Mallinson, Graham. 1987. "Rumanian." In *The world's major languages*, ed. Bernard Comrie. New York: Oxford University Press, 303–321.

Mallinson, Graham. 1988. "Rumanian." In *The Romance languages*, eds. Martin Harris & Vincent Nigel. London: Croom Helm, 391–419.

Manoliu-Manea, Maria. 1989. "Rumänisch: Morphosyntax/morphosyntaxe". In *Lexikon der Romanistischen Linguistik*, III, eds. Günter Holtus & Michael Metzeltin & Christian Schmitt. Tübingen: Niemeyer, 101–114.

Manoliu-Manea, Maria. 1993. "Un micromodel al genului românesc" [A micro-model of Romanian gender]. *Limbă şi literatură* 1–2: 21–29.

Marcus, Solomon. 1967. *Algebraic linguistics: Analytical models*. New York: Academic Press.

Miroiu, Mihaela. 1997. "Ana's land: The right to be sacrificed". In *Ana's land. Sisterhood in Eastern Europe*, ed. Tanya Renne. Colorado: Westview, 136–140.

Miroiu, Mihaela. 1998a. "(De)formatorii de opinie" [(De)former of opinion]. In *Revista 22* (16), 16–22 aprilie.

Miroiu, Mihaela. 1998b. "Dimensiunea de gen a educație" [The dimension of gender in education]. In *Revista 22* (8), 19–25 februarie.

Moghdan, Valentine M., ed. 1993. *Democratic reform and the position of women in transitional economies.* Oxford: Clarendon.

Nève, Dorothée de. 1998. "Zwanghafte Gleichberechtigung und kontrollierter Körper – Zu den Lebensbedingungen von Frauen im sozialistischen Rumänien". In *Frauen in Südosteuropa*, eds. Anneli Ute Gabanyi & Hans Georg Majer. München: Südosteuropa-Gesellschaft, 59–78.

Niculescu, Alexandru. 1990. *Outline history of the Romanian language.* Paduva: Unipress. (reprint from Bucharest 1981)

Popescu, Christian Tudor. 1998. "Femeia nu e om" [The woman is not a man/human being]. *Adevărul* (408), 10 martie.

Priestly, Tom M. S. 1983. "On 'drift' in Indo-European gender systems." *Journal of Indo-European Studies* 11: 339–363.

RLŞL = *Revista de lingvistică și știință literară.* [Journal of Linguistics and Literary Studies].

Rosetti, Alexandru. 1965. *Linguistica.* The Hague: Mouton.

Rosetti, Alexandru. 1986. *Istoria limbii române: Editie definitiva.* [The history of the Romanian language]. Vol. 1. București: Editura științifică și enciclopedică.

Tasmowski, Liliane. 1989. *Cours de grammaire roumaine.* Ghent: Communication & Cognition.

RUSSIAN

Doing gender in Russian

Structure and perspective

Ursula Doleschal
Wirtschaftsuniversität Wien, Vienna, Austria

Sonja Schmid
Cornell University, Ithaca, USA

1.   Introduction

Russian (*Russkij jazyk*) is the native language of about 153 million inhabitants of the Russian Federation and the former Soviet republics. An additional 61 million people in the former Soviet Union have learnt Russian as their first foreign language (Timberlake 1990:827). In the second half of the twentieth century Russian was also taught extensively in Eastern European countries that were under the Soviet sphere of influence. Russian belongs to the Slavic group of the Indo-European language family. Its closest relatives are Belorussian and Ukrainian which, together with Russian, form the subgroup of East Slavic languages.

The modern standard language is known as *Russkij literaturnyj jazyk*. It is regulated by the Institute of Russian Language of the Soviet Academy of Sciences, which publishes authoritative dictionaries and grammars. Russian is written in the Cyrillic alphabet, the major transliteration used by linguists is close to broad phonemic transcription.[1]

Structurally, Russian is an inflecting language, characterized by both affixational and fusional morphology and a productive system of word formation. The verb is inflected for tense (past, present, future), person (first, second, third), number (singular, plural), mood (indicative, imperative, subjunctive), voice (active, passive), aspect (perfective, imperfective) and – gender (in the past tense and in the subjunctive). The inflectional categories of the nouns, adjectives and some numerals comprise case (nominative, genitive, dative, accusative, instrumental, locative/prepositional), number, gender and animacy. Pronouns are inflected for the same categories as the word classes they substitute.[2]

2.   Structural properties

2.1 Grammatical gender

As in many other European languages, in Russian nouns are divided into three gender classes: feminine, masculine and neuter.[3] Nouns denoting persons normally belong to the masculine or feminine grammatical gender, i.e., nouns denoting male human beings are masculine, and nouns denoting female human beings are feminine (Švedova 1980:466). There is no separate class for reference to human beings in general. The neuter gender, which theoretically could take on such a function, has almost completely lost the capacity to classify animate nouns. The gender-specific classificatory function of grammatical gender can best be demonstrated with kinship terms and a few general personal nouns which also have lexical gender:

Table 1a. Kinship terms

f		m	
mat'	'mother'	*otec*	'father'
doč'	'daughter'	*syn*	'son'

Table 1b. General personal nouns

f		m	
ženščina	'woman'	*mužčina*	'man'
devuška	'girl'	*mal'čik*	'boy'

However, this symmetry is atypical of the majority of nouns denoting persons. It is far more common for feminine-female nouns to be derived from masculine-(male) ones – or to be lacking altogether, cf. the examples in Table 2.

Table 2. Feminine-female nouns derived from masculine-male ones

f		m	
moskvič-ka	'female Muscovite'	*moskvič*	'male Muscovite'
student-ka	'female student'	*student*	'(male) student'
(*vrač-ixa*)	'female physician'	*vrač*	'(male) physician'
(*professor-ša*)	'female professor'	*professor*	'(male) professor'
–		*politik*	'(male) politician'

Note that the nouns given in parentheses have derogatory connotations and therefore are no stylistically neutral equivalents of their masculine counterparts, which is indicated by question marks. While the relation between the nouns cited in Tables 1a and 1b is an equipollent one, it is privative for the nouns in Table 2. Therefore, in the latter case the masculine noun can (or must) be applied to female referents in Contemporary Standard Russian. One such context is the plural, where masculine nouns may be used even when denoting exclusively female groups (see Doleschal 1995, but cf. Martynyuk 1990 for a different view).

(1) *U vas sredi   poslušnic   sejčas nemalo studentov.*
at you among novices.FEM now not.few students.MASC
'Among your novices there are now quite a few students.'

The relation between grammatical gender[4] and referential gender can thus be symbolized as follows: M⊃m, f⊃F. It is therefore not a biunique one, i.e., masculine personal nouns denote males but may also refer to females, while feminine personal nouns can never refer to males. The same is true, mutatis mutandis, for pronouns and other word classes showing gender agreement.

2.2 Gender agreement

The constitutive feature of the grammatical category *gender* is agreement. The gender of a noun can unambiguously be determined only on the basis of the agreement with other words which are syntactically dependent on it. In Russian, gender is neutralized in the plural (with the exception of *oba* 'both' and *poltora* 'one and a half', which retain distinct forms in the oblique cases), so that gender agreement can be characterized as in Figure 1.

Singular	Plural	Singular	Plural		
Feminine		*dobr-aja*	'good-FEM'		
Masculine	Plural	*dobr-yj*	'good-MASC'	*dobr-ye*	'good-PL'
Neuter		*dobr-oe*	'good-NEUT'		

Figure 1. Target genders in Russian

Since grammatical gender is an inherent classificatory feature of every noun, the neutralization of gender agreement in the plural does not imply the loss of the category in the noun itself. It merely leads to a certain obfuscation of the category (especially in masculine underived nouns), but it remains salient in feminine derived nouns. The following syntactic contexts trigger gender agreement with a head noun (or nominal):

within the NP: attributive adjective or pronoun, relative pronoun, numeral ('one' and 'two') with the head noun
within the clause: predicative adjective or pronoun, numeral ('one' and 'two'), past tense, conditional form of the verb with the subject
beyond the clause: anaphoric or deictic pronoun and all anaphoric elements of the word classes adjective, possessive pronoun, numeral

('one' and 'two'), verb (past and conditional) with their
antecedent

Most of these contexts are illustrated by the following example:

(2) *Prišl-a   moj-a   byvš-aja   studentka,   kotor-aja očen'*
came-FEM my-FEM former-FEM student.FEM who-FEM very
umn-aja.   On-a   mogl-a   by   pomoč'.
intelligent-FEM she-FEM might-FEM COND help
'A former student of mine, who is very intelligent, has come. She might
help.'

Gender agreement is obligatory also exophorically, i.e., between the referential
or social gender of the speaker/hearer and the corresponding personal pronouns *ja* 'I', *ty* 'you' which have no distinct gender forms:

(3) *Ja èto   napisal-a.   Ty   gotov-a?*
I   that wrote-FEM you.SG ready-FEM
'I have written that. Are you ready?'

The pervasive obligatory use of gender agreement with antecedents (i.e., nouns,
personal or deictic pronouns, exophoric antecedents) means that grammatical
gender (and, by implication, referential or social gender) is expressed many
times throughout a text. The situation is different in the plural, where gender is
neutralized in agreement targets.

2.3 The morphological structure of personal nouns

2.3.1 *Derivation*
The examples in Table 2 suggest that there is a connection between the existence of grammatical gender and particular suffixes deriving female (or sometimes male) personal nouns. The situation is typical of languages with a highly
grammaticalized gender.

In what follows we will examine the mechanisms of personal noun formation in Russian from the perspective of gender-symmetry (as outlined in
Doleschal 1992, chap.1). The nouns in Tables 1a and 1b are lexically gender-
specific and belong to a corresponding grammatical gender category, but are
not semantically or morphologically derived from each other. Such a situation
also holds for common gender nouns, such as *plaksa* 'cry-baby', *sud'ja* 'judge'
(cf. also Doleschal 1999:118f, Nikunlassi 1999:775f). These nouns have only

one form but two grammatical genders (comparable to most personal nouns in English). They take feminine gender agreement with female referents, and masculine with male referents:[5]

(4) *tak-aja   plaksa*
     such-FEM cry.baby
     'such a female cry-baby'
     tak-oj   plaksa
     such-MASC cry.baby
     'such a male cry-baby'

Another class with paradigmatic gender-symmetry are feminine and masculine conversions of adjectives or participles, where both terms of the opposition may be derived separately from the corresponding adjective or participle and are equally marked formally, i.e., each gender has its own (adjectival) suffix:

(5) *vzrosl-aja*   *zavedujušč-aja*   *vzrosl-yj*   *zavedujušč-ij*
     adult-FEM   manager-FEM   adult-MASC   manager-MASC
     'female adult'   'female manager'   '(male) adult'   '(male) manager'

This symmetry holds to a lesser extent between Russian patronymics and surnames. Here the female term is positively marked by the nominative ending *-a*, whereas the derivational suffixes *-ovn-*, *-ovič-*, *-ov-* are parallel and apply separately to their bases, which are *Ivan* and *Mirt* in the following example:

(6) *Ivan-ovn-a*   *Mirt-ov-a*
     Ivan-daughter.of-FEM   Mirt-surname-FEM
     'daughter of Ivan's'   'Mirtov-FEM'
     Ivan-ovič   *Mirt-ov*
     Ivan-son.of.MASC.NOM   Mirt-surname.MASC.NOM
     'son of Ivan's.MASC'   'Mirtov.MASC'

The most prominent word formation process deriving female and male nouns in Russian is derivation by suffixes.[6] In suffixation the symmetry between female and male collapses, both on the level of content and on the level of expression, for the following reasons:

1. There are more masculine suffixes deriving personal nouns than there are feminine ones (almost twice as many, pace Švedova 1980: 142–219);

2. In many cases feminine and masculine suffixes do not function in a parallel way; rather, in order to derive a female noun, a lexically female and grammatically

feminine suffix has to be attached to an (existing or potential) masculine noun: *marksist* (m) → *marksist-ka* (f) 'Marxist';

3. There are other word formation devices deriving masculine nouns, such as compounding, zero derivation or clipping, from which feminine nouns can in some cases be derived by feminizing suffixes: *ėkskursovod* (m) 'guide' (< *ėkskursija* 'excursion' + *vodit'* 'to guide') → *ėkskursovod-ša* (f) (colloquial), *zav* (m) 'boss' (< *zavedujuščij* 'manager') → *zav-ka* (f) (colloquial);

4. Some (productive) feminine suffixes can be derogatory and are therefore restricted to non-official discourse: *-ixa, -ša*;

5. Many masculine nouns cannot be feminized at all *dramaturg* (m) 'playwright', *politik* (m) 'politician'. The reverse is also true for lexically female nouns, such as *ved'ma* (f) 'witch', but such cases are rare.

Nevertheless, there are quite a few feminine suffixes that may (also) operate autonomously, such as *-ka, -nica, -uxa*: *strjap-ka* (f) '(female) cook' (< *strjapat'* 'to cook'), *rodil'-nica* (f) 'woman in childbirth' (< *rodit'* 'to give birth'), *tolst-uxa* (f) 'fat woman' (< *tolstyj* 'fat'). This fact is usually obscured in grammars, where the main bulk of feminine nouns is treated under the heading of "modificational word-formation", implying that the meaning of the derivational base is not changed (as in "derivational" word formation), but only modified by the additional feature [FEMALE]. Zemskaja (1992: 148) even claims that "nouns denoting women always appear as correlative with male nouns and are formally derived from them" (our translation). This view has two implications that can be called into question: (1) all feminine nouns with a (potential) masculine base are actually derived from this base; (2) the masculine base is semantically gender-neutral. (1) is undermined by the fact that the patronymical suffix *-ovna* can be applied to any male name if need arises to derive a patronymic for someone's daughter, regardless of the existence of a son, and also by the occasional formation of feminine personal nouns in colloquial Russian, e.g., *ryb-nica* 'female lover of fish'. (2) is true for the majority of masculine personal nouns; however, there are also regular counterexamples, e.g., ethnonyms or nouns denoting athletes (see Tafel 1997: 142).

In Russian, unlike, e.g., German *-in*, there is no unique feminizing suffix, but a dozen of competing ones whose distribution is conditioned morph(on)-ologically. We will not go into details here, but rather exemplify the points made above, again proceeding from the more symmetrical cases to the asymmetrical ones, cf. Table 3.

Table 3. Derived personal nouns in Russian

	Feminine	Masculine	
(i)	*armjan-ka*	*armjan-in*	'Armenian'
	pervoklass-nica	*pervoklass-nik*	'first grader'
(ii)	*uči-tel'-nica*	*uči-tel'*	'teacher'
	beg-un'-ja	*beg-un*	'sprinter'
	marks-ist-ka	*marks-ist*	'Marxist'
(iii)	*profess-or-ša*	*profess-or*	'professor'
	vrač-ixa	*vrač*	'physician'
	filolog-inja	*filolog*	'philologist'
(iv)	–	*deja-tel'*	'activist'
	–	*politik*	'politician'
	–	*dramaturg*	'playwright'

In (i) both the masculine and the feminine personal nouns have a separate derivational suffix, so that there is symmetry on the expression level. In the case of *armjanin*, symmetry occurs also on the content level, since ethnonyms are in an equipollent opposition, whereas in the case of *pervoklass-nik/-nica* the masculine noun can refer both to men and women. In (ii), feminine nouns are derived by means of a feminine-female suffix from masculine nouns that are themselves derived from a verbal or nominal basis. Due to this asymmetry on expression as well as content level, the masculine nouns can be interpreted as the hyperonyms of the feminine ones. The feminine nouns in (iii) are derivations by colloquial suffixes from masculine nouns. The asymmetries on the content and expression levels are even more pronounced due to the fact that in this case the feminine suffixes are stylistically marked by a negative connotation, so that the resulting feminine nouns are derogatory and cannot be used in non-familiar, let alone official, contexts (cf. Mozdzierz 1999, Yokoyama 1999). The masculine nouns in (iv) lack any feminine counterparts altogether. This is explained morphonologically or by reference to underlying social asymmetries (cf. Mozdzierz 1999:173f, Tafel 1997:146f). As in other languages, e.g., German (cf. Oksaar 1976), in Russian high prestige is connected with masculinity (in a social sense), therefore female counterparts of personal nouns denoting prestigious occupations are avoided. When addressed or referred to by a corresponding feminine form, women feel downgraded or not treated seriously.

There is an unsolved contradiction between femininity and high social prestige (except for the concept of 'mother', cf. 6.1.4).

2.3.2   Compounding

Compounding in the strict sense is not used as a means of gender-specification in Russian. However, there is the possibility of juxtaposition of the word *ženščina* 'woman' with a masculine noun, as in *ženščina-kosmonavt* 'woman cosmonaut', *ženščina-toreador* 'woman torero', where both parts are inflected and the second lexeme is actually a syntactic apposition. These juxtapositions are not lexicalized, and their use is confined to contexts where the female gender has to be stressed, similar to the use of the English adjective *female*.

3.   The lexical representation of women and men

In Russian, gender-marked nouns belong to the group of personal nouns (and nouns referring to animals). Kinship terms and some general human nouns (like 'man', 'woman') are mostly separate lexemes or derivations that have become lexicalized (see Tables 1a and 1b). Feminist studies of the Russian lexicon usually search for lexical asymmetries, gaps and differing meanings.

In her study on women in the Russian vocabulary, Tafel maintains that the evidently higher frequency of masculine-male expressions in Russian public communication and written documents influences people's perception as well as the contents of normative grammars (cf. Tafel 1997: 126). There are a few quantitative studies of lexical asymmetries, lexical gaps, and semantic differences in Russian, including Yokoyama's analysis of the *Častotnyj slovar' russkogo jazyka* (Frequency Dictionary of Russian), and Martynyuk's frequency analysis of the standard Russian-Russian dictionary by Ožegov (cf. Yokoyama 1986, Martynyuk 1990). Martynyuk's study of the 1978 edition of Ožegov's dictionary reveals a frequency ratio of gender-marked units of 95 : 33 for masculine-male to feminine-female. In her text-frequency study, Yokoyama claims a ratio of the personal pronouns *on* (m) 'he' vs. *ona* (f) 'she' vs. *ono* (n) 'it' (in all case forms) of 13143 : 5836 : 522, and 5 : 2 for *on* (m) vs. *ona* (f) (excluding all incidents of *ono* (n) in oblique cases). As far as nouns are concerned, the ratio is more balanced.

More recently, we conducted a small survey of dictionary entries in four of the most common Russian-Russian dictionaries.[7] Using a short word list

(67 nouns including appositions, masculine and feminine forms, cf. Schmid 1998:247f), the dictionaries were checked for nouns with the feature [FEMALE]. Only few nouns are listed as independent entries in their feminine form, regardless of the size of the dictionary (in our word list these were *molodčina* 'splendid person'[8] and *supruga* 'wife'). In the dictionaries of 1950–1956 and 1981, the feminine entries are frequently followed by references to the masculine form (*ženskoe k* ... 'female/feminine equivalent to ...'). In some cases, the feminine form is described as directly dependent on the masculine form, referring to the "wife of the male referent". However, this is not the case in the more recent dictionaries of 1990 and 1993. Feminine nouns are often additionally labeled as *razg.* 'colloquial', *ustar.* 'archaic' or even *prost.* 'vulgar'. However, this labeling may be subject to diachronic change, e.g., shifting from 'archaic' to 'colloquial', as in the case of *aptekarša* 'female pharmacist', or losing its label 'colloquial', as in the case of *lingvistka* 'female linguist' and *aspirantka* 'female doctoral student'.

Also, a term may frequently lack at least one meaning when used in its feminine form. Usually the most prestigious and/or powerful meaning of a given term is reserved for its masculine form, e.g., *revoljucioner* (m) 'revolutionary' can denote 'one who opens up new perspectives', whereas *revoljucionerka* (f) 'female revolutionary' simply means 'participant in a revolution'; *master* (m) can denote 'artist', 'specialist', 'head of a department', while the feminine-female *masterica* (f) is simply 'skilled laborer', 'master' (cf. also Mozdzierz 1999:169–171).

4.   Gender and reference

4.1 Gender-specific reference and agreement conflicts

Since gender is highly grammaticalized in Russian, gender agreement is a formal phenomenon, i.e., a masculine antecedent triggers masculine agreement, and a feminine one feminine agreement. As has been mentioned above, there is a tendency to use masculine personal nouns with reference to women, since many occupational terms do not form a feminine counterpart or the respective suffix bears a negative connotation. This leads to the effect that in terms of grammatical correctness agreement should be masculine. And indeed, there are cases where a woman refers to herself exclusively by masculine forms, cf. the following example from Corbett (1991:232):

(7) *Ėkskursovod pered   Vami. On podnjal ruku.*
guide.MASC in.front.of you he raised arm
'The guide is standing in front of you. He has raised his arm.'

Although such examples occur in official (con)texts, their awkwardness is obvious, and different strategies may be applied to avoid semantic mismatches (cf. also Doleschal 1994). In written texts (especially in journalese), a masculine personal noun referring to a woman is usually accompanied by the name of the person in question. This indicates not only the referent's gender, but also allows for the use of feminine agreement (cf. Doleschal 1993, 1994, 1995; Tafel 1997). An alternative strategy is semantic agreement, which is used in less formal situations. "Semantic agreement" means that feminine agreement occurs – incorrectly from the point of view of grammar – with a masculine noun referring to a woman, as in the following example:

(8) *Direktor   instrukciju vypolnil-a   po-staxanovski.*
director.MASC instruction fulfilled-FEM like-Staxanov
'The headmaster followed the instruction in a Staxanov way.'

However, semantic agreement is only a partial remedy, since it cannot be applied consistently. Semantic agreement may be applied more easily in syntactically more distant positions of the agreement target from its controller, and the agreement may vary, sometimes even within the same clause:

(9) *Buduš̌c-ij   filolog   iz   Minska vyigral-a.*
future-MASC philologist.MASC from Minsk won-FEM
'A female future philologist from Minsk has won.'

Feminine semantic agreement is not allowed in the oblique cases of attributive pronouns and adjectives:

(10) **Videla naš-u   direktor-a.*
saw   our-FEM.ACC.SG director-MASC.ACC.SG
'I saw our headmaster.'

In contradistinction to the feminine, masculine semantic agreement is not subject to such restrictions, e.g., if a feminine noun is used to denote a male person, masculine agreement occurs in any case form:

(11) *A   ja, tak i   peredaj emu, skotine   èt-omu,   čto ja i   videt'*
and I   so just tell   him beast.FEM that-MASC.DAT that I   even see
ego ne želaju!
him not wish
'And I, tell that swine so, that I do not even wish to see him!'

4.2 Gender-indefinite reference and generic masculines

If the gender of the person(s) referred to is unknown or irrelevant in the
context, Russian uses masculine forms throughout:

(12) *Artist   dolžen   delat' iz sebja kul't.*
artist.MASC must.MASC make of self   cult
'An artist has to make a cult of himself.'

Likewise, the interrogative pronoun *kto* 'who' and the indefinite pronouns *kto-nibud'*, *kto-to*, *koe-kto*, *nekto* 'anybody, somebody', *nikto* 'nobody, no one'
trigger masculine agreement. Even if the referent in question can only be a
woman, there is no tendency to use semantic agreement as with personal nouns:

(13) *Nikto   iz ženščin ne prišel.*
nobody of women not came.MASC
'None of the women came.'

Likewise, in impersonal generalizing utterances, masculine gender is common
(14a), but feminine agreement is also possible, if the speaker is a woman (14b):

(14) a. *Neprijatno byt' obmanut-ym.*
unpleasant be cheated-MASC
'It is unpleasant to be cheated.'
   b. *Bystro zabyvaeš' sebja,   t-u,   kak-oj   byl-a   kogda-to.*
quickly forget   yourself that-FEM which-FEM were-FEM some-time
'You quickly forget yourself, the one you were some time ago.'

Further, there are two types of impersonal constructions which leave referential
gender unspecified: the impersonal plural form of the verb (corresponding to
English *one* or German *man*), cf. (15a), and impersonal predicates like *možno*
'(it is) possible', *nel'zja* '(it is) impossible' (15b):

(15) a. *Zdes' ne kurja-t.*
here not smoke-3PL
'One does not smoke here.'

b. *Zdes' možno/ nel'zja   kurit'.*
here possible/ impossible smoke
'One may/must not smoke here.'

4.3 The endearing use of the masculine gender

In specific contexts, women may be referred to by masculine forms, which can have an endearing or upgrading function:

(16) *Lizok   u   nas xoroš-ij.*
Lizok.MASC with us good-MASC
'Little Lizzy is a good sport.'

Such a use is characteristic of close interpersonal relationships, such as friendships between women, and occurs in motherese and the language of love, cf. Zemskaja (1983), Zemskaja & Kitajgorodskaja & Rozanova (1993); see also Tobin, this vol., on the corresponding phenomenon in Hebrew. Significantly, though, the feminine gender does not have such a function when referring to men. On the contrary, using feminine agreement when referring to men, as in *tak-aja* (f) *p'janica* 'such a (f) drunkard' is downgrading.

4.4 Summary

As we have seen, Russian has quite a few ways of referring to women: by feminine nouns (mostly derived ones), by semantic agreement, or simply by masculine nouns, sometimes accompanied by the apposition 'woman'. The choice of these possibilities is not random, but conforms to two distinct situational patterns, as described by Yokoyama (1999). In official contexts, feminine nouns are not appropriate, since they imply a sexualization of the referent. Therefore, stylistically neutral masculine nouns (and agreement patterns) are used in reference to women and in self-reference by women. However, in more informal situations (as in colloquial speech), the gender of the referent plays a role, therefore female forms are widely used, even if they are derived with the help of suffixes like -*ša*, which have a depreciative connotation.

5.   The interpretation of generic masculines: Empirical evidence

Masculine personal nouns are supposed to be gender-neutral, since they may denote men *and* women. The claim is often supported by evidence from female speakers who use masculine personal nouns when they talk about themselves or other females (cf. Comrie & Stone & Polinsky 1996: 231–248).

Gender neutrality of Russian masculine nouns is usually approached from the production side of communication, i.e., the speakers' perspective only (cf. Krongauz 1993).[9] By contrast, our tests investigate the hearers' perspective: how generic masculine nouns denoting persons are perceived in close-to-authentic contexts. The results of our studies show that once attention shifts from the speaker's to the hearer's perspective, the picture changes significantly: allegedly neutral masculine nouns are, in fact, predominantly perceived and interpreted as [MALE] (cf. Doleschal 1993, Schmid 1998).

5.1   Personal nouns with specific reference

The first two experiments aimed at determining to which extent masculine nouns referring to concrete persons are perceived as denoting males (cf. Doleschal 1992, 1995). Since it was hypothesized that the specification of referential gender increased with the number of corresponding grammatically masculine anaphoric expressions, the possibility of using nouns rather than anaphora was tested.

Doleschal (1993: 166–167, 1997) conducted an experiment in which informants were presented with a questionnaire containing sentences clipped out of a novel. Every sentence contained a masculine personal noun with a concrete singular reference. The informants were asked to name those persons both by their first names and their patronymics, which would guarantee gender-specificity. The results were as shown in Table 4.

Most of the test items were interpreted as [MALE], with the exception of two lexemes, *buxgalter* and *vrač*, which received higher female scores. This indicates that the [MALE] semantics of the masculine gender is generally quite pronounced in concrete singular reference. But it may be overruled by extra-linguistic factors, e.g., by the speaker's knowledge that some occupations are typically female (social gender).

Schmid (1998) investigated whether an allegedly generic masculine noun is interpreted as denoting a male or a female person. The informants were provided with five initial situations and were asked to compose five short

Table 4. Interpretation of masculine nouns [a]

Masculine test noun	Maleness (%)	M	F	Both	Uninter-pretable	Total
predsedatel' 'chairperson'	100.0	10	–	–	–	10
advokat 'solicitor'	100.0	10	–	–	–	10
sopernik 'rival'	94.1	16	–	–	1	17
vrag 'enemy'	90.0	9	–	1	–	10
aptekar' 'pharmacist'	90,0	9	–	–	1	10
ministr 'secretary of state'	90.0	9	–	1	–	10
avtor 'author'	87.5	14	–	1	1	16
korrespondent 'correspondent'	80.0	8	1	1	–	10
repetitor 'private tutor'	76.5	13	3	1	–	17
čelovek 'human being'	75.0	12	2	–	2	16
vrač 'physician'	40.0	4	5	1	–	10
buxgalter 'accountant'	35.3	6	10	1	–	17

[a] All figures except for the measure of "maleness" are given in raw values, since the number of subjects ("total") was too small for a percentage. Answers providing both male and female names were classified as "both", inadequate answers, such as e.g., *Saša*, a hypochoristic which is both male and female, as "uninterpretable".

stories. Each of the initial sentences contained a personal noun in its masculine form, while the remaining context was cleared of any hints as to that character's gender. The personal nouns used were *vrač* 'physician', *kollega* 'colleague', *učitel'* 'teacher', *repetitor* 'private tutor', *obmanščik* 'defrauder', and *specialist* 'specialist'. The results show a strong tendency towards interpreting these nouns as denoting men. In every single case at least 50% of the informants – male and female – associated the noun with a man, the others were not sure or opted for "rather male". The "female" categories remained empty.

5.2 Personal nouns with more generic reference

Doleschal (1993: 70–73, 1997) conducted an experiment in which informants were asked to describe typical representatives of several occupations. The occupational titles (four masculine, one common gender, one feminine noun) were given without any context. Only unambiguous hints of femininity or masculinity (such as "wears a short skirt", "deceives his wife") were taken as indicative of referential (or social) gender. The occurrence of masculine anaphora was not taken into account in order to avoid a circular interpretation.

As was the case in the test with referential NPs, an interaction between

Table 5. Interpretation of generic nouns

Test noun	Maleness (%)	M	F	Both	Uninter-pretable	Total
professor (m) 'professor'	66.6	12	–	–	6	18
politik (m) 'politician'	64.0	11	–	–	6	17
vrač (m) 'physician'	25.0	5	1	4	10	20
učitel' (m) 'teacher'	22.2	4	4	4	6	18
sud'ja (m/f) 'judge'	8.0	1	3	2	6	12
medsestra (f) 'nurse'	0	0	9	0	6	15

grammatical and social gender can be observed: there is a tendency to interpret masculine occupational terms as male rather than female, whereas the common gender and the feminine noun are instantiated by females rather than by males. In the case of conflicting items, like *vrač* and *učitel'*, which are masculine but denote typically female occupations (in the former USSR two thirds of the physicians and three quarters of the teachers were women in 1990), the male percentage is relatively low, but it is never lower than the female percentage. Even for professions where women are in the majority, their chances of being referred to by masculine nouns are not equal to those of men.

In the second part of Schmid's questionnaire, respondents were asked to spontaneously associate "generic" masculine nouns with a woman or a man (cf. Schmid 1998:245f). The answers showed that some nouns are clearly associated with men, e.g., *brodjaga* 'vagabond', *master* 'master', *p'janica* 'drunk', *rabočij* 'worker', *revoljucioner* 'revolutionary', while other nouns display interesting tendencies. Thus, the following expressions were interpreted as denoting male referents along a scale of decreasing distinctiveness (a) = most male-specific, (f) = least male-specific:

(a)   *ministr* 'minister', *predsedatel'* 'chairperson', *skul'ptor* 'sculptor';
(b)   *genij* 'genius', *kranovščik* 'crane operator', *lingvist* 'linguist', *prozaik* 'prose-writer', *skotina* 'scoundrel', *sopernik* 'rival', *suprug* 'spouse';
(c)   *arxeolog* 'archeologist', *kollega* 'colleague', *učenij* 'scholar', *istorik* 'historian', *poet* 'poet';
(d)   *lentjaj* 'sluggard', *repetitor* 'private coach', *student* 'student';
(e)   *molodec* 'splendid fellow';
(f)   *bednjaga* 'poor soul', *vrag* 'enemy', *sirota* 'orphan'.

However, *nedotroga* 'touchy person', *buxgalter* 'bookkeeper', *umnica* 'know-all' were interpreted as "female".[10]

In some cases, the answers of female and male informants differed significantly: male informants associated women, while female informants associated men with the Russian equivalents of 'lawyer', 'geographer', 'reporter', 'student', 'judge'. The opposite case was 'warden', classified by women as predominantly "female" and by men as "male".

5.3 Metalinguistic test

Schmid also asked her informants to rate the application frequency of 67 nouns denoting women (see above and Schmid 1998: 247–248 for a complete list). The test items included "generic" masculine nouns, feminine derivations, and appositions. Informants were asked to classify the nouns into the categories "very common", "quite common", "quite uncommon", "uncommon", and a neutral category.

The results show that the female informants classified "generic" masculine nouns as "very common" more often than the male informants. Apart from that, the commonness seems to depend on the noun. E.g., *buxgalter* 'book-keeper', *vrač* 'physician', *učitel'* 'teacher', *repetitor* 'private coach', as well as the derived feminine nouns *aspirantka* 'female doctoral student', *pessimistka* 'female pessimist', *pisatel'nica* 'female writer', *poètessa* 'female poet', *rasskazčica* 'female narrator', *sopernica* 'female rival', *studentka* 'female student', *učitel'nica* 'female teacher' were all classified as "very common" for denoting a woman.

In another part of the test, informants had to spontaneously produce "feminine equivalents" of a series of 21 "generic" masculine nouns (cf. Schmid 1998: 246). 61% of the informants preferred to stay with the masculine form, 38% derived feminine nouns by suffixes and the remaining 1% used appositions.

To sum up, our empirical studies show an interesting paradox: although respondents interpret "generic" masculine nouns as predominantly "male", such nouns are the most common form to denote women. This results in a significant discrepancy between intention and effect.

6. Linguistic gender studies in Russia

The question of language and gender has a long tradition in Soviet linguistics (Tafel 1997: 43), although it was not considered from a feminist perspective. The Soviet ideology took for granted the implementation of equal rights for women and men, therefore the problem of their unequal treatment by the language structure did not arise. The questions which have been addressed are essentially the use of female occupational terms as well as semantic agreement with reference to women. They have been approached both empirically and normatively (cf. Comrie et al. 1996, Tafel 1997). The results of these studies are directly reflected in Yokoyama's differentiation between official and unofficial contexts (Yokoyama 1999). Thus, normativists prefer the use of masculine nouns with masculine agreement when referring to women, while empiricists state that in informal contexts the need to mark referential gender (i.e. female) is adequately fulfilled by means of both word-formation and agreement, i.e., female forms may be used. The latter view is laid down in the Academy grammar of the Russian language (Švedova 1980: 468), while the former is reflected in lexicography, where hybrid nouns are consequently classified as masculine and generic. Since these discussions are documented by Comrie et al. (1996) and Tafel (1997), the following sections will concentrate on issues which have only recently been raised and discussed from a feminist point of view.[11]

6.1 Proverbs and idioms

Russian proverbs and idioms are an important source for cultural interpretation: they may be understood as "a stereotype prescription of popular self-consciousness, providing a wide field for self-identification" (Telija 1996: 240, our transl.). Today, proverbs are mainly used as a rhetorical device, in order to embroider one's speech, e.g., in a humorous way.

In an article on androcentrism in Russian proverbs, Kirilina (1999a) emphasizes the opposition of female and male perspectives. She maintains that the Russian language categorizes reality from a male point of view, but that there are opposite tendencies as well. She tries to determine the level of androcentrism inherent in the language by tracing different images of women in Russian proverbs and idioms. Dal's (1984) collection of proverbs (*Poslovicy russkogo naroda*) she calls "a mirror of Russian cultural stereotypes". 2.000 entries (i.e. less than 10%) from Dal's collection were analyzed[12] for the androcentric, female, and pseudo-female perspectives.

6.1.1 The androcentric perspective
In 1671 units subsumed under this category, i.e., more than 80% of the entries analyzed, Kirilina identifies several semantic clusters. First, it is a man who functions both as speaker and addressee, which Kirilina interprets as a sign of a male world view and male power, e.g., *Žena ne steklo – možno pobit'* 'A wife is

not (made of) glass – one can beat her up'.[13] Second, male space is portrayed as larger than female space, and women mainly appear as objects of male action. Finally, women are not even legitimate members of the category "human", e.g., *Kurica ne ptica, baba ne čelovek* 'A hen is not a bird, a woman is not a human being'. The opposition [MALE] vs. [FEMALE] is further polarized in proverbs which tell the woman what to do and how to do it. They invariably take the form of prescriptions and orders, e.g., *Ne pet' kurice petuxom, ne byt' babe mužikom* 'A hen must/should not crow like a rooster, a woman must/should not be (like) a man'.

In very few cases the relationship of dependence is reversed, and men (especially elderly ones) are pictured as dependent on women, e.g., *Rassypalsja by deduška, koli ego ne podpojasyvala babuška* 'Grandfather would fall apart, if grandmother did not belt him'.

6.1.2   *Ženskij golos* – 'The female voice'

Typically, the so-called "female world view" refers to the emotional sphere, with frequent use of diminutives, and with notions of fatalism and defenselessness. Kirilina claims that this "female voice" tendency, which she detects in about 15% of the data, neutralizes the general androcentrism of Russian proverbs. The major semantic fields mentioned within this category are marriage, kinship relations, love, and affection. Marriage in proverbs is predominantly perceived as inevitable reality, resulting in disappointed hopes, dependence and lack of freedom. Nevertheless a few proverbs do show female autonomy.

The most interesting category concerns women and kinship relations. In proverbs relating to kinship, women appear in various roles, e.g., as mother, sister, daughter, mother-in-law, stepmother, grandmother, etc. Telija (1996: 261) depicts the concept 'woman' *(ženščina/baba)* as the basic one, with all the other roles derived from it, whereas Kirilina adds another basic concept, namely that of 'mother', arguing that the concepts are quite opposite in terms of connotation.

6.1.3   'Woman/wife'

A wife is more often pictured as bad than as good, e.g., *Vsex zlydnej zlee zlaja žena* 'A bad wife is worse than all evils'. The androcentric (male) "I" attributes to women prototypical properties, which create a negative stereotype, whose prevalent message is the notion of a weak and illogical female intellect, e.g., *Volos dlinnyj, a um korotkij* 'Long hair, but short wits'. There are only few proverbs that highly value the female mind, e.g., *Ženskij um lučše vsjakix dum*

'The female mind is better than any thinking'. In general, female brightness is considered uncommon, and also somewhat undesirable, e.g., *Umnuju vzjat'* – *ne dast slova skazat'* 'Take a clever one (f) – [she] won't let you say a word'.

Other common notions related to women are stubbornness and unpredictability: *S baboj ne sgovoriš'/ne ubediš'* 'You will never persuade a woman [derogatory]'; or danger, witchcraft, and loquaciousness. The neutral verb *govorit'* 'talk' does not occur in this context at all. Instead, it is substituted by verbs with negative connotations. Female activity is envisaged as the opposite of male activity in terms of right and wrong, e.g., *Mužskoj um govorit: nado; babij um govorit: xoču* 'Male reason says: it's necessary; female [derogatory] reason says: I want'. A man's action is described as more important and complex than a woman's, e.g., *Muž v bedax, a žena v gostjax* 'The husband is in trouble, while the wife is paying a visit'. The two nouns very seldom exchange positions within a proverb. Finally, looks are often valued as less important than housewifely qualities, e.g., *Ne prigoža, da prigodna* 'Not pretty, but useful/effective.'[14]

6.1.4   *'Mother'*

A totally different picture emerges in proverbs on mothers: 'mother' is a positive image, protective and supportive. There are proverbs where the mother herself expresses opinions on the difficulties and responsibilities of motherhood and the social restrictions on childbirth. A general (male) perspective is expressed by proverbs where 'mother' is perceived as a source of comfort, care, and a symbol of light and warmth. This conception of 'mother' carries predominantly positive connotations. 'Mother' even lacks typical female attributes. The offensive nature of the popular Russian curse *eb tvoju mat'* (lit. 'I (male speaker) have fucked your mother') results from exposing the sacrosanct concept of 'mother' to an action which is considered "normal" for the concept of 'woman/wife'.

6.1.5   *The "pseudo-female" perspective*

Proverbs where female speech is imitated from a male perspective are assigned by Kirilina to the category "pseudo-female", which clearly reflects androcentric language and negatively stereotyped conceptions of women, e.g., as superficial: *Prodaj, muž, lošad' da korovu, kupi žene obnovu* 'Husband, sell your horse and cow, and buy your wife a new dress'. Considering that (Russian) women often accept and support (male) discourse devaluating women, the perspective of (negative) reference towards women appears to be more important here than the gender of the speaker.

To sum up, there is empirical evidence for the existence of femininity stereotypes in Russian proverbs (cf. Tafel 1997:181), since they contain the same images which exist in classical gender stereotypes and stereotyped role-models. It is indisputable that the drastic bias in a number of proverbs referring to men and women is a clear expression of androcentrism. However, the notion of a woman does not necessarily have a negative connotation. While this is the case for the concept of 'wife/woman', it does not hold true for that of 'mother'.

Women who use proverbs (especially those with instructive and evaluative function) and pass them on to their children, have not only accepted the dominant norms, but have also internalized the alleged *fait accompli* of men taking higher social positions. They do not question their own disadvantage, which prevents them from eventually creating "atypical" proverbs (cf. Tafel 1997:175).

Considering the origin of proverbs, we agree with Tafel's claim that gendered role models are extraordinarily persistent, lagging behind actual changes in social reality (cf. Tafel 1997:173). Similarly, Kirilina argues that in Russian proverbs men do not only dominate and control, but also provide a good or bad example, while women are subordinate and play an important role only in the family.

6.2 Obscene expressions – a male domain?[15]

The term "obscene" refers to words where either the referent is a taboo (e.g., sexuality, excretion), or where the referent appears in a non-euphemistic form (euphemisms may be paraphrases or Latin medical terms). Obscene expressions and curses (maledictions) are not identical, but partly correlating categories: obscene words within a curse (e.g., *pošel na xuj!* lit. 'go to the prick!')[16] may be substituted by a non-obscene expression without the phrase losing its curse character (*pošel k čertu!* lit. 'go to the devil!') In phrases other than curses (e.g., *na xuj mne èto nužno!* lit. 'to the prick do I need this'), the elimination of obscene words neutralizes the expression, as in *začem mne èto nužno!* lit. 'why do I need this'.

Russian obscene language, called "Russian *mat*" *(russkij mat)*, (cf. Il'jasov 1994) is a system of lexemes and idioms, derived from or composed with a few lexical roots referring to the sphere of sexuality. Diligently excluded even from contemporary scientific dictionaries, *mat* is primarily an oral phenomenon – although historically there is some written evidence in folk texts and formerly unpublished literary works.

The three main roots of *mat* are *xuj-* 'cock-', *eb-* 'fuck-', *pizd-* 'cunt-', which are combined with a wide variety of prefixes and suffixes. The literal meanings of the resulting invectives refer to (1) sexual organs and (2) sexual services and deviations (e.g., *xuesos* 'cocksucker', *pizdasos* 'cuntsucker', *žopoeb* 'assfucker'). However, more often these sexual *signifiants* are used in their secondary meaning, denoting offense, imprecation, rejection or reference to other semantic fields, e.g., the military sphere. The verb *ebat'* 'fuck' may thus denote an energetic movement, or emphatic and expressive emphasis of an action with a negative impact on another person.

"Importing" these obscene words into more neutral contexts – usually in order to enhance expressiveness – results in the (at least subconscious) association with prostitution, aggression, discrimination etc.

The uniqueness of Russian obscene vocabulary lies in its degree of interdiction as compared to Western European languages. Uspenskij (1994) shows that research on Russian *mat* is heavily impaired by its being a taboo, especially in academic circles. The *mat* taboo does not (or not as much) concern the content level (the *signifié*) of the relevant vocabulary, but the expression level (the *signifiant*), thus directly affecting linguistic/philological research. This inherent handicap of research prevents the empirical investigation of Russian *mat* in authentic contexts: there is no systematically obtained empirical data – and probably there will not be any in the near future. The fact that *mat* expressions in their literal meaning are extremely obscene is of significance from a gender perspective, since much of the relevant literature suggests that *mat* is mostly used by men and among men. Regardless of the changes due to 20th century emancipation, *mat* used by women is still considered improper, at least in academic circles (cf. Uspenskij 1994:56). By contrast, working-class women are reported to be "just as proficient as men in expectorating those four-letter *kaka*-phonous words" (Kauffman 1980:271).

The almost universal "mother curse",[17] which is not linked to Russian alone, stands in sharp contrast to "mother" as the only positive female concept throughout the canon of Russian proverbs (cf. Section 6.1).

From a gender-conscious point of view, Ermen (1993:288) observes an asymmetrical distribution of lexemes with sexual referents and sexual meaning. Among grammatically possible variants, only phrases denoting an action with a male subject and a female object are rated acceptable by Russian native speakers:

(17)   *on ee ebet/eb/ebal*   * *ona ego ebet/ebla/ebala*
     'he fucks/fucked (IPF/PF) her'   * 'she fucks/fucked (IPF/PF) him'
     * *on eben*   *ona ebena*
     * 'he has been fucked'   'she has been fucked'

Nomina agentis are distributed asymmetrically as well: while there are *ebar'* ('lover, friend, womanizer'), and its synonyms *ebaka, ebak, ebač*, there are no equivalents denoting women – *ebuška* is not common, and the conventional term for a promiscuous woman is *bljad'* which has a decisively negative connotation ('slut, whore').

Further evidence of a gender difference in denoting persons using *mat* expressions is offered by Žel'vis (1997:296), who conceives of *mat* as a kind of compensation for the profane lower body half as opposed to the sacred upper body half, a common association in the dichotomic scheme of masculine vs. feminine gender stereotypes. Quite similarly, Buj (1995) interprets *mat* expressions as tied to the "demon of sexuality", paying primary attention to the literal meaning, the "inner form" of *mat* expressions. This questionable thesis reminds one of common prejudices against "the female" as the location of negatively connoted sexuality.

Lexemes with non-sexual referents but sexual meaning, i.e., somewhat metaphorical notions of the sexual act, tend to adopt a male perspective. Many non-obscene synonyms for *ebat'* 'fuck',[18] are transitive and passivizable. They clearly denote a relationship with an object that may be used and/or abused. The female perspective, on the contrary, is expressed by verbs like *dat' komu-l.* 'allow (someone)', *podlezt' pod kogo-l.* 'crawl under (someone)', *leč'/ložit'sja* 'lie down', all expressing subjugation and devotion.

Kirilina (1998) in her study of the Russian *mat* identifies the following common semantic roots of idioms containing obscene words and sharing the meaning of "reaching superiority by intimidation and/or force": (1) physical contact is established between subject and object of a given action, (2) the physical contact leads the object of the action to a state of physical discomfort, which may vary in degree and may culminate in complete helplessness, e.g., *nastupit' na gorlo* 'to step on (someone's) throat'. The verbal threats of physical assault or rape do not only imply physical contact, but also penetration and absolute annihilation of a person's privacy.

Usually, *mat* is primarily performative: by pronouncing a *mat*-word or phrase, the speaker not only expresses something in a vulgar way, but also acts vulgarly (in the sense of Austin's speech acts; cf. Levin 1996:109). In non-performative utterances, usually a plan or a wish is expressed, e.g., *Ja budu ljubit' tebja* 'I will love you'. With invective words in a similar context, *mat* is used to utter threats, usually of force and rape, e.g., *Ja tebja vyebu* 'I will fuck you up' (cf. Kirilina 1999a).[19]

Apart from the literal meaning of *mat*, obscene expressions may signify dominance and power. This certainly holds true for the military sphere, where *vyebat'/vyebnut' kogo-libo* 'to fuck someone' is used in the meaning of 'to punish someone' in the context of someone using his/her higher (social) position. The phrase *načal'stvo ebet* (lit. 'the superiors fuck') hints at superiors who consciously use their higher and more powerful position to oppress their subordinates.

Kirilina's conclusion is a disappointing but typical compromise. Like most *mat*-researchers, she abstracts from actual language use, generalizing *mat* use in a way that mixes the gender perspective with the topics of the military, the prison camps etc. Her position as a woman studying *mat* does not make things easier: in order to avoid being accused of gender-bias herself, she has no other option but to adopt a general, abstract perspective, claiming the absence of gender differences despite empirical evidence that might support opposite claims.

7. Language politics

As to language politics, first steps have already been taken, aiming at the creation of guidelines for equal treatment of women and men. However, "Women and gender studies in Russia: future strategies and techniques", a large multidisciplinary project aiming at the implementation of gender studies in Russia also in the field of Russian linguistics (cf. *Ženščina v Rossijskom obščestve* 1998), was cancelled by the Ministry of Education of the Russian Federation for economic reasons. The linguistic part was initiated by Irina I. Xaleeva, Alla V. Kirilina, Tatjana Kirjuškina and Natal'ja Suxova from Moscow Linguistic University. We are not aware of any other measures to reform the Russian language nor of attempts within women's groups to use a gender-fair language, but we are convinced that this is no topic of public discourse.

The reactions of influential Russian linguists to feminist linguistics are on the whole negative. They range from outspoken scorn and irony to simply ignoring the field. Since no feminist critique of the Russian language, let alone guidelines for a gender-fair usage, have publicly been proposed in Russia so far, the goal of the negative reactions is Western feminist linguistics, especially the

American oeuvre on English. The semantics of gender and the resulting privileged position of men are not recognized as a problem. For instance, Zemskaja & Kitajgorodskaja & Rozanova (1993:94) conclude that "such facts [...] are no evidence of an unequal position of women and do not lead to their discrimination" (our translation). Works of Western linguists dealing with this problem in Russian (e.g., Weiss 1988, 1991, 1992; Doleschal 1993, 1997) are ignored. The line of argumentation is reminiscent of the debate between Kalverkämper and Pusch on German in the late 1970s (cf., e.g., Bulygina & Šmelev 1997).

8. Suggestions for future research

Russian feminist linguistics has a great variety of topics to explore in the future. Since little research has been done so far from a distinct gender perspective, it would be of great importance to take up this issue in the first place. With regard to "generic" masculines, it is time to shift emphasis from production to perception. As our test materials suggest, results can be expected to differ significantly from previous positions that took into account only the speaker's perspective. Gender-conscious perception research can be expected to provide new perspectives on deadlock concepts in the dominant structuralist theory.

In future research on gender stereotypes it will be essential to cross disciplinary boundaries. In particular, statistical tests common in sociology have not yet been applied to Russian in the field of gender stereotypes. Such tests concerning masculinity and femininity were conducted for English in the US in the 1960s (cf. Smith 1985:92–110). These studies tried to identify the semantic profiles of what is actual male/female behavior *(gender differences)* and what is perceived as typically feminine/masculine *(gender stereotypes)*. Also, positive and negative connotations of allegedly "typical" female/male features were tested by means of sociological content analysis. There are still too few data of this kind for the Russian context, so that, for instance, the relationship between perception and actual (sociological) facts, between gender-specific cognitive representations and their social correlates, are far from clear.

Notes

1. Signs not used by the IPA are the following: *è* for open /e/, *c* for a voiceless alveolar affricate, *č* for a voiceless palatal affricate, *š* for a voiceless palato-alveolar fricative, *y* for a central high vowel, *ž* for a voiced palato-alveolar fricative. The letter *e* is pronounced /je/ syllable-initially. The single apostrophe refers to a softening (palatalization) of the preceding consonant, while the double apostrophe is used by orthographic convention to indicate /j/ after prefixes.

2. Standard descriptions of Russian are Comrie & Stone & Polinsky (1996), Wade (1992), Švedova (1980).

3. Each of these genders has an animate and an inanimate subgender. However, these will not be discussed here as they are irrelevant to the present topic.

4. The abbreviations (f) and (m) will be used to indicate the grammatical gender of the Russian word, whereas FEM and MASC will be used for the grammatical category in the interlinear translations. Lexical or referential gender will be denoted by *female* or *male*, or F and M in Tables 4 and 5.

5. Note that all common gender nouns belong to the *a*-declension (nominative singular ends in *-a*), which is usually associated with the feminine gender. In our view, however, inflectional endings of personal nouns do not signal grammatical gender. The *a*-declension comprises both feminine, common gender, and masculine nouns (e.g., *mužčina* 'man', *papa* 'daddy') which are inflected identically.

6. Suffixation is a very complex phenomenon in Russian, but the intricacies are beyond the scope of this chapter (cf., e.g., Švedova 1980: 138).

7. *Slovar' sovremennogo russkogo literaturnogo jazyka* (Soviet Academy of Sciences 1950–1956), *Slovar' russkogo jazyka* (Soviet Academy of Sciences 1981), Ožegov (1990), Ožegov & Švedova (1993).

8. *Molodčina* is actually a common gender noun which usually refers to males.

9. There are some tests by Tafel (1997) who consulted 21 native speakers of Russian. Her test design, however, lacks some relevant aspects: e.g., when she asked her informants to complete sentences by means of a personal pronoun, she used single pronoun occurrence as evidence for the informant's interpretation in terms of referential gender, neglecting the possibility of denoting women – at least the first time – by means of a masculine pronoun. We suggest a different approach in classifying such data. In Schmid (1998: 248), the answers were classified according to the number of independent references to the referential or social gender of the person in question as "clearly male" (3 or more references), "rather male" (1 or 2 references), "unclear", "rather female" (1 or 2 references), "clearly female" (3 or more references). A reference was defined as a pronoun of any kind, a finite verb in the past tense or conditional, or an adjective. Semantic identification, e.g., 'son', was classified as "clearly male/female" even if it was the only reference to the referent's gender.

10. Although *bednjaga*, *kollega*, *sirota*, *skotina* and *sud'ja* are common gender nouns, masculine agreement is generally considered gender-neutral; therefore, we include these expressions here.

11. Kirilina (1999b) as well as the (Western) studies edited by Mills (1999) appeared after the completion of the manuscript and have therefore not been considered here.

12. However, Kirilina rules out units with generic or ambiguous meaning, even though they could be criticized in terms of female absence.

13. All translations of the proverbs are ours. We did not attempt to look for any fully or partially corresponding English proverbs, since our central interest is the way women are pictured in the Russian language.

14. This stands in opposition to Tafel's findings: she suggests that appearance is of central importance in proverbs referring to women (cf. Tafel 1997: 172).

15. We are indebted to Barbara Wurm for inspiration and comments on this chapter.

16. For the sake of a clear and explicit discussion, we deliberately refrain from using three dots which is still the prevailing way of writing about obscene vocabulary (at least in the Russian context).

17. *Mat* expressions, according to Uspenskij, offend "three mothers", namely God's Mother, one's "real life" (biological) mother, and Mother Earth, all perceived as sacred referents. Thus, it is their *signifiants*, rather than the actual referents, that are banned (cf. Uspenskij 1994: 85).

18. E.g., *dolbat'* 'carve', *napyrjat'* 'bump', *pixat'* 'bang', *traxat'* 'ash', *otrabotat'* 'work off', *ispol'zovat'* 'exploit', *otžarit'* 'fry', *upotrebljat'* 'use', *zapuzyrit'* 'blow up/inflate' (cf. Ermen 1993).

19. Kirilina lists some examples, collected by a Russian lawyer in the course of numerous trials, which, unfortunately, lack adequate source documentation.

References

Buj, Vasilij. 1995. *Russkaja zavetnaja idiomatika* [Russian classified idiomatics]. Moscow: Pomovskij.

Bulygina, Tat'jana & Aleksej Šmelev. 1997. *Jazykovaja konceptualizacija mira (na materiale russkoj grammatiki)* [The linguistic conceptualization of the world (on the basis of Russian grammar)]. Moscow: Jazyki russkoj kul'tury.

Comrie, Bernard. 1987. "Russian." In *The world's major languages*, ed. Bernard Comrie. London: Croom Helm, 329–347.

Comrie, Bernard & Gerald Stone & Maria Polinsky. 1996. *The Russian language in the twentieth century.* 2nd ed. Oxford: Clarendon.

Corbett, Greville G. 1991. *Gender.* Cambridge: Cambridge University Press.

Dal', Vladimir. 1984. *Poslovicy russkogo naroda* [Proverbs of the Russian people]. Moscow: Xudožestvennaja literatura.

Doleschal, Ursula. 1992. *Movierung im Deutschen. Eine Darstellung der Bildung und Verwendung weiblicher Personenbezeichnungen.* Unterschleissheim: Lincom Europa.

Doleschal, Ursula. 1993. *Genus als grammatische und textlinguistische Kategorie. Eine kognitiv-funktionalistische Untersuchung des Russischen.* Ph.D. dissertation, University of Vienna.

Doleschal, Ursula. 1994. "Näheres und Weiteres zur Genuskongruenz im Russischen." *Wiener Slawistischer Almanach* 33: 51–66.

Doleschal, Ursula. 1995. "Referring to women." In *Reference in multidisciplinary perspective: Philosophical object, cognitive subject, intersubjective process,* ed. Richard A. Geiger. Hildesheim: Olms, 277–298.

Doleschal, Ursula. 1997. "O vzaimosvjazi grammatičeskoj kategorii roda i pola" [On the interdependence of the grammatical category gender and sex]. In *Verbal'naja i neverbal'naja interpretacija polovych charakteristik* [Verbal and nonverbal interpretation of gender characteristics], ed. Aleksandr Xolod. Krivoj Rog: Meždunarodnyj Issledovatel'skij Centr Čelovek-Jazyk-Kul'tura-Poznanie, 134–155.

Doleschal, Ursula. 1999. "Gender assignment revisited." In *Gender in grammar and cognition,* eds. Barbara Unterbeck et al. Berlin: de Gruyter, 117–165.

Ermen, Ilse. 1993. "Die geschlechtsspezifische Ausrichtung des russischen sexuellen Wortschatzes" In *Zwischen Anpassung und Widerspruch,* ed. Uta Grabmüller & Monika Katz. Wiesbaden: Harrassowitz, 285–296.

Il'jasov, F., ed. 1994. *Russkij Mat: Antologija dlja specialistov-filologov* [Russian *mat*: An anthology for philology specialists]. Moscow: Lada M.

Kauffman, Charles A. 1980. "A survey of Russian obscenities and invective usage." *Maledicta* 4: 261–281.

Kirilina, Alla V. 1998. "Ešče odin aspekt značenija obscennoj leksiki" [Another aspect of the semantics of obscene vocabulary]. In *Vestnik tambovskogo universiteta. Serija gumanitarnye nauki 1998/4*: 13–16.

Kirilina, Alla V. 1999a. "Russkie poslovicy i pogovorki: ne tol'ko androcentrizm" [Russian proverbs and idioms: not only androcentrism] In *Vestnik tambovskogo universiteta. Serija gumanitarnye nauki 1999/3*: 41–47.

Kirilina, Alla V. 1999b. *Gender: lingvističeskie aspekty* [Gender: linguistic aspects]. Moscow: Institute of Sociology of the Russian Academy of Sciences.

Krongauz, Maksim A. 1993. "Sexus, ili problema pola v russkom jazyke" [Sexus, or the problem of gender in Russian]. In *Rusistika, Slavistika, Indoevropeistika* [Russian, Slavic, and Indo-European Studies], ed. Russian Academy of Sciences, Institute for Slavic and Balkan Studies. Moscow: Indrik, 510–525.

Levin, Jurij. 1996. "Ob obscennych vyraženijax russkogo jazyka" [On obscene expressions in Russian]. In *Anti-mir russkoj kul'tury: jazyk, fol'klor, literatura* [Anti-world of Russian culture: Language, folklore, literature], ed. Nikolaj A. Bogomolov. Moscow: Ladomir, 108–120.

Martynyuk, Alla. 1990. "A contrastive study of male and female occupational terms in English and Russian." *Papers and Studies in Contrastive Linguistics* 26: 103–110.

Mills, Margaret H., ed. 1999. *Slavic gender linguistics.* Amsterdam: Benjamins.

Mozdzierz, Barbara. 1999. "The rule of feminization in Russian." In *Slavic gender linguistics,* ed. Margaret H. Mills. Amsterdam: Benjamins, 165–182.

Nikunlassi, Ahti. 1999. "On gender assignment in Russian." In *Gender in grammar and cognition,* eds. Barbara Unterbeck et al. Berlin: de Gruyter, 771–791.

Oksaar, Els. 1976. *Berufsbezeichnungen im heutigen Deutsch.* Düsseldorf: Schwann.

Ožegov, Sergej I., ed. 1990. *Tolkovyj slovar' russkogo jazyka* [Russian-Russian dictionary]. Moscow: Russkij Jazyk.

Ožegov, Sergej I. & Natal'ja J. Švedova, eds. 1993. *Tolkovyj slovar' russkogo jazyka* [Russian-Russian dictionary]. Moscow: Az".

Schmid, Sonja. 1998. "Zur Bezeichnung weiblicher Personen im Russischen: Eine empirische Pilotstudie." *Wiener Slawistischer Almanach* 41: 239–262.

Smith, Philip M. 1985. *Language, the sexes and society.* Oxford: Blackwell.

Soviet Academy of Sciences, Russian Language Institute. 1950–1956. *Slovar' sovremennogo russkogo literaturnogo jazyka* [Dictionary of the contemporary literary Russian language]. Vol. 1–17. Moscow: Soviet Academy of Sciences Publication.

Soviet Academy of Sciences. 1981. *Slovar' russkogo jazyka* [Dictionary of the Russian language]. Vol. 1–4. Moscow: Russkij Jazyk.

Švedova, Natal'ja J., ed. 1980. *Russkaja Grammatika. Tom 1* [Russian grammar. Vol. 1]. Moscow: Nauka.

Tafel, Karin. 1997. *Die Frau im Spiegel der russischen Sprache.* Wiesbaden: Harrassowitz.

Telija, Veronika N. 1996. *Russkaja frazeologija. Semantičeskij, pragmatičeskij i lingvokul'turo-logičeskij aspekty* [Russian phraseology. Semantic, pragmatic, and lingo-cultural aspects]. Moscow: Jazyki russkoj kul'tury.

Timberlake, Alan. 1990. "Russian." In *The Slavonic languages,* eds. Bernard Comrie & Greville G. Corbett. London: Routledge, 827–886.

Uspenskij, Boris A. 1994. "Mifologičeskij aspekt russkoj ėkspressivnoj frazeologii" [The mythological aspect of Russian expressive phraseology]. In *Boris A. Uspenskij. Izbrannye trudy* [Selected writings] Vol. 2. Moscow: Gnozis, 53–128.

Wade, Terence 1992. *A comprehensive Russian grammar.* Oxford: Blackwell.

Weiss, Daniel. 1988. "Kurica ne ptica, (a) baba ne čelovek" [A hen is no bird, a woman is no human being]. In *Slavistische Linguistik 1987,* ed. Jochen Raecke. Munich: Kubon & Sagner, 413–443.

Weiss, Daniel. 1991. "Sexus distinctions in Polish and Russian." In *Words are physicians for an ailing mind,* eds. Maciej Grochowski & Daniel Weiss. Munich: Kubon & Sagner, 449–466.

Weiss, Daniel. 1992. "How many sexes are there? Reflections on natural and grammatical gender in contemporary Polish and Russian." In *Studies in Polish inflectional morphology and syntax. Synchronic and diachronic problems.* eds. Roman Laskowski & Gerd Hentschel. Munich: Kubon & Sagner, 71–105.

Yokoyama, Ol'ga T. 1986. "Lexical frequency and its implications: The case of contemporary edited Russian." *Slavic and East European Journal* 30: 147–166.

Yokoyama, Ol'ga T. 1999. "Russian genderlects and referential expressions." *Language in Society* 28: 401–429.

Žel'vis, Valerij. 1997. *Pole brani. Skvernoslovie kak social'naja problema* [Battle-field. Cursing as social problem]. Moscow: Ladomir.

Zemskaja, Elena A., ed. 1983. *Russkaja razgovornaja reč'. Fonetika. Morfologija. Leksika. Tekst* [Colloquial Russian. Phonetics. Morphology. Lexicon. Text]. Moscow: Nauka.

Zemskaja, Elena A. 1992. *Slovoobrazovanie kak dejatel'nost'* [Word-formation as an activity]. Moscow: Nauka.

Zemskaja, Elena A. & Margarita V. Kitajgorodskaja & Nina N. Rozanova. 1993. "Osobennosti mužskoj i ženskoj reči" [The peculiarities of male vs. female speech in the modern Russian language]. In *Russkij jazyk v ego funkcionirovanii. Kommunikativno-pragmatičeskij aspekt* [The Russian language in its functioning. Communication and pragmatics], eds. Elena A. Zemskaja & Dmitrij N. Šmelev. Moscow: Nauka, 90–136.

Ženščina v Rossijskom obščestve. 1998. = *Ženščina v Rossijskom obščestve* [Woman in Russian society] 1 (9): 1–9.

The communication of gender in Turkish[*]

Friederike Braun
University of Kiel, Germany

1. Introduction

Turkish (*Türk dili, Türkçe*) is the official language of the Turkish Republic, spoken by about 90% of its 56 million inhabitants. It is also the most widely spoken of the Turkic languages. Turkish is a left-branching language with modifiers preceding syntactical heads, Subject-Object-Verb as the unmarked word order, and postpositions. It has a typical agglutinating structure, expressing grammatical relations and derivational processes via suffixing morphology. The rich morphology is extremely regular, including predictable allomorphy due to vowel harmony and other morphophonological processes. During the Ottoman empire Turkish was heavily influenced by Persian and Arabic. Since the founding of the Republic in 1923, there have been efforts under the auspices of the *Türk Dil Kurumu* (Turkish Language Academy) to "turkify" the language, with varying degrees of success. For a structural overview of the language cf. Kornfilt (1987), for grammatical descriptions cf. Kornfilt (1997), Underhill (1976), and Lewis (1991). A standard Turkish-English dictionary is Redhouse (1997).

Gender is one of the most salient social categories in Turkey, a major determinant of patterns of behavior in all sectors of everyday life as well as on the various levels of public organization. For example, in schools different uniforms are prescribed for girls and boys, patterns of seat selection and seat allocation in busses are largely governed by considerations of gender, Turkish Civil Law confers different rights and obligations on women and men in marriage, and there are clear conceptions of what should be the characteristics, activities and interests of males or females.

Paradoxically however, gender does not appear to figure prominently in the Turkish language, as Turkish lacks grammatical gender distinctions and only rarely demands any overt indication of the gender of persons referred to. The Turkish language thus appears more or less indifferent to gender distinctions and to the category as a whole, a feature it shares with many other languages (see, e.g., the contributions on Indonesian and Creole languages in this volume). But how is gender communicated when it is not grammaticalized? How is gender signaled, and how is it perceived? Is it really less prominent in Turkish discourse than in the languages where it is anchored as an obligatory category in the grammar? What does language contribute to the social gender arrangement?

Until now, these questions have received little attention, the general assumption being that grammatical neutrality corresponds to neutrality in discourse. Although a handful of articles on language and gender have been published during the last decade, they focus on different aspects such as proverbs (Külebi 1989), personal names (Duman 1991), language behavior of women and men (König 1992a,b; Hayasi 1998), and terms of abuse (Özçalışkan 1994, Koçoğlu 1996). Many of these authors approach their subject on the basis of hypotheses formulated with regard to Western languages, i.e. languages with a very different structure, using unsystematic observation and introspection as linguistic methods. In 1995, I began to investigate the questions posed in the preceding paragraph in a more systematic manner. The core of that research was a series of empirical studies conducted at various universities in Ankara between 1995 and 1997.[1] Because the social gender arrangement was expected to be a major factor in the communication of gender, I examined the relevant sociological literature and conducted interviews with fellow Turkish scholars parallel to the main investigations. Results from various stages of this research have been published in earlier papers (Braun 1997a,b, 1998, 1999). The present contribution offers a synopsis of the major findings, as well as going into related topics such as terms of abuse (cf. Section 7) and feminist language critique (cf. Section 8) not treated in earlier publications.

2.   Gender in the Turkish language system

The majority of Turkish terms for person reference lack formal clues as to the gender of the person referred to, e.g., *komşu* 'neighbor', *işçi* 'worker' or *başbakan* 'prime minister'. Even pronominal forms, whether full pronouns or bound forms, do not differentiate referential gender, e.g. *o* (pronoun) 'she, he, it'; *ev* 'house', *ev-i* 'her house, his house'. A sentence such as (1) may thus refer to a woman as well as a man, and sentence (2) contains multiple gender-ambiguity.

(1)   *Bir   arkadaş ara-dı.*
       INDEF friend   call-PAST
       'A friend called.'

(2)   *Kardeş-im,   araba-sı-na   bin-di.*
       sibling-POSS.1SG car-POSS.3SG-DAT enter-PAST
       'My sister got into her car.'
       'My sister got into his car.'
       'My brother got into his car.'
       'My brother got into her car.'

However, Turkish does possess linguistic means for expressing referential gender; they comprise words with lexical gender, suffixing and compounding.

Nouns with lexical gender, i.e. an inherent specification of referential gender, are generally found in the fields of kinship terms and forms of address, cf. Tables 1 and 2. Consequently, gender distinctions are often inescapable when reference is made to family members as well as in direct address.[2]

Gender-indicating suffixes are not Turkish in origin, but loans from gender languages. Most of them occur only with those stems with which they were borrowed.[3] The most frequent suffix of this kind is Arabic *-e* (f). In spite of the anti-Arabic (and anti-Persian) language reform, which was launched after the foundation of the Republic of Turkey in 1923, neither Arabic lexemes nor the

Table 1. Kinship terms

Female	Male
anne 'mother'	*baba* 'father'
abla 'older sister'	*abi (ağabey)* 'older brother'
nine 'grandmother'	*dede* 'grandfather'
teyze 'aunt' (mother's sister)	*dayı* 'uncle' (mother's brother)
hala 'aunt' (father's sister)	*amca* 'uncle' (father's brother)

Table 2. Terms of address

Female	Male
hanım 'Mrs, Madam'	*bey* 'Mr, sir'
hanımefendi 'lady'	*beyefendi* 'sir'
bayan 'lady'	*bay* 'sir'
abla 'older sister'	*abi* 'older brother'
teyze 'aunt'	*amca* 'uncle'

-e suffix could be completely extinguished. Even modern texts contain forms like *sahib-e* 'female owner', *müdir-e* 'female director' or *memur-e* 'female official, employee'. They are used alongside the suffixless forms *sahip*, *müdür*, and *memur* for female reference. The ending *-içe* in *kral-içe* 'queen' or *impara-tor-içe* 'empress' was borrowed from Slavic and is used with a handful of stems. In addition to these, gender distinctions based on suffixes can be found in isolated word pairs of European origin, such as *prens/prenses* 'prince/princess' or *aktör/aktris* 'actor/actress'. None of the gender-indicating suffixes ever became productive in Turkish and no systematic gender distinction emerged from suffixation. Even so, the suffixes constitute a potential for overt gender marking which is exploited in everyday language.

Explicit gender marking can also be achieved through the combination of gender lexemes with other terms for person reference (as in the English expressions *girlfriend* or *male author*). Some combinations, among them *kız çocuğu* 'girl child (=girl)', *kız kardeş* 'girl sibling (=sister)', *erkek arkadaş* 'male friend (=boyfriend)', are rather frequent and almost routinely used even when gender is irrelevant to the utterance. Other combinations such as *erkek okuyucu* 'male reader' or *bayan sürücü* 'lady driver' occur more rarely and are more sensitive to contextual demands – but, as we shall see below (Section 4), even their use cannot always be explained by textual necessity.

3. Covert gender – the semantics of terms without overt gender distinctions

As noted above, gender can be overtly expressed in Turkish. But what about the many cases in which it is not expressed? Just what is the semantics of the numerous terms for person reference which do not contain gender markers and which give the language its neutral appearance? The following section will present results from a series of empirical studies which were designed to systematically investigate the gender semantics of such terms.

The initial assumption behind these studies was that the semantics of Turkish terms for person reference are determined by socio-cultural factors rather than by grammatical genderlessness. For example, a term referring to a typically male-occupied profession (e.g., *polis* 'police officer') can be expected to have a male-biased semantics. It was thus hypothesized that gender distributions in different occupations as well as gender stereotypes and gender roles – in short: the Turkish gender belief system (Deaux 1985:65) – have an impact on the semantics of Turkish terms for person reference. This gender belief system would produce gender biases or gender expectations that remain hidden beneath the grammatical neutrality of the linguistic structure.

3.1 Covert gender

In an initial study, gender associations evoked by different terms for person reference were elicited from 130 subjects (78 female and 52 male university students). Subjects were informed that the research was aimed at investigating Turkish forms of address. They were given a questionnaire which contained a list of person categories, such as *sekreter* 'secretary', *kuyumcu* 'goldseller', *taksi şoförü* 'taxi driver' etc., and were asked to write down the terms of address most widely used for these types of persons. Since many Turkish terms of address express the gender of the addressee (cf. Table 2 above), the subjects' responses usually indicated which gender they had associated with a stimulus term. When a subject chose, for example, *hanımefendi* 'lady' as a form of address for a secretary, it was evident that the stimulus *sekreter* had been interpreted as 'female'.

The pool of stimuli included terms from diverse domains (male-dominated, female-dominated and unspecific), "domains" being defined on the basis of the quantitative distribution of men and women. For example, *polis* 'police officer', *işportacı* 'street vendor', *kuyumcu* 'goldseller', *taksi şoförü* 'taxi driver', *postacı* 'mail man/woman' and *memur* here: 'bank employee' represented fields in which males constitute the statistical majority. These terms displayed a pro-nounced male bias: They were interpreted as 'male' in 69–98% of the cases, with an average of 85% 'male' interpretations. This finding is in keeping with the expectation that gender semantics is governed by socio-cultural factors. The male bias is in accordance with both the quantitative dominance of males in the respective occupations and the fact that certain aspects of these activities are considered not suitable for women: exposing oneself in public (street vendors, mail men/women), being in close contact with members of the opposite gender group (taxi drivers) or exercising power (police).

Stimulus-terms from predominantly female domains were the words *temizlikçi* 'cleaning person', *sekreter* 'secretary' and *tezgâhtar* 'salesperson'. They were clearly female-biased, with female interpretations ranging from 65% to 96% (average 85%). *Misafir* 'visitor' was also included as a female-oriented term, for visiting each other at home is rather a female activity in Turkey (institutionalized as *gün* 'day', a fixed day of the week on which women friends and relatives come together for tea and a chat while doing needlework or knitting). The female bias of this term was less pronounced, but still noticeable (46% 'female' interpretations vs. 19% 'male' interpretations).[4] The data thus reflect the gender distribution and the socio-cultural background: Cleaner (in a private household) and secretary are typically female occupations in Turkey; there are also a number of women who work as salespersons in shops (i.e., not in public and more protected than street vendors).

So far, the data confirm that even grammatically neutral forms can be gender-biased, as terms from gender-specific domains tend to develop corre-sponding gender biases in their semantics. More interesting, however, is the question of whether there are any gender biases in the semantics of terms from unspecific domains, i.e., domains where neither females nor males constitute the statistical majority. Table 3 will show whether the associations evoked by such terms are indeed neutral.

The data document a male bias for all of these words despite the fact that the number of men and women is roughly equal in these categories.[5] But why should a 'person' or 'someone', for instance, be more often thought of as male rather than female? Obviously, aspects other than actual gender distribution come into play here. Because the degree of representativeness or importance attached to male and female gender should be relevant, let us briefly consider the Turkish gender belief system from this angle.

The Turkish gender arrangement is characterized by a male dominance evident in almost all of the subsystems of Turkish society (economy, labor

Table 3. Terms from neutral domains

term	male interpret.	female interpret.	female & male	gender not determinable
köylü 'villager'	72%	5%	20%	3%
kişi 'person'	68%	8%	21%	3%
birisi 'someone'	68%	5%	28%	0%
yolcu 'passenger'	66%	6%	24%	4%

market, politics, law, religion). Men are simultaneously the privileged group and the leading figures in these subsystems. This is also reflected in the disproportionate representation of women and men in Turkish newspapers, in which general female representation lies at only 20%. Of the articles that deal with only one gender, 92% report about males (İmamoğlu & Gültekin & Köseoğlu & Çebi 1990). In general, males are more visible in many areas of everyday life in Turkey. Often there are more men than women to be seen in public places such as cafés and restaurants – and even where women are present in equal numbers (e.g., on the streets of city centers) they may be viewed as out of place. A reminder of this is the institution of the *aile salonu*, an extra room in traditional restaurants which is reserved for women and families. While this may seem a convenient institution at first glance (protecting women from harassment), the *aile salonu* emphasizes female presence as something special, something requiring special measures, and relegates women to the periphery of public space, for the *aile salonu* usually lies at the back of the respective building, upstairs or downstairs. In general, then, women seem to be a special case within the larger category of humans. To see them or discuss them is not expected, and this correlates nicely with the male bias in terms from neutral domains.

In sum, the results show that Turkish terms for person reference – even though structurally neutral – have an inherent gender bias, one which I refer to as "covert gender".[6] This covert gender is more than a simple reflection of the statistical likelihood of referring to a particular gender, because covert gender does not always correspond to the quantitative distribution of women and men in a given category.

3.2 Covert gender in context

In a natural interaction, person reference is always embedded in a linguistic and/or non-linguistic context. Since the context may contribute clues to the gender of a person mentioned, the question of how context information and covert gender interact arises. Do the effects of covert gender persist, for example, when countered by conflicting context information? These questions were examined in a second study with 386 subjects (239 female and 147 male students). This study had a 3×3 factorial design: The three terms *sekreter* 'secretary' (female domain, covert gender female), *kuyumcu* 'goldseller' (male domain, covert gender male), and *kişi* 'person' (neutral domain, covert gender male) were combined with three different contexts: household activities (cooking), sports (football), and watching television. These activities had been pre-determined in an earlier test as representing female, male and neutral fields of interest, respectively. From these combinations, nine different versions of a text were constructed, describing either a 'secretary', 'goldseller', or 'person' who is fond of spending leisure time with either cooking, football, or watching television. Each subject read one of the text versions and was then asked to assign the character a name and to specify the gender they had in mind when reading the story.

As the results show, context does have an impact on the covert gender of the terms, but to differing degrees, cf. Figure 1.

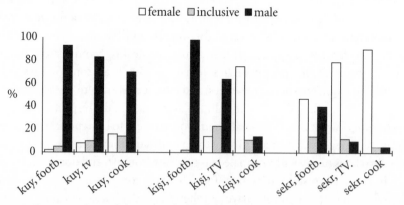

Figure 1. Interpretation of *kuyumcu* 'goldseller', *kişi* 'person', and *sekreter* 'secretary' according to context

kuy = *kuyumcu*, kişi = *kişi*, sekr = *sekreter*; footb = football, cook = cooking, TV = television

Covert gender was stable in the case of *kuyumcu* 'goldseller', with 'male' exceeding other interpretations in all three contexts. *Sekreter* 'secretary' was more sensitive to context effects, but its gender bias (female) was never completely reversed. Even in the male context, where female interpretations reached a low of 47%, they still exceeded male interpretations. *Kişi* 'person', however, the term with the most vague lexical meaning, was heavily affected by context and underwent a kind of "gender reversal": *Kişi* was female in the female context and even more male in the male context. But most interestingly, *kişi* retained its male bias in the gender-neutral context (television), though it was less extreme than in the male context. That *kişi* 'person', as a grammatically neutral term with a gender-neutral lexical meaning, showed a male bias in a neutral context, is another and very striking linguistic correlate of the greater representativity and importance ascribed to males in the Turkish gender belief system.

Proceeding from these results we can conclude that the covert gender of Turkish person reference terms functions as a default value: an interpretation which predominates at least when the context does not provide contradictory clues. But covert gender can be so pronounced as to be largely resistant to contextual factors (cf. *kuyumcu* 'goldseller'), in which case it may be on the way to becoming incorporated into the term's lexical meaning. This as well as the "gender reversal" of *kişi* 'person' shows that the susceptibility for context effects depends to a considerable degree on the respective lexeme.

3.3 Linguistic effects of covert gender

It could be argued that the covert gender of terms for person reference is not a strictly linguistic phenomenon. Covert gender could be understood as the mental image conjured up by certain terms, but outside of language itself. It is thus worth considering which traces of covert gender can be found in linguistic structures.

The study reported next was based on the observation that covert gender can affect the way sentences are formulated, for utterances are judged as problematic by native speakers when their predication contradicts the covert gender of the subject, as in sentence (3), which combines a predication associated with women with the male-biased term *kuyumcu*:

(3) $^?$*Köşe-de-ki   kuyumcu, altı ay-lık   hamile-ymiş.*
     corner-LOC-ADJ goldseller six month-ADJ pregnant-EVID
     $^?$'The goldseller at the corner is six months pregnant.'

In this study, terms for person reference were systematically combined with predications that either did or did not match their covert gender. Sentences (4) and (5) are examples from the experiment with the term *futbolcu* 'football player' (covert gender male) as the subject:

(4)   *Sadece iki gün-lük evli   ol-an   22*
     only   two day-ADJ married be-PART 22
     yaş-ı-nda-ki   bir   futbolcu   yaşıt-ı
     year-POSS.3SG-LOC-ADJ INDEF football.player agemate-POSS.3SG
     ol-an   karı-sı-nı   dün   Maltepe'de   meydan-a
     be-PART wife-POSS.3SG-ACC yesterday Maltepe-LOC place-DAT
     gel-en   feci   bir   trafik kaza-sı-nda
     come-PART tragic INDEF traffic accident-POSS.3SG-LOC
     kaybet-ti.
     lose-PAST
     'A 22 year old football player, who had been married for only two days, lost his[7] 22 year old wife in a tragic car accident in Maltepe yesterday.'

(5)   *Sadece iki gün-lük evli   ol-an   22*
     only   two day-ADJ married be-PART 22
     yaş-ı-nda-ki   bir   futbolcu,   yaşıt-ı
     year-POSS.3SG-LOC-ADJ INDEF football.player agemate-POSS.3SG
     ol-an   koca-sı-nı   dün   Maltepe'de
     be-PART husband-POSS.3SG-ACC yesterday Maltepe-LOC
     meydan-a gel-en   feci   bir   trafik kaza-sı-nda
     place-DAT come-PART tragic INDEF traffic accident-POSS.3SG-LOC
     kaybet-ti.
     lose-PAST
     'A 22 year old football player, who had been married for only two days, lost her 22 year old husband in a tragic car accident in Maltepe yesterday.'

105 native speakers (60 female students, 43 male students, and two who did not specify their gender) participated in the investigation. They were told that the study was designed to evaluate a program for computer translation and that they would be asked to judge the well-formedness of sentences translated by that program. Every subject then rated six stimulus-sentences on a 5-point-scale ranging from 1 'totally impossible', to 5 'perfectly possible'. Three of the sentences contained a conflict between covert gender and predication of the type shown in (5), three were matching sentences like (4). In all, six different

stimulus-terms were used: *sekreter* 'secretary' and *çocuk bakıcısı* 'nursery school teacher' (female domain, covert gender female), *Ankaralı* 'inhabitant of Ankara' and *genç* 'young person'[8] (neutral domain, covert gender male), *futbolcu* 'football player' and *işportacı* 'street vendor' (male domain, covert gender male). Each of these terms was presented both in the matching and the conflicting version of two different sentence frames, one of which is the "accident"-frame shown in (4) and (5). This resulted in a pool of 24 stimulus-sentences, from which every study subject received six. The results of the study are summarized in Figure 2.

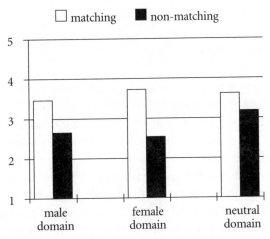

Figure 2. Mean ratings of matching and non-matching sentences by domain of terms for person reference

As the figure shows, sentences with non-matching predications received lower scores than matching sentences. The difference between matching and non-matching sentences in each domain was statistically significant.[9] Note that none of the non-matching sentences violated grammatical rules and that all of them were "logically" possible, as there are, e.g., female football players and male secretaries in Turkey.[10] What caused the reduced acceptability of non-matching sentences must therefore have been the semantic conflict between covert gender and predication.

In addition to the quantitative study, qualitative interviews were carried out with 42 native speakers of Turkish (22 females, 20 males), using the stimulus-sentences of the quantitative study as a starting point for discussion. The majority of the interviewees expressed uneasiness with the non-matching sentences referring to the problem as, for example, a "disruption in meaning".

It is unlikely that speakers would utter conflict sentences, such as the ones used in the study, in a natural conversation. Speakers share intuitions about the covert gender of terms for person reference and anticipate its possible effects on the interpretations and expectations of the hearers. Therefore they construct their utterances in such a way that semantic conflict will not arise. When the interviewees where asked how they would formulate the non-matching sentences, if they were to express the state of affairs with their own words, they came up with a number of solutions. Overt gender marking for example is a means of escaping the clash between covert gender and non-matching predication.

4. Asymmetrical gender marking

The final study reported here was designed to monitor the use of overt gender markers in language production, 404 students (176 female/227 male)[11] participated as subjects. The investigation was based on a translation from English to Turkish. Subjects were given a text relating a traffic accident in which one person was injured. The person concerned was introduced via a gender-unmarked term in most of the cases.[12] Referential gender was then expressed in subsequent pronominal references to that person (e.g., *she* or *he*). Every subject translated one version of the text into Turkish. Dependent variables were the use or non-use of overt gender markers in the Turkish translations, their number and position in the text. The following is an example of the stimulus text in the version *American/she*:

> **American injured in traffic accident**
>
> Thick fog over South England was the cause of several traffic accidents yesterday. Near London a thirty year old American was seriously injured when the car which she was in crashed into a tree. She was taken to Knightsbridge Hospital. This morning doctors reported that her condition was critical.

The text frame was held constant over all versions, but the term for person reference (the "main character") varied according to a 3×2 factorial design. Different stimuli were selected to represent a neutral, female and male domain: *American* and *child* (neutral domain), *secretary* and *househelper* (female domain), *basketball player* and *police* (male domain). The terms were combined with either *she* or *he* to make the main character female in one version of the text and male in the other.

The most conspicuous finding of the study was that gender marking was much more frequent when the person referred to was female. Translating a text about a female child, for example, subjects used expressions such as *kız çocuğu* 'girl child', whereas a male child was designated as *çocuk* 'child'. Explicit marking of this kind occurred with 50% of the female stimuli used in the study, but with only 5% of the male ones. Statistical analyses show this difference to be highly significant and the correspondence of gender and marking to be substantial ($\chi^2 = 104.104$; df = 1; p < .0001; φ = .508). In addition, there was a tendency to place gender markings for females at the earliest possible position in a text, while markings for males tended to appear in later positions. This difference, however, did not attain statistical significance. Gender marking was, of course, also dependent on the domain to which the stimulus referred. Table 4 shows the distribution of gender markings for the different stimuli.

As is evident from the table, gender marking was always more frequent for female than for male gender, but the difference was small in the case of *house-helper* and *secretary* (terms from a female domain) and was not statistically significant there. It seems only logical that female markings diminish when the covert gender of a term is female already, as with *hizmetçi* 'househelper' or *sekreter* 'secretary'. But what is striking is that male gender was marked rarely in these cases, even though male gender is the deviation from the norm here. Thus, a general rule extractable from the data is that male gender remains mostly unmarked regardless of context, whereas female gender tends to be overtly expressed. If, however, a specifically female domain is referred to, female marking becomes redundant and can be omitted.

5. The male-human ambiguity

5.1 Male = human

Whatever the asymmetries in covert gender and in overt gender marking, it would seem that Turkish is at least spared the problem of masculine generics, since there simply is no masculine in a genderless language. But are things really that simple? With regard to English, the term "masculine generics" is commonly used not only for grammatical phenomena (such as anaphoric *he* or *his* after *someone*), but also for lexemes of the type *mankind* or *chairman*, i.e., lexemes which have a 'male' meaning but are also used to refer to humans in general. This section will show that similar "masculine" generics exist in Turkish, a

Table 4. Distribution of gender marking by stimulus term and stimulus gender

Term	Gender	Marked	Unmarked
police	f	100%	0%
$p < .000001$; $\varphi = 0.972$	m	3%	97%
basketball player	f	26%	74%
$p < .005$; $\varphi = 0.382$	m	0%	100%
American	f	57%	43%
$p < .0005$; $\varphi = 0.487$	m	11%	89%
child	f	69%	31%
$p < .000005$; $\varphi = 0.682$	m	3%	97%
househelper	f	25%	75%
n.s.; $\varphi = 0.158$	m	13%	88%
secretary	f	7%	93%
n.s.; $\varphi = 0.189$	m	0%	100%

complement to the general tendency of treating males linguistically as the norm and females as the deviation. These forms will be called "male generics" to distinguish them from generics which involve grammatical gender.

Just like the English word *man*, Turkish *adam* means both 'male' and 'human being', which is not very surprising given the obvious origin of the word.[13] *Adam* can also be used as an indefinite pronoun in the sense of 'one, you', again equating males and humans in general, see example (6).

(6)   *Adam-ı   çile-den   çıkar-ıyor.*
      man-ACC hardship-ABL bring.out-PROG
      'She/he drives you (one) crazy.'

The ambiguous male-human *adam* moreover appears in a number of idioms which express a positive evaluation of the *adam* concept (also mentioned in Külebi 1989: 17 and Aliefendioğlu 1994: 2f): *adam gibi* means 'decent, respectable' (lit. 'like a man/human'), *adam olmak* 'to become a respectable, decent, educated person', *adama benzemek* 'to resemble a respectable, decent person', *adamdan saymak* 'to consider competent, to treat respectfully', *adam yerine koymak* 'to respect, honor' (lit. 'to place in the position of a man/human'). Even though humanness rather than maleness is the preferred reading in these expressions, they still carry a kind of "male flavor", for they can be used with reference to males without any difficulty, but (according to my informants) not all of them are considered totally appropriate in reference to a female (esp. *adam olmak* and *adama benzemek*).

Adam also functions as a component of a number of occupational terms, again collapsing the categories of males and people into a single term: *iş adamı* 'businessman', *devlet adamı* 'statesman', *bilim adamı* 'scientist' (lit. 'science man'), *din adamı* 'clergyman'. Although these terms appear to be acceptable (in the plural) in reference to a mixed group, my informants were slightly hesitant about using them in specific reference to a female as in (7):

(7) ?*Bir iş   adam-ı   olarak abla-m-ın*
    INDEF business man-POSS.3SG as   sister-POSS.1SG-GEN
    devamlı   toplantı-lar-a   katıl-ma-sı   lazım.
    constantly meeting-PL-DAT participate-INF-POSS.3SG necessary
    ?'Because she is a businessman my sister is always having to attend conferences.'

The case of *adam* might seem less serious when considering that Turkish has another word for 'human' which does not confound maleness and humanness: *insan* 'human'. In the sense of 'one, you' *insan* even seems to be more frequent than *adam*. However, *insan* is the base of another male generic in Turkish, *insanoğlu* 'human, man' (lit. 'son of a human'),[14] which is used instead of or alternatively to *insan* when humans are referred to as a species. *İnsanoğlu* is considered inappropriate by many speakers when combined with a specifically female feature (8), but is rather unproblematic in combination with male ones (9):

(8) ?*İnsan-oğl-u   ancak 50 yaş-lar-ı-na   kadar çocuk*
    human-son-POSS.3SG only 50 year-PL-POSS.3SG-DAT until child
    doğur-abil-iyor.
    bear-can-PROG
    ?'Man(kind) is only capable of giving birth up to the age of 50.'

(9) *Evrim   sürec-i-nde   insan-oğl-u-nun   vücut-kıl-*
    evolution process-POSS.3SG-LOC human-son-POSS.3SG-GEN body-hair-
    lar-ı   gittikçe azal-mış-tır,   sadece vücud-u-nun
    PL-POSS.3SG gradually diminish-EVID-3SG only   body-POSS.3SG-GEN
    belirli yer-ler-i-nde   kıl ve surat-ı-nda
    certain place-PL-POSS.3SG-LOC hair and face-POSS.3SG-LOC
    sakal-ı   çık-ıyor.
    beard-POSS.3SG appear-PROG
    'Man's body hair has gradually diminished in the course of evolution, it is now limited to facial hair (beard) and certain parts of the body.'

5.2   Human > male

A kind of counterpart to the male generics discussed above is the tendency towards semantic narrowing from 'human' to 'male' which can be observed in some Turkish words. The lexical core of the term *genç*, e.g., is the meaning 'young', as in *genç müdür* 'young director', *genç kız* 'young girl', *gençler* 'the young (ones)'. But when *genç* is used as the head of an NP and in specific reference (in the singular), it is generally male, as in (10):

(10)   *sev-diğ-i   genç-le   birlikte kaç-an   genç   kız*
       love-PART-POSS.3SG young-with together flee-PART young girl
       'the young girl who eloped with the young (man) she loved'

Although there are cases where *genç* is used in specific reference to a female, most native speakers perceive it as rather 'male' in meaning (cf. note 8). The semantics of *genç* thus seems to be undergoing a semantic narrowing from general to gender-specific, and comes to resemble English *youth* (in the sense of 'young man').

   Turkish language history supplies another example of semantic narrowing: In former times, the meaning of the word *oğul* used to be 'child', that is gender-neutral, but over time narrowed to mean 'son' (Clauson 1972:83). In modern Turkish it is a lexical gender word. Interestingly, the modern word for 'child', *çocuk*, seems to be undergoing a similar process: In specific reference to a single person, *çocuk* is more frequent for boys than for girls, for the latter are often referred to as *kız* 'girl' or *kız çocuğu* 'girl child' (cf. the corresponding results of the study described in Section 4). *Çocuk* is entirely 'male' when used to refer to young adults (up to ca. 25 years of age) as in sentence (11):

(11)   *Soner, çok hoş bir   çocuk.*
       Soner very nice INDEF child
       'Soner is a very nice child (i.e. young man).'

6.   Gender in Turkish proverbs

While terms of person reference communicate messages about gender in rather subtle ways (by means of their semantics, asymmetrical marking patterns etc.), proverbs elaborate on gender stereotypes very explicitly. Unfortunately, systematic studies on Turkish proverbs employing a sound methodology are lacking. There is, for example, no research on the frequency and usage of proverbs in everyday discourse, therefore we can only consult examples from more or less unsystematical observation (taken from Uğuz 1988, Ağaçsaban 1989, Arat 1989, Külebi 1989 and Yurtbaşı 1994).[15] Still it seems safe to point out one tendency found in other languages as well:[16] There are apparently more proverbs about women and female characteristics in Turkish than proverbs dealing with maleness – clues to an underlying male perspective. Cursory examination of the index of a Turkish proverb dictionary (Yurtbaşı 1994) reveals approx. 80 entries with the keyword *kadın* 'woman', but only about 30 with the keyword *erkek* 'man, male'.[17] This section gives a few examples of the way gender is depicted in Turkish proverbs (though claims no representativity).

Because proverbs tend to be overly conservative, it is not surprising that they define the female as responsible for the household and the male as the breadwinner:

(12) *Yuvayı dişi kuş yapar.*
'It is the female bird that builds the nest.'

(13) *Er olan ekmeğini taştan çıkarır.*
'The one who is a man digs his bread from stone.'

Turkish proverbs also document the preference of sons over daughters as well as the divergent evaluations of males and females:

(14) *Oğlan doğuran övünsün, kız doğuran dövünsün.*
'Let the one who bears a son be proud, let the one who bears a daughter beat herself.'

(15) *Oğlan büyür koç olur, kız büyür hiç olur.*
'A boy grows up to be a ram [strong, proud], a girl grows up to be nothing.'

The following proverbs describe power relations in marriage:

(16) *Karı sözüne uyan adam değildir.*
'He who takes heed of his wife's words is not a man.'

(17) *Kadının sırtından sopa, karnından sıpa eksik edilmez.*
'A woman should not be spared the rod on her back and the child in her womb.'

A double standard is expressed in example (18):

(18) *Kadının yüzünün karası, erkeğin elinin kınası.*
'The shame of a woman is the pride of a man. / Sexual relationships are a source of shame for a woman, but a source of pride for a man.'

It goes without saying that proverbs do not give a realistic picture of contemporary gender relations, nor do they express views shared by all members of a language community. But neither can they be dismissed as irrelevant. Proverbs communicate traditional beliefs about gender and, as part of the shared knowledge of the language community, contribute to gender stereotyping.

7. Gender in terms of abuse and verbal insults

In contrast to proverbs, terms of abuse and verbal insults convey their messages indirectly, by negating values that are vital for individuals' self-esteem or for their social acknowledgment. To the degree that the recipients feel degraded or provoked, insults reconfirm the norms a society has built up for women and men. The present section is an attempt to summarize some important aspects of what Turkish insults communicate with respect to the Turkish gender arrangement.

In many languages, insults aimed at women focus upon their sexuality as the target of the verbal attack. Insults of this kind are extremely frequent in Turkey, with words like *fahişe, orospu, kahpe, kaltak, şırfıntı* (all 'prostitute, whore') or *kaldırım süpürgesi* 'sidewalk broom' aiming to slight the woman in question. These terms are not only used in their literal sense (i.e., to express doubt of a woman's virtuousness), but also to voice any kind of discontent. Thus, speakers may use 'prostitute' terms when annoyed by a woman's driving in traffic or during an argument with a woman. The occasional use of a term like *orospu* 'prostitute' against males is felt to be secondary to the original use, which is against females. Therefore, *orospu çocuğu* 'child of a prostitute (bastard)' is a more wide-spread derogative for males. A Turkish speaker provided a typical example of this distribution when he referred to the former Prime Minister Tansu Çiller as *kaltak karı* 'whore woman (slut)' to express his political contempt, but to Süleyman Demirel, President of the Turkish Republic, as *orospu çocuğu* 'child of a prostitute (bastard)' within the same sentence. Even though 'bastard' terms[18] may serve as the male counterpart for the 'prostitute' terms, it is worth noting that they, too, derive their force from negating a woman's (i.e., the mother's) sexual virtue.[19]

The importance of female chastity in Turkish insults points to one of the core asymmetries in the Turkish gender arrangement, whose roots lie in the traditional Islamic paradigm. This asymmetry is embodied in the concept of *namus* that creates and explains much of the differences or inequalities between females and males. The Redhouse dictionary translates *namus* as 'honor, honesty, good name' and the corresponding adjective *namuslu* as 'honorable, honest, modest, chaste' (Redhouse 1997: 866) without, however, referring to the crucial point: the implications of *namus* are different for women and men. For women to be *namuslu* is to be sexually pure or virtuous, presupposing either virginity (unmarried women) or fidelity in marriage. On the other hand, a man who is *namuslu* is one who is honest, reliable and who is capable of protecting and controlling the *namus* of his female relatives. His own sexual virtuousness, however, is of no relevance, since concepts of sexual "purity" or "impurity" do not apply to males.

The ramifications of *namus* are numerous and far-reaching. Because any contact with unrelated men constitutes a threat to female virtue, *namus* demands and justifies the fundamental allocation of females to the house (or the private sphere) and the association of males with the public sphere. That *namus* must lead to severe restrictions on the self-determination of female sexuality is obvious. This may even go so far as to include "virginity checks" which are sometimes performed on girls in Turkish schools (without asking their consent, cf. Tavşanoğlu 1995). Effects of *namus* also manifest themselves in the unequal definition of *zina* 'adultery' in Turkish Criminal Law: According to the legislation, a woman commits adultery if she has intercourse just once with a man to whom she is not married. A man, on the other hand, is only guilty of adultery when having a permanent affair which is publicly known or when having intercourse with another woman in the conjugal house.[20] It is important to note that *namus* confers restrictions and obligations not only on women, but also on their male family members, because males are held responsible for the virtue of their mothers, daughters, sisters, or spouses. The ability to ensure the protection and control of female sexuality is just as vital for male identity as is sexual purity for female identity.

Since male *namus* is independent of male sexual behavior, it is more effective to call one of his female family members a prostitute than to call him a prostitute. This explains the existence of insult-exchanges centering around each other's mother (or other family members) observed among Turkish males. For the present purpose they will be labeled "mother insults". The following utterances are illustrative of mother insults:

(19) *Ana-n-ı*   *avrad-ın-ı*   *sik-er-im.*
      mother-POSS.2SG-ACC wife-POSS.2SG-ACC fuck-AOR-1SG
      'I'll fuck your mother and your wife.'

(20)   *Ana-n-ı*   *belle-r-im.*
       mother-POSS.2SG-ACC fuck-AOR-1SG
       'I'll fuck your mother.'

(21)   *Abla-n*   *var-sa*   *ban-a sik-tir.*
       elder.sister-POSS.2SG exist-COND I-DAT fuck-CAUS
       'If you have an elder sister let me fuck her.'
       (Dundes & Leach & Özkök 1986: 139)

An expression like *ebene atlarım* 'I'll jump on (assault) your midwife' indicates that this type of insult can be extended to any female vaguely associated with the interlocutor. Mother insults are used in the following functions: (a) as insults or provocations in fights and arguments among males, (b) as playful teasing among boys or grown-up (male) acquaintances, (c) as material in verbal duels among boys. Often the insult is countered by a similar and if possible stronger retort from the first speaker's rival, thus developing into more or less ritualized exchanges. Dundes & Leach & Özkök (1986) give detailed descriptions of verbal duels of this type among Turkish boys. Although the strongly ritualized and stylized types of such duels may be less frequent in the modern oral culture of big cities, less "artful" forms of verbal dueling were familiar to my male informants, all of whom spent the greater part of their lives in cities. Probably as a result of their extensive use, the mother insults have given rise to idioms such as *anasını sikmek* 'to ruin sth. (= to fuck its mother)' or *anası bellenmek* 'to have a hard time, be in a difficult situation (= one's mother is fucked)', which are current in Turkish (male) slang. An exclamation such as *Anasını siktin!* 'You ruined it! (= fucked its mother)' could be a reaction to someone's dropping a vase. A complaint about working conditions which are hard to endure can be voiced as *Anamız bellendi* 'We are having a real hard time (=our mother was fucked)'.

While chastity is the primary target when insulting females, questioning his masculinity is the central attack against a male. A mild form consists of ascribing to him "feminine" qualities: A man who is called *karı gibi* or *kadın gibi* 'like a woman' is thereby branded as fearful and unreliable. A man who is *karı kılıklı* 'looking like a woman, having the appearance of a woman' is a passive person without energy or drive, one who is *kadın ağızlı* 'with the mouth of woman' is overly talkative.[21] Such expressions highlight important aspects of the female stereotype, while at the same time providing evidence for the different evaluation of femininity and masculinity: Though it is disgraceful for a man to be compared to a woman, it is not insulting at all for a woman to be ascribed masculine characteristics. On the contrary, a woman who is referred to as *erkek gibi karı* 'a woman like a man' is thereby evaluated positively, as a person who is energetic, courageous and reliable.[22]

Probably the most damaging insult to masculinity is the suggestion that the respective male is a homosexual. Hence terms like *ibne* and *top* 'gay' or *göt veren* 'one who presents his ass' constitute rather severe insults in Turkish. Interestingly, however, it is only the passive role in a homosexual relationship that is depicted as disgraceful. Thus a speaker may well threaten to assault or to rape another male without losing face himself (e.g., *sana atlayayım mı?* 'shall I jump on [mount] you?'). It is not sexual intercourse with another male which is in itself degrading, but only the passive role in the relationship. Insults of the passive homosexual type are hurled during arguments among males or in other situations which call for expressions of anger directed against another male. They also occur in the same forms of ritualized verbal dueling as the mother insults (cf. Dundes & Leach & Özkök 1986 for various examples).

Abuse and insults are not exclusively concerned with gender (cf. expressions such as *salak* 'idiot'), but from this conventionalized area of language usage much can be learned about the core conceptions of gender and the asymmetries in gender roles operative in the Turkish language community.[23]

8. Feminist language critique and linguistic change in Turkish

While feminist language critique has led to noticeable changes in languages such as English or German – promoting symmetrical designations of women and men and discouraging the use of masculine (or male) generics – little criticism has focused on Turkish. One reason for this may be that the asymmetries discussed in Sections 3 and 4 are less immediately obvious than the much-discussed asymmetries of gender languages. For example, in her book discussing "bad" usage of Turkish, Hepçilingirler (1997:211f) points to the desirability of ungendered nouns and expressions and argues that they are already the rule in Turkish.

The only forms that have received some critical attention are the occupational terms containing *adam* (such as *bilim adamı* 'science man', cf. Section 5.1). In recent years female counterparts have been coined for some of these terms: There is, e.g., *iş kadını* 'business woman' or even *iş hanımı* 'business lady' and *bilim kadını* '(female) scientist' (lit. 'science woman'). Terms like *bilim insanı* 'scientist (science person)' instead of *bilim adamı* 'science man' have occasionally been suggested and used. Such usage is, however, far from institutionalized and even the new female forms cannot obliterate the fundamental asymmetry, for they mark their referents as specifically female and isolate them from the main category. A second point occasionally mentioned (e.g., König 1992a:26) is the widespread use of *bayan* or *hanım* 'lady' instead of *kadın* 'woman'. As English *lady*, *bayan* and *hanım* are judged to be euphemistic expressions which indirectly emphasize the fact that *kadın* 'woman' is a problematic, if not deprecatory, designation.

Furthermore, these few points of feminist language critique are discussed in extremely limited (feminist and academic) circles which are already aware of gender issues. There is no public debate, still less a public demand, for guidelines or regulations. Indeed, promoting feminist language change in a language which has covert – but not overt – gender, is quite possibly a fruitless endeavor. It may be comparatively easy to avoid the equation of 'male' and 'human' incorporated in the *adam*-expressions, to avoid explicit female markings or to get rid of other asymmetries,[24] but it would be difficult to find a remedy for the most subtle and most effective bias: covert gender. Especially desirable would be a change in the gender semantics of terms from neutral domains, such as *kişi* 'person' or *birisi* 'someone', for the pervasive pattern of equating males and humans can lead to a neglect of women's interests and rights. But a constant repetition of explicitly 'female' forms, in order to enhance female visibility and to directly evoke female associations, would be a strategy which is alien to Turkish language structure (hence promising little success), and would in addition enhance the existing tendency to treat females as the marked gender. It might therefore be more promising to avoid explicit female markings in the hope of including females in those categories whose covert gender is originally male. But it is difficult to predict to what degree or in which timespan such a strategy might produce results.

9.   Conclusion

As argued in this article, the absence of grammatical devices does not prevent the Turkish language – or rather, its speakers – from communicating messages about gender. Gender messages are encapsulated in (among other things) covert gender, explicit gender markings, proverbs and terms of abuse. As these linguistic elements correlate with the social gender arrangement, they reflect and reinforce existing social asymmetries. At this point I will briefly recapitulate the most important findings:

Gender stereotypes

Turkish terms for person reference contain information about gender-specific domains in Turkish society. This information is embodied in the terms' covert gender, e.g. the female gender bias of *çocuk bakıcısı* 'nursery-school teacher' or the male gender bias of *futbolcu* 'football player'. Although covert gender does not imply a definite gender assignment, it is substantial enough to affect the formulation of utterances. A certain term for person reference, for example, will not be used, when its covert gender might create false impressions or might lead to conflict with a gender-specific predication in the sentence. Covert gender provides initial clues regarding the gender of the person spoken about, but covert gender can fulfill this communicative function only because it is grounded in communal ideas regarding female and male occupations and roles, i.e., in gender stereotypes. That proverbs also have an important share in the explicit linguistic construction of gender stereotypes was discussed in Section 6 (e.g. *yuvayı dişi kuş yapar* 'it is the female bird that builds the nest').

The representative members of humanity

A pervasive message communicated in various forms in Turkish is that men are more representative of humanity. This message is conveyed through the male covert gender of terms whose lexical meaning should be gender-neutral (e.g., *kişi* 'person'). It is more openly communicated by the male generics of Turkish, above all, terms and idioms including *adam* 'man, human' in its various shades of meaning. But it is also reflected in the semantic narrowing of general terms to male meanings such as 'child' to 'son' or 'boy'.

The peripheral members of humanity

Since men are central to the 'human' category, a peripheral or secondary position is what remains for females. This "extra-ordinary" status of women is linguistically communicated by a pronounced tendency towards gender marking in female reference, as in *kız çocuğu* 'girl child' or *kız kardeş* 'girl sibling' (=sister)'. The "feminine" suffixes which exist and persist despite their foreign origin and all purifying efforts equally attest to the special status of females.

Evaluations of femininity and masculinity

A different evaluation of men and women is documented in some expressions used as insults. A man is devalued when he is compared to a woman (e.g., *karı kılıklı* 'with the appearance of a woman') or ascribed a passive (= female) sexual role (e.g. *göt veren* 'the one who presents his ass'). On the other hand, calling a woman *erkek gibi kadın* 'a man-like woman' can actually improve her standing. Evaluative tendencies are also documented in Turkish proverbs with, for example, the higher value of sons being made explicit in the saying *Oğlan büyür koç olur, kız büyür hiç olur* 'A boy grows up to be strong, a girl grows up to be nothing'.

The importance of female purity

One of the most important aspects and the basis of a fundamental asymmetry in the Turkish gender arrangement is the *namus* concept which makes sexual purity simultaneously the most valuable and the most vulnerable female characteristic. Its vital importance is communicated by making women's *namus* the primary target for insults and agents of abuse. Female *namus* is not only the target in insults aimed at women themselves (e.g., by calling them *orospu* 'whore' to their face), but is also one of the preferred targets in male-to-male fights and arguments (e.g., in expressions such as *ananın amına koyayım* 'I'll fuck your mother'). Although in the latter situation, the insult is aimed at the man and questions the male's *namus* as well, it can only do so because female *namus* is the focus of the whole family's reputation.

Whether grammaticalized in a language or not, gender will be communicated as long as it is a relevant social category in a language community. The lack of a grammatical gender distinction is thus of little diagnostic value for sexism or egalitarianism in the community and even in the language itself. In the final analysis, the decisive factor for "sexism" in a language is the social construction of gender and the social treatment of women and men and not its grammatical structure.

Notes

* This research was conducted at the Centre for Interdisciplinary Research on Women and Gender at Kiel University and profited greatly from the assistance of all my colleagues there. Special thanks go to Sabine Sczesny, who advised me in designing and evaluating the empirical tests. I am very grateful to my friend and colleague Geoff Haig for his assistance in all stages of this research. Last, but not least I would like to thank Marlis Hellinger and Hadumod Bußmann for their critical reading and their feedback on this contribution – but most of all for their patient, constructive and inspiring cooperation in the course of the entire project, which was as enjoyable as it was instructive.

1. I am greatly indebted to my friends and colleagues at the universities in Ankara who helped me collect the data: above all, Güray König and Ahmet Kaftanlı from Hacettepe University, Serdar Gökkuş, Zülfü Aşık and Helga Rittersberger-Tılıç from Middle East Technical University, and Hanneke van der Heijden from Ankara University.

2. Not all kinship terms and terms of address differentiate gender (e.g., *kardeş* 'younger sister/brother', *yeğen* 'niece/nephew'; *efendim* '(my) lady/sir', *canım* 'dear', *hocam* 'my teacher'), but kinship and address terms are those lexical fields where gender distinctions are comparatively frequent.

3. An exception is the derivation *patron-içe* 'female boss', where Slavic *-içe* is suffixed to the French stem *patron* 'boss'.

4. Inclusive interpretations (both genders) were given in 11% of the cases. For 24% of the responses, gender was not determinable.

5. Because of the design of the investigation (address terms) it was not possible to present these terms without any context. Thus *birisi*, e.g., was presented as 'someone who is waiting in the bus queue'. I have not seen any significant differences in the number of women and men waiting for busses in large Turkish cities, but an effect of context information cannot be excluded with absolute certainty. The results of the second study (cf. Section 3.2), however, confirm the male bias of terms from neutral domains.

6. Covert gender corresponds to what Hellinger (1990:61) and Baron (1986:175) call *social gender* with regard to English words like *nurse* or *mechanic*. But while the term *social gender* stresses the social causes of the bias, *covert gender* emphasizes its structural invisibility.

7. The Turkish possessive is of course not specified for gender, but the contexts provided make the given readings the only plausible ones.

8. To some speakers, the male bias of *genç* is so pronounced that they might hesitate to classify it as a term from a neutral domain or to translate it as 'young person'. Yet *genç* cannot be regarded as a 'male' lexeme such as *bey* 'sir', for even females are occasionally referred to as *bu genç* 'this young person'. In a series of interviews with native speakers of Turkish (cf. Section 3.3), 12 of 42 interviewees claimed to associate both men and women with the word *genç*.

9. This was tested by using t-tests for paired samples.

10. In addition, the cover story about the translation program encouraged respondents to judge the well-formedness of the sentences rather than the likelihood or credibility of the reported facts.

11. One subject did not specify her/his gender.

12. The only exception was the stimulus *police*, which displayed a lexical gender distinction (*policewoman* vs. *policeman*). This case of lexical gender distinction was included to determine the impact of the linguistic form of the stimulus.

13. In specific reference to a single person, only the male reading of *adam* is possible, e.g. *dün gördüğüm adam* 'the man I saw yesterday'.

14. The term *insanoğlu* apparently came into use at a time when *oğul* still meant 'child' (and not 'son' as it does today). Speakers of modern Turkish, however, must perceive *insanoğlu* as a male generic, since *oğul* has developed into a lexical gender word. See also Section 5.2.

15. Yurtbaşı (1994) is a proverb dictionary providing a classification of proverbs according to keywords, among others *kadın* 'woman' (interestingly enough, there is no section *erkek* 'man', even though *erkek* appears in the index). However, Yurtbaşı does not evaluate them from the perspective of gender stereotypes.

16. Cf., e.g., Daniels (1985: 18) on German proverbs.

17. There are many proverbs containing *adam* 'man, human', but they are often generic and do not focus on male-specific characteristics or activities as seen from a female perspective (cf. *Adam adamın şeytanıdır.* 'Man is man's devil = Humans treat each other cruelly.').

18. Apart from *orospu çocuğu* there are further terms with the same meaning, e.g., *onun bunun çocuğu* 'child of whoever (bastard)' or *piç* 'bastard'.

19. Moreover, 'bastard' terms can also be directed against females.

20. According to the newspaper *Sabah* (15 January 1997), the definition of *zina* as well as the punishment foreseen by Criminal Law are about to be revised. What the new version will be like, however, is not mentioned in the article.

21. Cf. the expression *kadınlar hamamı gibi* 'like a women's bathhouse', i.e., a noisy place full of voices and chatter.

22. Cf. the somewhat outdated expression *taşaklı kadın* 'woman with balls' which was used to describe an independent woman (e.g., a widow) who was the head and breadwinner of a household.

23. There are two investigations on the use of verbal insults by female and male Turkish speakers, Özçalışkan (1994) and Koçoğlu (1996). Both apply the questionnaire originally developed by Staley (1978) to elicit statements from Turkish subjects about their own use of insults and expletives under various conditions as well as those expletives they expect men or women to use. Unfortunately, these studies suffer from drawbacks which reduce the reliability of their results. Both Koçoğlu and (apparently) Özçalışkan apply Stayley's classification and ranking of expletives to Turkish without even considering that such classifications might be culture-specific. It is, moreover, regrettable that Koçoğlu does not always give literal translations for the Turkish expressions and that Özçalışkan does not quote in full the expressions about which she writes.

24. Cf., e.g., the asymmetry of *hayat adamı* 'playboy, experienced man' vs. *hayat kadını* 'prostitute'.

References

Ağaçsaban, Asuman. 1989. *Kız ve erkek öğrencilerde cinsiyetten kaynaklanan farklı dil kulla-nımı. (Ahmet Kanatlı Lisesinde Uygulamalı)* [Gender-based differences in the language use of female and male school children. (As occurring at the Ahmet Kanatlı High School)]. Yüksek Lisans Tezi. Anadolu University, Eskişehir, Turkey.

Aliefendioğlu, Hanife. 1994. *Konuşma dilinde cinsiyete dayalı farklılaşma: Kadın ve erkek dili* [Gender-specific differences in spoken language. Female and male language]. Yüksek Lisans Tezi. Hacettepe University, Ankara, Turkey.

Arat, Yeşim. 1989. *The patriarchal paradox. Women politicians in Turkey.* London: Associated University Presses.

Baron, Dennis. 1986. *Grammar and gender.* New Haven: Yale University Press.

Braun, Friederike. 1997a. "Covert gender in Turkish." In *VIII. Uluslararası Türk Dilbilimi Konferansı Bildirileri, 7–9 Ağustos, 1996* [Proceedings of the VIIIth International Conference on Turkish Linguistics, August 7–9, 1996], eds. Kâmile İmer & N. Engin Uzun. Ankara: Ankara Üniversitesi, 267–274.

Braun, Friederike. 1997b. "Genderless = gender-neutral? Empirical evidence from Turkish." In *Kommunikation von Geschlecht – Communication of gender,* eds. Friederike Braun & Ursula Pasero. Pfaffenweiler: Centaurus, 13–29.

Braun, Friederike. 1998. "Prototype theory and covert gender in Turkish." In *Discourse and cognition: Bridging the gap,* ed. Jean-Pierre Koenig. Stanford, CA: Center for the Study of Language and Information, 113–122.

Braun, Friederike. 1999. "Gender in a genderless language: The case of Turkish." In *Language and Society in the Middle East and North Africa. Studies in variation and identity,* ed. Yasir Suleiman. Richmond: Curzon, 190–203.

Clauson, Gerald. 1972. *An etymological dictionary of pre-thirteenth-century Turkish.* Oxford: Clarendon.

Daniels, Karlheinz. 1985. "Geschlechtsspezifische Stereotypen im Sprichwort." *Sprache und Literatur* 16 (56): 18–25.

Deaux, Kay. 1985. "Sex and gender." *Annual Review of Psychology* 36: 49–81.

Duman, Seyyare. 1991. "Türk kadınına verilen adlar" [The names given to Turkish women]. In *Dilbilim Araştırmaları* [Studies in linguistics] 1991, eds. Gül Durmuşoğlu & Kâmile İmer & Ahmet Kocaman & Sumru Özsoy. Ankara: Hitit, 40–42.

Dundes, Alan & Jerry W. Leach & Bora Özkök. 1986. "The strategy of Turkish boys' dueling rhymes." In *Directions in sociolinguistics. The ethnography of communication,* eds. John J. Gumperz & Dell Hymes. Oxford: Blackwell, 130–160. (1st ed. 1972).

Hayasi, Tooru. 1998. "Gender differences in modern Turkish discourse." *International Journal of the Sociology of Language* 129: 117–126.

Hellinger, Marlis. 1990. *Kontrastive feministische Linguistik. Mechanismen sprachlicher Diskriminierung im Englischen und Deutschen.* München: Hueber.

Hepçilingirler, Feyza. 1997. *Türkçe "off"* [Turkish "off"]. İstanbul: Remzi.

İmamoğlu, E. Olcay & Yeşim (Yasak) Gültekin & Bahar Köseoğlu & Afife Çebi. 1990. "Representation of women and men in Turkish newspapers." *Journal of Human Sciences* 9: 57–67.

Koçoğlu, Zeynep. 1996. "Gender differences in the use of expletives: A Turkish case." *Women and Language* 19: 30–35.

König, Güray Çağlar. 1992a. "Dil ve cins: Kadın ve erkeklerin dil kullanımı" [Language and gender: Language use by women and men]. In *Dilbilim Araştırmaları* [Studies in linguistics] 1992, eds. Gül Durmuşoğlu & Kâmile İmer & Ahmet Kocaman & Sumru Özsoy, Ankara: Hitit, 25–36.

König, Güray Çağlar. 1992b. "Cinslerarası ilişkilerde algılama" [Perception in relations between the genders]. *Department of American Culture and Literature, 1982, 10th Anniversary.* Special Issue, ed. David Laudrey. Ankara: Hacettepe Üniversitesi, 79–93.

Kornfilt, Jaklin. 1987. "Turkish and the Turkic languages." In *The world's major languages*, ed. Bernard Comrie. London: Croom Helm, 619–644.

Kornfilt, Jaklin. 1997. *Turkish.* London: Routledge.

Külebi, Oya. 1989. "Kadın hakları konusunda toplumdilbilim açısından bir yaklaşım" [A sociolinguistic approach to women's rights]. *Hacettepe Üniversitesi Edebiyat Fakültesi Dergisi* 6: 7–21.

Lewis, Geoffrey L. 1991. *Turkish grammar.* Oxford: Oxford University Press. (1st ed. 1967).

Özçalışkan, Şeyda. 1994. "Kadın ve erkeklerin küfür kullanımı üzerine" [On the use of swear words by women and men]. In *Dilbilim Araştırmaları* [Studies in linguistics] *1994*, eds. Kâmile İmer & Ahmet Kocaman & Sumru Özsoy, Ankara: Hitit, 274–287.

Redhouse. 1997. *Redhouse Yeni Türkçe-İngilizce Sözlük* [New Turkish-English Redhouse Dictionary]. İstanbul: Redhouse. (1st ed. 1968).

Staley, Constance M. 1978. "Male-female use of expletives: A hell of a difference in expectations." *Anthropological Linguistics* 20: 367–380.

Tavşanoğlu, Leyla. 1995. "Türkiye, namus cinayetleri ülkesi" [Turkey, the country of murder committed for the sake of honor]. *Cumhuriyet Hafta* 17–23 February 1995: 17.

Uğuz, Gülnur. 1988. *A preliminary study of idioms related to women in Turkish and English.* MA thesis. Hacettepe University, Ankara, Turkey.

Underhill, Robert. 1976. *Turkish grammar.* Cambridge, MA: MIT Press.

Yurtbaşı, Metin. 1994. *Sınıflandırılmış Türk atasözleri* [Classified Turkish proverbs]. Ankara: Özdemir.

Notes on contributors

Friederike Braun, born in Wetzlar, Germany. She received her doctoral degree und her *Habilitation* in General Linguistics from the University of Kiel, Germany, where she teaches Linguistics at the Department of General and Comparative Linguistics. Her main areas of research are: Sociolinguistics, language and gender, and Turkish linguistics.

(1988) *Terms of address. Problems of patterns and usage in various languages and cultures.* Berlin: Mouton de Gruyter.

(1997) with Ursula Pasero, eds. *Kommunikation von Geschlecht – Communication of gender.* Pfaffenweiler: Centaurus.

(2000) *Geschlecht im Türkischen: Untersuchungen zum sprachlichen Umgang mit einer sozialen Kategorie.* Wiesbaden: Harrassowitz.

Hadumod Bußmann, born in Frankfurt am Main, Germany. She received her doctoral degree in German Medieval Studies from the University of Munich, Germany. She was Senior Lecturer (*Akademische Direktorin*) of German Linguistics at the Institute of German Philology of the University of Munich. Her main areas of research are: Linguistic terminology, history of women in academia, and language and gender.

(1995) with Renate Hof, eds. *Genus. Zur Geschlechterdifferenz in den Kulturwissenschaften.* Stuttgart: Kröner.

(1996) *Routledge dictionary of language and linguistics.* London: Routledge.

(1997) with Hiltrud Häntzschel, eds. *Bedrohlich gescheit. Ein Jahrhundert Frauen und Wissenschaft in Bayern.* München: Beck.

Ursula Doleschal, born in Vienna, Austria. She received her doctoral degree in Russian Linguistics from the University of Vienna and her *Habilitation* in Slavic Linguistics from the Vienna University of Economics and Business Administration. She is an Assistant Professor of Slavic Linguistics at the Institute of Slavic Languages, Wirtschaftsuniversität Wien. Her main areas of research are: Morphology of Slavic languages, language and gender, and intercultural communication.

(1992) *Movierung im Deutschen. Eine Studie der Bildung und Verwendung weiblicher Personenbezeichnungen.* Unterschleissheim: Lincom Europe.

(1998) "Entwicklung und Auswirkungen der feministischen Sprachkritik in Österreich seit 1987." *Germanistische Linguistik* 139/140: 87–115.

(2000) "Gender assignment revisited." In *Gender in grammar and cognition*, eds. Barbara Unterbeck et al. Berlin: de Gruyter, 117–165.

Geneviève Escure, born in Perpignon, France. She received her PhD in Linguistics from Indiana University, Bloomington, USA. She is Professor of Linguistics at the Department of English at the University of Minnesota, Minneapolis. Her main areas of research are: Sociolinguistics, creole linguistics, pragmatics, Chinese dialect variation, language and gender, gender and ethnicity.

(1997) *Creole and dialect continua: Standard acquisition processes in Belize and China (PRC).* Creole Language Library Vol. 18. Amsterdam: Benjamins.

(1998) "Language contact: Gender and tense/aspect in Belizean Creole." In *SICOL (Proceedings of the Second International Conference on Oceanic Linguistics)*, eds. Jan Tent & France Mugler. Pacific Linguistics: Canberra University Press, 27–41.

(1999) "The grammaticalization of past in Creoles." *American Speech* 74: 165–202.

Atiqa Hachimi, born in Khenifra, Morocco. She is a PhD candidate at the Department of Linguistics at the University of Hawaii at Manoa, Honolulu, USA. Her main areas of research are: Dialect contact, language variation and change, and language attitudes.

(1996) *The acquisition of gutturals by native speakers of American English.* MA Thesis. University of Hawaii.

(2000) "Review of Niloofar Haeri (1997) The sociolinguistic market in Cairo: Gender, class and education." In *Arab Studies Quarterly* 22: 109–114.

Marlis Hellinger, born in Pirna/Dresden, Germany. She received her doctoral degree in English Linguistics from the University of Hamburg, Germany. She is Professor of English Linguistics at the Department of English and American Studies at the University of Frankfurt am Main, Germany. Her main areas of research are: Contrastive linguistics, sociolinguistics, language and gender, and creole linguistics.

(1985) *Englisch-orientierte Pidgin- und Kreolsprachen: Entstehung, Geschichte und sprachlicher Wandel.* Darmstadt: Wissenschaftliche Buchgesellschaft.

(1990) *Kontrastive feministische Linguistik: Mechanismen sprachlicher Diskriminierung im Englischen und Deutschen.* München: Hueber.

(1996) with Ulrich Ammon, eds. *Contrastive sociolinguistics.* Berlin: Mouton de Gruyter.

Janet Holmes, born in Liverpool, England. She received her postgraduate degree in Linguistics from the University of Leeds, England. She is Professor of Linguistics at the Victoria University of Wellington, New Zealand. Her main areas of research are: Sociolinguistics, language and gender, language in the workplace, New Zealand English, and social dialectology.

(1995) *Women, men and politeness.* London: Longman.
(2000) ed. *Gendered speech in social context: Perspectives from gown and town.* Wellington: Victoria University Press.
(2001) *Introduction to sociolinguistics.* 2nd edition. London: Longman.

Esther Kuntjara, born in Tegal, Central Java, Indonesia. She received her PhD from Indiana University of Pennsylvania, USA, und is currently an EFL Instructor at Petra Christian University, Surabaya, Indonesia. Her main area of research is: Women and politeness.

(1997) "Challenging the tradition of Javanese women." *Asian Journal of Women's Studies* 3: 77–100.
(1999) with Anita Lie. *Protocol analysis of students' reading and writing in gender perspective.* Pellba 13.

Florence Maurice, born in Munich, Germany. She received her doctoral degree in Slavic Linguistics from the University of Zürich, Switzerland. Her main areas of research are: Modality, computer-mediated communication, and language and gender.

(1995) "Die Verteilung von Notwendigkeit und Möglichkeit im russischen modalen Infinitiv. In *Linguistische Beiträge zur Slavistik aus Deutschland, Österreich und der Schweiz*, ed. Horst Dippong. München: Sagner, 147–158.
(1996) *Der modale Infinitiv in der modernen russischen Standardsprache.* München: Sagner.
(2001) "Einführung in die russische Chat-Kommunikation". *Zeitschrift für Slavische Philologie* 60: 79–104.

Bettina Migge, born in Hamburg, Germany. She received her PhD in Linguistics from The Ohio State University, Columbus, OH, USA. She is a Lecturer of Linguistics (*Hochschulassistentin*) at the Department of English and American Studies at the University of Frankfurt am Main, Germany. Her main areas of research are: Sociolinguistics, language contact, creole languages, and West African languages.

(1996) "Copula variability in the Belize continuum and the notion of the creole continuum." In *Sociolinguistic variation, data, theory, and analysis: Selected papers from NWAV 23 at Stanford*, eds. Jennifer Arnold et al. Stanford, CA: CSLI, 129–150.

(1998) "Substrate influence in creole formation: The origin of *give*-type serial verb constructions in the Surinamese Plantation Creole." *Journal of Pidgin and Creole Languages*
13: 215–265.
(2000) "The origin of property items in the Surinamese Plantation Creole." In *Language
change and language contact in pidgins and creoles,* ed. John McWhorter. Amsterdam:
Benjamins, 201–234.

Anne Pauwels, born in Antwerp, Belgium. She received her PhD in Linguistics
from Monash University, Australia. She is Executive Dean of the Faculty of Arts
and Professor of Linguistics at the University of Western Australia, Australia.
She is also a Fellow of the Australian Academy of Social Sciences. Her main
areas of research are: Language and gender, cross-cultural communication,
language contact, and bilingualism.

(1987) *Women and language in Australian and New Zealand society.* Sidney: Australian
Professional Publications.
(1995) *Cross-cultural communication in the health services.* London: Macmillan.
(1998) *Women changing language.* London: Longman.

Suzanne Romaine, born in Woburn, Massachusetts, USA. She received her
PhD in Linguistics from the University of Birmingham, England. She is
Merton Professor of English Language at the University of Oxford, England.
Her main areas of research are: Sociolinguistics, historical linguistics, and
pidgins and creoles.

(1989) *Bilingualism.* Oxford: Blackwell. (2nd ed. 1995)
(1994) *Language in society. An introduction to sociolinguistics.* Oxford: Oxford University
Press. (2nd ed. 2000)
(1999) *Communicating gender.* Mahwah, NJ: Erlbaum.

Sonja Schmid, born in Graz, Austria. She is a PhD candidate in Science and
Technology Studies at Cornell University, Ithaka, NY, USA. She has worked as
a Research Assistant at the Institute for Slavic Languages at the University of
Economics and Business Administration, Vienna, and teaches at the Institute
for Philsophy of Science and Social Studies of Science at the University of
Vienna. Her main areas of research are: Gender politics, discourse and ideology,
popular-scientific discourse.

(1998) "Zur Bezeichnung weiblicher Personen im Russischen. Eine empirische Pilotstudie."
Wiener Slawistischer Almanach 41: 239–262.
(1999) "Zur *zhenskaja proza* der Svetlana Vasilenko. Versuch einer feministisch-formalis-
tischen Annäherung." *Via Regia* 58/59, 81–91.

(2000) "Korrekturmechanismen in interkulturellen Verhandlungen. Zur Relevanz von interaktiven Mitteln der Verständnissicherung." In *Slawistik in Österreich. Beiträge zum 1.Arbeitstreffen, Innsbruck 24.-26.2.1999*, eds. W. Stadler & E. Binder & H. Kalb: Innsbruck: Institut für Sprachwissenschaft der Universität Innsbruck, 69–86.

Yishai Tobin, born in New York City, USA. He received his PhD in Linguistics from New York University. He is Professor of Linguistics at the Department of Foreign Literatures and Linguistics, and at the Department of Behavioral Sciences at the Ben-Gurion University of the Negev, Israel. His main areas of research are: Semiotics, discourse analysis, clinical phonetics, and phonology.

(1993) *Aspect in the English verb: Process and result in language*. London: Longman.
(1994) *Invariance, markedness and distinctive feature analysis. A contrastive study of sign systems in English and Hebrew*. Amsterdam: Benjamins.
(1997) *Phonology as human behavior: Theoretical implications and clinical applications*. Durham, NC: Duke University Press.

Name index

Subject index